# Carrara™ 5 Pro Handbook

# CARRARA™ 5 PRO HANDBOOK

## MIKE DE LA FLOR

CHARLES RIVER MEDIA, INC.

Hingham, Massachusetts

Copyright 2006 by Career & Professional Group, a division of Thomson Learning Inc.
Published by CHARLES RIVER MEDIA, INC.
All rights reserved.

Cover Design: Tyler Creative

CHARLES RIVER MEDIA, INC.
10 Downer Avenue
Hingham, Massachusetts 02043
781-740-0400
781-740-8816 (FAX)
*crminfo@thomson.com*
*www.charlesriver.com*

This book is printed on acid-free paper.

Mike de la Flor. *Carrara 5 Pro Handbook.*
ISBN: 1-58450-463-3

Library of Congress Cataloging-in-Publication Data
De la Flor, Mike.
  Carrara 5 pro handbook / Mike de la Flor.
    p. cm. — (Graphics series)
  Includes index.
  ISBN 1-58450-463-3 (pbk. with cd-rom : alk. paper)
 1. Computer animation. 2. Three-dimensional display systems. 3.
Carrara (Computer file) I. Title: Carrara five pro handbook. II. Title.
III. Charles River Media graphics.
  TR897.7.D394 2006
  006.6'96—dc22

Printed in Canada
06 7 6 5 4 3 2 First Edition

CHARLES RIVER MEDIA titles are available for site license or bulk purchase by institutions, user groups, corporations, etc. For additional information, please contact the Special Sales Department at 781-740-0400.

Requests for replacement of a defective CD-ROM must be accompanied by the original disc, your mailing address, telephone number, date of purchase, and purchase price. Please state the nature of the problem, and send the information to CHARLES RIVER MEDIA, INC., 10 Downer Avenue, Hingham, Massachusetts 02043. CRM's sole obligation to the purchaser is to replace the disc, based on defective materials or faulty workmanship, but not on the operation or functionality of the product.

*This book is dedicated to my fellow teachers, my students,*
*professional colleagues, and most of all to the Carrara user community.*
*Enjoy!*

# CONTENTS

# ACKNOWLEDGMENTS

As with the first edition of the *Carrara Handbook* this second edition was made possible through the hard work and dedication of many talented people. First and foremost I want to thank my publisher Jenifer Niles for her patience, support and direction, and also many thanks to the other people at Charles River Media whose expertise made this book possible.

At Eovia I would like to thank Charles Brissart and Bob Stockwell, for their patience and support in organizing this book. I am especially thankful to Ilya Melikov-Preys for technical support with Carrara and Thomas Roussel (merci beaucoup) for technical support with Hexagon.

Without the talent, know-how and willingness of the contributing authors to give of their time and share their skill this book would not have been possible. Special thanks to David Bell, Peter MacDougall, Andrea Newton, Patrick Tuten, Jack Whitney, and Eric Winemiller, and Lisa Yimm. Thanks guys and great job!

Most of all, I am grateful to my lovely wife Bridgette for her unending support and encouragement.

# PREFACE

## WHAT'S IN THE CARRARA 5 PRO HANDBOOK?

Carrara™ 5 Pro has a redesigned interface improved workflow, and it features dozens of new and advanced tools to model, texture, and animate better than ever before—and that is exciting news for all Carrara users.

The *Carrara 5 Pro Handbook* has been written by expert Carrara users to cover many of the new features in Carrara 5 with you, the end user, in mind. From the very first pages the *Carrara 5 Pro Handbook* guides you through everything you need to know to succeed with Carrara and also succeed as a 3D artist.

In *Part I: Understanding 3D* many of the concepts behind 3D modeling, texturing, animating and rendering are demystified. Did you ever want to know what a surface normal or an N-gon is but were afraid to ask? Chapters 1, 2 and 3 will provide you with the answers to those and many more questions.

The five chapters in *Part II: Getting to Know Carrara* will help you to get acquainted with Carrara's new look and feel. Explore the new interface and discover how to customize Carrara. Learn to work with objects, cameras, and lights and even begin to texture and animate.

*Part III: Modeling with Carrara and Hexagon* features five in-depth modeling tutorials that cover the topics and techniques that are of the most interest to you. In Chapter 9 learn to use splines to build a Delta rocket from scratch. Then box model a super hero from head to toe, and then take to the virtual skies with a detailed Piper Cherokee airplane modeled with Carrara's new 2D curves and cool surfacing tools.

As an added bonus there are two in-depth tutorials on modeling with Hexagon. Why are there Hexagon tutorials in a Carrara book? Simply put, because Hexagon rocks when it comes to modeling, and it was developed by Eovia® to integrate with Carrara seamlessly. The Hexagon tutorials not only teach you how to model in Hexagon, but they reinforce the modeling techniques you learned in the Vertex Modeling tutorials. By the time you are finished with Chapter 10 you will be able to model anything your heart desires.

In *Part IV: Texturing with Carrara* you will learn the ins and outs of working with different types of shaders, procedurals, layers, texture maps, and shading domains, and you will unleash the power of UV mapping. In Chapter 13 you will work with the subtle but fantastic effects of subsurface scattering to achieve ultra-realistic lighting. Then you will move on to modeling a mummy with nothing but the new displacement mapping tools.

With modeling and texturing out of the way, it's time to jump right into animation. *Part V: Animation with Carrara* tackles two of the most challenging things an animator can do: facial animation and walk cycles. In Chapter 14 you will discover how to make Nigel, the friendly troll, speak and emote with Carrara's superb morph targets. In Chapter 15 you will build a bones skeleton, apply constraint and IK and make a biped character walk with an attitude.

The final step in any 3D project is rendering, so in *Part VI: Rendering with Carrara* you will work with advanced rendering tools such as HDRI, caustics, indirect lighting, skylight, and motion blur to achieve the hyper-realistic results you've been looking for. When you are ready to go from realistic to abstract there is also a tutorial to guide you through Carrara's Non-Photorealist render engine.

At this point just about everything you probably wanted to know about Carrara has been covered, but there is still more. *Part VII: Carrara and Other Programs* features three chapters with comprehensive tutorials on exporting Carrara data to Flash and Illustrator with VectorStyle 2, importing Poser data into Carrara, and compositing renders in After Effects. Finally in *Part VIII: Carrara Plug-ins* you will learn to extend Carrara's built-in capabilities with popular plug-ins from Digital Carvers Guild.

## WHO THIS BOOK IS FOR

For the do-it-yourselfer new to 3D this book has everything you will need to learn at your own pace and achieve a confident proficiency with Carrara 5 Pro and Hexagon. For the veteran Carrara artist this book covers many of the new and sophisticated tools and techniques in Carrara 5 Pro.

This book has also been structured to be used in the classroom. Written with teachers and students in mind the *Carrara 5 Pro Handbook* provides high school and college teachers with a structured lesson plan and the tools necessary to successfully teach modeling, texturing, animation and rendering. The tutorials in this book are designed to keep students interested by providing them with engaging and challenging subject matter. For instance in the modeling chapters students learn to model characters, a concept car, an airplane, and a rocket. Beyond just the written

*ON THE CD*

word, the book's companion CD-ROM is full of incremental files, finished models, support files, and movies to help teachers help their students get past any challenge.

## ABOUT THE AUTHOR

Mike de la Flor (Houston, TX) is a freelance medical illustrator and writer. He is the author of *The Digital Biomedical Illustration Handbook* (Charles River Media 2004) and contributing writer for *3DWorld Magazine* and *Computer Arts Magazine*. He is also an adjunct instructor at Kingwood College where he teaches computer graphics. Mike has served as staff illustrator at the University of Texas Health Science Center in Houston, the University of Texas Medical Branch at Galveston, and Baylor College of Medicine. He has been a Professional member of the Association of Medical Illustrators since 1992. For more information visit *www.delaflor.com*.

# I

# UNDERSTANDING 3D

# 1

# CONCEPTS AND TECHNIQUES IN 3D MODELING

## In This Chapter

- Getting around in 3D: Cartesian Coordinates
- Vertices and Polygons
- Curves
- Surfaces
- Subdivision Surfaces
- Primitives

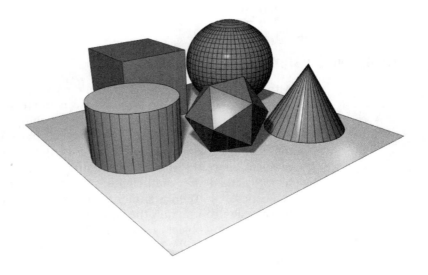

Polygons, points, curves, surfaces, and coordinates; this list sounds more like a syllabus from an algebra or geometry course than tools used by computer graphics (CG) artists. The truth is that behind all 3D programs, there exist very complex mathematics and programming. Fortunately, as artists, we do not have to be mathematicians to be proficient 3D modelers or animators. All of the mathematics and programming is neatly tucked into a stylized user interface (UI).

It is common sense that you do not have to be a mechanical engineer to drive and enjoy a car, which at an average of 5000 parts is a very complex machine. However, it is good to know something about how your car works to keep it running at its best. If you plan to be a race car driver you not only have to know how to drive a car, but you also need to understand its engineering, aerodynamics, and the physics of moving at 230 mph. Similarly, with Carrara, you can be content just knowing that by clicking on the right buttons you can create amazing 3D graphics and animations. However, if you plan to make a living as a 3D artist, consider that once you understand the basic concepts in 3D you can begin to harness the power of Carrara and develop your own style. More importantly, you can be more creative and make smarter decisions as a 3D artist.

Chapters 1, 2, and 3 of Part I were written to provide you with a basic understanding of 3D modeling, texturing, and animation. If you want to skip these chapters for now, feel free to jump to the tutorials in later chapters and have fun working in Carrara. However, when you feel curious about what is happening under the hood, come back and look—it will be worth your time.

## GETTING AROUND IN 3D: CARTESIAN COORDINATES

Although some astrophysicists would have us believe that there are possibly more than three dimensions in our universe, our brains, and consequently the computers and software we design, are wired to deal with only three dimensions. Since all 3D objects have width, height, and depth, there must be some method to describe these 3D attributes. To solve this problem, most 3D programs, including Carrara, use the *Cartesian coordinate system* (named after mathematician René Descartes) to describe the characteristics of a 3D environment and the objects within it (see Figure 1.1). In Cartesian coordinates the variables $x$, $y$, and $z$ are used to determine the location of any object in space. In Carrara the variable $z$ is used to describe up and down. At the center of Cartesian space is the *origin*, at which the value of $x$, $y$, and $z$ is zero.

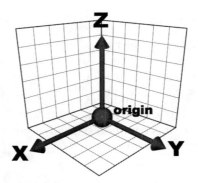

**FIGURE 1.1**    Carrara uses the Cartesian coordinate system to describe the location of 3D objects. The center of Cartesian space is the origin.

## Translation (Move)

In order to move in 3D space, an object must follow one, two, or all three of the *x*, *y*, and *z axes*. For example, if the center of a cube is located five units along the *z*-axis, two units along the *y*-axis, and three units along the *x*-axis, the location of the cube can be accurately plotted in 3D space. If the *x*, *y*, and *z* values of the cube change, then the cube has moved, or *translated*, in 3D space, as in Figure 1.2.

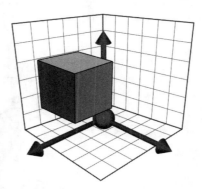

**FIGURE 1.2**    Translation in 3D space.

## Rotation

The *x*, *y*, and *z* values can also describe the rotation of an object. Like translation, rotation occurs along one axis or a combination of the *x*, *y*, and *z* axes. If the cube described earlier tilts to the left 5 degrees, then it is said to have rotated 5 degrees about the *y*-axis (see Figure 1.3).

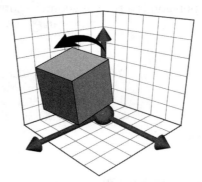

**FIGURE 1.3**    Rotation in 3D space.

## The Right-Handed Rule

An easy way to remember the Cartesian coordinate system is to use the *right-handed rule* model. Hold up your right hand and make a fist. Now, extend your index finger as if pointing up. Point the middle finger to the left and finally extend your thumb toward you. Your index finger represents the *z* axis, the middle represents the *x* axis, and the thumb, the *y* axis (see Figure 1.4).

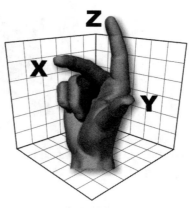

**FIGURE 1.4**    The right-handed rule helps orient the axes.

## VERTICES AND POLYGONS

A *vertex*, or *point*, is a fundamental building block of all 3D objects. Vertices are defined by their *x*, *y*, and *z* coordinates, but by themselves vertices have no volume or area and cannot be rendered; in other words, they are invisible. However, when three or more vertices are linked by segments called *lines*, or *edges*, a *polygon* is formed, as shown in Figure 1.5. A polygon is a type of geometric object that can either be open or closed, as in Figure 1.6A, and it can be empty or filled, as in Figure 1.6b.

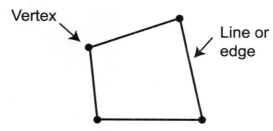

**FIGURE 1.5**    The parts of a polygon.

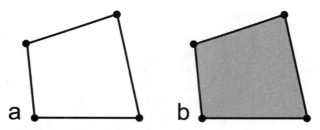

**FIGURE 1.6**    (a) An empty polygon and (b) a filled polygon.

Polygons can have any number of vertices to define their shape but commonly have three vertices to form a *triangle* or four vertices to form a *quadrangle* (*quad* for short). Moreover, a polygonal model composed of quads is generally smaller in file size than a polygonal model composed of triangles—assuming that both models have the same number of vertices. Polygons with more than four vertices, referred to as *N-gons* (where *N* stands in for a number greater than four), are not frequently used in finished models because they could cause problems with subdivision, rendering, and animation.

Unlike a single vertex, which is always invisible, when a polygon is filled, it becomes a visible 3D component that can be rendered. A filled polygon has surface characteristics that will interact with digital light; it can have color, reflect light, and cast shadows, among many other properties (see Figure 1.7).

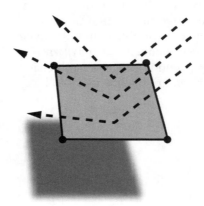

**FIGURE 1.7**   Filled polygons can interact with digital light.

## Face Normals

A *face normal* is an imaginary vector that points away from the polygonal face. When polygons are created in Carrara, they are automatically front-facing polygons. Front-facing polygons have normals that point away from the middle of an object or toward the outside and will render correctly (see Figure 1.8a). It is important to be aware of face normals because reversed face normals, as shown in Figure 1.8b, will not accept textures correctly or render correctly. Reversed normal polygons are common in imported 3D models, especially with DXF files. To correct reversed face normals with Carrara, open the model in the Vertex Modeler and choose Model/Reverse Polygon Normals.

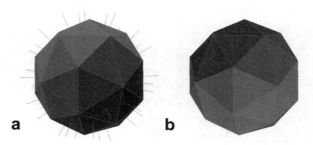

**FIGURE 1.8**   Face normals: (a) Front-facing normals and (b) reversed normals (normals turned on).

## Vertex Normals

When digital light bounces off a polygon, it appears faceted, like a cut gem (see Figure 1.9a). In other words, each polygon in the model will appear flat. To overcome this inherent property of polygons, *vertex normals* are used to give the model a smooth appearance. Simply put, vertex normals average the angles of the polygons that surround a particular vertex and calculate a smooth surface, as shown in Figure 1.9b. When switching from flat to *Gouraud* shading in Carrara, you are turning vertex normals off and on.

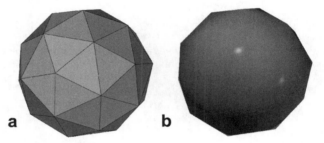

**FIGURE 1.9**    (a) Polygons are inherently flat. (b) Vertex normals give polygons a smooth surface. Note that the silhouette is not smoothed.

## CURVES

*Curves* are mathematical formulas that are graphically represented as 2D objects defined by points and the segments that connect those points. Curves may be arced or straight or open or closed, and along with the vertices, they form the basis of all polygonal modeling. Carrara features several types of curves including polyline, curve, interpolated curve, circle, rectangle, and Bézier.

Curve, interpolated curve, circle, and rectangle, are different implementations of polylines, which are the straight segments, or edges, between two or more vertices. As such, all polyline curve tools may be used to draw 2D profiles, cross sections, polygons, and N-gons.

*Bézier curves* (named after mathematician Pierre Bézier) are found exclusively in the Carrara Spline Modeler. The shape of a Bézier curve is determined by *edit points* and the segments that connect the edit points. The edit points in a Bézier curve have *control handles* that fine-tune the curvature, or arch, of the connecting line. Bézier curves can be used to create smooth shapes or smooth transitions between shapes (see Figure 1.10).

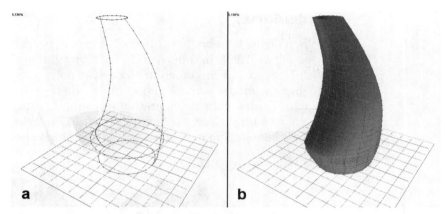

**FIGURE 1.10**    Curves are fundamental building blocks in polygonal modeling. In this figure the Gordon tool is used to generate a surface from a surface network of polylines.

## SURFACES

Now that we are familiar with vertices, polygons, and curves, we can move on to understanding *surfaces,* or *topologies*. Though a single filled polygon has a surface, by itself it is not very useful, as it has no volume or thickness and is rigid. However, when many polygons are joined by sharing their edges and vertices, they can form an open or closed surface. A complex surface is often referred to as a *polymesh*. Joining hundreds or thousands of polygons to form complex surfaces, or volumes, would be a daunting if not impossible task, so 3D programs like Carrara have specialized tools that easily generate surfaces. These tools fall into four basic categories: extrude, sweep, lathed, and loft. The new Vertex Modeler in Carrara 5 features Loft, Lathe, Sweep, Extrude, and Dynamic Extrusion tools and introduces Ruled Surfaces, Double Sweep, Gordon, and Coons, which are advanced surface construction tools.

Surfacing tools are closely related and may be easily confused. For instance, the Extrude and Sweep tools are similar and produce comparable results. Similarly, the Loft and Ruled Surfaces tools have analogous functions and produce like results. With a bit of experience you will find that while the functionality of some tools overlap, there are unique applications for each. Many of the modeling tools in Carrara will be covered later in the book, but the following quick tool descriptions will give you an idea of how each surfacing tool works.

The Loft tool generates surfaces by connecting polylines. The Lathe tool takes a profile and turns it around an axis defined by polyline to quickly create complex surfaces. The Sweep tool sweeps, or moves, a profile or cross section along a path defined by a polyline (see Figure 1.11).

**FIGURE 1.11**    Loft, Lathe, and Sweep.

Extrude and Dynamic Extrusion simply take a polygon or set of polygons or edges and moves them from their original position; in this way, new polygons and edges are created along the extrusion path (see Figure 1.12).

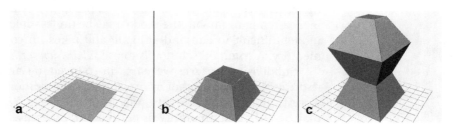

**FIGURE 1.12**    Extrusion is a basic surfacing tool.

Ruled Surfaces, Double Sweep, Gordon, and Coons are new in Carrara 5 and provide advanced surface construction options. Ruled Surfaces is a type of loft function that generates surfaces by connecting polylines. Unlike the Loft tool, Ruled Surfaces always generates surfaces with quadrangles. Whereas the Sweep tool sweeps a profile along a single path, the Double Sweep tool sweeps a profile along two paths. The Gordon tool is the ultimate sweep tool, as it generates surfaces from any number of polylines. Finally, Coons creates a surface composed of quadrangles from any closed polyline (see Figure 1.13.)

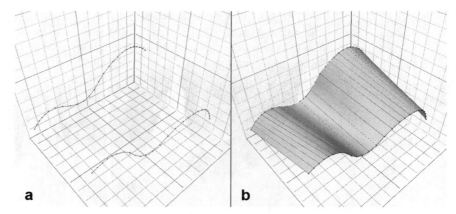

**FIGURE 1.13**    Carrara has advanced surfacing tools. Ruled Surfaces is used here to generate a surface from two polylines.

## SUBDIVISION SURFACES

Polygonal models with few polygons often appear boxy and rough around the edges (see Figure 1.14a). However, permanently adding more polygons in an attempt to smooth the model may be undesirable because it makes the model difficult to edit and animate and takes up considerable computer memory. A common solution is to use *subdivision surfaces.*

Subdivision surfaces were first introduced in Carrara 3, but Carrara 5 features improved subdivision surfaces implementing Catmull-Clark algorithms to subdivide any polymesh. In Carrara subdivision surfaces may be used to temporarily or permanently increase the number of polygons, thereby smoothing the model's surface. When subdivision surfaces are applied to a model, the number of polygons or edges is not displayed; instead lines called *isoparms* are displayed on the model surface. Isoparms indicate the general separations between subdivided polygons, as shown in Figure 1.14b. In Carrara not only can you apply subdivision surfaces to a completed model, but you can model using subdivision surfaces, which makes it simple to edit the surface of a complex model. In addition, Carrara can toggle a Smoothed Display that superimposes a *lattice* based on the geometry of the original low-polygon-count model onto the smoothed model, which further facilitates modeling (see Figure 1.14c).

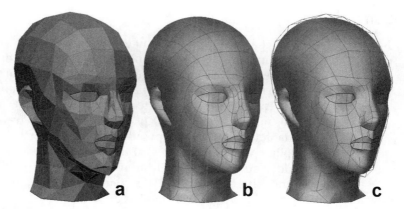

**FIGURE 1.14**    Subdivision surfaces make a low-polygon-count model appear smooth.

## PRIMITIVES

Geometric *primitives* are *parametric* objects that are defined by mathematical formulas and that cannot be readily broken down into parts unless they are converted into polygonal models. Carrara has seven basic geometric primitive shapes: sphere, cube, cone, plane, infinite plane, cylinder, and icosahedra (see Figure 1.15). Because primitives are defined instead of constructed, they use much less computer memory. This efficiency makes them ideal for building compound models.

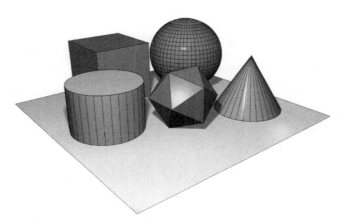

**FIGURE 1.15**    Carrara's geometric primitives.

## SUMMARY

This chapter introduced you to many of the basic concepts behind building 3D models. Although learning the concepts behind 3D modeling might not seem as glamorous as diving right in and creating cool 3D models and animations, it is an important step in becoming a well-rounded 3D artist.

Part III of this book features five extensive modeling tutorials that will put into practice all of the concepts and techniques learned in this chapter. Part III is composed of three chapters: Chapter 9 focuses on the Spline Modeler; Chapter 10 has two Vertex Modeler tutorials; and as an added bonus Chapter 11 has two detailed tutorials on modeling with Carrara's sister application Hexagon™. In the meantime, in the next chapter we will learn how 3D models are textured.

# 3D TEXTURING TECHNIQUES

**In This Chapter**

- What is 3D Texturing?
- Procedural Textures
- Projection Mapping
- UV Mapping
- Shader Channels

## WHAT IS 3D TEXTURING?

The process of building 3D models can yield impressive results, but by itself 3D modeling does not complete the illusion of realism. Once the modeling is completed, most 3D models usually look like plastic toys with a default gray color (see Figure 2.1). A 3D model that is not textured looks incomplete because real objects have surface characteristics such as color, texture, reflection, transparency, highlight, and so on. Common textures are so ingrained in our minds that we can identify an object by simply getting a glimpse of its texture. For example, most people can quickly identify a wooden picture frame, even if the wood has been milled, carved, cut, painted, and finished. Wood textures have distinctive surface characteristics that we immediately recognize as "wood."

**FIGURE 2.1** A 3D model of a Corsair WWII fighter plane. Without textures, it looks unfinished and it's difficult to discern its scale.

Because real-world textures are easily recognizable, it is important for 3D texture artists to be keen observers of their environment and pay close attention to the surface characteristics of the objects they intend to reproduce in 3D. Lack of attention in the texturing process inevitably leads to obvious flaws, which may give away the digital origin of the 3D model. A poor 3D model that has been expertly textured will probably look great, but the reverse is not true—a great 3D model with a poor texture will be easily picked out as a computer-generated object.

Texturing 3D models can be achieved using different methods such as projection mapping, procedural textures, and UV mapping. Each texturing method produces different results, and the decision to use one method over another is directly related to the type of 3D model being textured and whether the model is to be used for illustration, animation in film or video, or animation in games. It is important to understand how the different texturing methods work, so let's review procedural textures, projection mapping, and UV mapping.

## PROCEDURAL TEXTURES

Procedural textures are unique because they are typically created through a mathematical process instead of mapping a 2D image onto a 3D object, as with other texturing methods such as projection mapping and UV mapping. Common examples of procedural textures include marble, wood, cells, and checkers, as shown in Figure 2.2.

**FIGURE 2.2**    Procedural texture examples.

For example, once you have completed a 3D model of a wooden toy train, you will probably want to assign a wood texture to it (see Figure 2.3). You could use a scanned image of an actual piece of wood and apply that image to the model. While this approach might work, using an image as a texture has a couple of drawbacks. First, the amount of computing power needed to load, apply, and possibly animate the train model with its digitized texture is much greater than if a procedural texture simulating wood were used (see Figure 2.4). Additionally, there is the issue of texture distortion that often occurs when a 2D image is applied to a 3D object. Distortion can be particularly noticeable with texture that has a grain, like wood, as in Figure 2.5.

In this example you can see that the texture is being stretched in several places.

One advantage of procedural textures it that they can be animated. Procedural textures are created by defining a set of values. For example, in Carrara the wood procedural is defined by the values Global Scale,

**FIGURE 2.3** 3D model of a toy train ready for texturing.

**FIGURE 2.4** Using procedural textures saves on the amount of computing power needed to texture an object.

**FIGURE 2.5** Texture distortion is a common problem when 2D images are used as textures.

Vein Count, Undulation, Vein Blending, Perturbation, Direction, and Center. By assigning specific values to a procedural at the beginning of an animation and then changing the values at the end of the animation, a procedural texture can be made to appear to change over time. In Figure 2.6 the color and texture of the leaves is animated to change from green to yellow to simulate fall colors and textures.

Procedural textures can only be used as procedurals within the native program that created them. In other words, you usually can't export a procedural texture. If you export a 3D object with a procedural texture,

**FIGURE 2.6**   Procedural textures can be animated.

the connection between the mathematical process that created the procedural texture is lost and the procedural texture is exported as an imaged-based texture.

Procedural textures are also very flexible; for example, the wood procedural can be used to simulate ripples of water when it is used in the Bump channel of a shader. The marble procedural can be used to simulate clouds in a sky, and the checkers procedural can be used to create a tiled floor. The possibilities are endless, so try to keep an open mind when using procedural textures and don't let their names keep you from experimenting.

## PROJECTION MAPPING

Projection mapping works just as its name implies. In this texturing method a 2D image is projected onto a 3D object, much like a slide projector projects an image onto a screen (see Figure 2.7). Although projection mapping can be used to texture any 3D object, it works best when texturing shapes that resemble geometric primitives, such as cylinders, spheres, planes, cubes, and so on. The 2D image to be projected is always image based, such as a digital photograph or scan or an image painted with a program like Adobe® Photoshop® or Painter™.

The most common problem with projection mapping is texture distortion. All 2D images are flat and rectangular. When a flat, rectangular image is projected onto a 3D object, the image will be stretched, pinched, and distorted as it follows the contours of the 3D object. Projection types such as spherical, planar, cylindrical, and box help alleviate the distortion

**FIGURE 2.7**   In projection mapping a 2D image is projected on to a 3D surface.

problem. By assigning a specific type of projection, most, if not all, distortion can be hidden or eliminated. For example, if a cylindrical projection type is used when texturing a cylinder, then the chances of distortion are minimized (see Figure 2.8).

**FIGURE 2.8**   The cylinder on the far right uses cylindrical projection to minimize texture distortion. Note the pinching and severe distortion on the other two cylinders.

With projection mapping, you can achieve highly detailed and realistic results that are not possible with procedural texturing. By definition, procedural textures are limited by the procedure that created them. The amount of detail and realism in a projected 2D image is limited only by your imagination.

## UV Mapping

UV mapping is a texturing process where a 2D image is "applied" to a 3D object. Unlike projection mapping, UV mapping uses a 2D coordinate system represented by the axes *U* and *V* to assign the pixels in a 2D image to specific locations on the geometry of a 3D model. Therefore, instead of simply projecting the 2D image, the UV process applies an image to the 3D object, much like a roll of wallpaper is applied to a wall (see Figure 2.9).

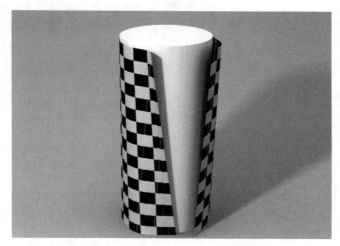

**FIGURE 2.9**    In UV mapping a 2D image is applied to an object using UV coordinates.

Once the image is applied using UV mapping, it will adjust itself to any changes in the shape of the 3D object, using the UV coordinate information. In other words, if the 3D object is animated, edited, or morphed, the image on the 3D object will move relative to the movements of the geometry (see Figure 2.10). A typical limitation of UV mapping is that you usually can't add or delete vertices on the 3D object once UV mapping is done because this will disrupt the UVs' relationship to the object's geometry.

In Carrara the UV Editor is in the Vertex Modeler, so any model you want to UV map has to either have been created in the Vertex Modeler or brought into the Vertex Modeler. Carrara's UV Editor has comprehensive tools that not only apply UV coordinates to a 3D object but also feature tools to move, scale, and rotate individual UVs to hide, minimize, or remove texture distortions. Removing or minimizing distortion is akin to smoothing out bubbles when wallpaper is applied to a wall. By moving the UVs in the UV Editor, you can eliminate any imperfections. Once an object is UV-mapped, the UV Editor will export a 2D image to use as a template in a

**FIGURE 2.10**    UV-mapped images "stick" to the geometry of a 3D shape, so when the shape is edited, the mapped image moves with it.

graphics program to create the textures. Once the texture is ready, it is applied to the model using Carrara's shaders.

ON THE CD

Now that you have an idea of how UV mapping works, let's try a quick tutorial. Open the file UVmap.car found in the Chapter 2 folder in the companion CD-ROM. With the Move tool, double-click on the cube in the scene. Carrara will open the Vertex Modeler because the cube was created in the Vertex Modeler. Next press Ctrl/Command-A to select all of the polygons in the cube. You know that the cube is selected because all polygons will turn red.

To open the UV Editor, click on the UV Map tab in the Properties tray and then press the UV Editor button. The large gray area on the left is the UV map; on the right are all of the UV mapping tools and a preview window. In the bottom-right corner of the UV Editor are three tabs: Edit, Projection, and Display; click on the Projection tab. From the small menu choose Box and check Frame and then in the Box Mode section click on the rightmost icon and press the Apply button. Notice that in the UV map Carrara applies box mode UV projection, as in Figure 2.11.

Once the cube is UV-mapped, the next step is to export a graphical template of the UV map so textures can be created for the cube. Click on the Display tab and press the Export button. Select a Map Size of 1024 (1024 × 1024 pixels) and save the map. Figure 2.12 shows the UV map template. Next, you would load the UV map in to a graphics program and create the textures, but for tutorial purposes the textures have already been created for you (see Figure 2.13).

Close the UV Editor and press the Texture Room button in the upper-right corner of the Carrara interface (the paintbrush icon). In the Texture Room you will see the shader tree and a preview of the cube. On the left

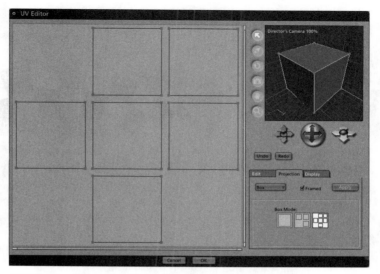

**FIGURE 2.11**    The cube with the box UV projection applied.

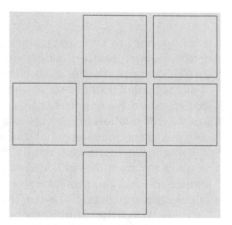

**FIGURE 2.12**    The UV map template.

side of the shader tree click on the Color channel menu and select Texture Map. Note the texture map options on the right side of the shader tree. Click once on the first folder icon and browse to the file cubeTexture.tif on the CD-ROM and press Open to load the texture. The preview window shows that the texture is applied perfectly onto the sides of the cube (see Figure 2.14). The texture fits perfectly because the cube was UV-mapped and the texture was created using the UV map as a template.

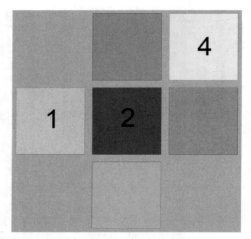

**FIGURE 2.13** The texture painted based on the UV map.

## SHADER CHANNELS

ON THE CD

It is important to note that using a procedural texture, projected texture, or UV-mapped texture is only one step in the process of creating the surface characteristics of a 3D object. Usually, the main texture for a 3D object is loaded into the Color channel of the object's shader. In Carrara shaders are the components that are used to store and apply all of the surface information for objects in a scene. Shaders will be covered more in depth in the following chapters and tutorials.

To illustrate the concept of channels in a shader, let's revisit the wooden toy train model. Once you have applied some form of wooden texture to the train, there are still other surface characteristics to be considered. For example, if the wood is finished, it might be shiny, even reflective. To set the shininess or reflective qualities, you would assign values to the Shininess and Reflection channels of the train's shader. If the wood is bumpy, you could simulate the bumps by using a grayscale texture in the Bump channel. If the train has plastic windows, you would set the transparency of the windows in the Transparency channel (see Figure 2.15). Striking a balance between the various channels in a shader is an important step in creating believable surface characteristics on 3D objects.

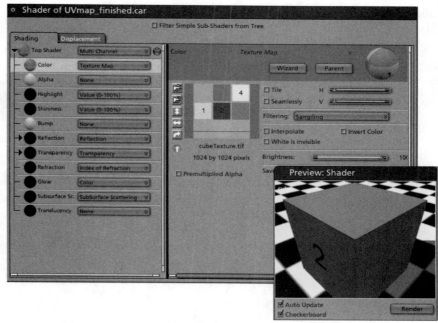

**FIGURE 2.14**    The UV-mapped texture applied to the 3D object.

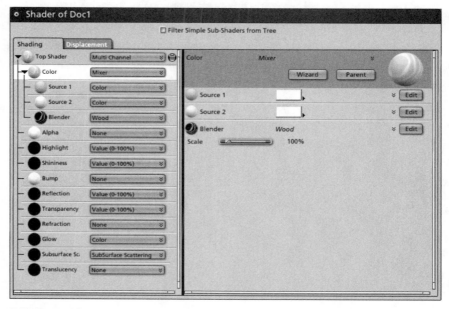

**FIGURE 2.15**    The Carrara shader tree.

## SUMMARY

Texturing is one of the important steps in creating good 3D models. Somewhere between 3D modeling and 3D lighting, texturing can make or break the illusion of realism in an animation or illustration. As with 3D modeling, a keen eye and careful observation are essential in creating believable textures. Texture mapping is definitely a challenge, but with a little practice and with a little help from Carrara, you will soon be texturing with the pros (see Figure 2.16).

**FIGURE 2.16**    The Corsair from the beginning of the chapter textured and rendered.

# 3D ANIMATION: MAKING THINGS MOVE

## In This Chapter

- What is Animation?
- Key Frames and Tweeners
- The Timeline
- The Graph Editor
- Animation Methods

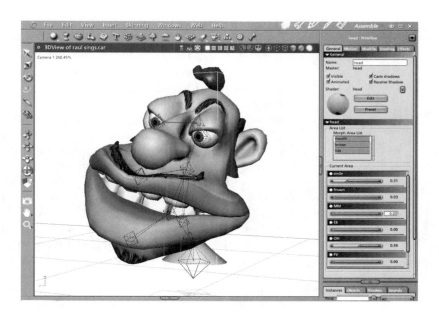

## WHAT IS ANIMATION?

The word *animation* comes from the Latin root word *anima*, which means life or to breathe. In essence, when something is animated, it is brought to life. In the case of 3D computer graphics, it means creating the illusion of life. The art of animation films dates back to the turn of the twentieth century, when early attempts at animation were simple and no more than a series of hand-drawn images that were photographed and then edited into a filmstrip. Even back then, animations were immensely popular. Animation techniques have evolved as fast as technology has allowed, yet in the almost 100 years that have passed, the basic concept of animation has remained the same.

Animations are composed of a series of still images. Each image is slightly different from the previous image; thus when viewed in quick succession, such as in a film, the illusion of movement is created. One of the main reasons this animation technique works is because of a neurological phenomenon known as *persistence of vision*, in which the human brain and eye retain an image for a fraction of a second after the image is gone. When hundreds or thousands of images are viewed in rapid succession (about 24 frames per second), the human brain can't see the flicker caused by the passing images, thus fooling the brain and creating the illusion of smooth movement.

## KEY FRAMES AND TWEENERS

3D computer animation works in much the same way as traditional 2D animation, but instead of having to hand-draw and photograph thousands of images as in traditional animation, the bulk of the work is done with a computer. In traditional animation hand-drawn *key frames* contain the key poses of an animated sequence. The numerous in-between poses are then drawn to create transitions between key frames.

Animation in Carrara works much the same way: you create key frames by editing the properties of objects, such as position, at specific points on the timeline. Then Carrara fills in the transitions between key frames through *interpolation*. The in-between frames, or frames between key frames, are known as *tweeners*. Two key frames contain all of the information the computer will need to interpolate the tweeners.

Let's take a quick look at a simple 3D animation that we will do in Chapter 5. In that animation you will make a fan oscillate back and forth. The first key frame in the animation has the fan in the start position facing to the left, and in the last key frame the fan is facing the right. When the computer creates the animation, it knows where to start and end the movement of the fan and where to place the fan in the tweeners to create the illusion of movement (see Figure 3.1). As you will see when you get to Chapter 5, the completed animation of the oscillating fan involves a bit more work, but setting the start and end key frames is all we need to know for now.

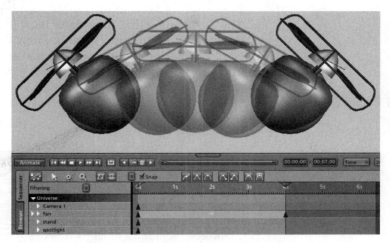

**FIGURE 3.1**    In the animation in Chapter 5 you will set the starting and ending key frames of the animation, and Carrara does the rest by creating the tweeners.

## THE TIMELINE

Key frames and tweeners have to exist somewhere, and that place is the *timeline*. The timeline is a graphical representation of time in an animation. In Carrara the timeline is located in the Sequencer tray, as shown in Figure 3.2. The timeline is where you set and edit key frames to choreograph all of the action in an animation. Key frames are represented on the timeline by a small triangle. Tweeners are the frames between key frames. In Carrara you can refine the motion of an object by adjusting tweener properties.

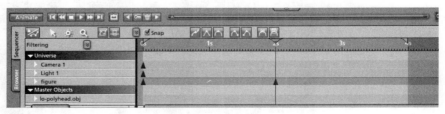

**FIGURE 3.2**    The Sequencer contains the timelines.

Each object in the scene that can be animated has a timeline assigned to it. The more objects you have, the more timelines appear in the timeline. This allows you to easily coordinate the movements of each object separately. Each timeline can have different properties and varying numbers of key frames. By positioning the key frames along the timeline and defining the tweeners' properties, you can easily orchestrate even the most demanding animations.

## THE GRAPH EDITOR

The Carrara 5 Graph Editor is a 2D graphical representation of an object's transform properties and location in the scene. The left side of the Graph Editor shows the value of the object's property, and the top shows its location in time. Key frames are represented by dots linked by curves. The curves represent the tweeners. The Graph Editor works in conjunction with the timeline; key frames must first be created in the timeline before the Graph Editor can be used.

For instance, to edit an object's height property using the Graph Editor, you would first scrub forward and move the object up or down along the z-axis to set a height key frame in the timeline. Then click once on the Timeline/Graph Editor toggle to open the Graph Editor. Once in the Graph Editor you have to drill down to the object's transform properties. The z-axis will be represented by a blue dot and curve. To edit the object's z value you move the dot up or down; to change timing or the position of the key frame you move the dot left or right.

By default, the curves between dots are straight, but you can change them to spline curves by clicking on a dot and then pressing the Spline Tangent button along the top of the Sequencer tray. Changing the curve from linear to spline allows you to fine-tune the object's transform property (see Figure 3.3).

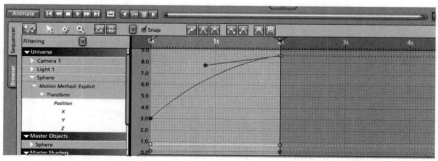

**FIGURE 3.3**    The Graph Editor is an alternate way to manage key frames and choreograph animation.

## ANIMATION METHODS

Now that we have a basic idea of what animation is and how to set key frames, let's take a brief look at several different animation methods that ship with Carrara: Explicit, Motion Paths, Physics, Kinematics, Morph Targets, and Bones.

### Explicit Animation

Imagine a simple key-framed animation where a ball rolls across the floor, as in Figure 3.4. Notice that in this animation, each position of the ball has a corresponding key frame in the timeline. In Explicit animation you are "explicitly" setting key frames that define the location of the object being animated. In other words, you are in control of exactly how the animated object will move. Explicit animation is probably the most common animation technique you will use in Carrara.

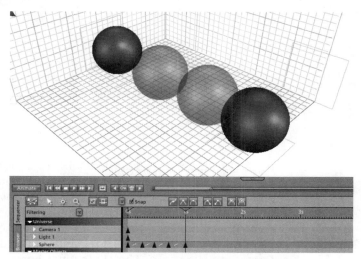

**FIGURE 3.4**    In explicit animation you control the animation by setting key frames.

### Motion Paths

When using motion paths, you draw a Bézier curve to create a visual representation of the path or trajectory an object will follow during the animation. The motion path, or curve, is drawn in the scene in much the same way you would draw any curve in any other part of Carrara. You can add points, delete points, move the points in 3D space, and refine the curve using its control handles. Motion paths also allow control over alignment to the path and banking around curves of the path. Motion paths are good for animating the fluid motion of objects on a trajectory such as, cars, airplanes, and bullets, but it is certainly not limited to those choices (see Figure 3.5).

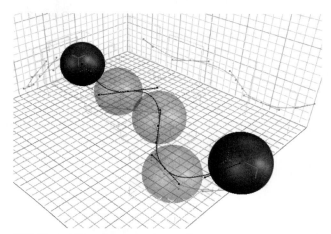

**FIGURE 3.5**   When using motion paths to animate an object, the object is attached to a path and will follow the trajectory of the path during the animation.

## Physics

In physics animation you control the motion of objects in a scene by defining their physical properties, such as initial velocity, friction, density, and bounce. To create motion in accordance with the laws of physics you insert a Physics Force object into the scene. For example, if you wanted to create an animated sequence with a ball bouncing, you would first set the physical properties of the floor and ball and then insert a Directional Force into the scene. The Directional Force moves the ball toward the floor, simulating gravity. When the ball collides with the floor, it bounces, but with each subsequent bounce the ball loses its virtual kinetic energy and eventually comes to rest. Using physics allows you to easily create complex animations that would be tedious to create by setting key frames (see Figure 3.6).

## Forward and Inverse Kinematics

Simply put, Kinematics facilitates the realistic posing or animation of an articulated system such as bone rig for a 3D character. Carrara supports two types of kinematics: forward kinematics (FK) and inverse kinematics (IK).

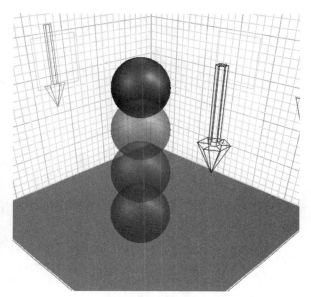

**FIGURE 3.6**   Creating complex animations that imitate the laws of physics is easy with physics animation.

FK is an animation system that relies on posing the articulated joints of a character over time. To make a character walk using FK, you would have to move and rotate each joint in sequence. For instance, first you would move the thigh, then the knee, and then the foot. Thus, FK propagates motion from a parent object (thigh) down to a child object (the rest of the leg). Though FK is more intuitive than IK, it is also more tedious for animating repetitive motion. In Carrara FK is the default animation method for any hierarchical, articulated system.

In IK motion is propagated up from a child object to a parent object. IK motion may seem odd at first, as it has no natural counterpart, but it allows repetitive motion such as walk cycles to be easily animated by moving the feet of the character instead of having to move all of the joints of the leg. With IK you move the child object, which is typically at the end of the IK chain, and Carrara solves the position of all of the joints and objects up the hierarchy. Thus, when you move the foot of a character in an IK chain, the rest of the leg follows along (see Figure 3.7).

## Bones

So far, all of the animation techniques we have covered involve the explicit motion of an object. Bones, however, are used to create character animations through the deformation of the character's polymesh. Bone-based

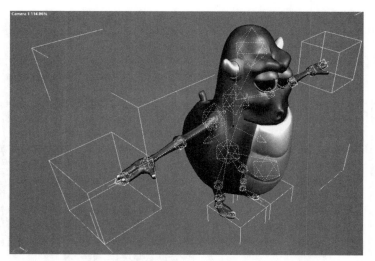

**FIGURE 3.7**    Forward and inverse kinematics facilitate the animation of 3D characters (modeled by Peter MacDougall).

character animation involves building a skeleton of bones and attaching it to the polymesh of the character, a process known as *skinning*. Characters are usually organic models, such as a person, a dog, an alien creature, a dinosaur, and so on. By building and attaching a bones skeleton to a character, you become a digital puppeteer. Moving the bones of the skeleton will animate the body of the character.

## Motion Capture

With Carrara you can build your own skeletons and attach them to any character and then animate them. However, Carrara can also import Biovision™ (BVH) and Kaydara® (FBX) *motion capture* files. Motion capture systems capture motion data by tracking sensors at key locations on a person's body, like the head, neck, shoulders, elbows, wrists, hips, knees, and ankles. The motion data is then applied to a bone system as key frames. When a motion capture file is imported into Carrara, it is displayed with Carrara's own bone system. A major benefit of using motion capture is that all the animation is already done, and the only thing you have to do is skin the bones to a character. A drawback to motion capture is that it tends to result in large files and the numerous key frames are difficult to edit (see Figure 3.8).

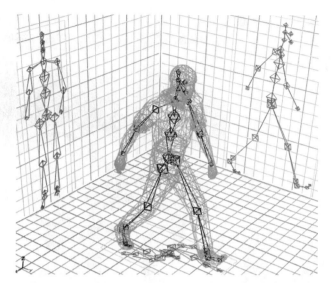

**FIGURE 3.8**    In bones animation a skeleton is built, attached, and moved to animate the body of a 3D character.

## Morph Targets

Like bones, *morph targets* are a form of polymesh deformation used in character animation, such as speech and facial expressions, though they can be used for other types of animation also. Though there are several morph targeting methods, they all work in essentially the same way. Typically, morph targeting requires a separate polymesh for each state of the object. In other words, if you have a character and you want to make him speak, you would have to create a separate polymesh for each *phoneme* of the words spoken. So if your character were to say "ouch!" there would be morph targets for each position of the mouth and lips when uttering "ouch!"

In Carrara morph targets do not use separate polymeshes as morph targets, but instead Carrara uses a more efficient method in which only the vertex positions of the deformations are saved as morph targets. Only one polymesh is needed, and morph targets are created by selecting vertices on the polymesh, creating the morph target, and then deforming the polymesh. Animation can then be created by using controls that transition between the saved morph targets. In Figure 3.9 Raul is made to speak to by using the phoneme morph targets shown in the Properties tray.

**FIGURE 3.9**   Morph targets are commonly used for facial animation such as speech and expressions (by Jack Whitney).

## SUMMARY

This chapter touched on some of the basics of 3D animation. Remember that good 3D animation takes more than just knowing the technical aspects of animation. A good animator, like a good 3D modeler or 3D texture artist, must be a keen observer of his surroundings and environment. Taking notice of how real-world objects move, understanding how to create emotions and moods in characters, and most importantly, knowing how to tell a story are the trademarks of a successful animator.

In Part V of the book you will work with several of the animation methods found in Carrara through step-by-step tutorials. In Chapter 14 you will use morph targets to make a character speak, and in Chapter 15 you will make a character walk using bones. But before you move on to the tutorials, the following five chapters in Part II will help you get acquainted with Carrara 5.

# GETTING TO KNOW CARRARA

# 4

# EXPLORING THE CARRARA WORKSPACE

## In This Chapter

- The Workspace
- The Document Window
- The Properties Tray
- The Sequencer Tray
- The Browser
- Customizing Carrara

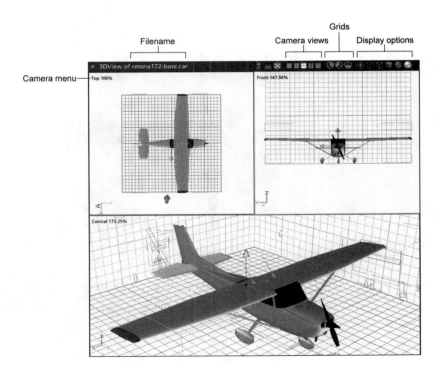

Grids

Filename      Camera views    Display options

Camera menu

*T*he purpose of the Carrara overview in Chapters 4 through 8 is to prepare
you for the tutorials in the subsequent chapters. Each chapter has a simple
exercise that will give you hands-on experience to concepts such as animation, texturing, and rendering. This overview is not intended to replace the information in the Carrara user manual, so have it handy. You will get much more out
of the tutorials if you become familiar with Carrara before attempting to work on
them.

## THE WORKSPACE

All of Carrara's powerful modeling, texturing, special effects, and animation tools can be easily accessed from the intuitively organized Carrara
workspace, or *graphical user interface* (GUI). One of the toughest challenges
in designing a software workspace is to organize the various windows,
buttons, and tools so that the desktop space is not cluttered and can be used
efficiently. The developers at Eovia have met this challenge by designing a
workspace that is customizable, elegant, and efficient.

When you first open a new or existing Carrara file, the default workspace is the Assemble room. The Assemble room is composed of the Document window, the Sequencer tray, the Properties tray, the Browser
tray, the Camera Navigation tools, the Primitive tools, and the 3D Object
Manipulation tools, as shown in Figure 4.1.

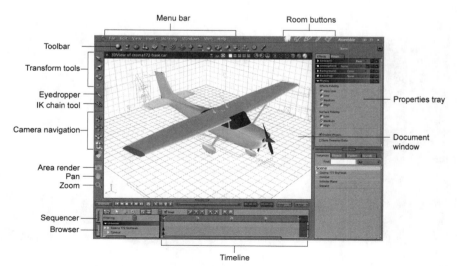

**FIGURE 4.1**    The Carrara graphical user interface.

Carrara was one of the first programs to use a unique working method to facilitate scene building, modeling, texturing, and rendering. In Carrara you build scenes in the Assemble room; if you want to model, you switch to the Modeling room; texturing is done in the Texture room and rendering in the Render room. Several other 3D and 2D programs are adopting some implementation of this working method. Using rooms to do different things might seem odd at first, but it is an efficient way to keep the workflow organized and the desktop uncluttered. To switch from room to room, click on the Room buttons in the upper-right corner of the workspace, as shown in Figure 4.2.

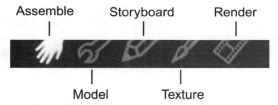

**FIGURE 4.2**    The Room buttons take you to each of the Carrara rooms.

## THE DOCUMENT WINDOW

The Carrara 3D universe exists within the Document window. A 3D scene is created when lights, cameras, and objects are placed and arranged inside the Document window. The Camera Navigation tools are used to track, pan, bank, and dolly around within the Document window.

One of the most useful features of the Document window is the View controls. Located along the top of the Document window, the View controls allow you to view a scene through up to four cameras at the same time. Having multiple views of a scene helps you build scenes quickly and precisely. You can switch to any other available camera from within the current camera view by selecting it from the Camera Name list in the upper-left corner of the camera view.

A useful feature of the Document window is the Object Preview controls. The Object Preview controls determine how the objects in a scene are rendered on screen. By default, objects are previewed in Gouraud shading, but sometimes it's more useful to switch to Flat preview, Wireframe preview, or even the Bounding Box preview. The computer will work faster in previews with less detail. However, if you want to see both shading and textures, switch to the Textured preview. Textured preview works best when you have a fast 3D graphics card that works with OpenGL.

The Working box is another important tool for building scenes and it is located inside the Document window. The Working box is composed of three orthogonal grids (also known as working planes) that help you move and orient objects within 3D space. Any object in the Document window will project 2D silhouettes on the plane of the Working box. You can use the projections to move, scale, and rotate objects. One or all of the planes can be hidden by clicking on the Grid controls located underneath the View controls. Sometimes it's easier to see the objects in the scene if some of the planes are hidden (see Figure 4.3).

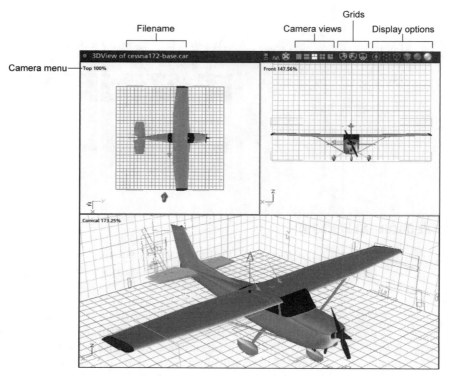

**FIGURE 4.3**    The Carrara Document window (split into three views).

Carrara 5 features a very useful scene manipulator, which facilitates the translation, rotation, and scaling of objects in the scene. When an object in the scene is selected, the scene manipulator appears as a gizmo that displays the *x*-, *y*-, and *z*-axes as arrows. By clicking and dragging on one of the arrows you can move the object along that axis. Switch to the Rotate tool and the Scene manipulator changes to a gizmo that has intersecting circles that represent the axes around which the object can be rotated. And finally, if the Scale tool is selected, the scene manipulator switches to a gizmo that displays vectors that can be used to scale the object along individual axes or all three axes at once.

## THE PROPERTIES TRAY

Next to the Document window, the Properties tray is probably the most important window in scene and model building. The Properties tray is divided into two parts. The top part is composed of five tabs that contain specific information about the object that is selected. Each tab is organized into sections. For example, if you select a sphere in the scene, its name (all objects can be renamed), shader assignment, visibility setting, and animation setting will be displayed within the General section of the General tab. In the View section of the General tab you can hide and display *backfaces*. In the Motion tab you can specify animation type, movement constraints, position, rotation, and scale. The Modifiers tab displays all of the deformers and behaviors that are available to apply to an object, and the Effects tab allows you to choose and apply different effects to the objects in the scene (see Figure 4.4).

**FIGURE 4.4**    The top half of the Properties tray in the Assemble room.

The bottom part of the Properties tray has four tabs: Instances, Objects, Shaders, and Sounds. The Instances tab displays single objects, groups of objects, and the hierarchical relationship between objects. You can also rearrange objects within the Instances tab by dragging them into a different location within the list. The Objects tab displays previews of all master objects, and the Shaders tab displays and stores all shaders in the scene. The Sound tab imports and stores sounds for use in the scene (see Figure 4.5).

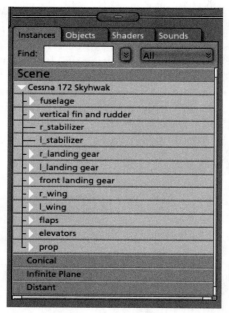

**FIGURE 4.5**    The bottom half of the Properties tray in the Assemble room.

In the Render room the Properties tray displays render settings such as render engine options, rendering options, raytracing options, advanced lighting, and motion blur settings. The Output tab of Properties tray displays render output settings such as render size, resolution, cameras, movie settings, and alpha mask settings.

## THE SEQUENCER TRAY

In the Assemble room the Sequencer tray gives you access to timelines for all objects in a scene, key frames, tweeners, animation playback controls, a scrubber, and the new Graph Editor. The timeline may be displayed in frames or time. The Sequencer tray has its own tools for selecting and placing key frames and for zooming in and out of the timelines. When you jump into the Render room, the Sequencer tray changes its content to display render information. In the Render room the Sequencer tray allows you to start and abort renders and also allows you to queue batched renders (see Figure 4.6).

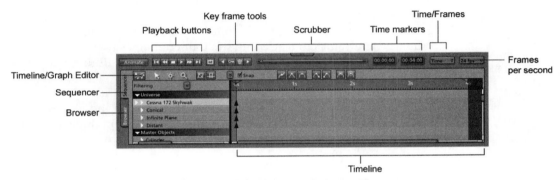

**FIGURE 4.6**    The Sequencer tray contains animation and object information.

## THE BROWSER

In Carrara 5 the Browser is found in the Sequencer tray, which is reminiscent of the manner in which Ray Dream Studio™ organized the Browser. The Browser is a drag-and-drop cataloging system that stores objects, lights, cameras, shaders, effects, and modifiers. In essence, the Browser helps keep things organized and provides quick access to the items stored in it. For example, if you build a bone skeletal system for a biped character, you can drag the bones into the Objects tab and store it for reuse in another biped character. There is no sense in building two bones systems when biped skeletons are essentially the same. Getting into the habit of using the Browser will make working in Carrara more efficient (see Figure 4.7).

**FIGURE 4.7**    The Browser stores various types of objects and files for quick access.

## CUSTOMIZING CARRARA

Carrara makes room for individual working preferences by allowing users to highly customize the way the user interface looks and works. To customize Carrara, open the File menu and choose Preferences. With the Preferences dialog window open, you'll notice that just about every part of the program is customizable, right down to the color of the camera names.

You will notice that figures in different parts of this book may look a bit different. That is because some of the colors in the 3D View Colors preference options have been changed. The document window Background color has been changed from the default dark blue to white, the Primary Wireframes to black, and the Camera names to black. If you like using keyboard shortcuts, make sure that the Toolbar Hotkeys are Sticky option is checked in General preferences. If you like a desktop that is as uncluttered as possible, you might consider turning off the clock and the background logo. Take a moment to experiment with the preferences to make your working environment as comfortable and productive as possible (see Figure 4.8).

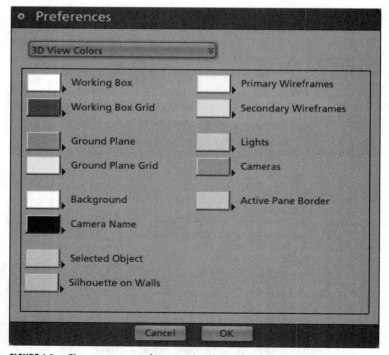

**FIGURE 4.8**    Choose your preferences in the Preferences dialog box.

## Moving the Tools

Besides customizing Carrara through the Preferences dialog box, you can also move the tools. For example, if you don't like the Camera Navigation tools on the left side of the window, simply drag it to a different location. You can also change its orientation from vertical to horizontal by Ctrl/Command-clicking on it. Just about everything except the menu bar and Room buttons can be relocated, as shown in Figure 4.9.

**FIGURE 4.9**    Move the components of the user interface to suit your style of working.

## Docking and Undocking the Trays

You can find one last bit of customizability in that the Sequencer tray and the Properties tray can be undocked, resized, and moved around. To undock the Sequencer tray, hold the Ctrl or Option key and drag the tray away from its docking spot, as in Figure 4.10. To put them back, hold the Ctrl or Option key again and drag them back into place. The Properties tray has a Dock and Undock button in the upper-right corner, so docking and undocking it is straightforward. Once undocked, each tray can be closed completely by clicking on the Close button in the upper-left corner. It might seem odd to want to undock the various trays, but if you have two monitors, you can move the undocked trays onto the desktop of one of the monitors to free up desktop space on the other monitor.

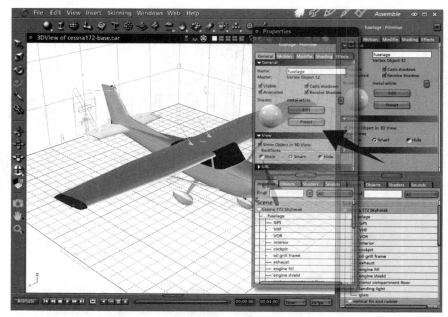

**FIGURE 4.10** All trays can be undocked and moved around.

## SUMMARY

Getting to know Carrara will take practice, but the people at Eovia have made it as easy as possible to be up and running in no time. This quick overview of the different parts of the Carrara workspace will help you feel right at home while working in Carrara and make learning the techniques in the following chapters more fun. Take time to review the manual for more information on customizing Carrara and customize Carrara to suit your style of working—it will pay off with higher productivity in the long run.

# 5

# WORKING IN THE ASSEMBLE ROOM

## In This Chapter

- Manipulating 3D Objects: Move, Scale, and Rotate
- Inserting and Positioning Cameras
- Inserting and Positioning Lights
- Creating a Simple Animation

## Manipulating 3D Objects: Move, Scale, and Rotate

Now that you are familiar with the Assemble room, let's perform some basic tasks. The first thing we are going to do is insert a sphere into the scene. Locate the Primitives toolbar at the top of the workspace. The button for inserting geometric primitives is located on the far left side of the toolbar (by default it has a Sphere icon). Click and hold the mouse over the button to reveal all of the primitives available. Choose the Sphere primitive by clicking on it once. Now, move the mouse over the working box in the main window and click once. Carrara inserts a Sphere primitive into the scene at the exact spot where you clicked, as shown in Figure 5.1. Repeat all of the steps, except this time when you are about to insert the sphere, click and drag in the working box. This action should allow you to insert and scale the new object at the same time. At this point, you should have a sphere somewhere in the scene.

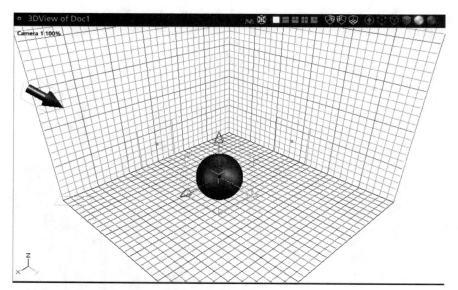

**FIGURE 5.1**    The sphere primitive in the scene.

### Working within a 3D Scene Using 2D Displays

Before attempting to manipulate the sphere we just inserted, let's solve a problem common to working in 3D: moving 3D objects within 3D space using a 2D display (screen) can be, to say the least, tricky. The problem is not so much moving the object as it is positioning it precisely. Computer displays cannot provide all of the information necessary to move around in 3D space from just one camera view, especially if you are using a *coni-*

*cal* camera (a camera that shows perspective). Carrara provides several tools to solve this problem.

First, the Document window has a working box planes that display *x*, *y*, and *z* projections of the objects in your scene. You can only move one projection at a time, so this effectively constrains movements to one or two axes, giving you better control (see Figure 5.2). With the Move tool (T), try moving one of the projections on the working planes.

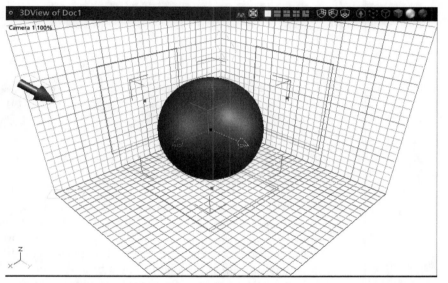

**FIGURE 5.2**   Projections on the working box grids and scene manipulators help position objects in the scene.

Second, the Document window has scene manipulators that permit accurate translation, rotation, and scaling of objects in the scene. Depending on which tool you have selected—Move (T), Rotate (R), or Scale (S)—the scene manipulator displays different graphical gizmos that allow precise manipulations. Holding the Shift key during translation, rotation, or scaling constrains the motion to straight, 45, and 90 degrees.

Third, you can view a scene through multiple camera views. Viewing the scene through more than one camera gives you more information on the position of an object in the scene. Choose the Four Views option from the View controls by clicking once on the icon that has four boxes, as in Figure 5.3. Carrara automatically changes the document window from a one-camera view to four cameras. Three of the four views will be *isometric* cameras, and one will be the view through the scene camera or the director's camera. However, you can change the camera view in any view by clicking on the menu in the upper-left corner and choosing a different camera.

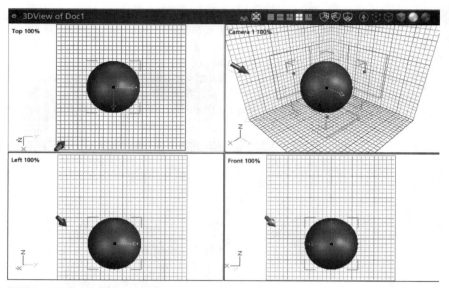

**FIGURE 5.3**    The Document window can be viewed through multiple camera views.

With a multiple camera view, it is very easy to see where you are moving an object. In addition, the isometric camera views restrain movement to only one or two axes. Use the Tab key to move from one camera view to the next. You can tell that a specific camera view has been selected because it is highlighted by a pink outline.

Now let's get back to our sphere manipulation exercise. Tab over to the Top camera view. Then click once on the sphere that you inserted earlier and move it by dragging the mouse. As you move the sphere in the Top camera view, you can see it moving in the other camera views as well. This feature allows you to precisely position any object because you can see all of the axes of movement at one time.

Carrara provides you with other options for moving and positioning objects; for example, you can use the Align tool (Edit/Align) to position objects relative to each other or relative to the working box. You can also position objects by entering *x*, *y*, and *z* coordinates in the Motion tab of the Properties tray (see Figure 5.4). You will get plenty of practice positioning objects and using different camera views in subsequent chapters. In the meantime, spend a little time experimenting with the various camera views and try inserting and positioning multiple objects.

## Scaling

Now that you've learned how to insert and position an object, let's take a look at 3D scaling. The Scale tool (S) allows you to change the size of an

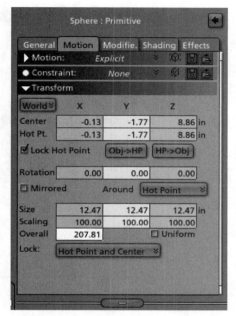

**FIGURE 5.4**    The Motion tab in the
Properties tray allows you to numerically
position an object.

object in any direction. Open a new Carrara document and insert a cube, but this time, insert the new object by selecting it from the Insert menu instead of the Primitives toolbar. To do this, open the Insert menu along the top of the main window and choose Cube. Carrara inserts a new cube object into the scene, perfectly centered at the origin of the Carrara universe. Next, move the cube so that it is off the floor or bottom grid, also known as the *xy* grid (see Figure 5.5).

Choose the Scale tool from the 3D Object Manipulation tools and note that the scene manipulator has changed to the scale gizmo. To scale the cube in any one axis, click and drag on one of the axes of the scene manipulator. If you hold down the Shift key, you will uniformly scale the whole cube in all three axes. Objects may also be scaled by entering values in the Motion tab of the Properties tray, as shown in Figure 5.6c.

## Rotate

The Rotate tool allows you to rotate objects around any one of the three axes or all three at the same time. Choose the Rotate tool (R) from the Object Manipulation tools and click and drag in the middle of the Cube primitive in the scene. Notice that as you drag, the cube is rotated freely.

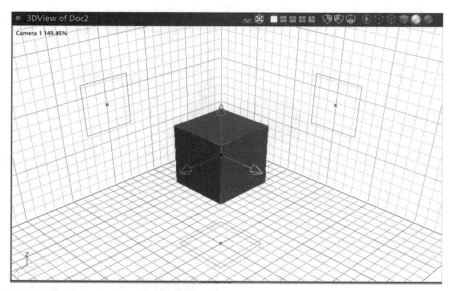

**FIGURE 5.5**  The cube primitive in the scene.

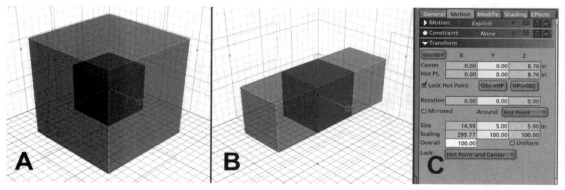

**FIGURE 5.6**  (a) Uniform scaling. (b) Scaling along the *x* axis. (c) Scaling numerically.

Reset the cube by choosing Undo from the Edit menu. This time rotate the cube by clicking and dragging on one of the circles of the scene manipulator gizmo. Notice that the rotation is constrained to one axis. Next, rotate the cube by clicking and dragging on the object projection on one of the grids. Try holding the Shift key to constrain rotation. As with moving and scaling, rotation can be done numerically in the Motion tab of the Properties tray (see Figure 5.7).

An important element to consider when rotating an object or grouped objects is the Hot Point. The Hot Point is represented by a small square at the center of the object. By default, the Hot Point is always centered

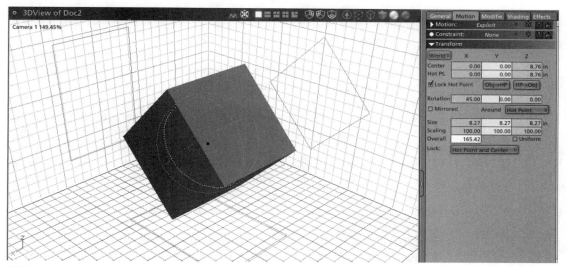

**FIGURE 5.7**    Rotating the cube.

within an object, so rotation makes an object spin around its center, as in Figure 5.8. However, the Hot Point can be moved away from the center of an object, causing rotation to appear like the object is orbiting around its Hot Point. Press the Caps Lock key and use the Move tool to move the Hot Point of an object or grouped objects.

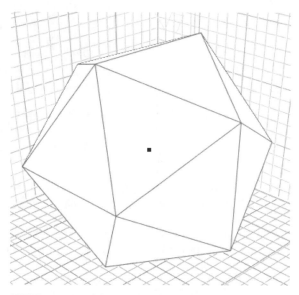

**FIGURE 5.8**    An object's Hot Point is the center of rotation.

## INSERTING AND POSITIONING CAMERAS

We have briefly covered how to insert and manipulate 3D objects in this section. Now we will cover how to position cameras and add more custom cameras to a scene. Why would you need more than one camera in a scene? Well, as with real-world filming, you will probably want more than one viewpoint of your scene. Can you imagine a movie with just one camera viewpoint? Although you could keep repositioning one camera to capture different viewpoints, it's much more efficient to have more than one custom camera and just switch back and forth between them.

As mentioned earlier, a default Carrara document will open with only one custom camera labeled "Camera 1." However, you also have access to six isometric cameras—Top, Bottom, Left, Right, Front and Back—and one Reference camera, as shown in Figure 5.9. Of all the cameras that a Carrara document has built in, you can only capture animation and still images with custom cameras. The six isometric cameras and the Reference camera are for working within the scene only.

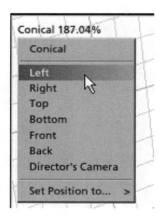

**FIGURE 5.9** The Camera Name list shows all available cameras in a scene.

Cameras are represented in the scene by blue, 3D camera objects, as shown in Figure 5.10. Camera objects can be manipulated in 3D space much like the primitives we worked with earlier. However, most of the manipulation you will do with a camera object is to move and rotate it to get it to point in the right direction. Scaling a camera object does not really do anything except make the camera object larger or smaller. It does not affect the view through the camera.

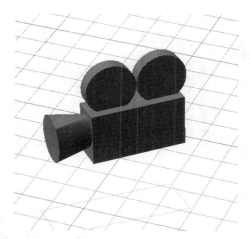

**FIGURE 5.10**    A camera is represented in a scene by a blue camera object.

Set up a new scene with any 3D object primitive. To insert a new camera, you can either select the Camera icon from the toolbar and click in the scene or choose Conical from the Insert menu. As mentioned previously, a conical camera sees perspective and an isometric camera does not see perspective. For animation and still images, you will almost always use a conical camera.

Once inserted, a new camera will be facing down on the *xy* grid, or the floor (see Figure 5.11a). As with any 3D object, you can use the Move and Rotate tools to position a camera. A quick way to get a camera to point in the right direction is to use the Point At command. Let's give it a try. Using the Move and Rotate tools, position the new camera that you've just inserted so that it roughly faces or points toward the primitive in the scene. With the new camera selected, Shift-click on the primitive to select it also. From the Edit menu, choose Point At. If you watch closely, you can see the new camera reorient itself so that the primitive is centered within its viewpoint (see Figure 5.11b). You can also use the Direct Manipulation wireframe to position a camera and to control its aim and zoom (see Figure 5.11c). The Direct Manipulation wireframe for a camera can be toggled on and off in the Camera section of General tab in the Properties tray.

So far, we have inserted a new camera and learned to position it within the scene. However, we are still looking at the scene through the original Camera 1. To switch to the new camera, click once on the Camera Name menu in the upper-left corner of any camera view to open it and select the new camera labeled Conical from the menu. Carrara will automatically change the point of view from Camera 1 to the new camera, as in Figure 5.12.

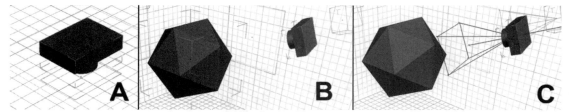

**FIGURE 5.11**    (a) A newly inserted camera. (b) Using the Point At command to position a camera. (c) The Direct Manipulation wireframe allows you to position, aim, and zoom a camera.

**FIGURE 5.12**    Choose the new camera from the Camera Name menu to switch views.

Camera 1 and Conical are not really good camera names, because they don't tell you much about the camera. It is a good idea to assign descriptive names to the cameras in your scene that will give you a clue as to what each camera does. For example, the main camera in a scene could be named MainCam (we like to shorten camera to cam), or a second camera could be named Bird's Eye View. The idea is to name the cameras so that they are easy to pick out in the Camera Name menu and the names describe what they do. To rename a camera, simply select it in the scene and type the new name in the Name field of the General tab in the Properties tray, as shown in Figure 5.13.

We have learned how to manipulate a camera exactly like any other 3D object, but because you can look through a camera, there is another way to position cameras. First, switch views to the camera you want to reposition. Once you are looking through the camera, you can use the Camera Navigation tools to change its location. The Camera Navigation tools, located along the left side of the main window, allow you to *track, pan, dolly,* and *bank* the camera that you are looking through. Each time you track, pan, dolly, or bank, the camera will be repositioned. If you get lost while positioning a camera and can't tell in which direction you're looking, you can reset the camera by using the Set Position to . . . option from the Camera Name menu. To do this, open the Camera Name menu, choose Set Position to . . . , and select Reference from the submenu. You could reset the camera position to any of the other cameras in the scene, but the Reference position gives you the best vantage point to reorient yourself (see Figure 5.14).

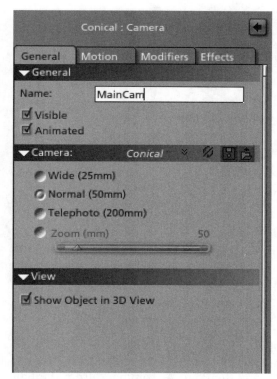

**FIGURE 5.13**   Giving a camera a descriptive name is a good idea.

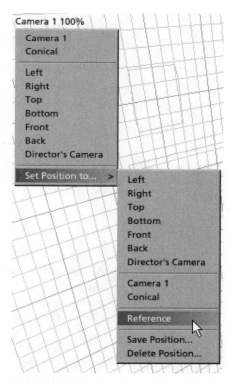

**FIGURE 5.14**   If you get lost while positioning a camera, choose the Set Position to. . . option from the Camera menu.

## INSERTING AND POSITIONING LIGHTS

By now you've probably figured out that inserting and positioning a light is similar to inserting and positioning cameras. However, let's go through a couple of quick exercises working with lights. To insert a new light, you can choose the type of light you want from the Light icon on the toolbar. Your basic options are Spotlight, Bulb light, Distant light, and Moon and Sun lights. The Spotlight will light a narrow portion of scene, the Bulb light shines in all directions, and the Distant light mimics sunlight. The Moon and Sun lights work best with the Atmosphere Sky and Realistic Sky presets. Carrara features other light objects, but they are for special effects, so we will stick to the basic lights for this chapter. Once you have selected the light type you want, click somewhere in the scene. The new light appears on the bottom grid pointing down, as shown in Figure 5.15.

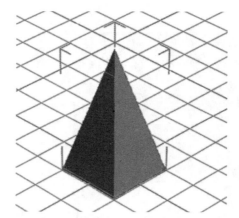

**FIGURE 5.15**   A new spotlight in the scene.

Once a light is inserted into the scene, it can be positioned using the Move and Rotate tools, just like a camera or another object. Select the Move tool and try moving the light around the scene. Remember that you can use the light's scene manipulator and silhouette projections on the working box grids to move it. If you inserted a spotlight or distant light, rotate it so that it doesn't point down. With the light selected, click on the Motion tab of the Properties tray. In the x field, type 90 and press Enter (see Figure 5.16). The camera is rotated 90 degrees. Like cameras, lights can also be positioned using the Point At command from the Edit menu or by using the Direct Manipulation wireframes.

While you can see where a camera is pointing by looking through it, that is not the case with lights. One way to see if a light is shining in the right direction is to use the Test Render tool (X) to see the effect the light has on the objects in a scene. To do this, point a Spotlight at an object. Select the Test Render tool and drag around the object and light (see Figure 5.17). The area will be rendered and you can see the effect the light is having on the object. If it isn't right, reposition the light or change the light settings in the Properties tray.

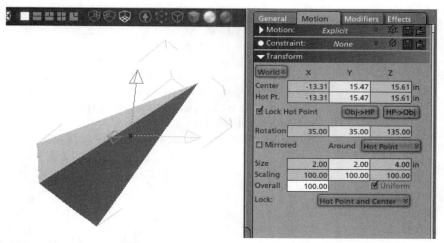

**FIGURE 5.16**    Lights can be manipulated by entering numbers in the Motion tab of the Properties tray.

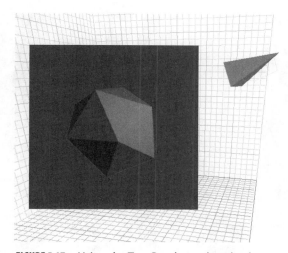

**FIGURE 5.17**    Using the Test Render tool to check on lighting effects.

## CREATING A SIMPLE ANIMATION

Now that we have covered most of the basics, we are ready to try a simple animation. In this next exercise, we are going to animate a spinning and oscillating fan. Although this might sound difficult, it's actually very easy to do.

Open the file fan-start.car located in the Chapter 5 folder on the accompanying CD-ROM. You should see a model of an old-style oscillating
fan on a plane (see Figure 5.18). Open the Sequencer tray so that you can
see the timeline of the fan group. First, we are going to extend the time
length of the movie to two seconds by moving the render range markers.
The render range is located at the top of the timelines and contains second or frame markers. The render range can be set by moving the yellow
half arrows. Click and drag the yellow arrow on the right or at the end of
the render range to four seconds (see Figure 5.19).

**FIGURE 5.18**     The oscillating fan that we will animate.

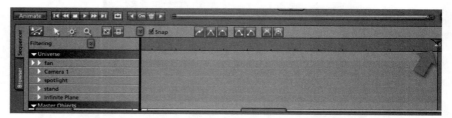

**FIGURE 5.19**     Setting the length of the animation by moving the render range markers.

Let's take a minute to review a few things about Carrara's interface.
In order to animate objects or groups of objects, you have to select them.
In Carrara you can select objects in the scene by clicking on them with

the Move tool, on their names in the Instances tab of the Properties tray, or in the object list in the Sequencer tray. How you select objects is up to you.

Before starting an animation, make sure that the time is set to zero, so click the Rewind button on the VCR-style controls. To set the starting point of the animation, select the fan group, and in the Motion tab of the Properties tray type "45" in the Z field of the Rotation fields or use the Rotate tool. Either method will rotate the fan. Now, click the Fast Forward button on the VCR controls to get to the end of the animation. Select the fan group once more, and this time enter "−45" in the Z field to rotate the fan in the opposite direction—this sets the end point of the animation. Note that a key frame has now appeared on the timeline for the fan group (see Figure 5.20). Try scrubbing the animation by dragging the small blue arrow in the scrubber located near the top of the Sequencer tray. You should see the fan move back and forth.

**FIGURE 5.20**    At time zero set the Z rotation of the fan to 45 degrees, and at time four seconds set the rotation to −45 degrees.

To play the animation click the Rewind button once and then click the Play button. The fan should turn from left to right one time. The fan moves back and forth once, but what we want is for the fan to oscillate several times. We could manually animate the fan to oscillate by setting key frames, but there is a better way. Instead of using key frames, we will apply the Oscillate behavior to the tweener between the key frames.

Click once on the space between the first keyframe and the last keyframe on the timeline for the fan group; notice that it turns yellow. In the Properties tray, Carrara displays the properties for the tweener—by default it should be set to Bézier (or Linear). Switch to Oscillate by clicking on the Tweener menu and selecting Oscillate. Once you have the Oscillate properties open, set the Number of Oscillations to 2 and play again (see Figure 5.21). Now the fan should oscillate a couple times during the animation.

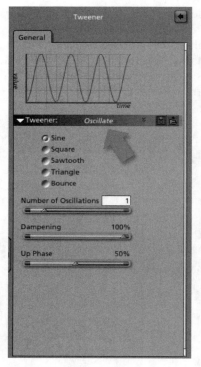

**FIGURE 5.21**  The Oscillate behavior makes the fan oscillate back and forth.

We are almost done; the only thing missing is that the fan blades are not turning, but this is also simple to do. In the Sequencer tray, open the fan group and select the fan blades group. In the Properties tray click on the Modifiers tab, and then click on the + symbol and choose Behaviors from the menu and Spin from the submenu. Set the Cycles per Second to 10 and set the Axis of Rotation to Y, as in Figure 5.22. When you play the animation this time, the fan should oscillate and the fan blades should spin.

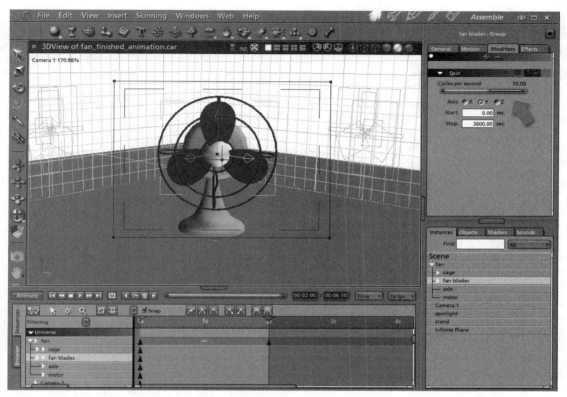

**FIGURE 5.22**   Setting the Spin behavior for the fan blades.

Congratulations on completing your first animation! This simple exercise introduced working with modifier behaviors and tweeners and reviewed several of the concepts that we discussed in previous chapters such as setting key frames, using the Rotate tool, setting properties in Properties tray, and using groups.

## SUMMARY

With Carrara, it's easy to build scenes and create animations. From simple animations to complex animations, the concepts and tools are the same—all it takes it is a bit of know-how and time. Experiment with the animation we just completed; try inserting different lights or changing the camera angles. The only real way to become proficient is to practice. In the next chapter, we will learn basic shader techniques to add color and texture to the oscillating fan, and in Chapter 8, we will render the fan animation into a movie.

# 6

# BUILDING SHADERS IN THE TEXTURE ROOM

## In This Chapter

- The Texture Room
- Working with Shaders

## THE TEXTURE ROOM

The Carrara Texture room has all of the tools you will need to texture the 3D objects you build or import. To open the Texture room, either select an object in the scene and click on the Texture room button or double-click on a shader button in the Properties tray. Once in the Texture room, you will see the Shader Tree Editor for the shader that you want to modify. You will also see a preview window that displays in real-time the surface characteristics of the object that you are texturing. The Camera Navigation tools can be used to get a better look at the object in the preview window (see Figure 6.1).

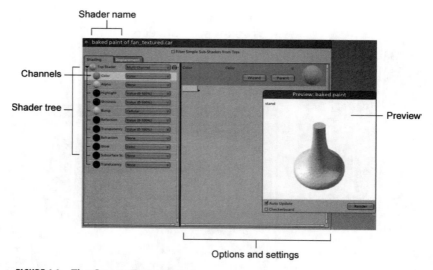

**FIGURE 6.1**    The Carrara Texture room.

## WORKING WITH SHADERS

The shader tree stores surface information that can be applied to any object in the scene. A single level, multichannel shader is composed of 11 channels: Color, Alpha, Highlight, Shininess, Bump, Reflection, Transparency, Refraction, and Glow, Subsurface Scattering, and Tranlucency (see Figure 6.2). Each channel can be customized with colors, texture maps, procedurals, operators, and many other functions. A custom shader is built by defining the values of each channel. Not all channels have to be defined, however. For example, if you are creating a shader for a window, you will use the Transparency channel to set the level of transparency, but if you are creating the shader for a metal, you would leave the Transparency channel value set to zero, or None.

Complex shaders can have multiple levels; thus, the Shader tree branches out into nested channels. The most common method to create multiple levels is to use the Mixer operator as the component for a top-level channel, as shown in Figure 6.2. If an object's surface is a gradient between red and blue, the only way to create this effect is to use a Mixer that has red for Source 1, blue for Source 2, and the Gradient component for the Blender. In this chapter we are going to stick to single-level shaders to keep things simple. However, in subsequent chapters we will delve into the more complex shaders.

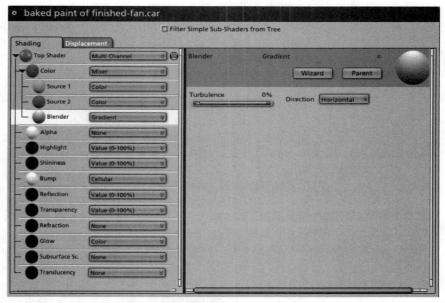

**FIGURE 6.2**    A multichannel shader tree with nested channels.

The following exercise illustrates the basic steps in texturing objects in the Texture room. We are going to use the oscillating fan model once more, so open the file fan_untextured.car in the Chapter 6 folder in the file in the accompanying CD-ROM. Click on the Shaders tab of the Properties tray. The only shader present should be the Default shader, as shown in Figure 6.3. Now, click once on the Default shader icon and take a look at the General tab in the upper half of the Properties tray. The Name field should show the Default name, and the Instances box displays all of the objects to which the Default shader has been applied (in this case its all of the objects in the scene).

Now we are going to set the surface qualities for the stand object of the fan. Select the stand object in the scene or in the Instances tab and then click once on the Texture room button. When Carrara asks if you

ON THE CD

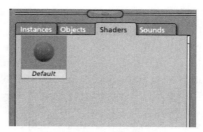

**FIGURE 6.3**   The Default shader in the Shaders tab of the Properties tray.

want to Edit the Master or Create a new Master, select the Create a new Master option and click OK. This will create a new shader for the stand object, leaving the Default shader untouched (see Figure 6.4).

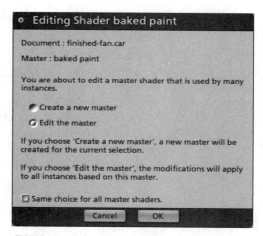

**FIGURE 6.4**   Select Create a New Master.

### Assigning a Color

The first step in setting the surface qualities of the stand object is to assign it a color. You can be creative later and make the fan any color you want, but for now let's give the fan a 1950s look by giving it an avocado green color. In the shader tree click on the Color channel and then on the right side click on the color chip (see arrow in Figure 6.5). The Color Picker will appear in the bottom-right corner of the window. The Color Picker allows you to numerically select the color you want in HLS, RGB, CMYK, and various other formats. For this exercise, let's use the HLS format. In the fields for the HLS Color Picker, enter H23, L62, S48. The color should be a pale green.

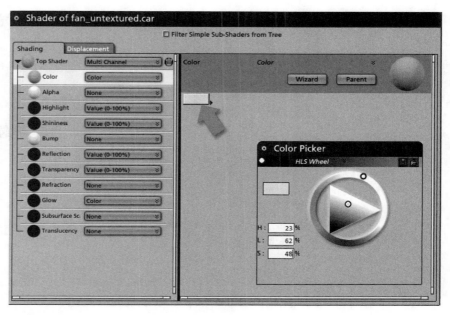

**FIGURE 6.5**    Set the color in the Color Picker.

## Using a Procedural Texture as a Bump Map

Now that the color has been applied, let's give the stand a texture so that the surface looks like the paint has been baked on. Click on the Bump channel in the shader tree and then click on the menu to open it. Choose Natural Functions and from the submenu, choose the Cellular procedural. You can see in the Preview window that the surface now appears to be wrinkled. To refine the Cellular effect, choose the fifth option down from the Shape menu. Then, set the Intensity to 8% and the Scale to 25%. Now the texture looks more like baked-on paint (see Figure 6.6). Recall that in Chapter 2 we discussed using procedural textures for tasks other than their name implies. In this example we are using the Cellular procedural to create a bumpy texture on a fan, not on a cell. Procedurals are great for all types of surface effects.

The finish of the stand is metal with a glossy, enamel paint, so it will require a sharp highlight. Set the Highlight value to 35% and the Shininess value to 5%. The Highlight value controls the intensity of the highlight, and the Shininess value controls the size of the highlight. Highlight and Shininess work together to define the specular quality of the surface. Most surfaces that have a high specular value usually also reflect light. To finish creating the surface characteristics of the stand object, set the Reflection value to about 11%. When you are done adjusting the shader settings, jump back into the Assemble room. To see the color in

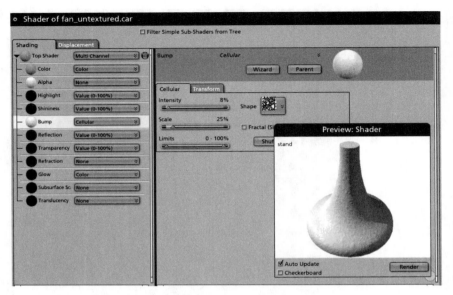

**FIGURE 6.6** The bump map effect is used to add textures.

the scene, press the Test Render tool (X) and draw a box around the stand. The result of assigning a color, adding a bump map, and setting the Highlight, Shininess, and Reflection values is that the stand object now looks like a painted metal surface (see Figure 6.7).

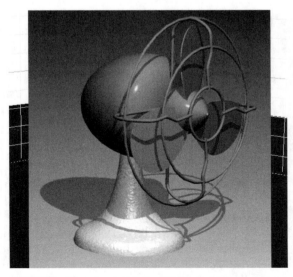

**FIGURE 6.7** The stand object with the finished shader applied.

Click on the Shaders tab of the Properties tray. You should now see two shaders: the original Default shader and the new shader you just created. Name the new shader "baked paint." To name the new shader, select it from the Shaders tab and type the new name in the Name field of the General tab in the Properties tray. Naming shaders is a good idea so that you can keep them organized, as shown in Figure 6.8.

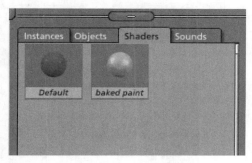

**FIGURE 6.8**    Name the new shader.

### Dragging and Dropping Shaders

Now we are going to apply the baked paint shader to another object, but we are going to do it without going to the Texture room. Instead, we are going to simply drag the shader from the Shader tab on to the object in the scene. Locate the fan group in the Instances tab of the Properties tray. Click once on the small, white arrow next to the group name to open the group. Click once on the motor object so that it is highlighted in the scene (this just makes it easier to see in the scene). The motor is the object behind the fan blades. Now, click once on the Shaders tab and drag the baked paint shader onto the motor object in the scene; when you are over the motor, it will turn red. The motor object immediately takes on the qualities of the baked paint shader (see Figure 6.9).

### Using Stock Shaders

To texture the fan blades and the protective cage around the fan blades, we are going to use a stock shader that comes with Carrara. While creating custom shaders can be a lot of fun, and using them on your 3D objects gives them a unique look, there is no sense in spending time recreating a shader that already exists. In this case, the finish of the metal cage and metal fan is polished metal. In the Instances tab of the Properties tray click to open the fan blade group so you can see the three blade objects. Next, open the Browser in the Sequencer tray and click on the Shaders tab and in the Basic Metals folder locate the Chrome shader. Finally, drag and drop the chrome shader onto each fan blade, as shown in Figure 6.10.

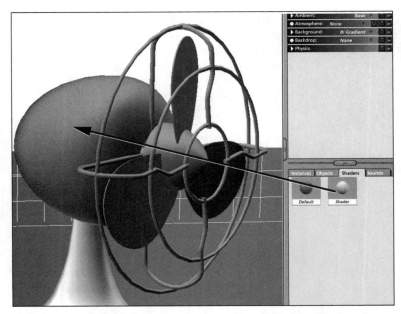

**FIGURE 6.9** Apply the baked paint shader to the motor object by dragging and dropping the shader from the Shaders tab onto the object in the scene.

**FIGURE 6.10** From the Shader Browser drag and drop the Chrome shader onto the fan blades.

## Using the Eyedropper Tool

To add the Chrome shader to the cage, we are going to use the Eyedropper tool. The Eyedropper tool allows you to sample an object's shader and then apply it to another object. The Eyedropper tool is located on the left side of the Carrara window under the Rotate tool. Select the Eyedropper tool and click once on one of the fan blades. You know that the Eyedropper tool has sampled the color because the tip turns black. After sampling the Chrome shader on one of the fan blades, click once on any part of the cage. The Eyedropper tool applies the Chrome shader to the cage object. Repeat these steps until all of the parts of the cage have been shaded with the Chrome shader (see Figure 6.11).

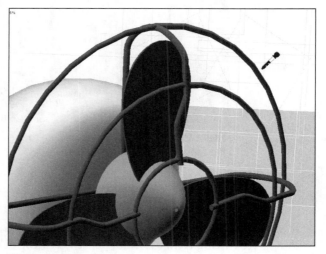

**FIGURE 6.11**    Use the Eyedropper tool to copy shaders from one object to another.

The last object to texture in the fan assembly is the fan spinner. The spinner is located in the center of all three blades. The spinner is a white version of the green baked paint shader we used earlier, but take a few moments to decide how you want to texture the spinner object. There is no right or wrong way to do it, and experimenting with shaders can be a lot of fun. When you are finished applying textures, use the Test Render tool once more to see what the fan looks like with all textures applied (see Figure 6.12).

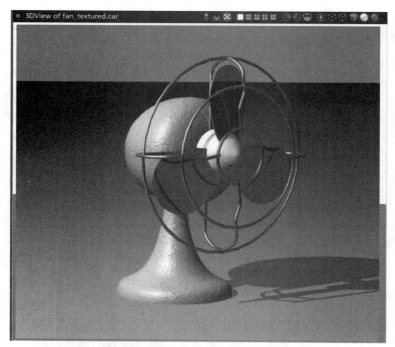

**FIGURE 6.12**     Use the Test Render tool to see what the textures look like on the fan.

## SUMMARY

Texturing is an essential part of creating 3D images and animations. With Carrara's shader tools, building complex textures is not only easy but fun. In this chapter we have learned how to use the shader tree in the Texture room to build shaders and apply them to objects in the scene. In addition to just adding color we created a rich shader that made the surfaces of the fan appear to be painted metal. We also learned that Carrara ships with dozens of ready-to-use shaders that can save us time. The chapters in Part IV will extensively cover the different methods of texturing models in Carrara, but for now the next chapter will review the modeling rooms in Carrara.

# 7

# THE CARRARA MODELING ROOMS

### In This Chapter

- Exploring the Spline Modeler
- Exploring the Vertex Modeler
- The Carrara UV Editor

## EXPLORING THE SPLINE MODELER

The Spline modeler is a powerful modeling tool that allows you to create complex 3D objects with ease. The Spline modeler generates surfaces by extruding cross sections along a sweep path, as in Figure 7.1. As long as a Spline object is not exported out of Carrara or converted into another type of modeler (e.g., Vertex modeler), the Spline object can always be edited, or even animated, by manipulating the cross sections, curves, sweep paths, and extrusion envelopes that define its shape. The Spline modeler does not allow the direct editing of vertices, edges, or polygons.

**FIGURE 7.1** The Spline modeler generates surfaces from cross sections that are extruded along a sweep path.

The Spline modeler is a great tool for modeling objects like machines, tools, furniture, and architecture. It can also be used for simple organic objects, such as cartooned or stylized figures, but its strength lies in creating 3D technical illustrations, as in Figure 7.2. The best way to work with the Spline modeler is to model the individual parts of an object and then assemble them in the Assemble room, as in Figure 7.3.

### The Spline Modeler Window

To open the Spline modeler, you can either choose Spline Object from the Insert menu or you can click once on the Spline Object button in the object bar and click once anywhere in the scene. Although similar in appearance to the Assemble room, the Spline modeler window displays a

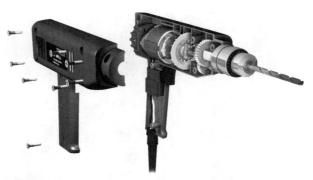

**FIGURE 7.2**    Technical illustrations are easily created in the Spline modeler.

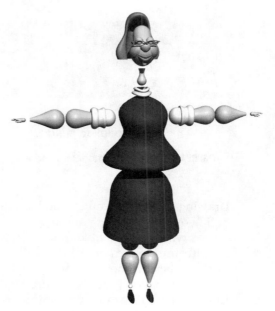

**FIGURE 7.3**    Complex objects can be assembled from parts modeled in the Spline modeler (modeled by Jack Whitney).

different toolbar and makes new menu commands available, as in Figure 7.4. The first thing you will see when the Spline modeler opens is a working box made up of *x*, *y*, and *z* planes. More importantly, inside the modeling box is the Drawing plane. The Drawing plane is where you will begin modeling any new Spline object. As soon as you draw a cross section on the Drawing plane, the Spline modeler will extrude it along the Sweep path. When the Spline modeler is first opened, you only have one

Spline Modeler tools

Properties tray

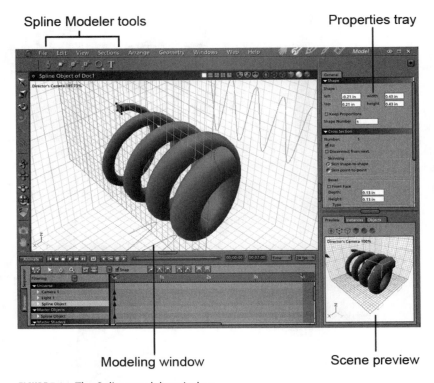

Modeling window

Scene preview

**FIGURE 7.4** The Spline modeler window.

Drawing plane, but you can add as many Drawing planes as you need to build your 3D shape.

As with the Assemble room, you can work with a single camera view or with multiple camera views. If you are working on small details, it might be best to zoom in with a single camera view; just click on the One View button along the side of the Modeling window to switch to a single camera view. However, if you are trying to position cross sections or are working with the Extrusion envelopes, multiple views are a better choice (see Figure 7.5).

You can use the Camera Navigation tools to move around the 3D space in the Spline modeler. Because Drawing planes can be rotated, it can easily become difficult to see or edit the cross sections that are in them. To address this problem, select the Drawing plane you want to work in and from the Camera List menu, select Current Section. The Current Section view allows you to see the contents of any Drawing plane by temporarily positioning the current camera directly in front of the Drawing plane, as in Figure 7.6. The Move, Rotate, Scale, Zoom, and Test Render tools are also available in the Spline modeler.

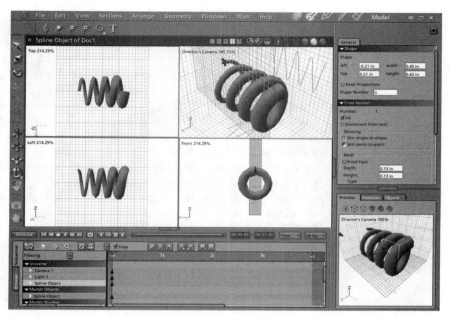

**FIGURE 7.5**    Like with the Assemble room you can use multiple camera views in the Spline modeler.

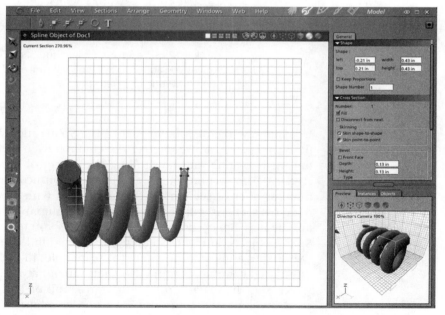

**FIGURE 7.6**    Use the Current Section from the Camera List menu to force a camera to view the cross section from the front.

## The Spline Modeler Tools

As mentioned earlier, when the Spline modeler is opened, you have access to a new toolbar and new menus. The Pen tool is the first button in the toolbar. The Pen tool works much like the Pen tool in Adobe Illustrator®, Adobe Photoshop, or Macromedia® Flash®. You use the Pen tool to draw curves on the Drawing plane. The curves are then extruded along the Sweep path. The Convert Point tool allows you to toggle from a smooth curve to a curve with corners. The Delete Point tool and the Add Point tool do exactly what their names imply. However, the Delete Point tool will also delete the line segments between edit points. The Add Point tool adds new control points along any curve in the Spline Modeler, whether a curve on the Drawing plane or the curves of the sweep path or envelopes. The next tool is the Primitives Shapes drawing tool. Click and hold on to the small arrowhead below this tool and you will get a fly-out menu that gives you access to four 2D primitives: rectangle, rounded corner rectangle, oval, and polygon. Last but not least is the Text tool, which makes it easy to create 3D text and logos (see Figure 7.7).

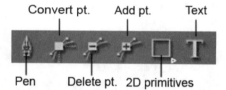

**FIGURE 7.7**    The Spline modeler toolbar gives you access to the tools you will need to build your 3D objects.

The new menus that appear in the Spline modeler window are Sections, Arrange, and Geometry. The commands in these menus are essential in managing and controlling the shape of the 3D object you are creating. The Sections menu provides you with commands to manage the number of cross sections in the model and with options to control how the cross sections will behave. The main commands in the Arrange menu are the new Bevel command, which allows you to easily create bevels on Spline objects, and the Combine as Compound command, which takes two shapes and combines them to create holes in the extrusion. The most often used commands in the Geometry menu are the Extrusion Method, which sets the extrusion type to Translation or Pipeline, and the Extrusion Envelope, which inserts Extrusion envelopes. The Geometry menu also provides Extrusion presets that come in handy for creating quick spline models.

### The Spline Modeler's Properties Tray

Because the Properties tray (Figure 7.8) provides you with detailed information about the shapes, points, and cross sections that make up the model, it is an essential tool when working in the Spline modeler. The values in the Properties tray can be edited, giving you precise control over how your model is built.

The Properties tray also gives you access to the Bevel tool and to the Scene Preview window. The Bevel tool allows you to easily add various types of bevels in the direction of the extrusion. The Preview window gives you a view of the Assemble room, so that you can monitor the progress of your model. The Preview window becomes critical when you are trying to model Spline objects in relation to other 3D objects in the Assemble room, as in the bottom of Figure 7.8.

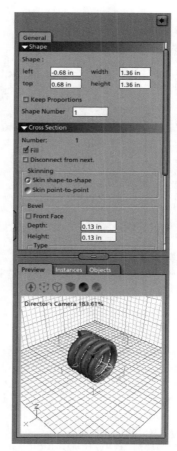

**FIGURE 7.8**    Spline modeler's Properties tray.

## EXPLORING THE VERTEX MODELER

The Vertex modeler is the quintessential polygonal modeler. Stocked with powerful modeling tools, yet easy to use, there isn't an object that can't be built with the Vertex modeler. The Vertex modeler gives you the freedom to create smooth organic models and allows you to build precise technical models. By positioning individual vertices, edges, and polygons, the Vertex modeler also provides unprecedented control over the object you are modeling (see Figure 7.9).

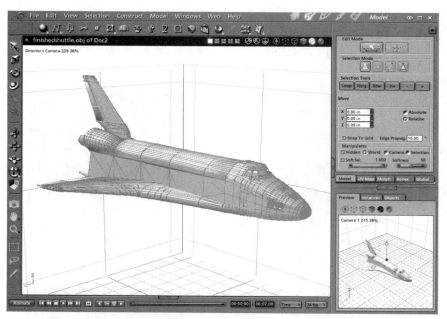

**FIGURE 7.9** The Vertex modeler can create detailed organic models and precise technical models.

### The Vertex Modeler Window

To work in the Vertex modeler, click on the Vertex Object icon from the Primitives toolbar in the Assemble room and click once in the Document window. You can also choose the Vertex Object option from the Insert menu. Eovia has done a great job keeping the design of the modeling rooms consistent, so when you go from room to room you know where to find the tools you need. However, the Vertex modeler does have its own toolbar, menus, and working box. Like the other modeling tools in Carrara, the Vertex modeler shares the Camera Navigation tools, Manipulation tools, and View Controls (see Figure 7.10).

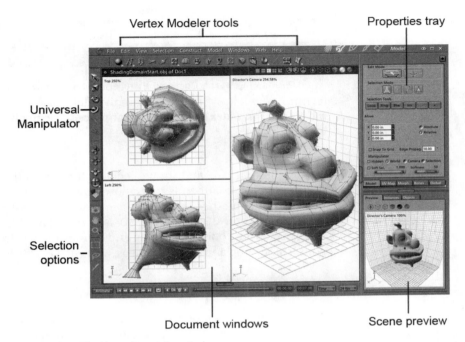

Vertex Modeler tools

Properties tray

Universal Manipulator

Selection options

Document windows

Scene preview

**FIGURE 7.10**    The Vertex modeler window.

## The Vertex Modeler Tools

The Vertex modeler has powerful tools that make modeling any object a snap. It has the standard modeling tools found in any good polygonal modeler, including connect, weld, add, delete, subdivision surface, extrude, lathe, sweep, loft, tessellate, and so on. Carrara 5 introduces new modeling and selection tools in the Vertex Modeler such as fillet, edge extraction, ruled surfaces, double sweep, Gordon, Coons, and many more. Used individually, each tool does a great job, but when used together, these tools make short work of creating any model. The new selection tools include loop, ring, lasso, marquee, and paint selection. In addition, the Vertex modeler features the Universal Manipulator, a unique transform tool that expedites move, scale, and rotate functions (see Figure 7.11).

The menus in the Vertex modeler provide access to additional tools and commands that help refine the shape of your model. The menus specific to the Vertex modeler are View, Selection, Construct, and Model. The View menu has commands that control the working box and the drawing

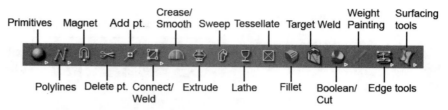

**FIGURE 7.11**   The Vertex modeler's toolbar has several new tools.

planes and that hide and show specific selections of the model. The Selection menu has commands that allow you to name, organize, and select polygons, polymeshes, edges, and vertices. The Construct menu provides access to the new 2D curve and 3D surfacing tools. The Model menu features numerous tools for welding and connecting vertices, managing polygons, smoothing and creasing edges, and edge extraction.

### The Vertex Modeler Properties Tray

As with the Spline modeler, the Properties tray in the Vertex modeler is very important when building models. However, the Properties tray in the Vertex modeler contains more information than the Spline modeler's version.

In the Vertex modeler the Properties tray is divided into several sections. The top section is the Edit Mode, which toggles between modeling mode and Animation Mode. The animation mode is used for creating morph targets and working with bones. Next, the Selection Mode section toggles between selecting polygons, vertices, and edges. The Selection Tools section has shortcuts for creating loops and rings and managing selections. Directly below the Selection Tools the Properties tray displays tool information and settings. For instance, if you select the Move tool, then the Properties tray displays numerical options for moving parts of the model. If instead you select the Dynamic Extrusion tool, it will display options for extrusion.

The middle section of the Properties tray is organized into five tabs. The Model tab allows access to subdivision surfaces, the UV Mapping tab contains tools for mapping and for accessing the UV Editor, the Morph tab manages and creates morph targets, the Bones tab allows control over bones influences, and the Global tab has tools for managing shading domains and the backdrop reference images. The bottom third of the Properties tray has the scene Preview window, which allows you to see your progress in the Assemble room, as shown in Figure 7.12.

**FIGURE 7.12**    The Vertex modeler
Properties tray.

## THE CARRARA UV EDITOR

Beginning with version 3, Carrara has featured a comprehensive UV Editor, as shown in Figure 7.13. UV mapping is the most common method used for texturing models for gaming and film. The Carrara UV Editor allows objects to be easily UV-mapped, edits UVs, and exports UV map templates for painting in another program such as Photoshop.

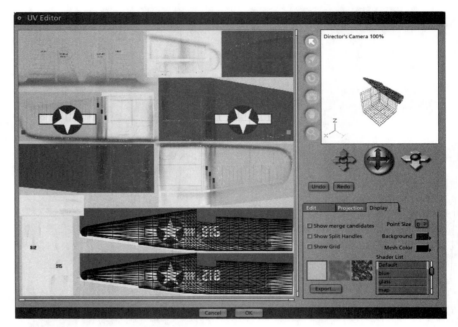

**FIGURE 7.13**  The Carrara UV Editor.

The Vertex modeler is unique among the Carrara modeling tools in that it provides unmatched control over the final shape of your object. However, more than just providing control, it is intuitive and simple to use. With new advanced modeling and selection tools that allow you to create morphs, UV map, control bone weighing, and manage shading domain tools you will find that you have everything you need within the Vertex modeler.

## SUMMARY

With the Carrara modeling tools, you can build anything you can imagine, from fantasy and realistic characters, to commercial products, to any type of vehicle. In this chapter we touched on the features and strengths of the Spline and Vertex modelers. In the chapters that follow you will work through challenging modeling tutorials that will provide you with hands-on experience with each modeler. By the time you're finished with this book, you will feel right at home with any of the Carrara modelers.

# RENDERING SCENES AND ANIMATIONS

## In This Chapter

- The Render Room
- Photorealistic Rendering
- Non-Photorealistic Rendering
- Rendering an Animation

If 20 years ago you were asked to render a scene, you probably would have pulled out your favorite drawing pencils, or oils and canvas, or maybe even your trusty Paasche VL airbrush (veteran artists know what a Paasche VL airbrush is) and proceeded to create an illustration or drawing. Today, however, if you were asked to render a scene, you would fire up Carrara, build and texture 3D models, arrange a scene with lights and cameras, and then click the Render button. The term *render* refers to the digital process of creating a 2D image from 3D data.

One of the best features in Carrara is its ability to render ultra photo-realistic scenes and animations using *raytracing, global illumination, caustics,* and *high dynamic range image* (HDRI). If you want just the opposite, you can also render images that appear to have been painted with oils on canvas—a process known as *non-photorealistic* rendering. Carrara offers a state-of-the-art render engine that allows you to control, down to the pixel, exactly how you want your rendered image to appear (see Figure 8.1).

**FIGURE 8.1**    Outdoor scene rendered using HDRI (image by David Bell).

## THE RENDER ROOM

After the models are built and textured, the light and cameras are in place, and the animation has been choreographed, you are ready to render. In Carrara the place for rendering a scene or animation is the Render room. The Render room is made up of the Properties tray, the Render tray (a.k.a. the Sequencer tray), and the Render window, as shown in Figure 8.2.

Render window                                        Properties tray

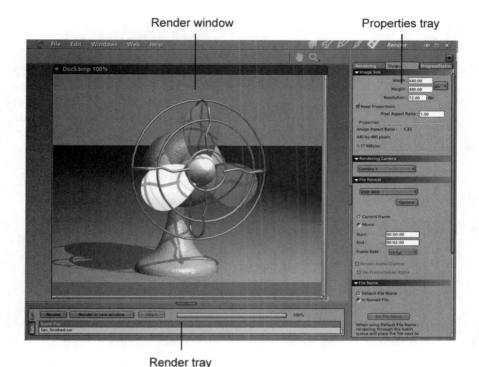

Render tray

**FIGURE 8.2**    The Carrara Render room.

The Properties tray organizes the different render settings into three tabs: the Rendering tab, the Output tab, and the Progress/Statistics tab, as shown in Figure 8.3. The Rendering tab allows you to choose the type of renderer you want to use. The Output tab lets you choose the size and resolution of the render, which camera will be used for the render, the file format, file name, and G-Buffers. The Progress/Statistics tab displays information about the render.

In the Render room the Render tray takes the place of the Sequencer tray. The Render tray organizes files that are about to be rendered. In the Current Scenes mode the Render tray manages the current scenes that are opened in the Assemble room. The Render in New Window feature allows you to make multiple renders of a scene for comparison without having to save each one. In Batch Queue mode the Render tray allows you to queue up multiple files and automatically render and save them while the computer is unattended, as in Figure 8.4.

Once you have clicked on the Render or Render in New Window button, the Render window appears. The Render window shows the progress of the image as it is being rendered and displays the finished ren-

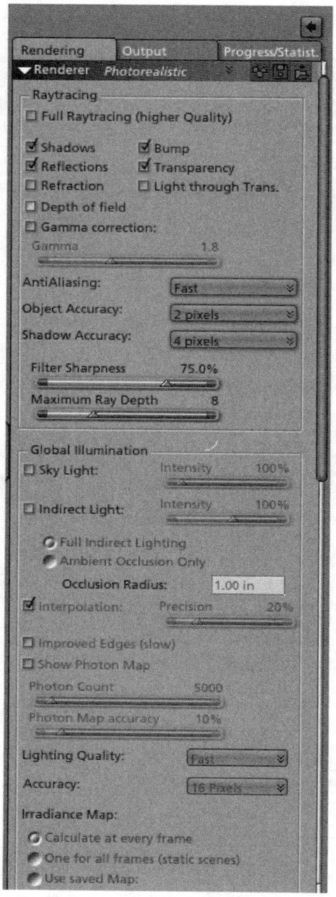

**FIGURE 8.3** The Render room Properties tray.

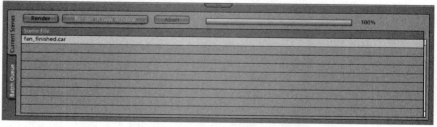

**FIGURE 8.4** The Render tray organizes files to be rendered.

der, as shown in Figure 8.5. Use the Pan and Zoom tools to inspect the rendered image. When you are happy with the render, save it by choosing Save As from the File menu.

**FIGURE 8.5**    An image in the process of being rendered.

If you are rendering an animation, the Render window shows which frame of the animated sequence is being rendered, and when the animation is complete, the Render window will have VCR controls to play the new movie. Choose Save As from the File menu to save the animation (see Figure 8.6).

**FIGURE 8.6**    The Render window with a finished animation.

## PHOTOREALISTIC RENDERING

Photorealistic, raytraced rendering has always been the hallmark of Carrara. However, in version 5, Carrara takes realism to a higher level with HDRI, improved global illumination, more efficient caustics, and *motion blur* and by introducing *subsurface scattering*, making Carrara one of the best photorealistic programs on the market. While each of these new features will be covered in later chapters, let's take a moment to see what lies behind the fancy names.

### HDRI

HDRI is a lighting method that more accurately reproduces the lighting effects created by the outdoor lighting. When lighting a scene with HDRI, a special file (*.hdr) designed to hold more detailed lighting information than standard image files is loaded into the Background of the scene. With Skylight enabled in the Render room, Carrara uses the information in the HDRI file to realistically light the scene, as in Figure 8.7.

**FIGURE 8.7**    HDRI rendering creates realistic highlights and light and dark areas (image by David Bell).

### Global Illumination

Global illumination is an advanced lighting method in which the diffuse characteristics of light are calculated. If visible light were not diffused, a

room lit by a single lamp would be completely dark except in the imme-
diate area where the light from the lamp falls. However, we all know that
when a lamp is turned on in a room, it lights up the entire room. This
happens because the light from the lamp bounces off the ceiling, walls,
and other objects in the room, filling the room with diffuse light, creating
a mix of soft and harsh shadows and different levels of lighting. With
global illumination enabled, Carrara calculates indirect lighting caused by
the diffusion of light, as shown in Figure 8.8.

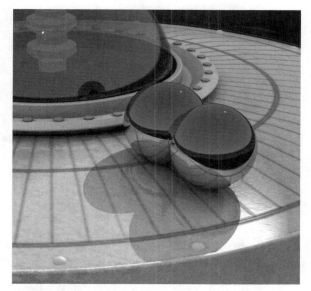

**FIGURE 8.8**  Global illumination calculates the diffuse
characteristics of light (image by David Bell).

## Caustics

As light passes through transparent objects, it is focused into distinct patterns called caustics. A typical example of caustics can be seen in the illumination patterns that water creates on the bottom of a pool on a sunny
day or in the focused highlights cast on to a table top as light passes
through a glass. Carrara can reproduce caustic lighting effects to add realism to an image (see Figure 8.9).

### Motion Blur

When software like Carrara renders moving objects, the objects often
have perfectly crisp edges, producing an unrealistic effect. In an effort to
create more natural movement, motion blur introduces the natural blur-
ring that we see and that film records when objects move.

**FIGURE 8.9**    Caustics create distinctive patterns of illumination (image by David Bell).

### Subsurface Scattering

Subsurface scattering is a natural phenomenon produced when light interacts with translucent surfaces. In subsurface scattering light partially penetrates the upper layers of a translucent surface such as skin, bounces around within the surface, and exits at a different point than where it entered. The result of subsurface scattering is that the surface appears to subtly glow or appear translucent. All nonmetal materials have some factor of subsurface scattering. In Carrara subsurface scattering is produced and managed in the Texture room and works much like other shaders.

## NON-PHOTOREALISTIC RENDERING

If you burn out on creating the perfect photo-realistic image, take a moment to work with Non-Photorealistic (NPR) rendering in Carrara. NPR creates painterly images that appear to have been drawn using traditional art techniques. NPR rendering goes beyond just mimicking traditional art techniques in that it allows you to express your own unique artistic style. NPR can be used to create paintings, drawings, and outlines from your 3D scene. Use NPR in your next animation and you will see a whole new world of rendering possibilities, as in Figure 8.10.

**FIGURE 8.10**    NPR creates painterly renders.

## RENDERING AN ANIMATION

ON THE CD

In the exercise in this chapter we will take the animated sequence of the oscillating fan created in Chapter 5 and render it to a QuickTime® movie. You can also use the fan_finished.car file from the Chapter 8 folder on the accompanying CD-ROM. Let's review what we did in the animation exercise in Chapter 5. In Chapter 5 the 3D model of an oscillating fan was animated using key frames to set the starting and ending points, a tweener Oscillate function was used to make the fan oscillate, and the Spin behavior to make the fan spin. If you worked through the animation exercise in Chapter 5, you probably discovered that creating complex animation is fairly simple with Carrara. Taking the next logical step and rendering the animation to a movie is just as easy—so let's get started.

The first thing we are going to do is define what part of the camera view is going to be in the movie. Pointing the camera at the scene or at an object is only part of deciding what will be captured in the animation. To define what part of the camera viewpoint will be in the render, we'll use a framing tool called the Production Frame (see Figure 8.11). Make sure you are looking at the scene through Camera 1. To see the Production Frame for Camera 1, go the to the View menu and choose Show Production Frame. The Production Frame should appear in the view of the camera as a rectangle. If you set your preferences to match the book's figures, then the Production Frame will be black; if not, it will be white by default. The Production Frame can be moved and scaled by using the Move tool.

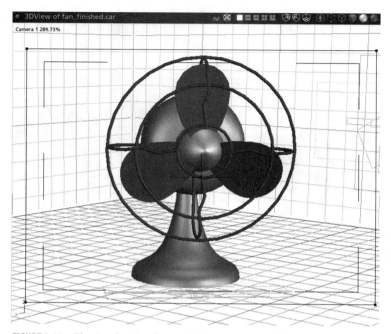

**FIGURE 8.11** The Production frame helps crop what will be in the render.

To move the entire Production Frame, click on the crosshairs in the middle of the rectangle and drag; to resize it, click on one of the corners and drag. In the final animation we want to be able to see the fan oscillate back and forth without any part being cropped out. To make sure all of the movement is in the animation, rewind the animation to 0 seconds and check to see that the fan is still in the frame. Now, fast forward to the end of the animation and check again. If you can see the fan at the beginning and the end, then you're okay. If not, move or resize the production frame until all of the fan is visible in the production frame during the animation.

With the Production frame in place, let's define the animation settings, so jump into the Render room and click on the Rendering tab of the Properties tray. By default, the Photorealistic option is selected; check Raytracing and make sure the Shadows, Reflections, and Bump options are checked. Uncheck the remaining options to speed rendering. We are not using global illumination or caustics in this animation, so leave everything else as default (see Figure 8.12).

Next, click on the Output tab in the Properties tray and check the Keep Proportions check box; this will keep the image size ratio constant. In the Width field enter 320; notice that the Height field is automatically updated to 240. Since many animations are played back on computer screens or displays of some type, 72 dots per inch (dpi) is perfect. Skip down to the File

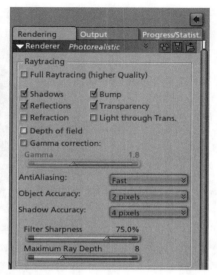

**FIGURE 8.12**    The settings in the Rendering tab.

Format section and make sure the QuickTime Movie option is selected from the menu. Set the frame rate to 24 fps (frames per second). Usually, 15 frames per second is good enough for Web, CD-ROM, or any other type of nonbroadcast media. In this case, however, since we have a spinning fan, a higher frame rate is necessary. If a low frame rate is used, then the spinning motion of the fan would be offset by the low frame rate and the fan would appear to be still or the spinning motion would not be smooth, as in Figure 8.13.

The physical size, resolution, and fps will determine the final uncompressed file size of an animation. Even simple animations can end up being composed of thousands of frames, creating files that can be very large. Another issue to consider is render time; high-resolution animations, with special effects like global illumination and motion blur, will take much longer to render. Time and computer storage space are expensive commodities, so take time to factor in all the variables and make sure to optimize animations.

With the Production frame in place and the render/animation settings specified, all that is left to do is to click on the Render button in the Sequencer tray. Once the Render button is clicked, Carrara will begin rendering each frame of the animation. You can see the rendering progress in the Rendering window. Once the rendering process is complete, you can play back the animation to see what it looks like. If you are not satisfied with how it looks, try a new position for the Production frame or maybe tweak the render settings in the Properties tray.

**FIGURE 8.13**    The settings in the Output tab.

## SUMMARY

Animation is one of the most satisfying and challenging aspects of 3D computer graphics. With Carrara and a little practice, you will be able to manage even the most complex animations. By walking you through the steps in rendering a simple animation, this chapter concludes the Carrara introduction. In previous chapters we touched on the basics of getting around in Carrara, choreographing an animation in the Assemble room, and texturing in the Texture room. At this point, you should have a general understanding of how Carrara works and can move on to working through the tutorials with confidence.

# MODELING WITH CARRARA AND HEXAGON

# MODELING WITH THE CARRARA SPLINE MODELER

## In This Chapter

- Modeling the Rocket Body
- Modeling the Rocket Engine Nozzle
- Assembling the Rocket

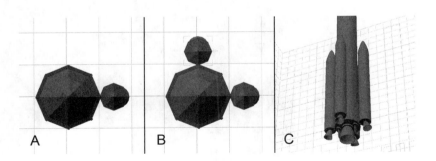

The Carrara Studio Spline modeler is a versatile modeling tool. With its cross sections, sweep path, and extrusion envelopes, you can create almost any object. The strength of the Spline Modeler lies in creating technical models or stylized character design (see Figure 9.1). The tutorial that follows focuses on that strength, and by the time you are finished with the tutorial, you will have enough experience with the tools in the Spline Modeler to venture out and start modeling whatever your heart desires.

## MODELING THE ROCKET BODY

ON THE CD

In this tutorial the Carrara Spline Modeler will be used to model a Delta rocket, a NASA workhorse used to launch satellites and deep space probes. The reason for picking a specific type of vehicle is to show that with Carrara it is easy to quickly build precise 3D models, as in Figure 9.1. If you get stuck during this tutorial or just want to see the model complete before starting the tutorial, the Chapter 9 folder in the accompanying CD-ROM has incremental files of the modeling steps in addition to the finished model.

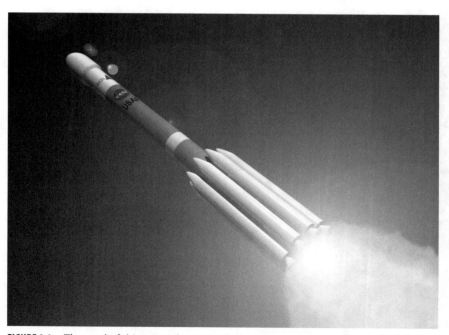

**FIGURE 9.1**   The goal of this tutorial is to teach you how to model a technical model, like a Delta rocket.

## Getting Started: Reference Images

Before starting any technical model, you will need reference materials, such as drawings, diagrams, photographs, or scale models. The reference materials are used as modeling guides and will help you model accurately and quickly. In the case of the Delta rocket model we will use a side-view drawing of the rocket. Because the rocket's cross section is circular, one view is all we need. The rocket is composed of the long rocket stages, or body, the payload at the top, the engine at the bottom, and eight solid booster rockets (see Figure 9.2).

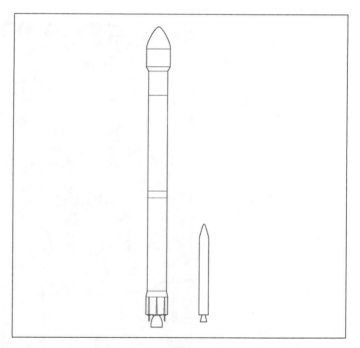

**FIGURE 9.2**    The reference drawings that we will use to model the Delta rocket.

**ON THE CD**

Open the file delta_step1.car from the Chapter 9 folder in the book's CD-ROM. The scene contains two lights, a camera, and a plane that has been textured with the reference image. The reference image has been carefully prepared so that it displays properly inside the Assemble room when Textured Display is toggled on. First, the reference image itself has high contrast so that the lines of the drawing are easily seen. Second, the reference image is a high resolution image at 1024 × 1024 pixel resolution and 300 points per inch (ppi). The ppi do not matter as much as the pixel resolution. For best display, use images whose size is in multiples of eight such as $128 \times 128$, $512 \times 512$, or, ideally, $1024 \times 1024$.

If you cannot see the reference image on the plane, you can do a couple things to fix the problem. The display settings located in the upper right corner of the document window control the how objects appear in the scene. Click on the Textured display button; it is the very last sphere in the display settings. If you still cannot see the reference image on the plane, click on Interactive Render Settings; it is the small arrow pointing up, to the left of the display settings, and in the Rendering Mode section click on 512 (see Figure 9.3). The reference image should look like Figure 9.4.

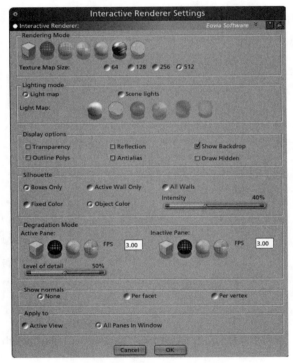

**FIGURE 9.3** The Interactive Render settings.

## Modeling with Cross Sections and Extrusion

Now that you can see the reference image in the Assemble room, we can start modeling the rocket. In Carrara all modeling is done in the modeling rooms. In this case we are using the Spline Modeler, so from the Insert menu choose Spline Object and click once in the scene. Carrara should immediately jump into the Spline Modeler. The Spline Modeler will display the standard working planes and a single drawing plane, as in Figure 9.5.

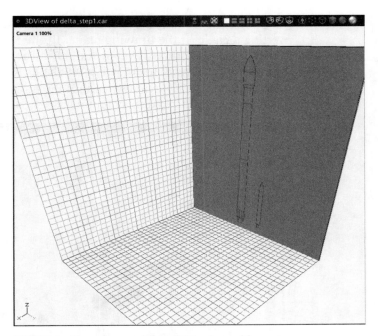

**FIGURE 9.4**     The reference image in the Assemble room.

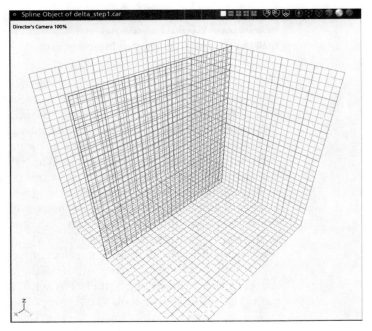

**FIGURE 9.5**     The Spline modeler working box.

Since the Delta rocket has a circular cross section, we will start by inserting a circle in the drawing plane. In the Spline Modeler toolbar click once on the 2D primitives tool and select Draw Oval. Then click once on the drawing plane. Carrara will immediately extrude the oval into a tube (see Figure 9.6).

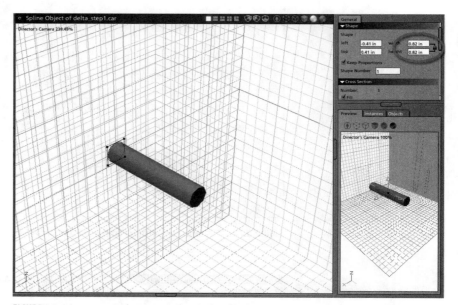

**FIGURE 9.6**   Insert a circle to start the rocket body.

Next, we have to scale the circle to the right size. Usually this takes some experimentation, but for tutorial purposes we will provide you with the correct size. Select the circle in the drawing plane by clicking on it. In the Properties tray locate the Shape section, check Keep Proportions to constrain scaling, and in the Height or Width fields enter ".82 in." Now that the circle is the right size, we need to center it on the drawing plane to facilitate modeling later. Select the circle again and from the Sections menu choose Center; note that the circle centers itself on the drawing plane.

Now we will increase the length of the tube by moving the end points of the sweep path. On either the *z,y* or *y,x* grids click on one of the ends of the sweep path (the pink line) to select one of the end points (see Figure 9.7a). Now hold the Shift key and drag the end point to the edge of the working box. Repeat the same steps with the other end of the sweep path. The result should look like Figure 9.7b.

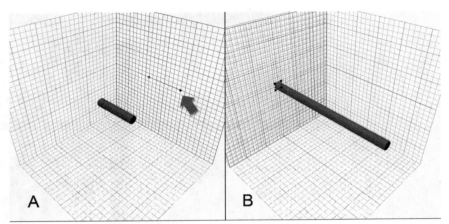

**FIGURE 9.7**    The rocket body is starting to take shape as the cross section circle is sized and the tube lengthened.

### Checking Scale against the Reference Image

Before we proceed, let's take a moment to see what the rocket looks like in the Assemble room. Jump back into the Assemble room by clicking on the Hand icon in the room buttons in the upper right corner of the Carrara interface. The rocket you just created is probably lying on its side on the floor of the Assemble room. We need to rotate the rocket so that it is upright. Click on the rocket and then select the Rotate tool. Hold the Shift key and click and drag on the red, or *x*-axis, circle. The rocket body should rotate 90 degrees (see Figure 9.8).

Now that the rocket is upright, you have probably noticed that it is too large, so we will have to correct that problem also. Switch to the Left Camera view, as this view will make it easier to scale the rocket. Select the rocket and locate the Motion tab in the Properties tray. In the Transform section of the Properties tray locate the Scale All field and type "200." You should see the rocket scale down. Use the Move tool to position the rocket body over the rocket in the reference image to check for scale, as in Figure 9.9. The rocket body should match the reference image closely in height and width, albeit not necessarily perfectly.

Before we jump back into the Spline Modeler to continue modeling, let's name the rocket object. Click on the Instances tab of the Properties tray. There should be an object named Spline Object. Click on this object and in the General tab (at the top of the Properties tray) locate the Name field and name the object "rocket." Naming the objects in a scene is a good way to keep things organized.

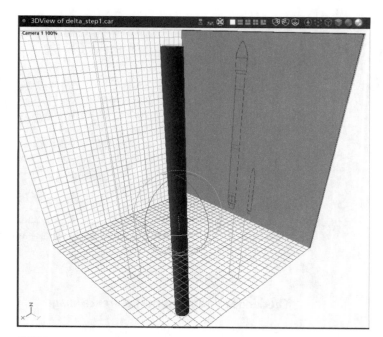

**FIGURE 9.8** Rotating the rocket body upright.

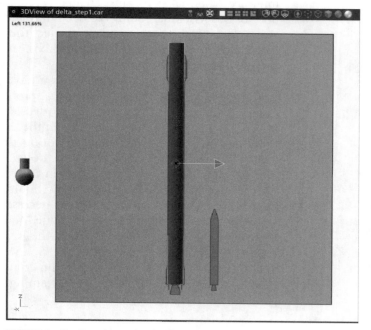

**FIGURE 9.9** Scaling the rocket body.

### Roughing-In the Payload and Engine

Most of the rocket is a straight tube, but at the top the payload capsule flares out and then ends in a rounded point. At the bottom also the rocket engine causes the rocket body to flare out. In the next few steps we will add new cross sections to create these details.

Double-click on the rocket to jump back into the Spline Modeler. Right now the rocket only has one cross section at the start of the sweep path. Let's add a new cross section at the other end of the sweep path. Click once on the drawing plane and from the Sections menu choose Create. Notice the new cross section at the end of the sweep path (see Figure 9.10).

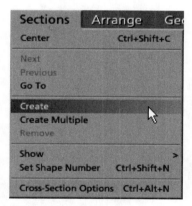

**FIGURE 9.10**    Adding a cross section at the end of the sweep path with the Create command.

To model the changes in diameter created by the payload and the engine, we have to add five more cross sections between the two end cross sections. Click on the first cross section and from the Sections menu choose Create Multiple. In the Create Multiple Cross Sections dialog box enter "5" and click OK. Carrara instantly adds five evenly spaced cross sections between the cross sections at the ends, as in Figure 9.11.

The new cross sections have to be positioned along the sweep path so that they correlate with the changes in diameter created by the payload and engine. Moving the control points on the sweep path moves the cross sections, so switch to the Left Camera view and with the Move tool click once on the sweep path (the pink line) to make the control points for each cross section visible. Next, move the control points one by one, as in Figure 9.12.

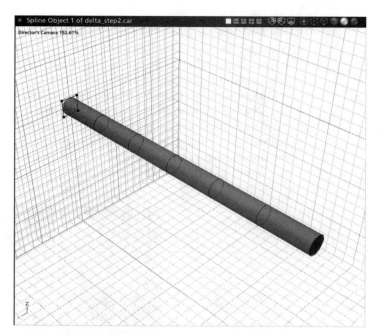

**FIGURE 9.11** New cross sections added to shape the rocket.

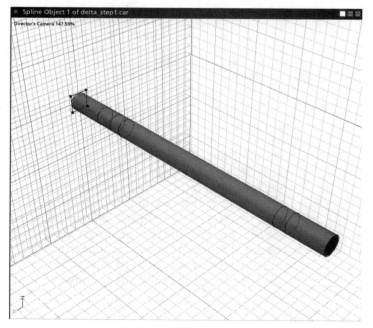

**FIGURE 9.12** The cross sections moved into position.

Now that we have the cross sections in roughly the right spots, we can start shaping the rocket. However, when working with multiple drawing planes it can be difficult to select individual cross sections or drawing planes. Luckily each drawing plane is numbered sequentially; the original drawing plane is 1, the next 2, the next one 3, and so on.

The rocket model has seven drawing planes, so to select drawing plane 1, open the Sections menu, and choose Go To. In the Go To dialog box enter "1" and click OK. The first drawing plane becomes active. Press Ctrl/Command-A to select the cross section on drawing plane 1. This cross section is the very tip of the rocket, so we have to scale it down considerably. With the cross section selected, hold the Shift key down and drag one of the corner points toward the middle (see Figure 9.13).

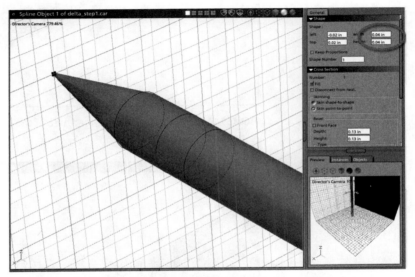

**FIGURE 9.13**    Scaling the first cross section to form the tip of the rocket.

Activate drawing panel 2 and select the cross section in it. Scale the cross section so that its height and width are 1 inch. You can see the height and width in the Properties tray. Go to drawing plane 3 and scale the cross section in it to the same size as the cross section in drawing plane 2. The payload area of the rocket should look like Figure 9.14.

Now we will model the change in diameter at the bottom of the rocket caused by the engine. Go to drawing plane 6 and scale the cross section in to 1 inch. Do the same for the cross section in drawing plane 7 (see Figure 9.15). Make sure that the cross sections remain perfectly centered on their respective drawing planes. You can do this by selecting the cross section and going to Sections/Center.

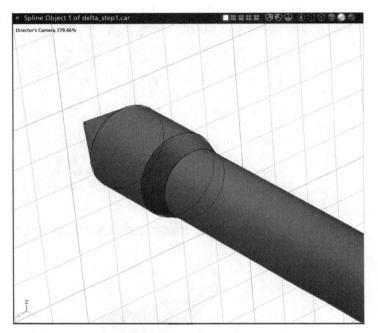

**FIGURE 9.14**    Roughing-in the payload area of the rocket.

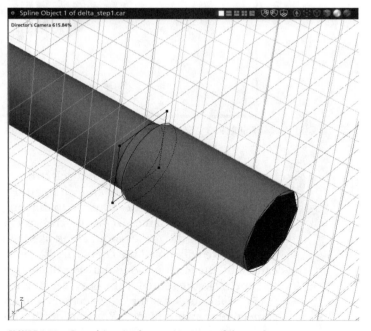

**FIGURE 9.15**    Roughing-in the engine area of the rocket.

## Working with the Properties Tray Preview Window

We have roughed-in the payload and engine compartments of the rocket but we need to check that the changes in diameter are in the right locations. We could jump into the Assemble room and check against the reference image and then jump back into the Spline Modeler to make adjustments, but that would be very time consuming. Instead, we can use the preview window in the Spline Modeler's Properties tray to see how the model is shaping up when compared to the reference image in the Assemble room.

The preview window in the Assemble room is located at the bottom of the Properties tray. Drag the separation line right above the preview window up to open it as large as you can, but before you can work with the preview window you have to adjust its settings to see the model and the reference image clearly. First, click on the camera menu in the properties window and select the Left Camera view. Next, select the Textured display by clicking on the rightmost sphere at the top of the preview window. Finally, if you still cannot see the reference image, click on the small arrow pointing up to open the Interactive Render Settings and choose 512 for Texture Map Size (see Figure 9.16).

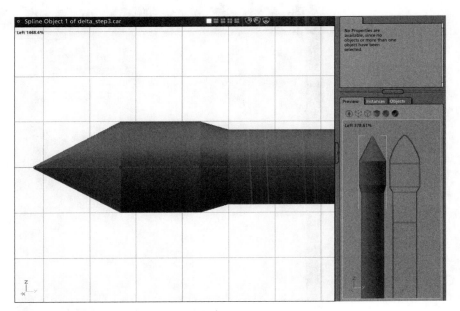

**FIGURE 9.16**    Setting up the preview window.

In the Spline Modeler window switch to the Left Camera view. Click on the sweep path to make the control points visible. Now move the control points one at a time to move the cross sections that define the transitions between the payload, the rocket, and the engine. As you move the cross sections in the Spline Modeler, you can see in the preview window the model updated in real time. This way you can compare the model against the reference image in the Assemble room as you model in the Spline Modeler. Take time to make sure that the payload area and the engine area correlate closely to the reference image.

## Refining the Payload and Engine with Extrusion Envelopes

You have probably noticed that the payload at the top of the rocket is pointy and blocky and not rounded as in the reference image. To round out the tip of the payload we will use extrusion envelopes. Extrusion envelopes are tools that help shape the silhouette of an object in the Spline Modeler.

Go to the Extrusion menu, choose Extrusion Envelopes, and then select Symmetrical, as in Figure 9.17. Notice that there are blue lines that silhouette the shape on the $z,x$ grid and green lines on the $x,y$ grid; these are the extrusion envelopes.

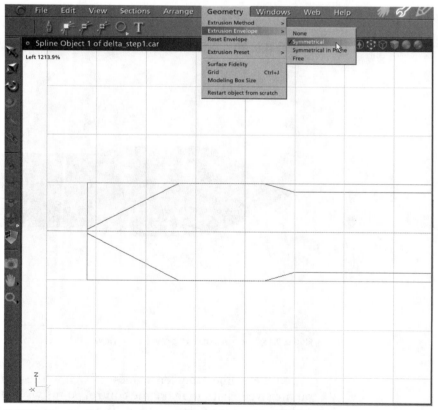

**FIGURE 9.17**    Applying extrusion envelopes (shown in wireframe preview).

It may be difficult to see the extrusion envelopes because they hug the shape of the rocket closely, but if you temporarily switch to a wireframe display, you should be able to see them. Switch to the Left Camera view and click on one of the blue lines of the extrusion envelope. Notice that there are points on the extrusion envelope much like there are on the sweep path. The points on the extrusion envelope and sweep path correlate to each other; if you move the points on one the other also moves.

### Control Handles

In order to round the payload area we have to add control handles to the points that define the transitions in diameter. Select the Convert Point tool from the toolbar and then slowly click and drag on the second point from the left on the top extrusion envelope. Notice that as you click and drag, control handles appear on either side of the point (see Figure 9.18).

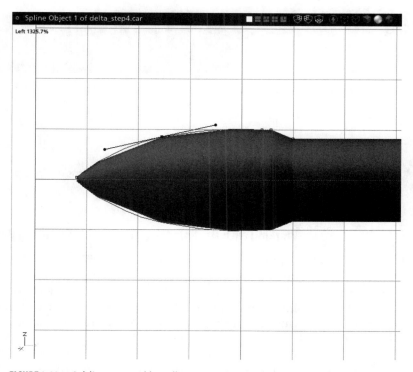

**FIGURE 9.18**    Adding control handles to a point on the extrusion envelope.

You have probably noticed that as you dragged to add the control handles, the silhouette of the rocket became more rounded. If you continue to drag on the control handles, that shape will continue to change. Control handles can be extended out, back in, or rotated, giving you the flexibility needed to control the shape of the object. Add control handles to all of the points that define the silhouette of the payload and move them until the payload area looks like Figure 9.19. Use the preview window (on the right of Figure 9.19) to see how the shape of the payload compares to the reference image.

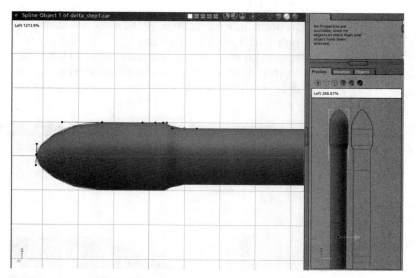

**FIGURE 9.19**    Control handles on the extrusion envelope points are used to smooth or round the payload.

## Working with Multiple Cross Sections on a Drawing Plane

With the payload area done, we will move to the other end of the rocket and add detail to the engine compartment. If you look carefully at the end of the rocket on the reference image, you will notice that there are vertical lines representing raised areas on the surface of the rocket. We will model this detail using multiple cross sections in the last two drawing planes.

Go to drawing plane 6 (the next to the last drawing plane) and from the Sections menu choose Show and from the submenu select Current, as in Figure 9.20. This will hide the cross sections on all other drawing planes, leaving only the current cross section visible.

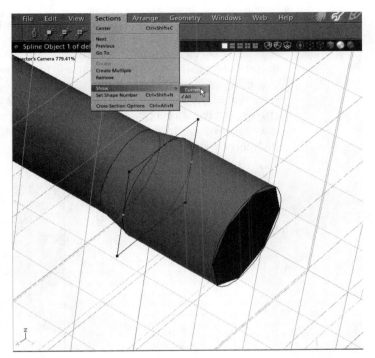

**FIGURE 9.20**   Hide all cross sections except the current one with the Show/Current command from the Sections menu.

Next switch to the Front camera and change the display mode to Bounding Box so that all you see is the cross section outline from the front, as in Figure 9.21a. Then from the 2D Primitives tool select the Rectangle tool and draw a very small square in the top part of the circle, as in Figure 9.21b. Copy and paste the square until you have eight copies distributed around the circle, as in Figure 9.21c. You will have to rotate four of the squares 45 degrees with the rotate tool.

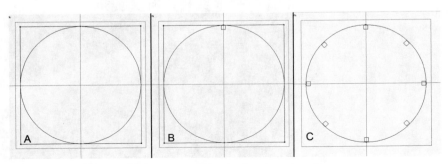

**FIGURE 9.21**   Adding multiple cross sections to drawing plane 6.

Select all of the cross sections on drawing plane 6 and press Ctrl/Command-C to copy them into memory. Next, go to drawing plane 7 and select and delete the single cross section that is there and press Ctrl/Command-V to paste the cross sections from drawing plane 6 into drawing plane 7. In drawing plane 7 move the squares so that they are on the outside of the circle cross section, as in Figure 9.22. Notice that the round cross sections connect and the small, square cross sections connect from drawing plane 6 to drawing plane 7. Also notice that the surface of the rocket now shows evenly spaced ridges.

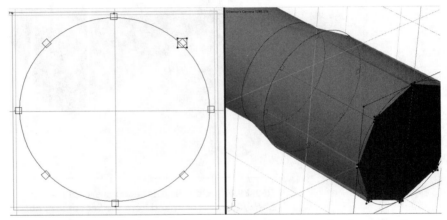

**FIGURE 9.22**    Copying the cross sections in drawing plane 6 into drawing plane 7.

The rocket payload, body, and engine areas are now complete. Click on the Test Render tool (X) and drag the rocket around to see a quick render of the completed rocket. It should appear as in Figure 9.23.

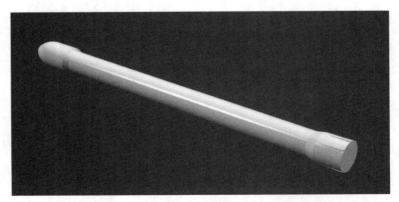

**FIGURE 9.23**    The finished rocket body (test render in the Spline Modeler).

## MODELING THE ROCKET ENGINE NOZZLE

In the next steps we will model the engine nozzle at the bottom of the rocket. This is the part of the rocket that spews out hot exhaust gasses to propel the rocket. The nozzle is made up of two parts: the nozzle base and the nozzle.

### Modeling the Nozzle Base with Primitives

If you are in the Spline Modeler, jump out into the Assemble room. We will use a cylinder primitive to model the base of the engine nozzle, so from the Primitives tool select and insert a Cylinder into the scene, as in Figure 9.24. In the Motion tab of the Properties tray enter the following values in the Size fields: for the X and Y field enter ".85" and for the Z field enter ".10." This will scale the cylinder as seen in Figure 9.24. Name the new part "nozzle base."

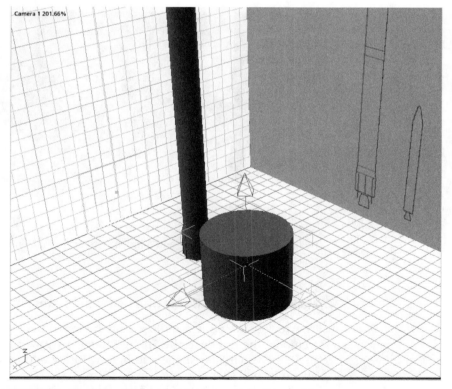

**FIGURE 9.24**    Modeling the nozzle base from a cylinder primitive.

## Using the Align Tool

The next thing we need to do is position the nozzle base under the rocket. Use the Move tool to move the nozzle base underneath the rocket (see Figure 9.25a). The base has to be centered under the rocket, which is difficult to do with just the Move tool. The best we can do with the Move tool is approximate the position. However, with the Align tool we can center the nozzle base perfectly underneath the rocket, so click on the rocket first and then on the base to select them. It is important to select the rocket first because this tells Carrara to center the base under the rocket. If you select the base first, then the rocket will be centered over the base. This may not be a problem when there are only two objects in the scene, but when there are many objects this feature comes in handy. Next, open the Edit menu and choose Align. In the Align dialog box click on the X and Y arrows, make sure that Align and Hotpoint are displayed in the menus, and click on OK (see Figure 9.25b). The base should move and center itself under the rocket.

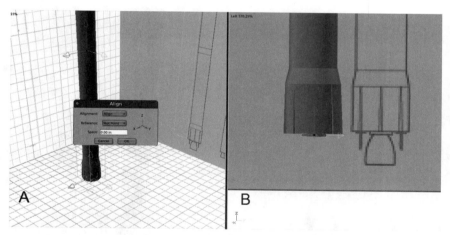

**FIGURE 9.25** Using the Move and Align tools to position the nozzle base under the rocket.

## Modeling the Rocket Nozzle with Compound Curves

The rocket nozzle is a hollow bell shape with some thickness. In order to model the nozzle in the Spline Modeler, we will use compound curves to define its circular shape and hollow inside and extrusion envelopes to give it its bell shape.

Jump back into the Spline Modeler and insert one circle in the drawing plane. Carrara will extrude the circle into a solid short tube. Select the circle and center it in the drawing plane by going to the Sections menu and choosing Center. Now, copy and paste a new copy of the circle back into the same drawing plane and scale one of the circles so that one is inside the other, as shown in Figure 9.26a. Make sure that both circles are selected and go to the Arrange menu and select Combine as Compound. Notice that the short tube is now hollow and has thickness (see Figure 9.26b). The thickness of the tube is defined by the distance between the two cross sections in the drawing plane. If you want to increase or decrease the thickness, select the circles on the drawing plane, go to the Arrange menu, and choose Break Apart Compound to release the circles. Then scale the circles so that the distance between is greater or smaller and then reapply the Combine as Compound command.

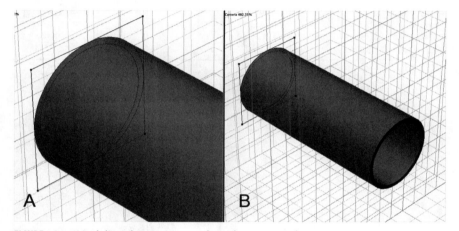

**FIGURE 9.26**    Modeling the engine nozzle with compound curves.

To create the bell shape of the nozzle we will use extrusion envelopes much as we did with the rocket body. Switch to the Left Camera view and go to the Geometry menu, select Extrusion Envelopes, and from the submenu choose Symmetrical. Now, with the Convert Point tool add control handles to both points on the extrusion envelopes and shape the nozzle as shown in Figure 9.27.

Now that the nozzle is finished, jump back out into the Assemble room. The nozzle will be on its side on the Assemble room floor. Scale the nozzle to about 30% so that it matches the nozzle in the reference image and use the Move tool and Align command to position it under the nozzle base (see Figure 9.28). Remember to name the new part "nozzle."

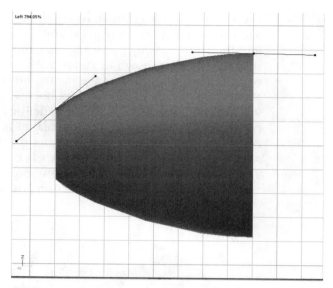

**FIGURE 9.27** The nozzle is shaped with extrusion envelopes.

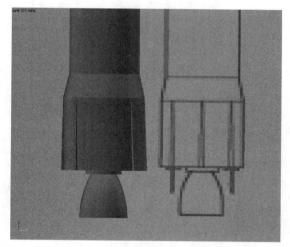

**FIGURE 9.28** The nozzle in position under the rocket.

## Modeling the Directional Vectors

The directional vectors help steer the rocket by changing the direction of the exhaust (see Figure 9.29). The vectors are modeled in the much same way as we modeled the rocket and the nozzle. We will insert a cross section on a drawing plane, center it, and then use extrusion envelopes to shape the silhouette.

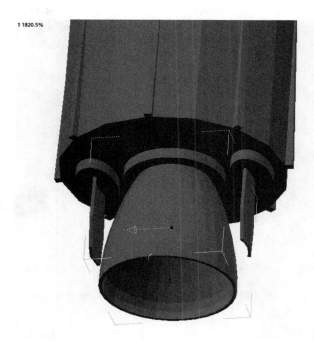

**FIGURE 9.29**    The directional vectors we are about to model.

### Editing Cross Section Shapes

Jump back into the Spline Modeler and insert a rectangle that is approximately 1.5 inches in width and 0.33 inches in height, as in Figure 9.30a. Make sure that the rectangle is centered and from the Edit menu choose Ungroup. When it is ungrouped, you should be able to see points and their control handles at each corner of the rectangle. To see the rectangle better, switch to the Front Camera view. Use the control handles to shape the top and bottom curves the rectangle as in Figure 9.30b. If you switch back to the Director's Camera, the extruded shape now has a dip in it.

### Working with Extrusion Envelopes that Are Symmetrical in One Plane

Next we will add extrusion envelopes to shape the vector, but this time we will use extrusion envelopes that are symmetrical within only one plane. Previously we have been using extrusion envelopes that are symmetrical in all planes, so that when you edited one set of extrusion envelopes the others were edited also. Switch to the Top Camera view and from the Geometry menu select Extrusion Envelopes and then from that submenu select Symmetrical in Plane to add extrusion envelopes. Select the Add Point tool from the tool bar and add a point to the extrusion envelope and move it away from the center, as in Figure 9.31.

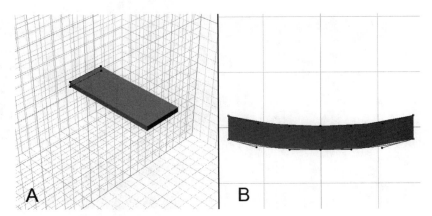

**FIGURE 9.30**    Editing the shape of the cross section.

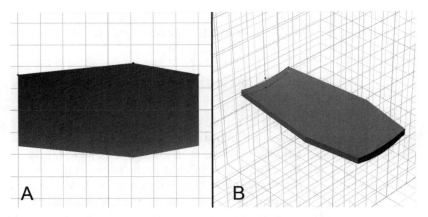

**FIGURE 9.31**    Shaping with extrusion envelopes that are symmetrical in one plane.

As with the nozzle we modeled previously, jump back out into the Assemble room to continue working on the directional vector. Take a look at the reference image and notice that there are two directional vectors, one on each side of the nozzle. Also notice that each directional vector has a base just like the nozzle.

Create a base for the first directional vector and position it under the rocket. The base for the directional vector is not a perfect circle but an oval. Remember that we created the nozzle base from a scaled cylinder primitive, so you can do the same for the base of the directional vector.

Position the directional vector base under the rocket using the Move tool (see Figure 9.32a). Next, scale and position the directional vector itself under the rocket, as in Figure 9.32b.

**FIGURE 9.32**    Assembling the directional vector under the rocket.

## Working with Groups

At this point we have the rocket body, the nozzle base, the nozzle, the directional vector base and the directional vector in the scene. That is five separate objects that we have to manage to keep organized. Naming objects goes a long way to keeping things organized, so go to the Instances tab of the Properties tray, click on each object to select it, and then name it (if it's not already named) (see Figure 9.33).

There is one more thing that we can do to stay organized and that is grouping objects together. For example, the nozzle and its base can be grouped as well as the directional vector and its base. To group objects, select each object to be grouped and press Ctrl/Command-G (alternatively you can go to the Edit menu and choose Group). Carrara will group the objects and a new group object will appear in the Instances tab. Groups can be named, so be sure to name each group appropriately. Groups can be opened and closed by clicking on the small triangle next to the name (see Figure 9.34). If you need to ungroup objects, select the group and simply press Ctrl/Command-U.

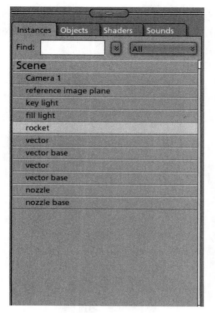

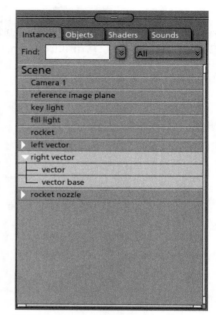

**FIGURE 9.33**   Naming the objects in the scene.

**FIGURE 9.34**   Grouping objects.

A major benefit of using groups is that many objects can behave as one object. For instance, instead of having to move the directional vector and its base separately, when they are grouped you can move them together.

Let's complete the rocket by creating the second directional vector. If you have not done so already, group the directional vector and its base into one group and name it "directional vector." Now all that is left to do is to make a copy and position it on the other side of the rocket nozzle. To make a copy select the directional vector group and either press Ctrl/Command-D for duplicate or copy and paste a new copy into the scene. Once you have the copy, position it on the other side of the nozzle as in Figure 10.35. The main Delta rocket is now complete. Next, we will model one of the solid rocket boosters.

### Modeling the Solid Rocket Boosters

The following description will be brief, as the steps to model the solid rocket booster and its nozzle are the same as, albeit much simpler than, the steps to model the main rocket.

In the Spline Modeler insert and center a circle in the drawing plane and lengthen the sweep path. Go into the Assemble room and rotate and position the booster so that it can be compared to the reference image.

**FIGURE 9.35**    Modeling the second directional vector by copying the first one.

Back in the Spline Modeler use the Preview window to see the reference image in the Assemble room.

Add two new cross sections, one at the end and another in between the two end cross sections (see Figure 9.36a). Use symmetrical extrusion envelopes to shape the tip of the booster, as seen in Figure 9.36b. The body of the booster is now complete (see Figure 9.36c).

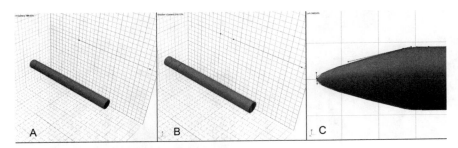

**FIGURE 9.36**    Modeling the solid rocket booster.

The exhaust nozzle of the booster is basically the same as the exhaust nozzle of the main rocket. To save time, copy the rocket nozzle and edit the copy. The first time you edit a copy of an object that is already in the scene Carrara will ask you if you want to Edit the Master or Create a New

Master. In this case we want to create a new master object so that the booster's nozzle is separate from the rocket's nozzle. If we had chosen to edit the master object, then any changes made to the booster's nozzle would have also been applied to the rocket's nozzle—and that is not what we want to happen (see Figure 9.37).

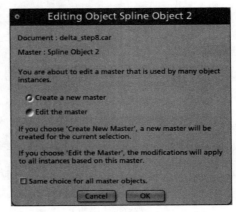

**FIGURE 9.37**  Creating a new master object for the booster nozzle.

Double-click on the nozzle copy to jump into the Spline Modeler. The only difference between the two nozzles is that booster nozzle has less of a bell shape, as in Figure 9.38.

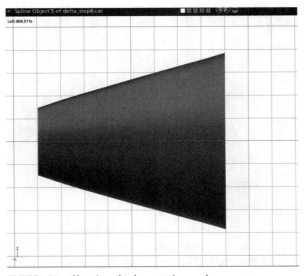

**FIGURE 9.38**  Shaping the booster's nozzle.

Back in the Assemble room position the new nozzle under the booster, as shown in Figure 9.39a. While the main rocket nozzle is vertical, the booster nozzle is rotated out about 30 degrees (see Figure 9.39b). Group the booster and its nozzle.

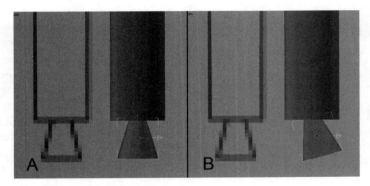

**FIGURE 9.39**    Assembling the booster rocket.

## ASSEMBLING THE ROCKET

We now have all of the parts to assemble the Delta rocket. Prior to launch, Delta rockets are configured with a different number of booster rockets depending on the weight of the payload, so you can have as few as two boosters or as many as eight. In our case let's assemble the rocket with four boosters. Before we proceed, group the rocket and its nozzle so that they can be moved as one object. Since we don't need the reference image anymore, hide it by selecting the plane and unchecking the Visible property in the Properties tray.

Switch to the Top Camera view and select the booster. Position it next to the rocket at the 3 o'clock position (see Figure 9.40a). Copy the

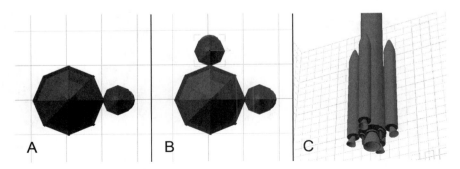

**FIGURE 9.40**    Assembling the main rocket with four booster rockets.

booster and position it at the 12 o'clock position. Since the nozzle at the bottom of the booster has to face out, rotate the booster at the 12 o'clock position 90 degrees, as in Figure 9.40b. Copy, position, and rotate the remaining two boosters. The end result should look like Figure 9.40c.

## SUMMARY

In this tutorial we have covered all of the basic and some of the advanced modeling techniques found in the Spline Modeler, such as extrusion envelopes and multiple cross sections. The good news is that at this point you have learned enough about the Spline Modeler and the Assemble room to customize the rocket any way you like, build a different one, or model your creations from scratch. In the next chapter we will thoroughly cover Carrara's Vertex Modeler, which in version 5 features numerous advanced modeling tools.

# 10

# MODELING WITH THE VERTEX MODELER

## In This Chapter

- Box Modeling a Low-Poly Character
- Modeling an Airplane

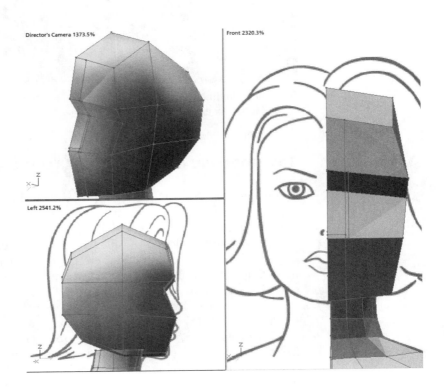

arrara 5 features a completely updated Vertex Modeler. Through an enhanced interface, improved workflow, and advanced modeling tools, the new Vertex Modeler makes it possible to model any object. In the first tutorial of this chapter we will box model a low-poly (short for low polygon count) character from head to toe. In the second tutorial we will build a model of a Piper Cherokee airplane with the Vertex Modeler's new curve and surfacing tools (see Figure 10.1). When it's all done you will have learned to use many, if not most, of the Vertex Modeler's tools and gained practical experience with modeling 3D objects.

**FIGURE 10.1**    In the first tutorial we will model a low-poly character and then in the second tutorial we will model an airplane.

**TUTORIAL 10.1**    **BOX MODELING A LOW-POLY CHARACTER**

Loosely defined, box modeling is a modeling technique where you build an object by starting with a primitive such as a cube, sphere, or cylinder. Then you model the character by moving, rotating, scaling, and extruding polygons, edges, and vertices. Typically box modeling begins by roughing-in the general shape of the object and then progressively refining the shape. Box modeling works well for any object but it is generally used to produce low-poly characters that can then be refined with subdivision surfaces.

To get started, launch Carrara and select the Vertex Object tool from the toolbar and click once in the scene. Carrara will jump immediately into the Vertex Modeler. Before moving on to modeling, we need to place the front and side reference images in the working planes. Having good reference drawings of the character from at least the front and side is important because it will greatly facilitate the modeling process. The reference images are used as guides only, and at any time you may deviate from them for creative purposes.

To place the reference images in the Vertex Modeler click on the Global tab of the Properties tray. In the Backdrop section check the Front/Back and Left/Right checkboxes. In the Front/Back load the front.jpg image, and in the Left/Right load the side.jpg image (see Figure 10.2). An important note about the Vertex Modeler is that reference images can only be viewed in the isometric camera views. In other words, the front and side reference images will appear in the Front, Back, Left, and Right camera views but not in the Director's camera view.

You may have noticed that the character we are about to model does not quite fit into the standard human form. We are modeling a female superhero, so her proportions are exaggerated. She is very tall, with long, muscular legs and arms, and her chest and back are broad and she is in very good shape.

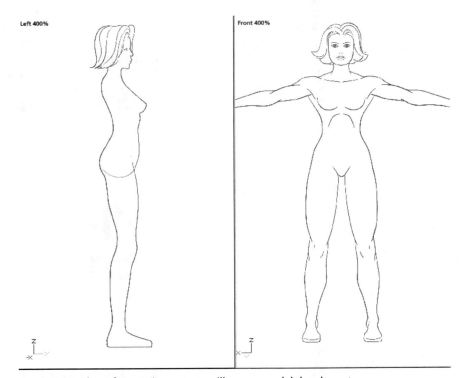

**FIGURE 10.2**    The reference images we will use to model the character.

## Getting Started with Primitives

Rendering the human figure with polygons or pencils can be a challenging task, so learning to see the human figure as geometric shapes and proportions provides an accurate starting point before adding details. When broken down into geometrical shapes, the human figure is essentially cylindrical, so we will start modeling the character by representing her legs, arms, and torso with cylinders.

If you are in the Assemble room double-click on the Vertex object in the Instances tab of the Properties tray to jump into the Vertex Modeler. Once in the Vertex Modeler, click on the Primitives tool in the toolbar and select the Cylinder primitive. Insert a cylinder with eight sides and five segments for the torso. You can press the plus (+) or minus (−) keys to increase or reduce the number of sides and segments of the cylinder or enter the number in the Object Definition field in the Properties tray. The number of sides and segments of the cylinder are the same; for instance, if the number of sides is eight, then the number of segments is also eight. To keep the sides at eight but reduce the segments you will have select and delete two segments off the top or bottom. Switch to the Front camera view and select the bottom two cross sections and from the Edit menu choose Delete. The number of polygons in the cylinder is purposely kept down to facilitate modeling and to control the final number of polygons in the finished model. Use the Move tool or Universal Manipulator to position and scale the cylinder. Once it is positioned, use the Delete tool to remove the caps of the cylinder so that it becomes a hollow tube (see Figure 10.3).

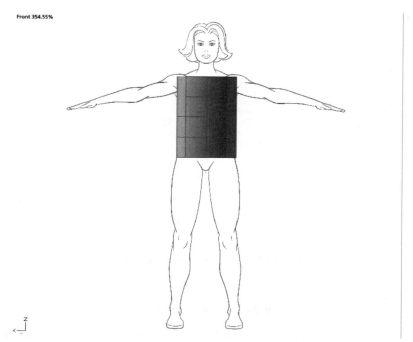

**FIGURE 10.3**    Modeling will start with a cylinder for the torso.

Either insert new cylinders or copy the torso cylinder to rough-in the left arm and left leg. You can copy the existing cylinder by copying and pasting or by using the Duplicate command in the Edit menu. Next select each cylinder and name them by going to Selection > Name > Polymesh, as shown in Figure 10.4. Naming objects helps keep things organized and will make it easy to select and hide parts as modeling progresses.

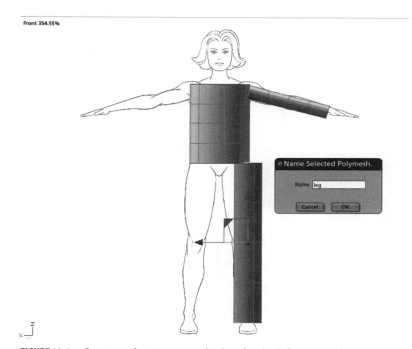

**FIGURE 10.4**   Create and name new cylinders for the left arm and leg.

## Shaping the Leg

We will begin modeling the leg first, so select the torso and arm, and from the View menu choose Hide Selection. Hiding the parts we are not working on removes clutter and helps us clearly see the parts we *are* working on. To transform the cylinder into a leg, we will position and rotate the cross sections with the Universal Manipulator and add new cross sections with the Edge tool and Add tool as needed. The Universal Manipulator is a new tool in Carrara 5 that combines the move, rotate, and scale functions into one tool. The Universal Manipulator is graphically represented in the Vertex Modeler by red, green, and blue arrowheads, cubes, and circular lines. Red indicates the *x*-axis, blue the *z*-axis, and green the *y*-axis. The arrowheads move objects, the cubes scale, and the circular lines rotate.

The cylinder that will become the leg is probably straight up and down, so rotate it so that it matches the leg in the reference figure. Once the cylinder is in place, select each cross section one at a time and then move, scale, and rotate them so that they line up with the general shape of the leg as seen from the front and side reference images (see Figure 10.5).

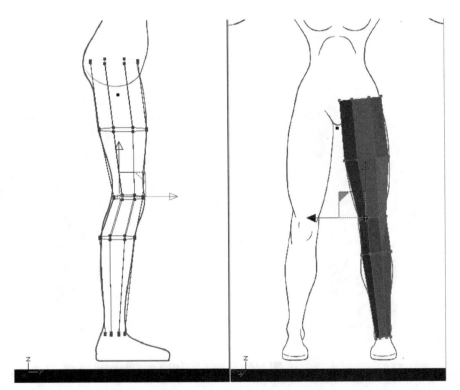

**FIGURE 10.5**    Roughing-in the shape of the leg.

Since the initial cylinder has only four or five segments, it is difficult to accurately shape the leg. To overcome this limitation we will add new vertices and edges. However, instead of randomly adding new vertices and edges with the Subdivide command or Tessellate tool, we will selectively place the new geometry with the Edge tools. The Edge tools will add new edges and vertices by extracting them from existing edges and vertices. In effect, the Edge tools are types of tessellation tools that add new polygons, but unlike the Tessellate tool, the Edge tools allow precise placement of the new vertices and edges.

At this point the thigh is defined by only three cross sections: one at the top, one in the middle, and one at the start of the knee, which makes the thigh appear triangular (see of Figure 10.6a). To give the thigh a more natural appearance add two more cross sections by selecting an edge on the middle cross section and then pressing the Loop button in the Properties tray to select all of the edges in the cross section. Next, select the Extract Around Edge tool from the toolbar and click and drag along the surface of the leg near the selected cross section to create two new cross sections, as shown in Figure 10.6b. Once you have the new cross sections added, refine the shape of the thigh using the reference image as a guide.

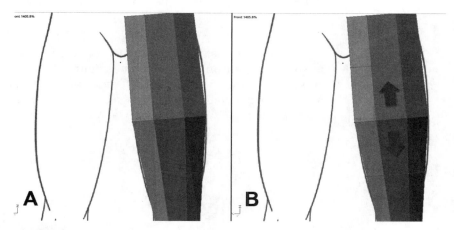

**FIGURE 10.6**    Refining the thigh by adding new cross sections with the Edge tools.

Refine the rest of the leg in a similar manner. Add two new cross sections around the knee and two new cross sections in the lower leg to shape the shin and calf (see Figure 10.7a). The top of the leg where it will meet the hip needs an extra cross section and needs to be shaped, as shown in Figure 10.7b. Remember to use the front and side reference guides to help shape.

## Shaping the Torso

The cylinder for the torso is probably hidden, so go to View > Reveal Hidden Vertices to reveal the torso. Next, select and hide the arm and leg so we have a clear view of the torso. To speed up and simplify the modeling process we are modeling the left side of the body only, so select half of the cylinder that makes up the torso and press the Delete key (see Figure 10.8a).

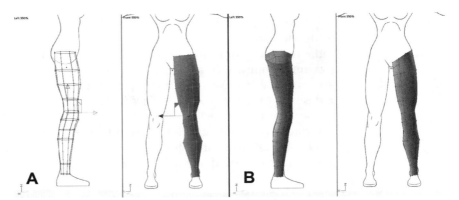

**FIGURE 10.7**    Once the new geometry is added, it is easy to shape the leg.

Move the initial number of cross sections to rough in the shape of the torso in comparison to the reference figure. As with the leg, the existing cross sections of the cylinder are not enough to accurately shape the torso, so begin adding new cross sections with Edge tools and continue shaping the torso with the Universal Manipulator (see Figure 10.8b).

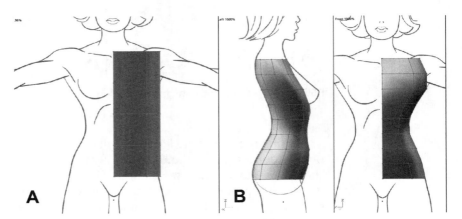

**FIGURE 10.8**    The torso begins as a half cylinder that is then shaped to match the reference images.

## Shaping the Arm

Reveal the cylinder of the arm and hide the torso and leg. As you have probably guessed by now, the arm is modeled by initially roughing-in the arm with the existing cross sections based on the reference image and then adding new cross sections to add detail (see Figure 10.9). It is important to plan where the new cross sections are placed. This will influence subdivision and animation later on, so do your best to place the cross sections as you see them in the figures.

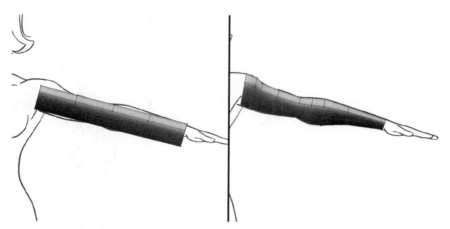

**FIGURE 10.9**    Modeling the arm as seen from the front.

Once you have modeled the arm, dolly around it and you will notice that the arm appears distorted because we have not shaped the top of the arm. Click on the Global tab of the Properties tray and check the Top/Bottom checkbox and load the top.jpg image. Now, shape the arm as seen from the top, as shown in Figure 10.10.

At this point you should have the leg, torso, and arm modeled, as shown in Figure 10.11. We were able to quickly and efficiently model major parts of the character because of three important modeling techniques. First, we started with clear reference images, which guided the modeling process. Second, we simplified the shape of the leg, torso, and arm by representing them with low-resolution, geometrical cylinders, which controlled the number of initial polygons. Finally we refined the shapes by adding new cross sections as needed, keeping the overall complexity of the model simple. As we move on we will continue to use these techniques to quickly model the rest of the character.

## Joining the Leg and Arm to the Torso

The next step in modeling the character is to join her arm and leg to her torso. To accomplish this task we will refine the joint areas by moving and adding vertices and then using the Weld tools to join the separate objects.

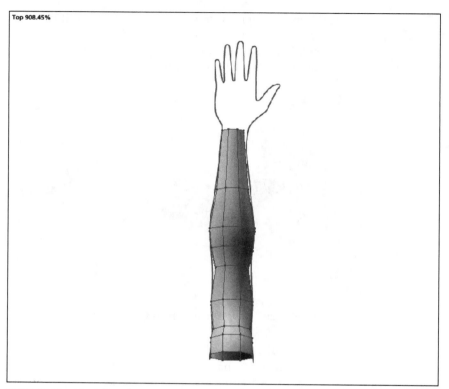

**FIGURE 10.10**    Modeling the arm as seen from the top.

Because we have kept the polymeshes simple in terms of resolution and the number of polygons, joining the separate parts will be straightforward.

To join the leg to the torso shape the bottom two cross sections of the torso so they line up with the top of the leg, as shown in Figure 10.12a. Ideally the vertices on the top of the leg should have corresponding vertices on the bottom of the torso that can be joined to each other. However, because the cylinder for the torso was split in half, it has fewer sides than the leg, so the number of vertices at the bottom of the torso and top of the leg are not the same. In this case with the Add tool we can easily add a new line of vertices and edges along the front, sides, and back of the torso, as shown in Figure 10.12b. The new vertices and edges will also help with refining the torso later on.

Once the new vertices are in place, use the Universal Manipulator to bring the edges of the torso and leg closer together (see Figure 10.13a). To select the Weld tool click and hold on the Link (the Link and Weld tools are toggled by pressing G on the keyboard) tool in the toolbar until the Weld tool appears. Next, join the top of the leg to the bottom of the

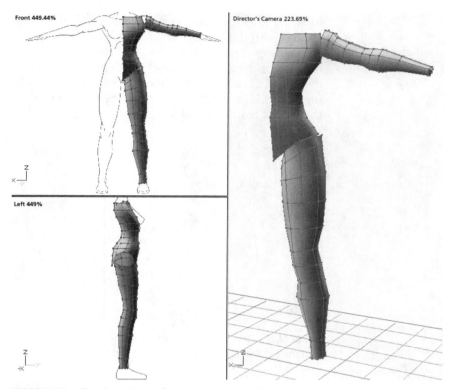

**FIGURE 10.11**    The character so far.

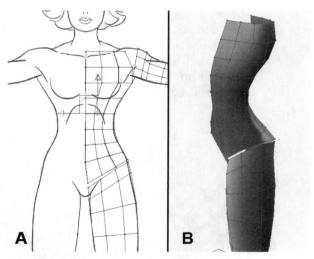

**FIGURE 10.12**    Line up the edges of the leg and torso.
Add new vertices and edges to facilitate joining.

torso by clicking on a vertex from the top of the leg (the first vertex clicked with the Weld tool will turn yellow) and then clicking on the corresponding vertex at the bottom of the torso. Work your way around the new seam, welding vertices between the leg and torso. When finished, inspect the seam for any defects, distortions, or missed vertices by dollying around the mesh. If you find any problems, this is the time to correct them. The result should look like Figure 10.13b.

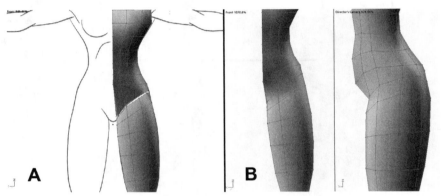

**FIGURE 10.13** Bring the torso and leg edges close together. Select the Weld tool and join the leg and torso two vertices at a time.

Next we will join the arm to the torso, but this is a bit more challenging than joining the leg to the torso because we have to prepare the upper torso to receive the arm by adding and shaping new geometry, while maintaining the shape of the shoulder, and then create the underarm.

The first step in joining the arm to the torso is to add new vertices and edges to the upper torso because the arm cross sections have eight vertices, and we want to have the same number of vertices in the upper torso as on the end of the arm. With the Edge tools add a new line of vertices and edges, as in Figure 10.14a. Reshape the cross sections of the

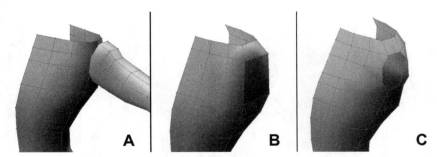

**FIGURE 10.14** Preparing the torso to receive the end of the arm. (The arm is hidden in panels b and c.)

upper torso as in Figure 10.14b. Notice that there is now one large polygon on the side of the torso that faces the end of the arm. Add two more lines of edges along the front and back of the torso. Model the polygons that face the arm into roughly the same shape as the end of the arm (see Figure 10.14c). We will use the new vertices to join the arm to the torso.

Now that we have prepared the torso to receive the arm, let's prepare the arm. We want the shape of the shoulder to be maintained during the joining process. To accomplish this we will add a new cross section as shown in Figure 10.15a. Next, move the arm close to the torso as in Figure 10.15b. Select the Weld tool and join the arm to the torso two vertices at a time. The finished seam should be similar to Figure 10.15c. Remember to inspect the seam for any problems and to correct any problems found.

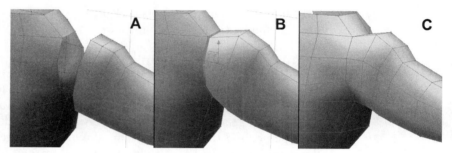

**FIGURE 10.15**    Preparing the end of the arm and then joining the arm to the torso.

With the arm joined to the torso, we can now model the underarm. However, before modeling the underarm it helps to understand how the underarm is formed in a real person. The underarm is primarily formed by two large muscles: the pectoralis major (pecs) in the front and the latissimus dorsi (lats) in the back. Unless the arm is raised above shoulder height, the underarm is not really noticeable, so at the most we will only suggest the underarm and not spend too much time on it.

To create the underarm we have to add new polygons, so with the Add tool add new vertices and edges as shown in Figure 10.16a,b. Then nudge the polygons in the underarm area toward the center of the body—just enough to suggest and underarm. Don't move them so much that you create a large recess (see Figure 10.16c).

So far we have modeled the leg, torso, and arm and then joined the parts together to complete nearly half of the character's body. In the next section we will complete the limbs by modeling feet and hands.

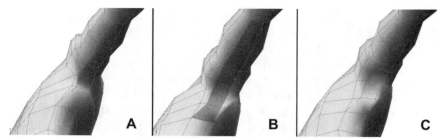

**FIGURE 10.16**   The underarm starts out as new polygons that are then shaped to create the recess of the underarm.

## Modeling the Feet and Hands

The character is wearing boots and gloves, so we don't have to model too much detail in her feet and hands. In fact, we don't have to model feet at all—just her boots.

To model the boots we will use the Dynamic Extrusion tool and extrude new polygons from the bottom of her leg, thus creating the start of the boot. Select the last cross section at the end of the leg, click on the Dynamic Extrusion tool, and click and drag down on one of the edges of the cross section. Stop about half way between the end of the leg and the floor plane, and then click and drag down once more all the way to the floor (see Figure 10.17a). Widen the polygons seen in the Front camera view of Figure 10.17b so that the front of the boot can be extruded. With the Dynamic Extrusion tool extrude three times and then shape the new polygons to create the front of the boot, as shown in Figure 17c.

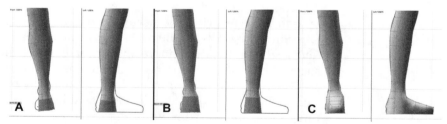

**FIGURE 10.17**   The boot begins as two extrusions from the bottom of the leg. The extrusions are shaped and then extruded three more times to create the front of the boot.

All that is left to do is to shape the boot into a basic shoe form. It may help to get out one of your own shoes to get a good idea of the shape of a shoe. Start by shaping the sole of the boot as in Figure 10.18a. Next, shape the upper part of the boot. Try not to add too many new polygons as you model the boot. The finished boot should look similar to Figure 10.18b.

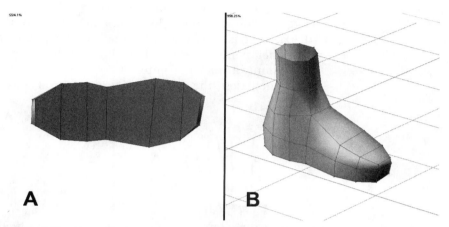

**FIGURE 10.18**    Shape the boot into a general shoe shape. (Part of the character is hidden.)

Now that the character has a foot, let's move on to modeling her hand. Modeling a human hand can be an intimidating challenge. However, if we simplify as we did with the leg, torso, arm, and boot, we will discover that convincing hands can be easily modeled. Take a look at your hands, but look beyond the wrinkles, creases, nails, and knuckles. You will soon notice that hands can be broken down into geometric shapes; a flattened cube for the palm and back of the hand and extruded cubes for the fingers (see Figure 10.19).

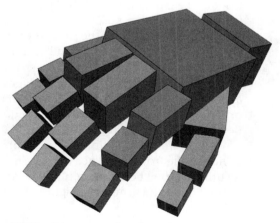

**FIGURE 10.19**    Human hands can be simplified into cubes.

Switch to the Top camera view and make sure that the top.jpg image is loaded. We will begin with the palm of the hand. From the Primitives tool select the Grid and click in the scene. Reduce the number of polygons by pressing on the minus (−) key until you get a grid that is 4 by 4 polygons. Position and scale the grid at the end of the arm, as in Figure 10.20a. Next, add volume or thickness to the grid by selecting it and from the Model menu choose Add Thickness. When Carrara prompts you for the amount of thickness enter −0.17. Your value may be a bit more or less. Nonetheless, the grid should be similar to Figure 10.20b.

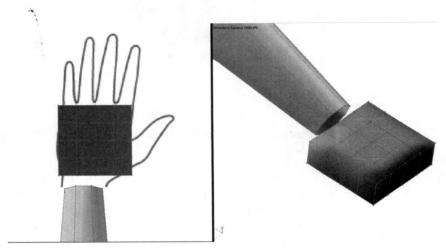

**FIGURE 10.20**    Modeling the palm of the hand from a grid primitive.

The fingers can be easily created by selecting the four polygons at the front of the palm and using the Dynamic Extrusion tool to create three extrusions (see Figure 10.21a). The thumb is formed from three extrusions starting from the one of the side polygons, as shown in Figure 10.21b.

Next, shape the fingers and thumb using the reference image as a guide. Not all fingers are the same size, so you will definitely want to indicate the differences. Use the Universal Manipulator to move, rotate, and scale the fingers' cross sections. Do the same for the thumb. The top of the hand should be slightly rounded, and the palm should suggest the fleshy part of the thumb (see Figure 10.22).

When the hand is finished, position it close to the wrist and rotate it to match the front reference image. Then use the Weld tool and the same techniques used before to join the leg and arm to the torso. Join the hand to the end of the arm, as in Figure 10.23.

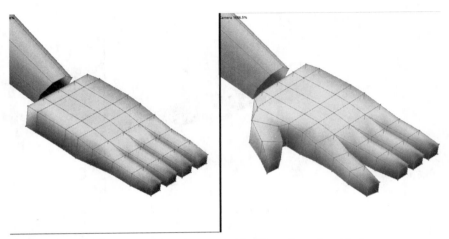

**FIGURE 10.21**    The fingers and thumb are extruded from the palm object.

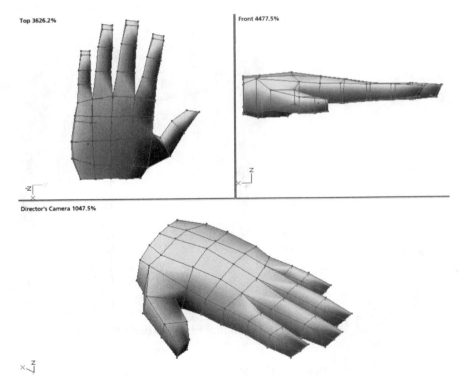

**FIGURE 10.22**    The back of the hand should be round, and the palm should indicate the fleshy part of the thumb. (Part of the character is hidden.)

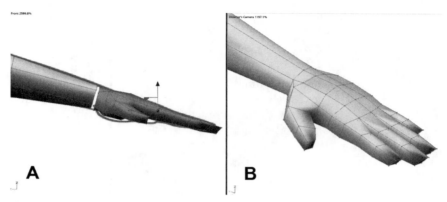

**FIGURE 10.23** The hand joined to the arm.

At this point you should have half of the body minus the head, and it should look similar to Figure 10.24. Select the entire object by pressing Ctrl/Command-A, and in the Properties tray click on the Model tab. Then select Smooth in the Subdivision section. You should see the body become very smooth.

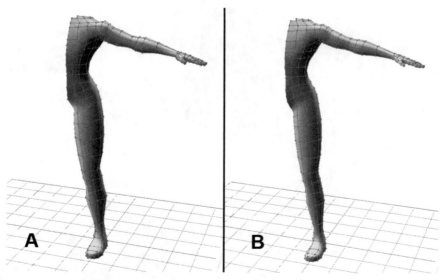

**FIGURE 10.24** Half of the character's body, not smoothed and smoothed.

## Modeling the Head

We have learned some very important box modeling techniques. We have learned to use the Move, Rotate, and Scale tools and the Universal

Manipulator to adjust edges, vertices, and polygons for shaping surfaces. We have used the Edge, Add, and Delete tools to extract and create new edges. We also used the Weld tool join surfaces and we have learned to use the Dynamic Extrusion tool to create new polygons. We have learned the importance of using good reference images to assist modeling. In the next steps we will use all of these tools and techniques to model the head and face of the character, which is probably the most challenging part of the process.

The first task in modeling the head is creating the neck. Select the edges along the top of the torso and with the Dynamic Extrusion tool extrude up three times and model to match the reference images, as in Figure 10.25.

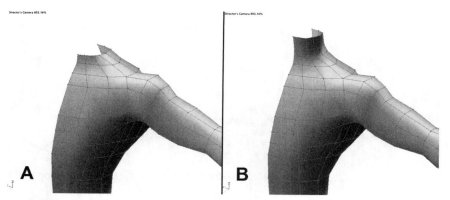

**FIGURE 10.25**   The neck is created from three extrusions.

The head starts out as a cube. Click on the Primitives tool in the toolbar and select the Cube. Click in the scene to insert the cube and press the minus (−) key until there are only four polygons on each side of the cube. Scale and position the cube on top of the neck as shown in Figure 10.26.

As with the torso, we will model only half of the head to save time, so select the right half of the cube and delete it. Next, add new edges that line up with the nose and brow when compared to the reference images, as shown in Figure 10.27. With the Move tool or Universal Manipulator, shape the vertices of the cube to rough-in the head (see Figure 10.28). Modeling the features of the face is a straightforward process that entails adding new polygons to the head in a controlled manner to progressively define the facial features. Rough-in the features and then refine them, all the time using the reference images as guides. The new polygons needed to model the face can be added with the Edge tools or with the Add tool or a combination of both.

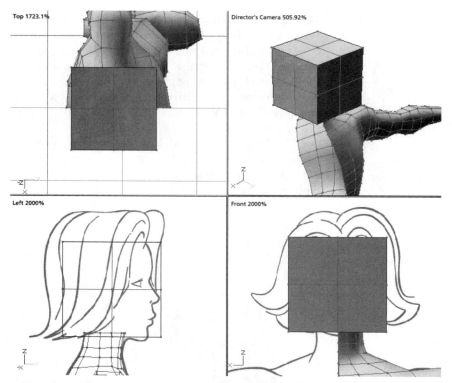

**FIGURE 10.26** The cube that will become the head on top of the neck.

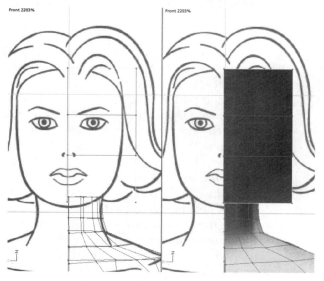

**FIGURE 10.27** Delineating the areas of the face.

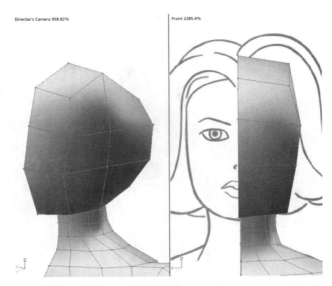

**FIGURE 10.28**    The head roughed in.

Create new edges as shown in Figure 10.29a. To start defining the brow and the nose, move the edges that cross over the eye and bridge of the nose back toward the back of the head (see Figure 10.29b). Create a new set of edges along the side of the edge that defines the nose and at the tip of the nose, as in Figure 10.30. These new edges will be used to rough-in the bridge of the nose and tip of the nose.

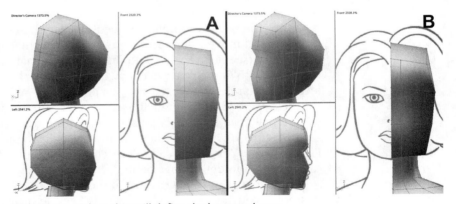

**FIGURE 10.29**    Edges that will define the brow and nose.

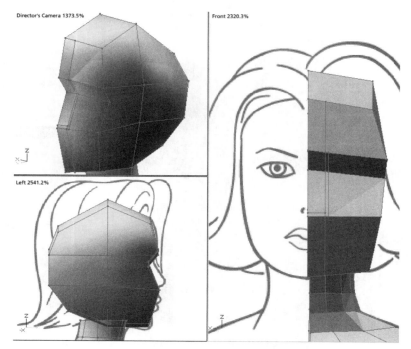

**FIGURE 10.30** The edges that will define the nose.

Before roughing in the nose, select the vertices shown in Figure 10.31 and weld them. This will allow the nose tip to be moved without any problems. You may use the Weld tool found in the toolbar or the Weld command from the Model menu (shown). If you use the Weld command, select the Weld Selected Vertices option.

Once the weld is complete, select the edge that is across the bridge of the nose and move it forward. Do the same for the edge that is at the tip of the nose (see Figure 10.32). Refine the edges that define the cheek and face outline to fit the reference images better. It's okay if the fit is not perfect with the reference images at this point.

Next we will begin modeling the eyelids, but in order to model eyelids we will need more polygons to move around, so create the edges you see in Figure 10.33. Once they are in place, shape the edges as shown in Figure 10.34. You may need to switch to wireframes temporarily so you can see the reference image behind the character.

Add a new ring of edges around the eye, as shown in Figure 10.35. At this point you should be able to clearly see the brow, eyelids, nose, and cheek. Everything, except the nose, is pretty much on the same plane, which is not the case in a real human face, which is essentially round. Select the rings of the edges that make up the eyelids and push them back

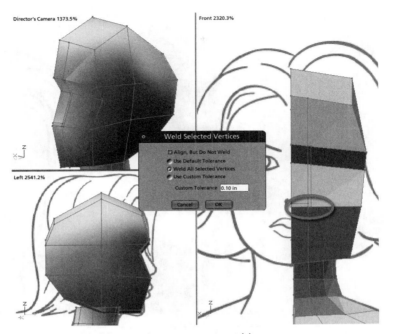

**FIGURE 10.31**    Welding vertices to prevent problems.

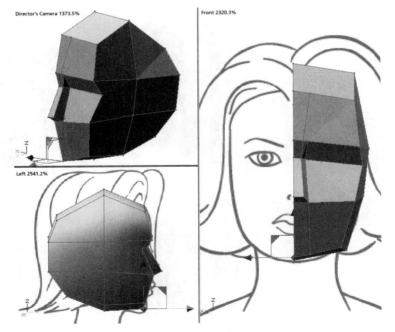

**FIGURE 10.32**    Shaping the nose and face.

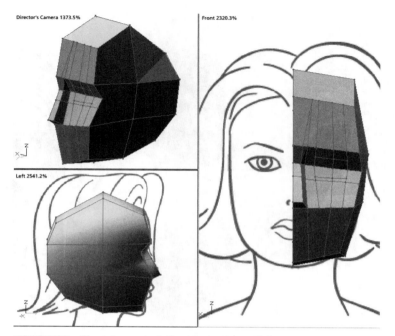

**FIGURE 10.33** The edges needed to shape the eyelids.

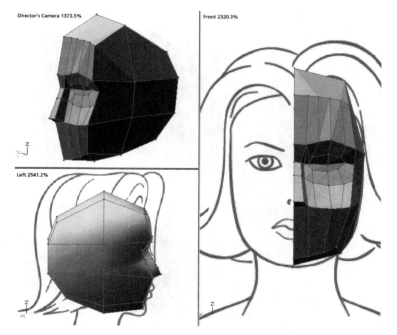

**FIGURE 10.34** The eyelids roughed in.

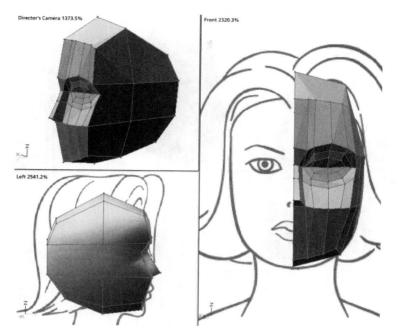

**FIGURE 10.35**    The edges needed to shape the eyelids.

and shape the eyelids, brow, and cheek as in Figure 10.36. If you look at your face in the mirror, you will see that your brow and cheek follow a circular path as they recede back toward the sides of your face. The eyelids are shaped by the eyeball, which is also round. At this point rough-in the eyelids. We will refine them later.

We have done quite a bit of work on the top of the face, so let's move to the mouth and chin. Like the eyes, the mouth will be modeled from a series of concentric rings of polygons. To start the rings add the edges shown in Figure 10.37a. Zoom in on the mouth and connect the edges you just created (see Figure 10.37b). Extract one more set of ringed edges, as shown in Figure 10.37c. At this point all of the geometry for the lips is in place, but the chin area needs some help before it can be modeled, so add the edges shown in Figure 10.38.

With the new edges for the lips and chin ready, it's time to model the mouth. The lips have three planes, as shown in Figure 10.39. Because we are modeling a low-poly model, we will use only the minimum number of polygons necessary to model the lips, so do not try to make the model perfectly smooth by increasing the number of polygons. As with the upper part of the face, the mouth and chin follow a curved path. Using

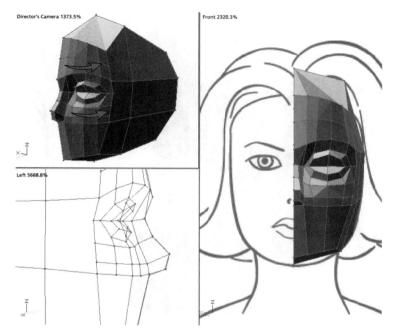

**FIGURE 10.36** Carefully shape the edges that make up the brow, eyelids, and cheek and model them in a more natural round shape.

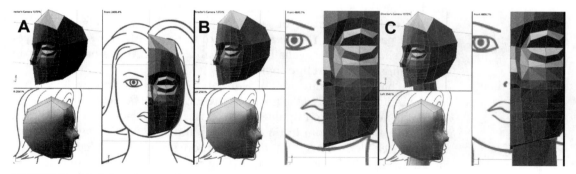

**FIGURE 10.37** Modeling the mouth.

the reference images as a guide, model the lips and chin as shown in Figure 10.40. The edges between the lips are pulled back into the mouth to create a slight parting of the lips and to accent the separation between to top and bottom lip (see Figure 10.40).

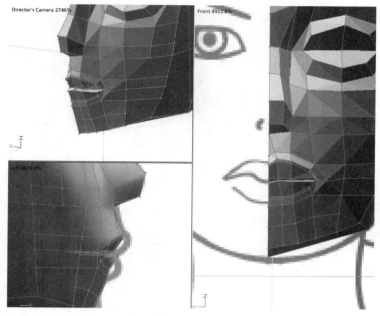

**FIGURE 10.38**    Adding edges to the chin.

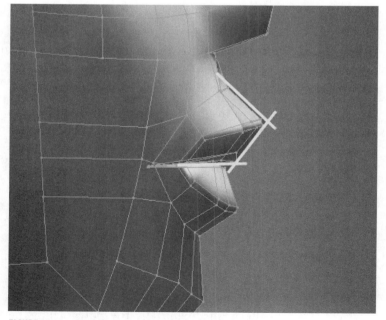

**FIGURE 10.39**    Each lip can be simplified into three planes.

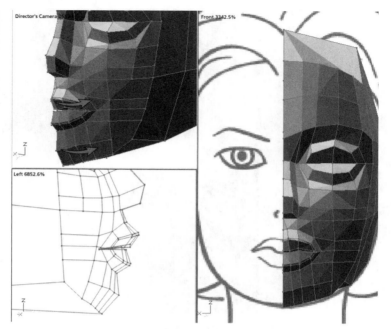

**FIGURE 10.40**    The face follows a round contour going back.

At this point the face is fairly well defined, with distinct areas for the forehead, brow, eyes, nose, cheeks, mouth, and chin. However, we have to do a bit more work to refine the entire face. Let's begin with the eyelids. Insert a sphere with about 16 sides and scale and position it as in Figure 10.41a. It is important that the sphere's poles point from front to back, so insert the sphere in the Front camera view. The sphere is the eyeball, so shape the eyelids so that they drape over the eyeball. You may have to add new edges to get a good fit (see Figure 10.41).

The nose is just about finished, but the tip of the nose needs to be refined. Because we are modeling a low-poly model, we will not model every detail of the nose. We will add just enough detail to suggest nostrils. Begin by adding new edges along the side of the nose and across the tip of the nose. Model the new polygons on the nose tip so that it appears round and move the edges on the nose tip that are near the face to suggest the nostrils (see Figure 10.42).

The only thing left to do now is to shape the rest of the head and clean up the edges and polygons on the face. This character will have hair covering most of her head, so it is not necessary to model ears or the back of the head. Eventually the polygons at the back of the head will be deleted. To clean up the polygons on the face, side of the face, and chin

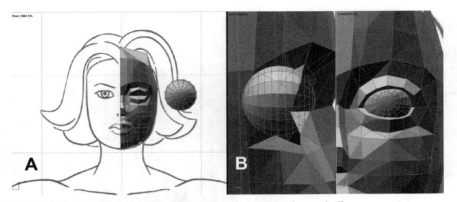

**FIGURE 10.41**    Model the eyelids so that they drape over the eyeball.

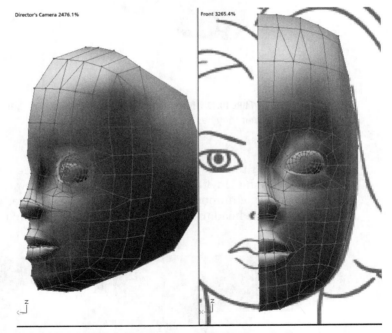

**FIGURE 10.42**    The tip of the nose is modeled so that it is round and the nostrils are only suggested.

subdivide polygons with more than four sides with the Link tool. Carefully continue to model the face by eliminating problem areas and rounding out the face. When complete, the face should look similar to Figure 10.43.

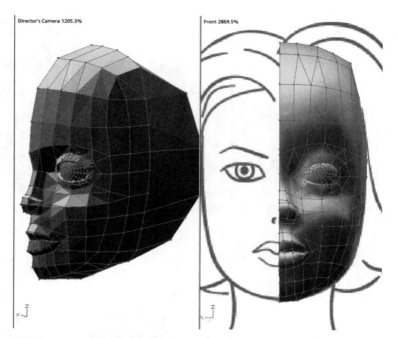

**FIGURE 10.43**    It is important to clean up the polygons on the head and face so that they have three or four sides.

It's time to join the head to the rest of the body. Prepare the bottom of the head with a hole that is roughly the same size as the neck and has the same number of vertices as in Figure 10.44a. Then with the Weld tool join the head to the neck two vertices at a time (see Figure 10.44b).

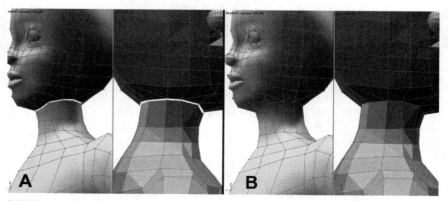

**FIGURE 10.44**    Prepare the bottom of the head to be joined to the neck and then use the Weld tool to join the head to the neck.

The last thing to do in modeling the left half of the character is to create the breast. This is easily accomplished by inserting and shaping a sphere and joining it to chest. It is important to position the sphere correctly on the body; otherwise the breast will look unnatural. Use the reference image to position and shape the breast, as shown in Figure 10.45a. Delete the half of the breast that is inside the body. Next prepare the torso to receive the breast by creating corresponding vertices on the chest as shown in Figure 10.45b. Delete the polygon on the chest that is directly under the breast to create a hole and then join the breast to the chest with the Weld tool. Use the reference images to shape the breast (see Figure 10.45c).

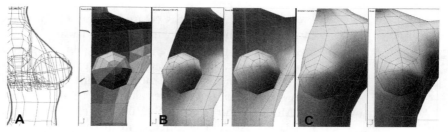

**FIGURE 10.45**    The breast starts out as a sphere that is shaped according to the reference image and joined to the chest.

If you like, you can add details to the body such as modeling the edge of the rib cage, suggesting the shoulder blades or the dip along the middle of back caused by the back muscles, or defining the lats or pecs. You can add as much or as little detail as you want. However, since we are modeling a low-poly character, whatever you do has to be done very efficiently so as to not add too many polygons. Also consider that many of these details can be effectively suggested with textures.

At this point you should have half of the character's body. The next steps are to create the other half and join the two haves together. First we will create the right half, so press Ctrl/Command-A to select everything in the Vertex Modeler. To set the axis along which the copy will be created, click the *zy* plane on the Working Box Controls button (see arrow) see Figure 10.46a). Next, Ctrl/Command-click on any of the vertices along the cut edge to move the working plane to the midline of the model, as in Figure 10.46b. Finally, select Duplicate with Symmetry from the Edit menu, and Carrara will create the other half of the body as shown in Figure 10.46c. To reset the working box plane go to View and choose Reset Working Box.

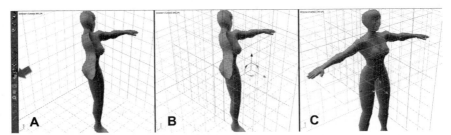

**FIGURE 10.46**    The right half of the character's body is created with the Duplicate with Symmetry command.

After the right half is created the two halves have to be joined. You can accomplish this task in one of two ways. Since the model has very few polygons, it would be possible to join the halves by using the Weld tool to weld two vertices at a time. However, the Weld command from the Model menu might be more efficient than using the Weld tool. Carefully select all of the vertices along the midline of both halves. Then from the Model menu select Weld. In the Weld Selected Vertices dialog box select Use Custom Tolerance, and in the Custom Tolerance field enter a very small value such as 0.01 in. and press OK (see Figure 10.47). The Weld command will join all vertices along the midline to the nearest

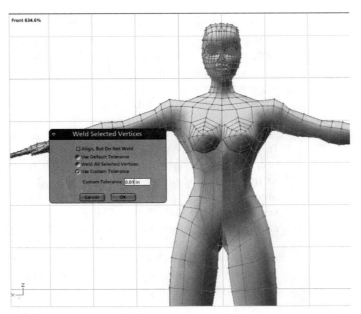

**FIGURE 10.47**    Use the Weld command to quickly join the left and right halves.

other vertex. The amount of tolerance sets the minimum distance that any two vertices will be joined. The tolerance value for your model may be more or less than the 0.01 value we are using in this tutorial. When the weld function is complete, check to make sure that you have not inadvertently welded vertices that were not supposed to be welded. This problem may occur in the details of the face where vertices are closer together.

Though the Weld command joined the halves together, the crotch is not closed completely, so use the Link tool to connect opposing vertices and then from the Model menu select the Fill Polygon command to fill the open areas.

ON THE CD

At this point the model is complete but hairless. In the Chapter 10 folder of the CD-ROM locate and open the character-hair.car file, select the hair object, and copy and paste it. Close the character-hair.car file. Now back in the Carrara file for your model, paste the hair and position it on the character's head. To reduce the polygon count even more, delete any polygons from the head that are underneath hair and will not be seen. The completed character should like Figure 10.48.

**FIGURE 10.48**    The finished superhero.

**TUTORIAL 10.2**    **MODELING AN AIRPLANE**

In this tutorial we will build a model of a Piper Cherokee airplane. However, instead of using box modeling as we did in the previous tutorial, we will use the Vertex Modeler's new curve and surfacing tools to generate the objects needed to model the airplane. Unlike box modeling, surface modeling requires that curves be drawn to define the profile or cross sections of an object. Then tools such as Lathe, Ruled Surface, and Double Sweep are used to generate surfaces based on the curves. Surface modeling is appropriate for technical models where precision is important. Since we will model an airplane, we want to be as accurate as possible (see Figure 10.49).

**FIGURE 10.49**   The subject of this tutorial.

**ON THE CD**

Launch Carrara and from the Insert menu choose Vertex Object. This will place a vertex object in the scene and instantly jump into the Vertex Modeler. The first thing we will do is place reference images in the Top, Left, and Front working planes for use as guides during the modeling process. Click on the Global tab of the Properties tray, and in the Backdrop section click on the Load Image File button in the Front/Back area. Browse to the file front.tif and check Enable. In the Left/Right area load the side.tif image and in the Top/Bottom area load top.tif. The reference images can be seen in any of the isometric camera views but not in the perspective view (see Figure 10.50).

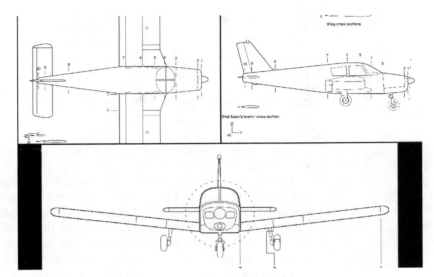

**FIGURE 10.50**    The reference images in the Vertex Modeler.

## Modeling the Fuselage

The first thing we will do in modeling the fuselage is create the curves or cross sections that will define the shape of the fuselage. Unlike box modeling, which we used to model the character in the previous tutorial, the fuselage is modeled from curves that will be lofted to generate a surface.

Switch to the Front camera view and notice that toward the bottom of the reference image is a series of curves numbered 1 through 10. These are the curves that we will use to quickly build the fuselage. With the Zoom tool (Z) zoom in on the curves. Now that you are zoomed in you should be able to clearly see small squares along the curves. These squares represent the vertices that make up the curves. The vertices on the curves have been carefully planned so that when the curves are lofted it will be easy to detail the fuselage. Now select the Polyline tool (Y) from the toolbar and create each curve by tracing the curve and clicking once at each vertex as shown on the reference image. To terminate a curve once you are done tracing it press Enter and then start the next curve (see Figure 10.51).

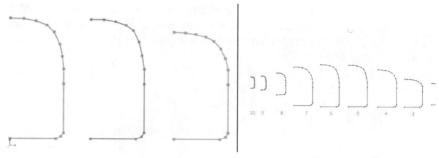

**FIGURE 10.51**   Trace the curves on the reference image with the Polyline tool.

Now switch to the Top camera view and you will see that all of the new curves you just created are on the *xz* plane. Notice that the reference image of the airplane from the top also has markings numbered 1 through 10. Each of those marks represents the position of a cross section with the same number along the fuselage. Select curve 1 and using the top and left views as referenced, position the curve on the mark labeled 1 with the Move tool (T) or the Universal Manipulator (U). Repeat the process until all of the curves you created are positioned along the fuselage as seen from the top or side (see Figure 10.52).

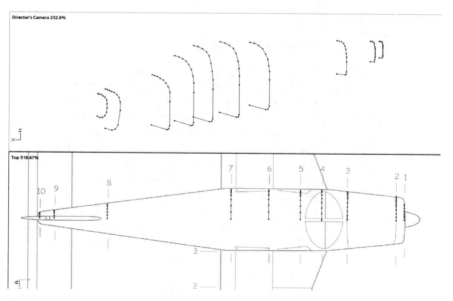

**FIGURE 10.52**   Once each curve is created, it is positioned along the fuselage.

With the curves in position, select the Ruled Surface tool from the toolbar and click on each curve in succession. Either click on curve 1 and proceed to curve 10 or click on curve 10 and work your way up to 1. As you click from curve to curve, a surface is lofted between each curve. When finished, the result should look like Figure 10.53.

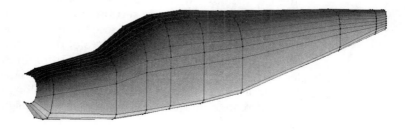

Director's Camera 294.45%

**FIGURE 10.53**    The surface of the fuselage is created by clicking on the curves with the Ruled Surface tool.

Carrara has a unique feature in which the original curves that were used to generate the surface remain in the scene. In other words, there are now 11 objects in the scene: the original 10 curves and the new surface. We do not need the original curves any longer, so they should be deleted. Double-click on any polygon of the new surface you just created to select it; the entire surface should turn red when selected. Now from the Selection menu choose Name and then select Polymesh from the submenu. In the Name Selected Polymesh dialog box type in the name of the fuselage and press OK, as shown in Figure 10.54. From the View menu choose Hide Selected Vertices to temporarily hide the fuselage. Then select all of the curves in the scene and delete them by pressing the Delete key. When the curves are gone, go back to the View menu and select Reveal Hidden Vertices to unhide the fuselage.

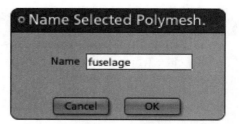

**FIGURE 10.54**    Name the new surface fuselage.

In the next few steps we will refine the shape of the airplane and out-line the windows by adding new cross sections and edges. At this point there are only three cross sections that mold the nose of the airplane. That is not enough to give the nose the right shape, so we will add a new cross section. Select one of the edges of the second cross section by click-ing on it once. Then press on the Loop button in the Properties tray to se-lect the entire cross section. Next, select the Extract Along tool from the Edge tools in the toolbar and click and drag along the surface of the fuse-lage to create a new cross section as shown in Figure 10.55.

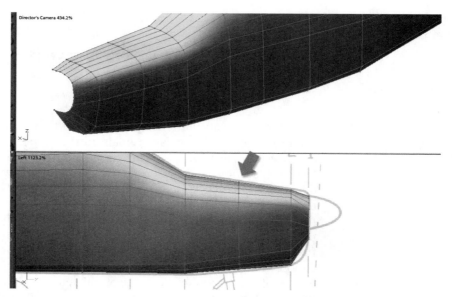

**FIGURE 10.55**    With the Extract Along tool create a new cross section between the second and third cross sections to help define the nose.

Repeat the process to create a new cross section between the first and second cross sections (see Figure 10.56). Once the new cross sections are created, position and shape them so that they match the fuselage's outline on the reference images.

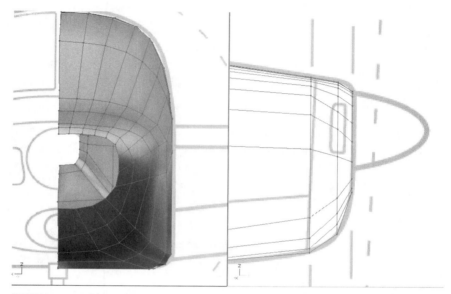

**FIGURE 10.56**    Add another cross section between the first and second cross sections.

In the next steps we will create the outlines of the cabin windows. Switch to the Left camera view so that you can see the outlines of the cabin windows in the reference images. Zoom in on cross section 6. Remember that each cross section has a number assigned to it on the reference images, so at this point it is easy to know which cross section is which. Select all of the edges of cross section 6 and move it back so that it lines up with the front edge of the small cabin window, as in Figure 10.57a. Next use the Extract Along tool to create a new cross section and move the new cross section so that it lines up with the back of the large cabin window (see Figure 10.57b).

With the Add tool create new edges along the back of the small cabin window and create new edges along the front of the large cabin window as shown in Figure 10.58a,b (red arrows). Since adding new edges creates polygons with more than four sides, subdivide those polygons into two polygons with three or four vertices by connecting their vertices with the Link tool (the blue arrow points to an example of a subdivided polygon). Adjust the edges near the top and bottom of the cabin windows with the Move tool so that they line up with the top and bottom of the cabin windows.

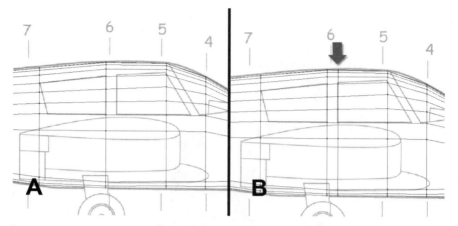

**FIGURE 10.57** Create the new edges to begin defining the side cabin windows.

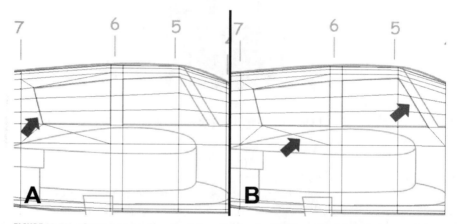

**FIGURE 10.58** Create new edges to define the back of the small cabin window and the front of the large cabin window.

With the cabin windows outlined, next we will outline the front windshield. However, since the front windshield wraps around from the side to the front, you will have to use two views to correctly place the new edges that will outline the windshield. In the Left camera view create new edges to define the back of the windshield. Then create the bottom of the windshield (see Figure 10.59a). To finish creating the windshield you will have to switch to the Top view and continue the new line of edges, as shown in Figure 10.59b. Don't forget that the windshield is made of two parts, so you will want to create a line edge that creates the partition (see the arrow in Figure 10.59b). Figure 10.59c shows the windows highlighted for clarity.

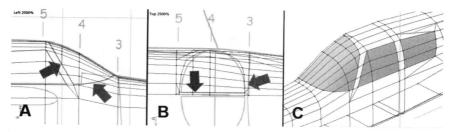

**FIGURE 10.59**    Define the windshield with new edges.

We will complete the fuselage detail by modeling the air intakes and landing light at the very front of the fuselage. First add new cross sections to the nose as shown in Figure 10.60a. Switch between the Top, Left, and Front camera views to make sure that the new cross sections follow the contours of the reference images as well as possible. To close the first cross section select the Polygon tool (found with the Primitives tools in the toolbar) and click on each of the vertices of the first cross section, as in Figure 10.60b.

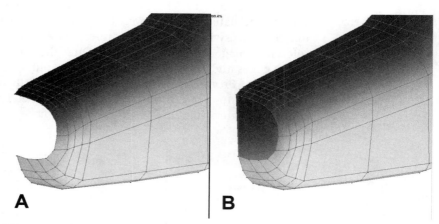

**FIGURE 10.60**    Close the first cross section to prepare it for modeling the nose details.

To be able to model the air intakes and landing light we need to add more polygons, so progressively add new polygons with the Add and Link tools (see Figure 10.61).

Before proceeding with modeling the nose details, it is important to hide most of the fuselage so that it does not interfere with modeling the nose as we try to use the reference images. Select the fuselage from the last cross section at the tail all the way to the front windshield. Then go to the View menu and choose Hide Selection to hide the selection.

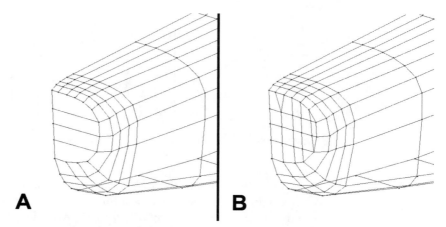

**FIGURE 10.61** Subdivide the new polygon at the front of the nose.

Switch to the Front camera view and with the Add and Link tools outline the air intake. Don't be afraid to experiment as you rough-in the intake. Once it looks good, clean it up by moving edges and vertices to fit the reference image. Wherever you create polygons with more than four sides triangulate those polygons by connecting vertices (see arrow). You may have to switch to the Left camera view to compare it with the side reference image (see Figure 10.62a). Once the intake is outlined, select all of the edges and vertices that make up the outer perimeter and inside of the intake. From the Model menu choose Detach Polygons and then press Delete to create the hole of the air intake. The result should look similar to Figure 10.62c.

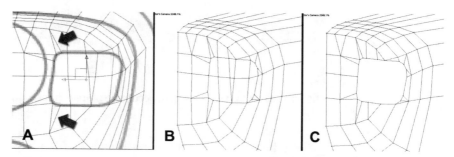

**FIGURE 10.62** Create the air intake with the Add and Link tools and then detach the inside and delete to create the hole of intake.

The next bit of detail is the landing light. The landing light is a round recessed area on the front of the airplane. To begin modeling the landing light switch to the Front camera view and rough-in the landing light by tracing it from the reference image (see Figure 10.63a). Next refine the circular path by adding more edges and vertices and then detach and delete the inside polygons to create a hole, as in Figure 10.63c.

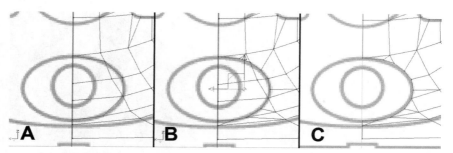

**FIGURE 10.63**    Like the intake, create the shape of the landing light and then detach and delete the inside.

The landing light is a recessed area, not a hole, so to finish modeling the landing light select all of the edges around the hole of the landing light and with the Dynamic Extrusion tool extrude inward as in Figure 10.64a. Then with the Polygon tool close the extruded edges (see Figure 10.64c).

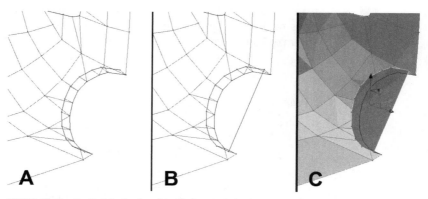

**FIGURE 10.64**    To finish the landing light extrude the edges inward and cap the inside with a polygon.

To complete the fuselage (for now) go to the View menu and select Reveal Hidden Vertices to unhide the rest of the airplane. Dolly around to the last cross section and use the Polygon tool to cap the end as shown in Figure 10.65. Since the fuselage is complete, let's move on to the wings.

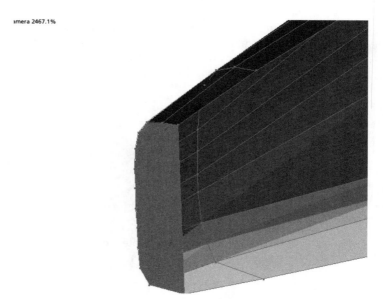

**FIGURE 10.65**   Cap the end of the fuselage with a polygon.

## Modeling the Wing

The wings of a Piper Cherokee are very simple in shape, as they are mostly rectangular. To begin the wings switch to the Left camera view and trace the three wing cross sections labeled 1, 2, and 3. Use few vertices to define the cross sections but make sure there are vertices where the arrows indicate (see Figure 10.66).

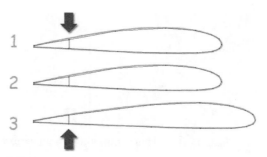

**FIGURE 10.66**   Trace the wing cross sections with the Polyline tool.

Switch to the Front camera view and position cross section 3 close to the fuselage and the other two on the cross section lines indicated in Figure 10.67. Now switch to the Director's camera view and with the Ruled

Surface tool connect all three cross sections to generate the wing surface, as in Figure 10.68. Remember that when you use the Ruled Surface tool the original curves are left behind. In other words, the wing surface is separate from the curves you traced a moment ago, so you have to remove the original wing curves by hiding the wing and fuselage and selecting the curves and then deleting them.

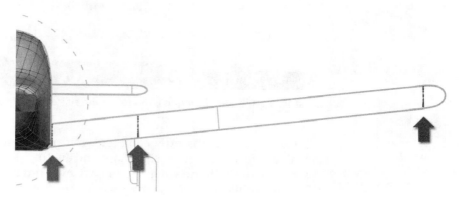

**FIGURE 10.67**    Position the cross sections along the wing.

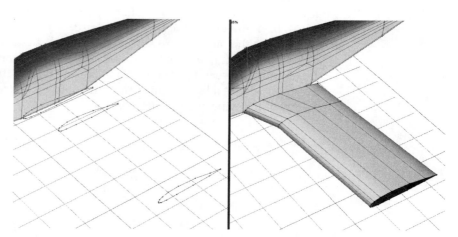

**FIGURE 10.68**    Use the Ruled Surface tool to generate the wing's cross section.

Once the wing surface is generated, use the front and top reference images to make sure the wing is in the correct position. The next item to model on the wing is the wingtip. The wingtip on the Piper Cherokee can be flat or round. For our model we will create a round wingtip. Select the last cross section on the wing, the one furthest from the fuselage, and fill it by pressing Ctrl/Command-F. Select the new polygon and with the Dynamic Extrusion tool extrude four times; each time make the extrusion smaller. Use the top and front reference images to shape the wingtip (see Figure 10.69).

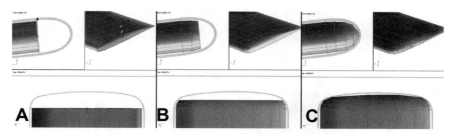

**FIGURE 10.69**    The round wingtip is modeled with successive extrusions.

The wing shape is now complete, but our model is going to have movable control surfaces such as flaps and ailerons, so we have to do a bit more work to finish the wing. If you have ever traveled near the wing on a jet, you could probably see the wing's control surfaces in action. The ailerons are the control surfaces at the end of the wing near the wing tip. The flaps are the large control surfaces near the wing root that move down on landing or take off and back up during flight.

To begin modeling the flaps and ailerons add a new cross section to the wing. Select the second cross section (see arrow) as shown in Figure 10.70a and with the Extract Along tool create a new cross section and position it at the division between the aileron and flap (see Figure 10.70b). The top surface of the flap is a bit narrower than the bottom, so create a new edge on the top of the wing as in Figure 10.71.

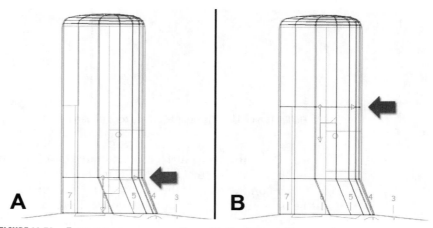

**FIGURE 10.70**    Extract a new cross section with the Extract Along tool.

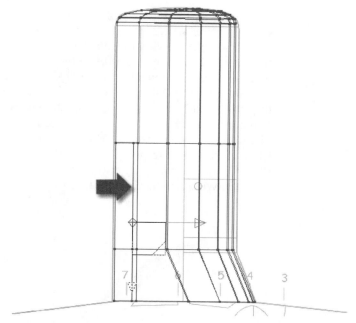

**FIGURE 10.71**    Extract one more edge to define the upper surface of the flap.

Next carefully select all of the polygons that make up the flap and aileron. Then from the Model menu choose Detach Polygons to separate the flap and aileron from the wing (see Figure 10.72). Once the flap and aileron are separated from the wing, separate the flap from the aileron so that there are three objects: wing, aileron, and flap. Remember to name the new objects (Selection > Name).

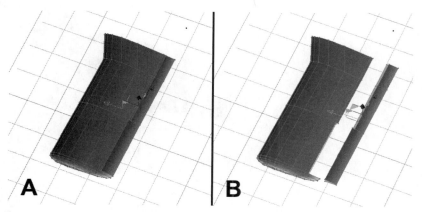

**FIGURE 10.72**    Separating the aileron and flap from the wing with the Detach Polygon command.

Now that the wing, flap, and aileron are separate objects, they are not solid. In other words, they have open areas as shown in Figure 10.73a. To make the objects solid once more we will use the Polygon tool. Hide everything except the flap. With the Polygon tool begin closing up the long side by clicking on each vertex. You will know that you are clicking on the vertices because the Polygon tool will snap to the vertices and the cursor will display a small square. Next select the edges at each end and use the Fill Polygon command to cap the ends (see Figure 10.73b). Repeat the process of closing all open areas on the wing and the aileron. When you are finished closing up the wing, flap, and aileron, reveal everything and move the flap and aileron back into place. At this point you should have a complete left wing and left half of the fuselage, as shown in Figure 10.74.

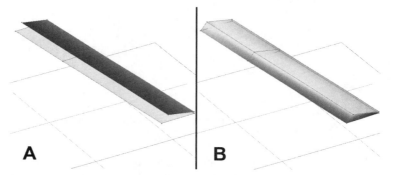

**A**          **B**

**FIGURE 10.73**   Closing the open areas of the flap with the Polygon tool.

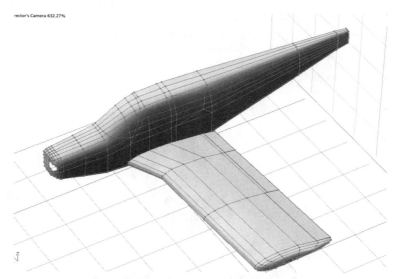

**FIGURE 10.74**   Once all areas are closed, move the aileron and flap back into place.

## Modeling the Fin and Stabilizer

The fin and stabilizer are the small vertical and horizontal wings at the back of the airplane. The fin has the rudder and the stabilizer has the elevator, which are control surfaces much like the aileron of the main wing. The fin and stabilizer are modeled in exactly the same way as the main wing. For instance, to model the stabilizer trace the cross section on the side reference image labeled stabilizer. Then create a second cross section and use either the Loft or Ruled Surfaces tool to generate the stabilizer surface, as shown in Figure 10.75a. Model the tip of the stabilizer by capping the end with a polygon. You can do this by selecting the cross section at the end and then from the Model menu selecting Fill Polygon. Once you have a polygon at the end, use the Dynamic Extrusion tool to model the tip (see Figure 10.75b). Finally, detach the elevator and make the stabilizer and elevator solid, as in Figure 10.75c.

The steps in modeling the fin and rudder are more involved than the stabilizer and elevator, but it is still essentially the same as the main wing. Trace the cross sections on the top reference view, position the cross sections, loft with the Loft or Ruled Surface tool, add details like the round tip and flare at the bottom, and then detach the rudder (see Figure 10.76). Remember to reposition the elevator at the back of the stabilizer and the rudder at the back of the fin.

**FIGURE 10.75**    Modeling the stabilizer and elevator.

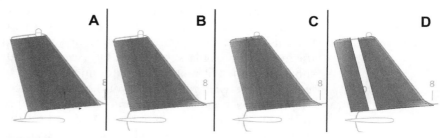

**FIGURE 10.76**    Modeling the fin and rudder.

### Creating the Right Half of the Airplane

At this point the left half of the airplane is basically complete, so it is time to create the right half and join the fuselage halves together. Much like the character modeling tutorial in this chapter, creating the right half is accomplished by selecting the parts to be duplicated, using the Duplicate with Symmetry command to make a copy, and then using the Weld command to join the fuselage halves.

Select the fin and rudder and hide them because these objects are complete and should not be part of this process. Next, press Ctrl/Command-A to select everything else that remains in the scene, as in Figure 10.77a. Then Ctrl/Command-click on any vertex along the cut edge of the fuselage to move the working plane along the midline of the fuselage. Before duplicating, we need to set the axis along which the duplication will happen, so click once on the *zy* plane in the Working Box controls (see arrow) (see Figure 10.77). Then from the Edit menu choose Duplicate with Symmetry to instantly create the right half as shown in Figure 10.77c. Once the right half is created, send the working planes back to their normal positions by choosing Reset Working Box from the View menu.

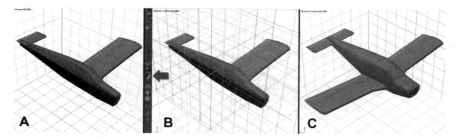

**FIGURE 10.77**   Creating the right half of the airplane.

The next step is to join the halves of the fuselage, stabilizer, and elevator. To join the fuselage, first hide everything but the fuselage to cut down on interference from other objects in the scene. Next carefully select all of the vertices along the middle as shown in Figure 10.78a. Then from the Model menu choose Weld. In the Weld Selected Vertices dialog box check Use Custom Tolerance, enter a small value such as 0.10 in. (the value you use may be more or less), and press OK (see Figure 10.78b). The two halves should be joined instantly. Dolly around the model to check for any problems with the weld function. If you find any vertices that are welded but should not be, press Ctrl/Command-Z to undo and use a larger value in the tolerance. On the other hand, if you find vertices that are not welded but should be, simply use the Weld tool to join those two vertices. The only other objects that need to be joined in a similar fashion as the fuselage are the stabilizer and elevator, so repeat the steps we just went through to join those objects.

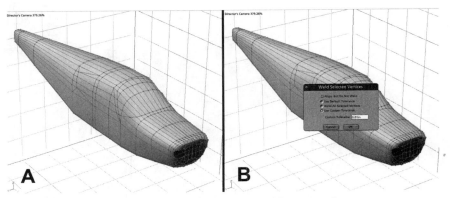

**FIGURE 10.78**    Joining the fuselage halves with the Weld command.

## Modeling the Landing Gear

In the next steps we will model the wheel, tire, fairing, and strut of the main landing gear. The Piper Cherokee has a tricycle landing gear configuration, meaning that it has one wheel under each wing and one at the nose. To begin the modeling process, move the *xz* drawing plane so that it intersects the airplane at approximately the same place as shown in Figure 10.79. Remember that you can quickly move the working box planes by Ctrl/Command-clicking any vertex. In this case the vertex where the blue and red grid lines intersect on the model was clicked. The drawing plane is moved into this position because we are about to draw the profiles for the tire and wheel with the Polyline tool and the curves are drawn under the wing with the *xz* drawing plane in this position.

Switch to the Front camera view and zoom in on the left wheel. With the Polyline tool trace the upper part of the tire and wheel as seen in Figure 10.80a. Now switch to the Director's camera and zoom in on the new curves so that we can see them in perspective. Select the curve for the wheel and click on the Lathe tool in the toolbar. Next click on the edge indicated by the arrow in Figure 10.80b. This will instantly create the wheel as shown in Figure 10.80c. Press the plus (+) key until the wheel has about 18 sides and press Enter to terminate the Lathe command. You can see the number of sides in the Properties tray.

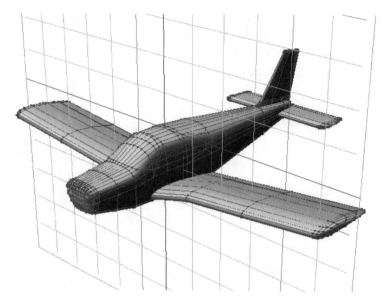

**FIGURE 10.79**   The *xz* drawing plane is moved to facilitate drawing the curves for the wheel and tire (*xy* and *zy* working planes hidden).

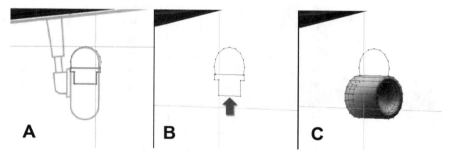

**A**          **B**          **C**

**FIGURE 10.80**   The wheel is created by lathing the curve that defines the profile of the wheel.

The tire is created in the same way as the wheel. Name the wheel and then hide it. Notice that the original curves are still in the scene. Select the curve of the tire, click on the Lathe tool, and then click on the edge shown in Figure 10.81a. It may seem odd to click on the same edge used for the wheel, but we want the tire to rotate around the same axis as the wheel so that they fit together. Once again the new object, in this case the tire, is instantly created. Press the plus (+) key until the tire has 18 sides. Make sure to name the tire and delete the original curves, as they are not needed anymore. Figure 10.81c shows the tire and wheel completed.

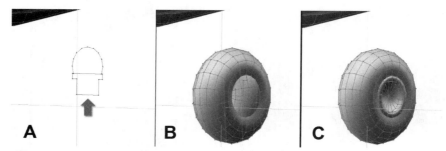

**FIGURE 10.81**    The tire is created the same way as the wheel.

The rest of the main landing gear is made up of a fairing that streamlines the landing gear, the struts, shock absorber, and brake. The fairing is modeled from two cross sections as shown in Figure 10.82a. The rest of the landing gear is easily modeled from cylinder primitives (see Figure 10.82b). To create the right landing gear duplicate all of the parts of the left landing gear. Use the reference images to position the completed landing gear under the wings.

**FIGURE 10.82**    Cross sections and cylinder primitives make up the rest of the landing gear.

The front landing gear is very similar to the main landing gear. In fact, you may duplicate the main wheel and tire and quickly create the wheel and tire for the front landing gear. To create the fork that holds the wheel in place switch to the Front camera view (remember to move the working plane to the position that you want to draw the curves) and with the Polyline tool trace one side of the fork, as in Figure 10.83a. Next create a square cross section at one end of the curves (see Figure 10.83b). To complete the fork from the curves we will use the Double Sweep tool. Select the Double Sweep tool from the toolbar, click on the square cross section once, and then click once on each curve. The Double Sweep tool will instantly generate the surfaces shown in Figure 10.83c. Remember to delete the original curves, as they are not needed anymore.

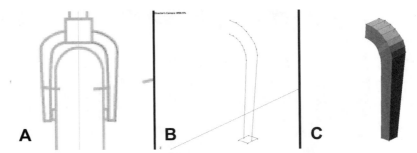

**FIGURE 10.83**    The fork that holds the front wheel in place is created with the Double Sweep tool.

Duplicate the left half of the fork to model the other side. The rest of the front landing gear will be modeled from cylinders, much like the main landing gear (see Figure 10.84). Use the reference images as guides to position the front landing gear at the nose of the airplane. When it's all assembled, the landing gear looks remarkably detailed, though it is really quite simple.

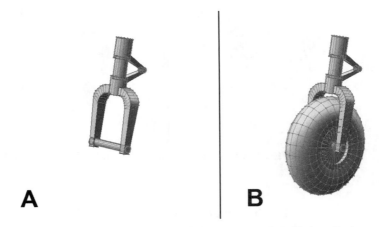

**FIGURE 10.84**    The rest of the front landing gear is modeled from cylinders and a couple of cubes.

### Prop and Spinner

The propeller is modeled by creating one blade from curves lofted with the Ruled Surface tool. Open the file prop.car from the Chapter 10 folder in the book's CD-ROM. Though the file appears empty, there is a vertex object named prop in the Instances tab of the Properties tray. Double-click on the prop object to jump into the Vertex Modeler. Zoom in on the 12 curves in the scene that will be used to create the propeller (see Figure 10.85a). From the toolbar select the Ruled Surface tool and click on each of the curves to generate the propeller's surface (see Figure 10.85b). Remember to delete the original curves that were used to generate the propeller's surface. Then cap the tip of the propeller with the Fill Polygon command. Select the propeller blade and copy and paste it into your model's document. Create the other half with the Duplicate with Symmetry command. Finally, model the spinner from half of a sphere primitive that is scaled into a half oval shape. When completed, position the prop and spinner using the reference images. The final result should look similar to Figure 10.86.

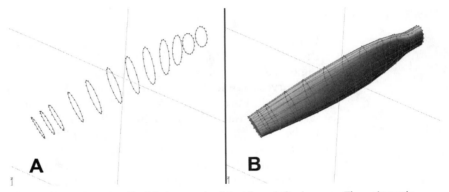

**FIGURE 10.85**    The propeller blades are modeled from lofted curves. The spinner is modeled from a scaled half sphere.

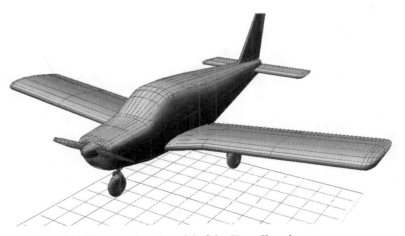

**FIGURE 10.86**    The completed model of the Piper Cherokee.

Though the model may be completed, there is still room to add details such as an interior, antennas, and navigation lights. You may also select the polygons that make up the windshield and cabin windows and detach them from the fuselage so that they can be textured separately. A final detail is to crease the edges of all of the airplane's parts so that sharp corners are possible. For instance, the edges of the control surfaces should be creased, as well as the back of the wings or any other place where there should be sharp corners. Use the Crease tool to crease individual edges or the Crease command from the Model menu to crease the entire model based on a tolerance value.

## SUMMARY

Congratulations on completing two very challenging modeling tutorials. In the first tutorial you learned to box model a character by pulling and pushing on edges, vertices, and polygons. In the second tutorial you learned to use curves to generate the surfaces needed. You have worked with many of the tools in Carrara's new Vertex Modeler and after working through this chapter you have the modeling skills to create just about anything you want. The logical next step is to texture and animate your models, and the subsequent chapters will give the insight you need to bring your models to life. As an added bonus, the next chapter features two in-depth modeling tutorials with Carrara's sister application Hexagon.

# 11

# MODELING WITH HEXAGON

## In This Chapter

- Tutorial 11.1. Modeling a Character Head
- Tutorial 11.2. Modeling a Concept Car

Hexagon is a new 3D modeling application developed by Eovia to work in conjunction with Carrara, but unlike Carrara, which has animation, modeling, and rendering tools, Hexagon is a dedicated modeler, so Hexagon's only task is to build 3D models. As such, Hexagon is an ideal tool to quickly and easily build polygonal models that can then be exported directly to Carrara for animation and rendering. Because Hexagon was designed with Carrara in mind, we have included two comprehensive Hexagon tutorials in this book.

As we will see in the next two tutorials, Hexagon is a powerful modeler and features three types of polygonal modeling: face, edge, and vertex modeling; surface modeling; and spline modeling. Hexagon also has a complete set of editing tools such as tessellation, edge extraction, welds, chamfer, fillet, and many more including a suite of utilities and deformers. Well, enough about Hexagon. Let's get elbow deep in polygons!

---

**TUTORIAL 11.1**   **MODELING A CHARACTER HEAD (BY JACK WHITNEY)**

In this tutorial we will use Eovia's new polygonal modeler Hexagon to model the head of a character named Raul, and as you can see in Figure 11.1, Raul is quite a character. You may think that Raul's expressive face was difficult to model, but quite the opposite is true. Raul's features are caricatured; in other words, they are exaggerated and simplified to emphasize those features that give Raul personality. The caricature works to our advantage because it reduces and simplifies the number of facial features we will have to model. We will use Hexagon's comprehensive modeling tools to model Raul from the ground up.

### Getting Started: Reference Images

All three of the current Eovia modeling products, Carrara, Hexagon, and Amapi, allow reference images to be projected onto the working planes within the modeler. Reference images are 2D graphics that show the subject about to be modeled in different views, which are important because they serve as guides during the modeling process.

The reference images were carefully created so that each is square and on the same scale. Grids or guides were used to ensure that the different parts of the head are aligned on both views. For instance, the horizontal lines at the top and base of the nose will be the same on both views (see Figure 11.2).

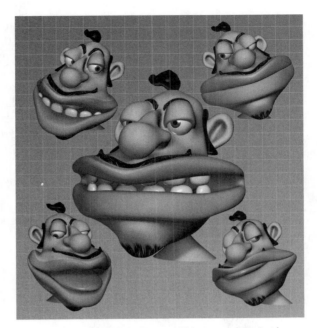

**FIGURE 11.1**    In this chapter we will be modeling Raul.

**FIGURE 11.2**    The front and side view reference images we will use to model Raul.

### Applying the Reference Images to the Hexagon Working Planes

ON THE CD

The reference images are provided for you in the book's companion CD-ROM in the Chapter 11 folder; the files are side.jpg and front.jpg. However, if you load the files into Hexagon from the CD-ROM, you will have to keep inserting the CD-ROM each time you want to work on Raul, as Hexagon keeps an absolute path to the images on the CD-ROM. It is better to copy the Chapter 11 folder from the book's companion CD-ROM to your desktop before proceeding.

Start up Hexagon and click on the Properties tab in the Scene palette, where you will find the options to display reference images on the left, right, and floor working planes. Activate the left and right grids by clicking on the small square next to the grid name. Click the Browse button for the left grid and locate the side.jpg image and for the right grid, browse to front.jpg, as in Figure 11.3. Now that the reference images are loaded, we are ready to begin modeling. Remember to save your work often.

**FIGURE 11.3**    The front and side view reference images in Hexagon.

## Modeling Raul

We will start Raul's head with a simple circle. Rough-in the shape of the head with extrusions and add details with good old fashioned vertex modeling—which means we will be working with vertices and edges to get just the shape we want. We will also use symmetrical modeling to add details both sides of the head.

## Modeling the Head

To begin, click on the Lines toolbar and select the Circle from Center tool. To easily draw the circle so that is parallel to the *zx* plane, or on the floor grid, you may want to dolly (Alt-MMB) the camera so you can see the floor grid better or switch to Four Views mode and draw the circle in the Top view. Draw the circle by clicking once to place the center of the circle and then dragging out from the center to set the radius. The size of the circle is not critical at this point, but the number of vertices is important. Once you have clicked to set the radius, the Circle from Center tool remains active and the cursor has changed to a +/− cursor. Hexagon is asking how many vertices you want the circle to have, so in the Tool properties enter "16" in the Nb Points field and press Validate. Using the manipulator move the circle up along the *z*-axis by clicking and dragging up on the green arrowhead so that the circle is about level with Raul's mouth, as shown in Figure 11.4.

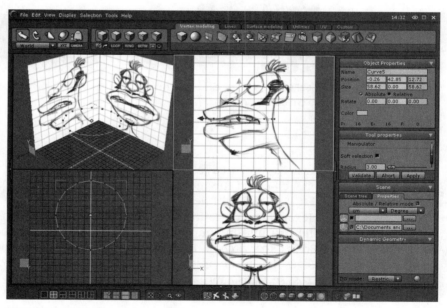

**FIGURE 11.4**    Raul starts out as a circle.

We will add volume to the top of Raul's head by creating new polygons with the extrusion tools. Switch to the Vertex Modeling toolbar and select the Sweep Surface tool. Click on the circle you created in the previous step and press the spacebar a couple times until the Extrude option (third option from the left) is highlighted in the Tool Properties palette. Drag upward and toward the center to create a shallow inverted funnel and click to complete the first extrusion. With the Sweep Surface tool still active, continue to drag upward and in toward the center to create a second extrusion, then extrude a third and fourth time. The result should produce a tapered cylinder with four sections along the cylinder, as in Figure 11.5. Take a look at the Dynamic Geometry palette; if Dynamic Geometry is turned on, collapse the Dynamic Geometry tree by clicking once on the lightning bolt icon. Unless you want to experiment with Dynamic Geometry, you can turn it off, as we will not be using it.

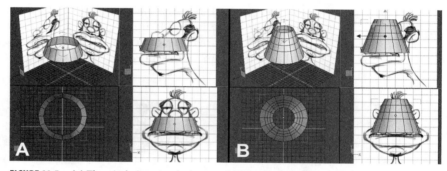

**FIGURE 11.5**    (a) The circle is extruded once. (b) Then is it is extruded three more times to create a funnel.

Let's adjust the shape we just created so that it fits better with Raul's head as compared to the reference images. To be able to see the reference image behind the model, turn on the Transparent Display. Click on the left half of Raul's head and in the Control toolbar at the bottom of the Hexagon user interface locate the three buttons at the far right. Click on the first button and notice that you can now see through Raul's head. Press 6 to switch to the Right view. To adjust the shape, we will select the edges that make up the cross sections and then move and scale until the cross sections approximate the reference images.

In the Manipulators toolbar select the Universal Manipulator (U) and in the Select toolbar choose the Select Edges tool (F3). Next, click on any of the edges that make up the first cross section and then press L to loop or select all edges in that cross section. To move the selection, simply click and drag on the manipulator's arrowheads. To scale, click and drag on the squares and to rotate, click and drag on the semicircles. This may take a bit of practice, but once you have the hang of it, it makes modeling go a lot faster. Move the edges as in Figure 11.6a and repeat the process until the shape looks like Figure 11.6b.

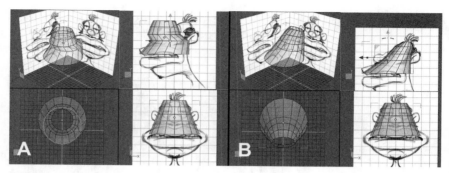

**FIGURE 11.6**   The cross sections are moved and scaled until the shape approximates the reference image. Transparency Display has been turned on to see the reference image behind the model.

Next we will rough-in the lower jaw and neck. Remember, we are working with the reference image in the Right view, so manipulate the new extrusions to fit this view. This time we will extrude using a keyboard shortcut instead of an extrusion tool. Select the first cross section (bottom cross section), press the Ctrl/Command key, and click on the green arrowhead (Z). When it turns white, drag it down to create a new extrusion. Once the first extrusion is done, create another extrusion (see Figure 11.7a). As with the top of Raul's head, use the Universal Manipulator and the Select Edges tool to model the lower part of the head. Remember, select an edge of the cross section you want to move, press L to create a loop, and use the various tools in the Universal Manipulator to move, rotate, and scale the cross sections into position (see Figure 11.7b). To complete the jaw and neck as seen from the Right view, create more extrusions with the extrusion tools or keyboard shortcut and then move the new extrusions into position. Better yet, you can extrude with the shortcut and manipulate the extrusion into position at the same time. Once you are finished with the head as seen from the

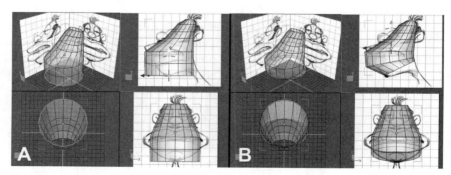

**FIGURE 11.7**   (a) Create new extrusions for the lower jaw. (b) Move the cross sections into place.

right, use the same tools to adjust the cross sections of head, lower jaw, and neck as seen from the front. When you are finished, your model should like Figure 11.8.

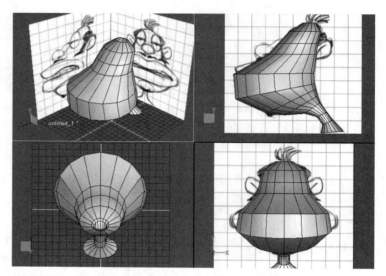

**FIGURE 11.8**    Model the lower jaw and neck as seen from the front.

### Increase Smoothing and Decrease Smoothing Tools

We are currently working with a model that has a very few polygons, which is good for quickly roughing in the head, but it does not show us what the final model may look like. Hexagon provides smoothing and un-smoothing tools to preview and can eventually subdivide the model's topology. To smooth Raul's head, select it by clicking on it in the scene or in the Scene Tree in the Scene palette, and in the Vertex Modeling toolbar click once on the Increase Smoothing tool. Notice that Raul's head is smoother, as in Figure 11.9. Clicking on the Increase Smoothing tool again will smooth the model again, but be careful not to click on the Increase Smoothing tool more than two or three times because each click doubles the number of polygons and this can quickly bog down even the fastest computer. To return Raul to his original number of polygons, click on the Decrease Smoothing tool. As you continue to model Raul's head, occasionally turn smoothing on to keep tabs on the modeling.

### Cloned Symmetrical Modeling

Since humans (and caricatures of humans) have right and left sides that are mostly symmetrical, it is smart to model one half of the body, then copy

**FIGURE 11.9**    Raul's head smoothed.

and flip the complete half to make the missing half and then weld the halves together. However, modeling one half and then copying and flipping to produce a whole may introduce time-consuming modeling errors. To get around this problem Hexagon has *cloned symmetrical modeling*, also known as *mirrored modeling*. This means that we can clone half of Raul's head and position the clone next to the original, and as we work on either half the changes are instantly updated in both halves. For instance, when you model an ear on the left half, an ear simultaneously appears on the right half.

To set up clone modeling, we have to first delete half of Raul's head. Deleting half of the head can be accomplished in several ways, but the most straightforward method is to switch to the Front view (2 on the number pad), select Raul's head, choose the Select Points tool (F4), and right-click anywhere in the document window. Notice that the cursor changes to a square with an arrow, indicating that the Lasso selection mode is active. With the Lasso tool click and drag to draw a box around the vertices that make up the right side of Raul's head as seen from the front, but do not select the vertices along the midline. This may take a few tries, but you'll get the hang of it. The selected vertices will turn light blue. Now press Delete; half of Raul's head should disappear (see Figure 11.10).

To create the clone, select the half that remains in the scene and select the Symmetry tool in the Vertex Modeling toolbar; it is the next to the last tool. In the Tool Properties toggle Clone On and move the cursor into the scene. Notice that as you mouse near the head with the Symmetry tool active, blue planes appear that represent the plane across which the clone will appear. When you get to the side of the head where you want the clone to appear, click once and notice that Raul's head appears to be whole. However, there are two cloned halves, or two objects, as shown in Figure 11.11. Now that cloned halves are ready, we are prepared to model the rest of Raul.

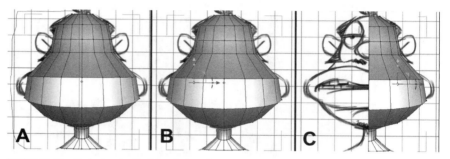

**FIGURE 11.10**    Deleting half of Raul's head.

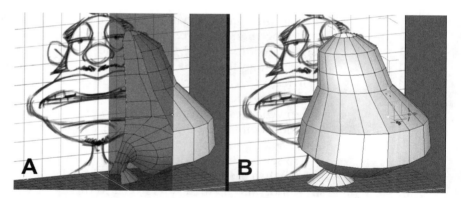

**FIGURE 11.11**    Creating a clone of the left side.

## Modeling the Mouth

Modeling Raul's lips and mouth is more challenging than roughing in the general shape of the head. The following steps will require patience and considerable edge and vertex modeling to achieve the desired result. Use the reference images as guides only, keeping in mind that the reference images are 2D and the model is 3D. Achieving a perfect correlation between the 2D images and the 3D model is not possible, because the 3D model has much more information. Before you begin modeling, it may be a good idea to study the finished model of Raul, finished-raul.hxn, and the incremental steps provided for you in the book's CD-ROM in the Chapter 11 folder. Studying the finished models will give you a good idea of the 3D aspects of Raul's caricatured face. Be patient and deliberate as you work, paying close attention to what you are doing, as modeling in 3D is challenging. Working too fast, especially if you are new to Hexagon (or 3D modeling), will slow you down in the long run, as you will have to correct errors later on.

To model the mouth, we need more polygons, so select the edges, as shown in Figure 11.12a, and in the Vertex Modeling toolbar subpalette choose the Extract Edge Along Edge tool (yes, that is the name of the tool). Two white arrowheads will appear along the selected edges. Click and drag on the arrowhead that points toward the inside of the mouth to create the new edges, as in Figure 11.12a. Repeat the steps to create another set of new edges further inside the mouth as in Figure 11.12c. The edges we just created will help define the edge of the lips and the inside of the mouth.

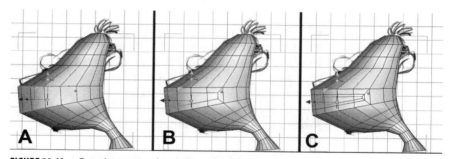

**FIGURE 11.12**    Creating new edges to model the lips and inside of the mouth.

The outer edge of the lips also has to be defined, so create edges on the outside of the mouth (see Figure 11.13). At this point you should be able to see the polygons that will become the lips and those that will make up the inside of the mouth.

Modeling the lips and mouth will require considerable modeling at the edge and vertex level, so to move things along we will use Hexagon's very cool Tweak tool. The Tweak tool quickly moves faces, edges, and vertices without having to use the selection tools. The Tweak tool works best in the Top, Left, Right, Front, Back, and Bottom views but it also works in the perspective view. Like any Hexagon tool, the Tweak tool is activated by selecting it from the appropriate toolbar (in this case the Vertex Modeling toolbar) and then terminating it when done by pressing on the Validate button in the Tool Properties.

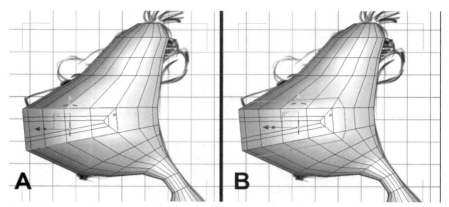

**FIGURE 11.13**    Creating new edges on the outside of the mouth to define the outer lips.

Before getting to the Tweak tool, let's move the polygons that will become the inside of the mouth a bit toward the back of the head. This will help us see which polygons will become the inside of the mouth and which will become the lips. Select polygons as shown in Figure 11.14a. Press U for the Universal Manipulator, locate the yellow cube in the middle of the Universal Manipulator, and click and drag to scale down the polygons, as shown in Figure 11.14b. Because we are working with cloned symmetrical modeling, the polygons inside the mouth of the right side were also scaled down, creating a small gap in front. To close the gap, move the middle edge toward the center (see Figure 11.14c).

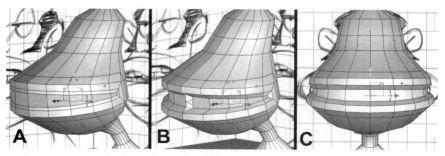

**FIGURE 11.14**    Roughing-in the inside of the mouth.

Select the left side of Raul's head, and if you have turned off the Transparency Display turn it back on, as you need to see the reference images to model the lips. If you still can't see the reference image clearly (especially from the Right view), try hiding the right side of the head by pressing the eye icon next the right side of the head in the Scene Properties Scene Tree. Now select the Tweak tool in the Vertex Modeling toolbar, and in the Front view (2) arrange the edges or vertices (whichever you like) that make up the top of the lip so that they conform to the front reference image. Switch to the Right view (6) and arrange those vertices so that they follow the reference image. Now move to the bottom of Raul's top lip and roughly position those vertices or edges so that they conform to the reference image, as in Figure 11.15. When you are finished with the Tweak tool, remember to terminate it by pressing Enter or the Validate button in the Tool Properties.

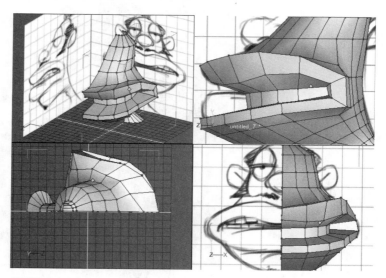

**FIGURE 11.15**    Modeling the top lip (right half hidden and transparency turned off for clarity).

With the top lip roughed-in (we are not trying to get things perfect just yet), move on to the inside of the mouth. The only thing to do here is carefully move and arrange the polygons that make up the inside of the mouth to the back of the mouth, as in Figure 11.16. Pay close attention to the polygons at the corners of the mouth, as they jut out from Raul's face. This is an area that can easily become jumbled. See Figure 11.17.

By now you should be getting the hang of the Tweak tool and should be able to model the lower lip in the same fashion as you did the upper lip. Remember, there is no trick or shortcut to modeling; you simply have to get in there and push and pull vertices and edges until things fall into place. Arrange the edges and vertices of the lower lip so that they line up as well as possible with the front and side reference images, as in Figure 11.18. Try smoothing Raul's head to see what it will look like.

To create the chin, select the large polygon in the chin region and create a new extrusion with the extrusion tools. You may also create the ex-

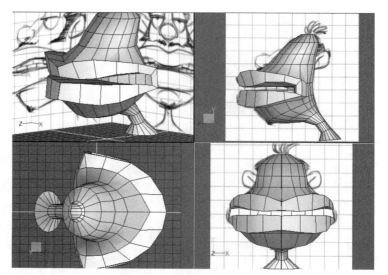

**FIGURE 11.16**    Once the lips are roughed-in begin the back of the mouth.

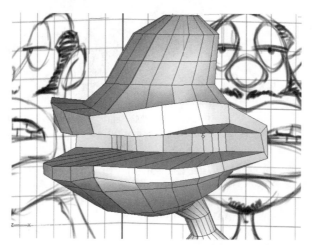

**FIGURE 11.17**    Creating the inside and back of the mouth (transparency turned off for clarity).

trusion by simply selecting the polygon and holding the Ctrl/Command key while clicking and dragging the blue arrowhead, as shown in Figure 11.19a. The new extrusion for the chin has created an unwanted polygon along the midline of the model. The added polygon is a normal result of extrusion, and you will encounter the same situation when you model the nose. To delete the unwanted polygon, select the right side of Raul's head

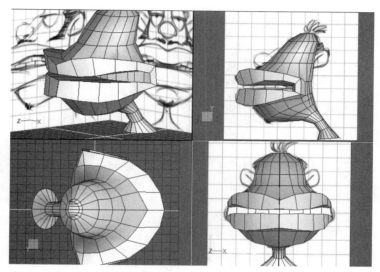

**FIGURE 11.18**    Modeling the lower lip (transparency turned off for clarity).

in the Scene Tree tab of the Scene palette and toggle off the eye icon of the highlighted object to temporarily hide it. Next, select the polygon to be removed and press the Delete key (see Figure 11.19b). Now un-hide the right side of the head and move the polygon you extruded a moment ago so the chin halves meet at the midline. If you want to give Raul a chin dimple, move the inside edge inward, as in Figure 11.19c.

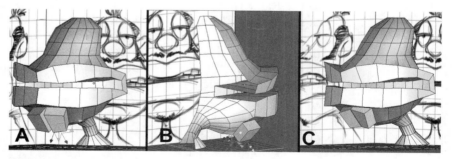

**FIGURE 11.19**    Modeling the chin.

## Modeling the Nose

The first thing we need to do to model the nose is to add new polygons. In Figure 11.20a you can see that new edges have been added. These new edges were added by creating an edge loop to select all edges along the cross sections and then using the Extract Edge Along Edge tool to create the new edges. In Figure 11.20b you can already see the outline of the nose.

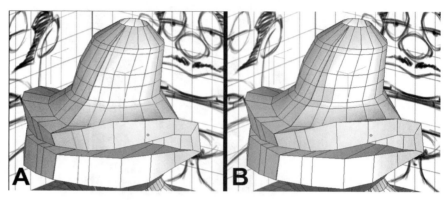

**FIGURE 11.20** To begin the nose, new edges are needed.

To give the nose volume, select the Extrude Surface tool, set its properties to Extrude and By Block, and extrude away from the face, as in Figure 11.21a. If it's not perfect, don't worry; we will be refining the nose in a few moments. Remember that performing an extrusion along the midline creates unwanted polygons on the inside of the head. These polygons have to be removed before proceeding. Refer to the instructions on removing unwanted polygons when you modeled the chin earlier. Switch to the Right view and move the vertices and edges along the top of the nose so they match the side view (see Figure 11.21b). Switch to the Front view and do the same. As with the lips, there is no strict set of instructions or formula to model the nose. You just have to get in there and move the edges and vertices that make up the nose until they conform to the reference images, as in Figure 11.21c.

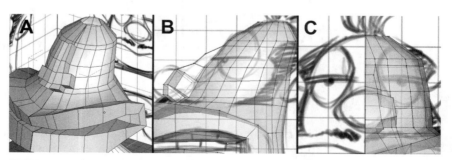

**FIGURE 11.21** The nose is extruded and shaped.

To model Raul's bulbous nose tip, select the two polygons at the top of the very tip of the nose. Select the Extrude Surface tool, set its properties to Extrude, and turn on By Block. Extrude up and away from the nose, making the new polygons a larger than the tip. Extrude again to finish the tip, as in Figure 11.22. Continue to model the nose so that it matches the reference images. You may want to check on how the model is progressing by temporarily smoothing, as in Figure 11.22b.

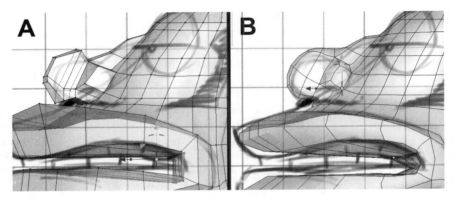

**FIGURE 11.22**    The large bulb on Raul's nose is also started as extrusions and then shaped.

Next we will create Raul's large nostrils by creating a new set of polygons to work with and then extruding into the nose. Create a new set of edges, as shown in Figure 11.23a. The edges on the outside of the nostril will help stabilize the shape when the model is smoothed. Next, dolly the camera so that you can see up Raul's nose and select the single polygon that is where the nostril should be. Use the Extrude Surfaces tool to create a radial extrusion. A radial extrusion is different from axial and sweep extrusions in that it creates new polygons on the same plane as the original polygon. Select the Extrude Surfaces tool and in the Tool Properties

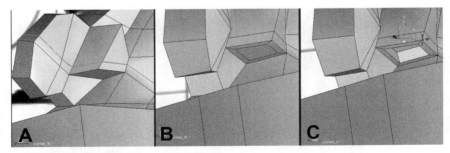

**FIGURE 11.23**    The nostril is started with new edges, then an axial sweep, and finally an extrusion into the nose.

select the Radial option and click and drag inside the polygon. The result should be similar to Figure 11.23b. You probably have figured out what will happen next. Select the inner polygon you just created and extrude up into the nose (see Figure 11.23c). With that last step the nose has been roughed-in and we can move on to the ears.

### Modeling the Ears

Raul's ears are very simple, as they are basically flattened circular disks with indentations to indicate the insides. To begin modeling the ears, select the two or three polygons on the side of the head, as in Figure 11.24a. With the Sweep Surface tool extrude the polygons away from the head (see Figure 11.24b). Make sure the Extrude and By Block options are selected before you extrude. You will probably extrude two or three times to rough-in the ear. The model in the figures has three extrusions, as shown in Figure 11.24c. With the Tweak tool shape the ear as seen from the Front view. Ultimately you can decide what type of ears you want Raul to have. To create the inside of the ear, create new edges and extrude into the ear, as in Figure 11.25. Continue to model the ear as you like with the Tweak tool and every now and then smooth the model to see how it is shaping up.

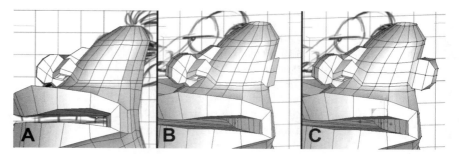

**FIGURE 11.24**  The ear extrusion starts here.

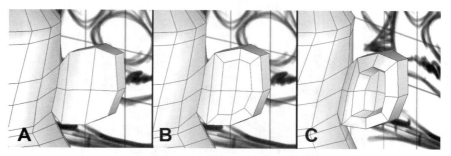

**FIGURE 11.25**  Create new edges inside the ear and then extrude inward.

## Modeling the Eyelids and Eyes

Raul has droopy eyelids over beady eyes, giving him a sly look. Modeling the eyelids will be a straightforward process involving extrusion and some tweaking of vertices and edges to get the right shape. The eyes are spheres that are rotated and positioned under the eyelids. Keep in mind that to create convincing eyelids, even for a caricature, the eyelids must look as if they are draped over the eye. To begin the eyelids, select four polygons (it may more or fewer polygons for your model) on the front of the face approximately where the eyes will be (see Figure 11.26). With the Sweep Surfaces tool, create a shallow extrusion, as in Figure 11.26b. Now, use the Tweak tool to rough-in the eyelid, as shown in Figure 11.26c.

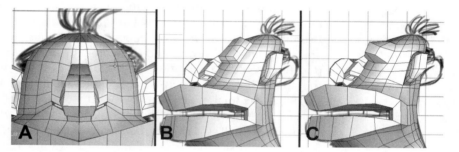

**FIGURE 11.26**    Modeling the eyelids.

Next insert a sphere by selecting the Create Sphere tool in the Vertex Modeling toolbar, and in any view click to start the sphere and click again to set the radius. The sphere should be approximately 12 units in size. You can adjust the size of the sphere numerically in the Size fields of the Object Properties palette or you can scale with the Universal Manipulator. The sphere just inserted has poles pointing north and south. The sphere needs to be rotated so that the poles point east and west (see Figure 11.27a). Next make a copy of the first sphere and position both under the eyelids, as in Figure 11.27b. The bottoms of the eyelids need to be modeled so that they fit the eyeballs nicely, so add new edges and use the Tweak tool to make the edits. The final results should look like Figure 11.27c.

## Refining the Geometry

At this point the basic geometry of the head is complete. The only thing left to do is add details such as a mustache, goatee, hair, eyebrows, tongue, and teeth. But before we move on to those details let's take some

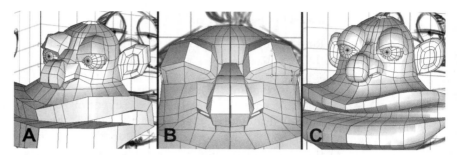

**FIGURE 11.27** The eyes are spheres that have been rotated to so that the poles point from side to side. The eyelids are tweaked until they fit the eyeballs nicely.

time to refine the geometry of the head. Refining the head simply means that you will correct any problem areas and add detail where needed. Usually, this means you will be adding new edges to increase definition and doing a lot of vertex and edge modeling. You can also take this opportunity to customize your version of Raul. If you want a bigger nose, then make it bigger. If you want a pointy head, then make it pointier.

Since the final model will be smoothed, we will take cues as to where to refine by smoothing one half of the head while working on the other unsmoothed half. If this has you scratching your head, do the following. Select the left side of the head and in the Scene Tree and click on the F next the object name to freeze it. Freeze means that the object is locked and cannot be changed. Now select the right side of the head and smooth it. Notice that only the right side is smoothed and the left side is not. Now unfreeze the left side by clicking on the U next to the object name. Now you can work on the unsmoothed head and see the results on the smoothed side.

Inspect the model by zooming in and dollying around the smoothed side of the head; if there are areas that have odd wrinkles or creases, have shrunk, or show any other unwanted artifacts, then that is a clear indication that this area needs some work. After inspection, it should be obvious that the lips need work because they do not look natural even for a human caricature. Add new edges and refine the lips via vertex modeling to get a more natural appearance, as in Figure 11.28. Though we did a good job of roughing-in the nose according to the reference images, let's make the nose a bit bumpier and larger. This is the fun of caricature modeling. You can do just about anything you want to get just the right character (see Figure 11.28). Take time to refine the rest of Raul's head and face. Once you are happy with your work, move on to adding details like hair and teeth.

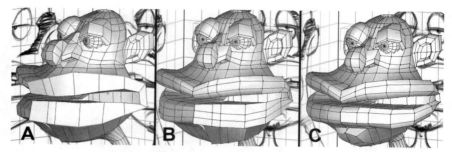

**FIGURE 11.28**    Refine Raul's head. Fix problems such as creasing and add detail to make the features more natural.

## Details: Hair, Teeth, and Tongue

Raul's head was started by roughing-in the shape of the head and neck with extrusions. Before modeling the facial features, the head was split into cloned halves to speed up modeling. Now that the head, face, and neck are done, the head needs to be joined into one object once again.

### Joining the Cloned Halves of Raul's Head and Orienting Normals

Before joining the halves of Raul's head, save the file that has the two halves and make a copy of it. This is done to preserve the original work on Raul's head and face. Open the new file and select both halves of the head. In the Vertex Modeling subpalette choose the Average Weld tool and in the Tool Properties increase the Distance by clicking once or twice on the up arrow. After one click on the up arrow you should see that all of the vertices along the midline are welded. If some of the vertices are not welded, increase the weld distance once more. Now Raul's head is one object (see Figure 11.29).

Once the halves are joined, it is a good idea to make sure that the face normals point in the right direction. A face normal indicates whether a filled polygon points toward the inside or outside. Sometimes with operations such as duplicate, flip, and symmetry, face normals may become inverted. This may cause problems with modeling tools such as adding thickness and texturing tools. To prevent problems, select Raul's head (after it has been joined) and from the Utilities subpalette choose the Orient Normals tool. In the Tool properties click once on the A to select all faces. Next, click on the Unify Normals tool until you see a yellow arrow pointing outward, indicating that all polygons or faces are pointing outward.

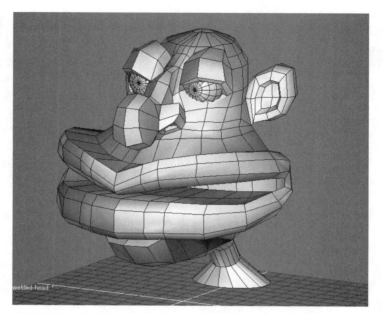

**FIGURE 11.29** Before you add details like hair and teeth, the halves of the head are joined.

Finally, we modeled much of Raul with symmetrical modeling, meaning that both ears, eyelids, nostrils, lips, and so on, are identical. Humans are symmetrical, but we are not perfectly symmetrical. As you continue to model and refine Raul's head, try to introduce subtle asymmetry to give him a more natural and less of a computer-generated look.

Now that we are ready, let's tackle the hair at the back of Raul's head and his sideburns first. This patch of hair will eventually be a separate object, but it is based on polygons that are already present on the side and back Raul's head. First make a copy of the head. Select the head and from the Edit menu choose Copy and then Paste or simply press Ctrl/Command-D for duplicate. Notice the new object in the Scene Tree and name it "Hair." (Note: Hexagon has an object naming bug that may cause the object name to revert to its previous name. Be aware of this.) Hide the original head by clicking the eye icon associated with it in the Scene Tree. Select the polygons that will become the hair and shape them as you like (see Figure 11.30). Since all we need are the polygons that make up the hair, select those polygons and choose the Extract tool from the Vertex Modeling toolbar. Hexagon will immediately separate the selected polygons from the rest of the head. Delete the rest of the head so that only the hair remains. Make the original head visible once more so you can see the hair polygons and the head together.

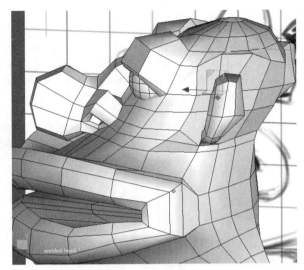

**FIGURE 11.30**   The hair is modeled from polygons on the back and side on a copy of the head.

With the hair selected, choose the Thickness tool from the Surface Modeling toolbar and make certain that the Outside option is selected in the Tool Properties palette. Thickness may be increased by pressing the plus key on the numeric keypad or by typing in numerical values in the Value field in the Tool Properties palette. Once you are satisfied with the thickness of the hair, press the Enter key. Smooth the head and the hair models to see how they look together, as in Figure 11.31. Now that the hair has volume, use the Tweak tool to shape and model the hair as you like.

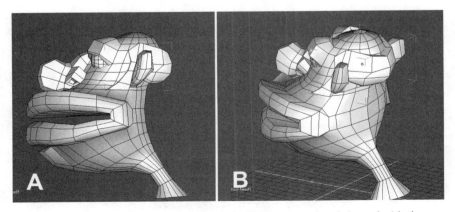

**FIGURE 11.31**   The hair is given volume with the Thickness tool and shaped with the Tweak tool (reference images turned off for clarity).

To cap the top of the head, zoom in and select the Close tool from the Vertex Modeling toolbar. All openings in the model are indicated by a white edge. Click the top opening with the Close tool and press the Enter key to close the hole. The tuft of hair on top of Raul's head is created by extruding the polygon at the very top of the head away from the head and manipulating the extrusions to form the curl (Figure 11.32).

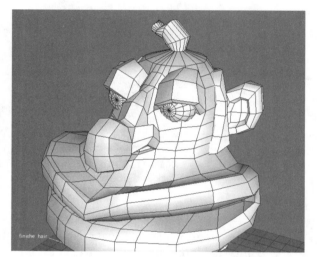

**FIGURE 11.32**    The tuft of hair on top of the head is created with extrusions (reference images turned off for clarity).

The mustache is modeled by creating new edges on the upper lip as shown in Figure 11.33 (three steps). The new polygons are extruded up and shaped. The handle bars at the end of the mustache are simple extrusions of the end polygons (see Figure 11.34) (two steps). The eyebrows are created in a similar fashion as the mustache. The edge between the eyelid

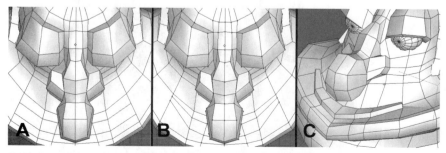

**FIGURE 11.33**    Create new edges with the Connect tool to delineate the mustache and then extrude the new polygons up.,

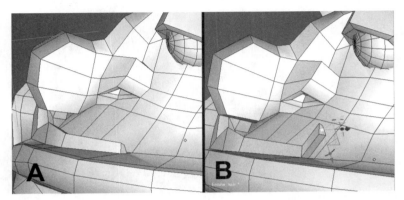

**FIGURE 11.34**   The curl at the end of the mustache is done by extruding the end polygons and moving them up a bit.

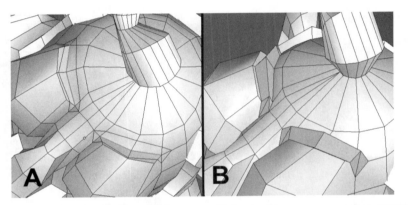

**FIGURE 11.35**   Use the Extract Edge around Edge tool to create new edges around the selection and then move the middle edge up to form the eyebrows.

and head is selected and new edges are created around the original edge with the Extract Edge around Edge tool. The eyebrows are then modeled from the edges in the middle, as shown in Figure 11.35. The beard, or goatee, is modeled from two simple extrusions (see Figure 11.36).

The teeth are very simple to create. Each tooth is a cube created with the Create a Cube tool in the Vertex Modeling toolbar. Create the upper right teeth first by moving, rotating, and scaling each tooth so that they follow the general shape of the mouth, as shown in Figure 11.37a. Delete the top polygon of each cube so that when the teeth are smoothed they don't become small spheres but instead retain a general cube shape. Next, mirror the initial row of teeth to create a complete set of upper teeth with the Symmetry tool, as in Figure 11.37b. Group the new row of teeth by selecting all teeth and choosing Group Selection from the Selection menu. Grouping the teeth makes it easy to move them as a single unit instead of

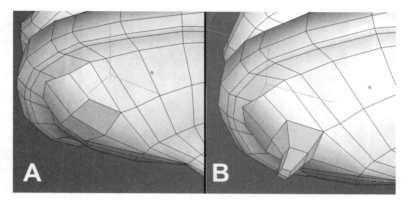

**FIGURE 11.36**    The mustache, eyebrows, and goatee are all modeled with new edges and extrusions and bit of tweaking.

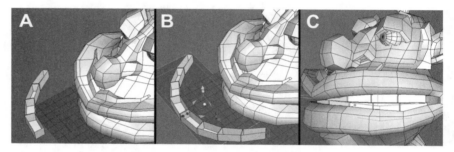

**FIGURE 11.37**    The teeth are modeled from cubes.

having to move each tooth separately. Move the row of teeth into the mouth and continue to position and scale as necessary. The lower teeth are created by creating a copy of the upper teeth and rotating and moving them into place (see Figure 11.37c). Feel free to change the teeth as you like. You can add teeth, make his teeth crooked, or take out a few teeth.

The tongue is modeled by inserting a new sphere into the scene and flattening it along the z-axis and tweaking it into shape, as in Figure 11.38. When done, move it into the mouth.

If you have gotten this far, then you have acquired the skills to model just about anything you can imagine with Hexagon. Pat yourself on the back for a job well done. In this tutorial we have used many of Hexagon's tools but we have concentrated on polygonal and edge modeling with extrusions and edge extractions. We learned to use symmetrical modeling and orient normals and we have practiced extensively with the Tweak tool to get things just right (see Figure 11.39). In the next Hexagon tutorial we will practice what we have learned and add new tools to our arsenal, such as tessellation, ruled surfaces, and the very nifty Bend tool.

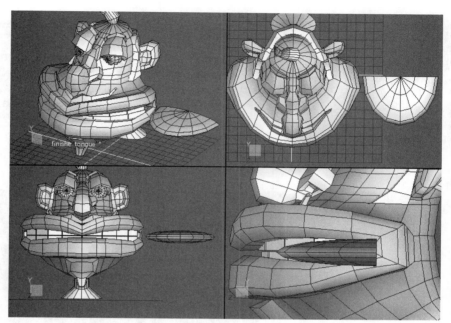

**FIGURE 11.38**    The tongue is a flattened sphere.

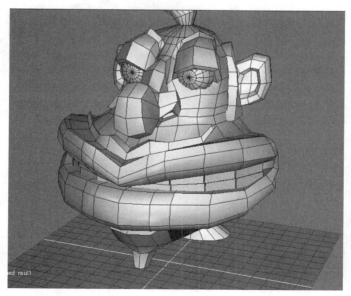

**FIGURE 11.39**    Raul finished.

| TUTORIAL 11.2 | **MODELING A CONCEPT CAR (BY PATRICK TUTEN)** |

In this tutorial we will use Hexagon to model a futuristic concept car. Concept cars are generally used by car designers to experiment with possible production designs. However, some concept cars are designed simply for the love of designing a cool car that will probably never enter the production line. Designing a concept car can be fun, as we are free to use our imaginations and to design whatever we like. The car we will model in this tutorial is a sleek, sporty roadster (see Figure 11.40).

**FIGURE 11.40**    In this tutorial we will model a sleek concept car.

If you have never modeled a concept car (or any vehicle) before, it is good to study reference material such as drawings and photographs to see how concept cars are designed and assembled. Many examples of concept cars can be found on the Web, in books, or in magazines. It is much easier to model your vehicle if you have a design in mind before you sit down at the computer. Sketching out the rough design beforehand will make the modeling process much easier. In the case of a concept car, it is not as important to have all the views drawn. A side view is enough to start modeling as long as you have some idea of what the other views will look like. Sketching a rough perspective view is also helpful, as in Figure 11.41.

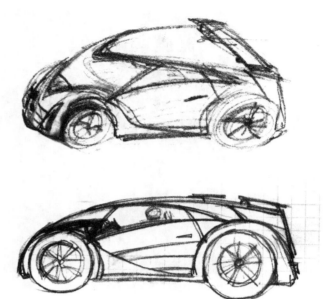

**FIGURE 11.41**    Concept sketches.

## Getting Started

As with the character modeling tutorial earlier in this chapter, the sketch of the car needs to be placed in Hexagon so that we can use it as a guide during the modeling process. We want the sketch to appear on the right, or *xy*, working plane, so in the Properties tab of the Scene palette, click on the small check box for the right grid (that's the third option) and browse to the sketch of the car. As with the first tutorial in this chapter, it is best to copy the sketch to your hard drive and then browse to the sketch (see Figure 11.42). However, we will use a line drawing version of the sketch to use as a reference image, or modeling guide.

In the Control palette at the bottom of the Hexagon user interface there are three icons located in the far right corner. The first icon toggles selection transparency, the second icon toggles backfaces, and the third icon toggles between perspective and orthographic views. The perspective view displays objects in the scene with perspective, and the orthographic view does not show perspective. Click once on the third button to toggle on the orthographic view. The orthographic view facilitates the modeling process when we view front, sides, top, or bottom by eliminating clutter or distortion caused by perspective. Press 2 on the number pad to switch to the Front view and you should see an undistorted view of your reference sketch, as shown in Figure 11.43. At the top of the interface there are two

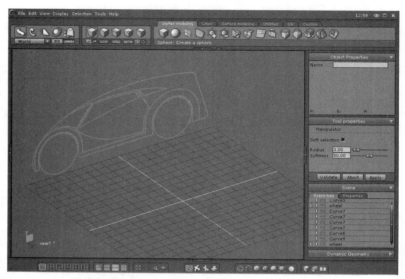

**FIGURE 11.42**    The reference image in Hexagon.

**FIGURE 11.43**    The Front view with perspective turned off.

tiers of tool palettes to pull down. They can be left open for easy access to all the tools.

In the previous tutorial in this chapter we modeled Raul using a process known as box modeling, in which extrusions are used as the primary modeling tool. In this tutorial we will take a different approach. Instead of box modeling, we will use polyline curves to define the general shape of the car and then create surfaces with Ruled Surfaces tool. We will use the Tessellate tool extensively to refine and add details.

ON THE CD

In the book's companion CD-ROM we have provided incremental steps of the modeling process from beginning to end. If at any point you become confused, simply open one of the files and take a look at the model. There is also a finished model, called finished-car.hxn, that you can study to become familiar with the topology.

## Roughing In the Car Body Shape

We will start by choosing the Polyline tool under the Lines toolbar. Click the first point at the bottom of the front of the body and then continue to draw the polyline by adding points and working your way all the way to the back of the car. This first polyline will become the midline of the car. Use only enough points to create the rough shape (about 14). More points are not necessary, as shown in Figure 11.44. Press the Validate button in the Tool Properties window to terminate the polyline tool. Press Alt-LMB or use the arrows to rotate the scene so that you can see where the polyline is in relation to the $z$-axis. The small XYZ icon, located on the bottom left, allows you to see which way the modeling grids are oriented. At the top left are the Manipulation tools and the Selection tools. The Universal Manipulator (U) allows you to move, scale, and rotate all in one tool. Very handy! The Selection tools, Select Faces, Select Edges, and Select Points allow you to select whole objects, groups of, or individual polygons, edges, or vertices. The Auto Select tool anticipates which type of selection you are trying to make and can select polygons, edges, or vertices.

**FIGURE 11.44**    The first polyline.

If you want to move the polyline, click on the Select Object tool (F1) and move the polyline by clicking and dragging on the appropriate arrowhead (probably the Z or blue arrowhead) of the Universal Manipulator tool. Next copy and paste the polyline and move it over a little along the *z*-axis and then paste one more polyline and slide it over a little further. When you are done, there should be three identical polylines aligned along the *z* axis as shown in Figure 11.45.

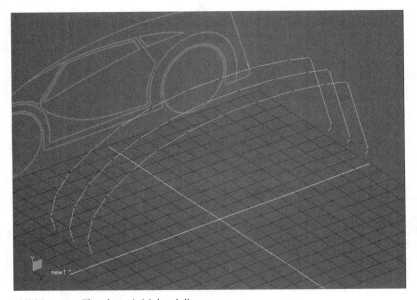

**FIGURE 11.45** The three initial polylines.

### Tire Placeholders

To help visualize the car body, we will insert two cylinders as proxies for the wheels and tires. Click on the Cylinder tool located in the Vertex Modeling subpalette. Then click and drag to create a short, squat cylinder. Close or cap each end of the cylinder by clicking once on the open ends and validate the cylinder tool. Now rotate the cylinder 90 degrees by typing "90" in the pink Rotate field in the Object Properties window. Resize and place the tire proxy in position by aligning it with the image on the grid and approximating its position on the *z*-axis. Make a copy of the first tire and position it on the back, as in Figure 11.46.

### Generating the Surface Mesh

Don't worry about getting things perfect at this point. We will be doing a lot of modeling to refine the shape in later steps. Copy and paste several

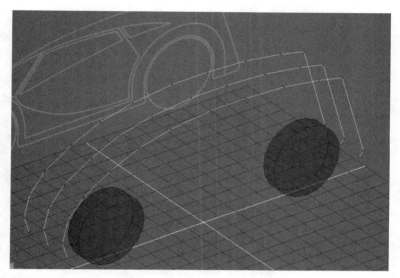

**FIGURE 11.46**    The proxy wheels.

more polylines and distribute them along the z-axis. The purpose of re-peatedly copying and pasting the first polyline is that when we create a surface with the Ruled Surface tool, the resulting shape will have a uni-form surface with an equal number of vertices in each direction. You should have about seven polylines spaced more or less evenly between the midline and the outer edge of the wheel proxy (see Figure 11.47).

After copying the first polyline a few times and inserting the proxy tires, there will be several objects in the Scene Tree tab of the Scene win-dow. Notice that each object in the Scene Tree has two icons next to it: an F and an eye icon. Clicking the eye icon toggles the hide function on and off. Clicking the F or U toggles the freeze/unfreeze function. The freeze function locks and object so that it cannot be accidentally altered, and the unfreeze function unlocks the object so that it can be worked on once more. Freeze both proxy tires since we will not be modeling them any-more at this point.

In the next steps we will edit the polylines so that they roughly rep-resent the cross sections of the car. Press 2 on the numeric keypad to re-turn to the orthographic view of the side of the vehicle. All the polylines should appear stacked one in front of the other. Select the first polyline (the one nearest to the car edge), choose the Select Points (F4) tool from the Selection toolbar, and move the vertices so that it conforms to the bottom of the wheel fairings. It will be necessary to rotate the scene peri-odically to see the location of each point on the polyline in relation to the

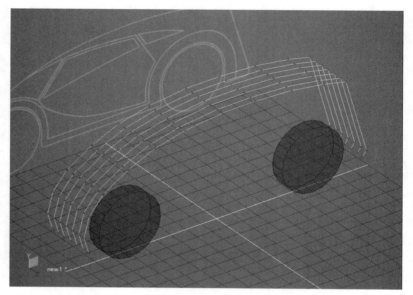

**FIGURE 11.47**    The polylines that will make up the car body.

others. Move on to the next polyline and model it so that it conforms to the top of the wheel fairings. Continue this process with each polyline until the polylines look like Figure 11.48.

**FIGURE 11.48**    Shape the polylines to conform to the contours of the car.

Now that we have the basic shape of the car outlined with the polylines, we will generate the surface or mesh of the car with the Ruled Surfaces tool. Select the Ruled Surfaces tool from the Surface Modeling toolbar
and click on each polyline in order from midline to outer edge and then
press Enter or Validate. You should be able to see a rough approximation of
the car body as in Figure 11.49. Now, from the Surface Modeling toolbar
click on the Smooth tool (the first icon) to smooth the blocky shape into a
nice curved form.

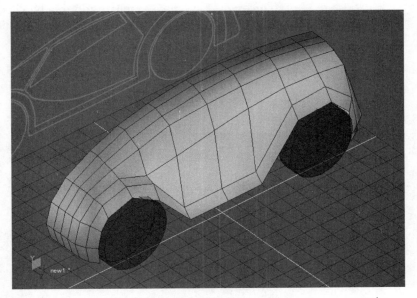

**FIGURE 11.49**   Apply the Ruled Surfaces tool to the polylines to generate the
mesh surface.

Now that we have a preview of things to come, remove the smoothing
by clicking the small curved arrow next to the object named Form2 (yours
may be named Form1 or some other number) in the Dynamic Geometry
window. It is better to remove the smoothing in this manner, rather than
using Undo or pressing Escape. Often during the modeling process, you
will want to apply smoothing to see how the model is shaping up and then
remove it to continue working. It is important that you keep the seam
plane as flat as possible where the two halves will be eventually joined.
Try not to move any of the vertices on first polyline in the $z$ direction. It
may be useful to click on one of the points on the seam and jot down the
$z$ coordinate value for reference, just in case a point is mistakenly moved.

### Refining the Car Body

At this point some areas of the car body are not well defined, especially the wheel fairings, as they look very blocky instead of round. To refine the car body, we need to add more vertices and edges to the mesh. To add new edges spanning across the car body from the outer edge to the midline and back to front, choose the Tessellate tool from the Vertex Modeling toolbar and set its mode to Tessellate by Slice in the Tool Properties window. The Tessellate by Slice setting quickly creates a continuous loop of edges starting from where you clicked, then "slicing" through the mesh.

Once you have the Tessellate tool ready, click on either the midline or on the outer edge of the wheel wells or running boards. Note that the Tessellate tool immediately creates new edges, as in Figure 11.50. After adding a few new edges move the edges and vertices with the Tweak tool to round out the wheel wells, as in Figure 11.51. To see the reference image behind the model, click on the Transparent Display toggle in the Control panel.

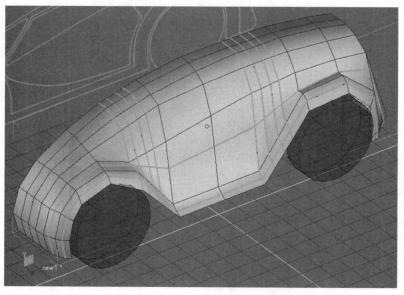

**FIGURE 11.50**   New edges running across from the midline to the running board and from front to back are added with the Tessellate tool, creating geometry to refine car body.

So far, we have been smoothing to preview the car shape and then unsmoothing to model on the less complex unsmoothed shape. However, there is another way to have the best of both worlds: a smooth shape and the simplicity of an unsmoothed shape to work on. To turn on

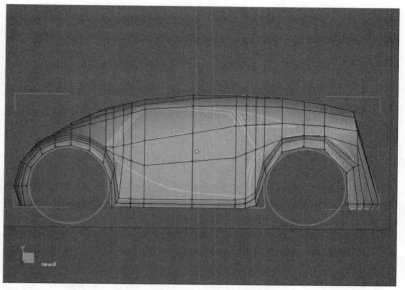

**FIGURE 11.51**    Begin modeling by moving edges and vertices with the Tweak tool to match the reference image.

Hexagon's Smoothing Control Shape function, click on the small spherical button in the bottom-right corner of the Dynamic Geometry window. This button toggles the smoothing control shape on and off. To smooth the car shape, click once on the Smooth tool in the Surface Modeling toolbar (see Figure 11.52). Once it is smoothed, it is very important that you do not click the small lightning bolt icon next to car body object in the Dynamic Geometry window because that triggers the Collapse Dynamic Geometry function, which permanently smoothes the model, meaning you would not be able to unsmooth the model once again to work on the simpler shape. Working with the Smoothing Control Shape over a smoothed object takes practice, so if you feel more comfortable unsmoothing the car shape and working at that level, that is okay too. Just remember to smooth every now and then to see how things are shaping up. At this point in the modeling process you simply need to continue modeling the shape of the car until it conforms to reference image—or your imagination.

While modeling the car, be sure to dolly around the entire car to see it from different angles. Work on the model from the front, back, and sides to make sure that no part is left untouched. It is not uncommon, even for experienced modelers, to inadvertently leave part of the model undone because of focusing too much on another part. There are no shortcuts to good modeling techniques. Remember to be patient and thorough as you shape the car body.

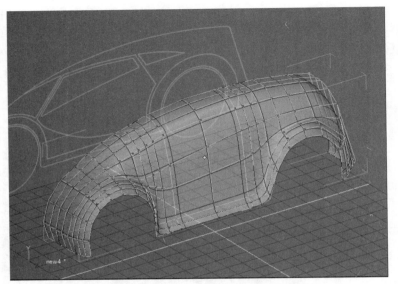

**FIGURE 11.52**   Toggle on the control shape feature to model over the smoothed shape.

Up to this point the car mesh has a very flowing aerodynamic shape, but there will be areas, such as the fenders and running boards, that need to be detailed with sharp bends or corners. Before modeling these details it is helpful to understand how the smoothing works in Hexagon. Hexagon 1.01 does not have a Crease Edges tool as does Carrara's Vertex Modeler. To create a sharp defined edge in Hexagon, you must place parallel edges in close proximity to each other. Select the edge that is between the outer running board and the body. With the Extract Edge Along Edge tool create two new edges, one on either side of the first edge (see Figure 11.53). Smooth the car body to see how the new edges create a nice crease between the running board and car body.

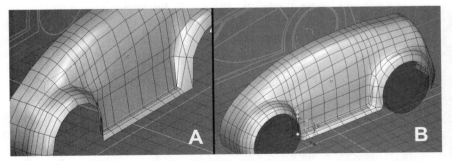

**FIGURE 11.53**   Add new edges along the bend between the running board and body to create a crease.

## Adding Thickness to the Car Body

You have probably noticed that we are modeling the outer metal or plastic panels of the car body, but so far our panels have no thickness. Even the thin metal or plastic panels of a car have some thickness. The thickness is especially noticeable around the doors, windows, wheel wells, and bottom edges of the car body. However, we have not modeled the doors or windows yet, so we will add thickness to the bottom edges and the inside of the wheel wells at this point. Adding thickness to the car body will make a more convincing model. Select the edges shown in Figure 11.54a. With the Fast Extrude tool create two small extrusions as in Figure 11.54b. That is it for the wheel wells and the bottom of the running boards. However, we still have to create the same thickness for the front and back fenders.

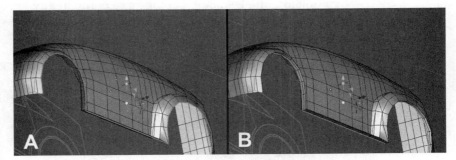

**FIGURE 11.54**    Adding thickness to wheel wells and running boards.

Select the bottom edges of the front fender and extrude inward, as in Figure 11.55a. Now arrange the vertices as in Figure 11.55b. You may have to weld together some of the vertices around the corner, depending on how you arrange the extrusion. Do the same for the rear fender. Try smoothing the car to see the results of the extrusions. You should see what appears to be thickness along the edges.

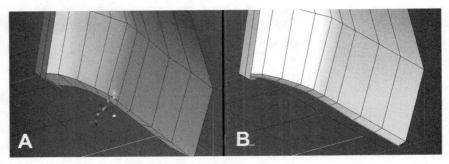

**FIGURE 11.55**    Adding thickness to front and rear fenders.

## Modeling the Doors and Windows

At this point the shape of the car body is complete. In the following steps we will make permanent changes to the car, including increasing the number of polygons and cutting out openings for the doors and windows. So this is a good time to make a final inspection of the car body. Dolly around to view the car from all angles and make sure there are no out of place vertices or odd creases or any artifacts. Since we will be making permanent changes to the model, it is a good idea to make a copy of the current file and then continue work on the copy. This will save the original car in case it is needed for future changes.

Select the car body and from the Vertex Modeling toolbar select the Smooth tool to smooth the car. You can also use the Smooth tool in the Surface modeling toolbar, but make sure that the Range value is set to 1. Collapse the Dynamic Geometry to permanently keep the smoothed car. You should see an increase in the number of polygons as in Figure 11.56.

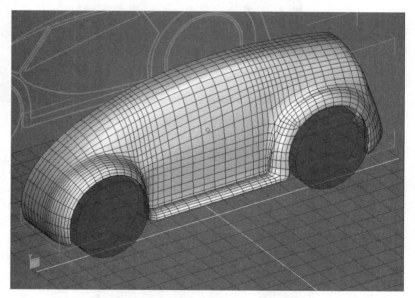

**FIGURE 11.56**   Smoothing the car body prior to cutting out the doors and windows.

To delineate the doors and windows, we will use our trusty Tessellate tool set to Tessellate by Segment. In essence we will use the Tessellate tool to "draw" the lines that will outline the doors and windows. From the side view, we can see where the edges of the doors and windows are located. However, remember that the reference image is just a guide. Since the reference image is 2D and the model is 3D, the door and window lines may not correlate exactly.

Before we dive into cutting out the windows and doors let's review how the Tessellate tool works. When the Tessellate tool is set to Tessellate by Segment, it allows you to create a slice through the mesh by defining the start and the end of the slice with clicks of the mouse. However, the Tessellate tool has a unique feature that makes it even more useful—you can precisely position the slice by dollying around with the Tessellate tool active until you find the perfect spot on the mesh. Here is how it works: select the Tessellate tool and click to define the starting point of the slice and then press Alt-LMB to define the end of the slice. As long as you hold the Alt key and left mouse button you can dolly around the mesh, and the slice (highlighted in yellow) will creep along the surface of the mesh, always facing the camera (see Figure 11.57). When you are happy with the position of the slice, release the Alt key and click once to create the slice. Remember to validate the Tessellate tool by pressing Enter or the Validate button. This may take a bit of practice at first, but it sure makes slicing precisely much easier.

**FIGURE 11.57**    Positioning the slice created by the Tessellate tool by holding the Alt key.

To create the slice for the top of the windshield and door, select the Tessellate tool. Set it to Tessellate by Segment and click once on the starting point of the slice and once on the ending point. Use the technique described above to position the slice (see Figure 11.58). It's okay if your slice is in a slightly different place.

**FIGURE 11.58**   The first set of edges created to delineate the windows and doors (shown selected).

Now all that is left is to create the rest of the slices for the door and door window as in Figure 11.59. The slices that define the outline of the door, door window, and small window are best created from the Front (2) view. Take your time when creating the slices for the doors and windows. There is no hurry. You can also create slices for the back window.

As you create the slices for the doors and windows, you are adding new polygons, which in turn adds new edges and vertices. Adding new polygons may introduce problems, such as existing polygons that are emptied as the slice passes by. It is easy to correct this problem. Simply select the Close tool (Vertex Modeling toolbar) and click on the open polygon to refill it. Another problem the slices may create is vertices that are very close together. If you see two or more vertices that are very close, simply use the Weld Points tool to combine the vertices into one vertex. Finally, be aware of polygons that have more than four vertices, known as N-gons, as these polygons may not slice or subdivide well. To prevent N-gons, use the Connect tool (Vertex Modeling toolbar) to create triangles or quadrangles from them. After all of the doors and windows have been outlined with slices and any problems corrected, it is time to separate the windows and doors from the car body.

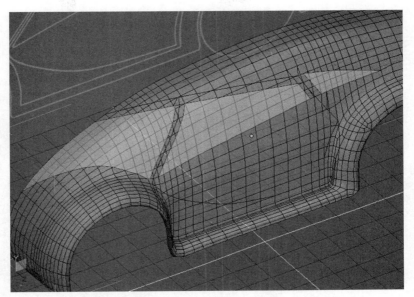

**FIGURE 11.59**    Edges created to delineate the doors and windows (polygons selected for clarity).

## Extracting the Doors and Window

To separate the doors and windows from the car body, we will use Hexagon's handy Extract tool, which neatly extracts selected polygons from a mesh in one step. Select all of the polygons that make up the door windows. Zoom in to make sure you have selected even the small polygons. Then, from the Vertex Modeling toolbar, press the Extract tool. Hexagon immediately separates the selected polygons from the mesh (see Figure 11.60). Repeat this process for the small window, the rear window, the doors, and the windshield. Take your time selecting all of the polygons that make up each object before extracting.

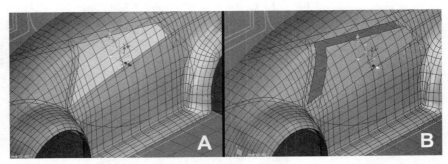

**FIGURE 11.60**    Separating the widows and doors with the Extract tool (polygons moved for clarity).

Too see the results of the extract action take a look at the Scene Tree. Notice that there are new forms in the list. Select all of the new forms and hide them. You should be able to see the car body without the windows and door, as in Figure 11.61. Congratulations on completing the tutorial so far. You have almost completed the car.

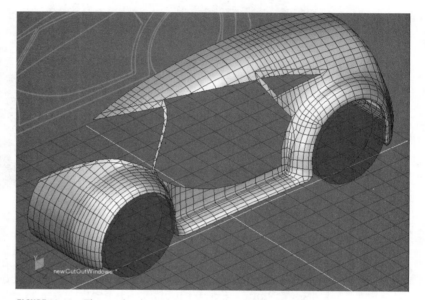

**FIGURE 11.61**    The car body without the doors and windows.

## Details 1: Lights and Air Intake

The headlights have two parts: the glass cover and the inside of the headlights. We will model the headlight glass first. Select edges as shown in Figure 11.62a. Next use the Edge tools (found in the Vertex Modeling toolbar) to create a new edge as in Figure 11.63b. Then select the inner

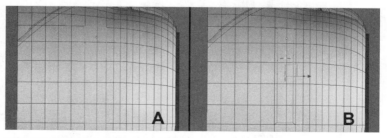

**FIGURE 11.62**    The headlight starts with new edges.

polygons as in Figure 11.63a and extract them. If you temporarily hide the new form, the result should look like Figure 11.63b. Make sure to name the new form "headlight glass" in the Scene Tree.

To create the inside of the headlight, make the headlight glass object visible (if you hid it in the previous step), select it, and copy and paste a new copy into the scene. Name the copy "headlight-inside." Hide the headlight glass object once more so that we can work on the inside of the headlight. Select the headlight-inside object and extract twice inward with the Extrude Surface tool set to Axial extrusion (see Figure 11.64).

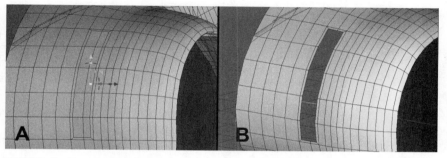

**FIGURE 11.63**    Extract the polygons created by the new edges to model the headlight glass.

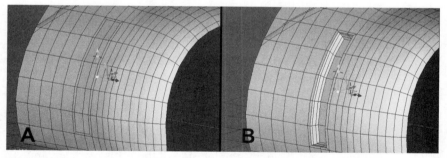

**FIGURE 11.64**    The inside of the headlight is modeled by extruding a copy of the headlight glass.

The air intake on the front of the car is modeled with extrusions much the same way as the headlights. Figure 11.65a shows the new edges extracted to begin the air intake. Select the polygons created by the new edges and extrude inward with a couple of shallow or small extrusions and then create a deeper extrusion as in Figure 11.65b,c. Note that the air intake extrusions will create polygons along the midline of the model. Those polygons have to be deleted.

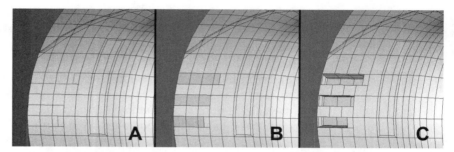

**FIGURE 11.65**    The air intake is created with new edges and extrusions.

A single taillight is modeled from a cylinder and a sphere. Insert a cylinder and cap the ends. Model the outside of the cylinder with extrusions (see Figure 11.66a). The taillight bulb is just a sphere, as shown in Figure 11.66b. Once the single taillight is complete, it is copied to create all of the taillights (see Figure 11.66c.)

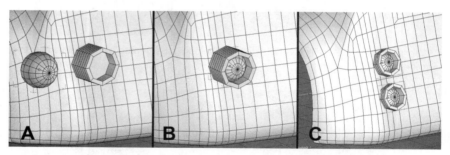

**FIGURE 11.66**    Modeling the taillight.

### Mirroring the Left Side to Create the Whole Car

At this point the left side of the car is modeled and is made up of at least six objects: the car body, windshield, small rear window, door, door window, and rear window (not counting the proxy tires). All of these objects will have to be duplicated and mirrored to create the right side. To accomplish this task, select all the objects that make up the car and from the Vertex Modeling toolbar select the Symmetry tool. Dolly around so that you can see the inside of the car and when the blue plane appears along the midline click once (see Figure 11.67a). The right side should appear as in Figure 11.67b. At this point you can select both halves and scale them.

Now that we have two sets of all of the parts we still do not have one car. To create one car we have to join the two car body halves together as well as the windshield and back window. If the right half is in a group,

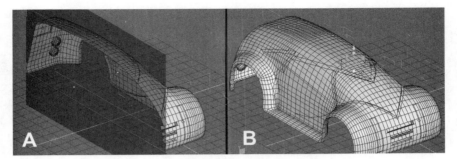

**FIGURE 11.67**    Use the Symmetry tool to create the right side of the car.

ungroup it by going to the Selection menu and choosing Ungroup Selection. Luckily, Hexagon's Average Weld tool will do the job nicely. In the scene select both halves of the car body and click once on the Average Weld tool, click on the Average Weld tool once more, and enter a value between 0.02 and 0.04 units and Validate (see Figure 11.68). You can test the weld by selecting a vertex or two along the seam and moving them. If the weld was successful, there should be no gaps along the seam when you move the vertex. Press Ctrl/Command-Z to put the vertices back after moving them. Now there is one car body. Repeat the weld process for windshield and back window.

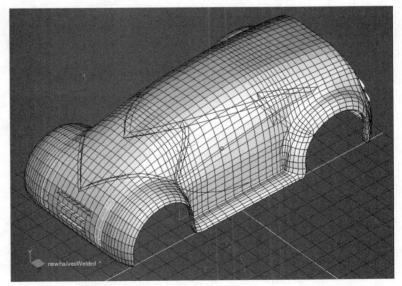

**FIGURE 11.68**    The Average Weld tool is used to join the halves of the car body, windshield, and back window.

### Details 2: Tires and Wheels

Tire treads make modeling tires one of the most challenging aspects of modeling a car, but with Hexagon's tools we can take on that challenge and easily model even the most complex tires with treads. However, we have modeled a concept car, so the tires will also be concept tires and we will model a unique tread pattern. After all, what's the point of modeling a cool concept car and then modeling the same tires you would find on an old Chevy truck?

Before modeling the tire, it is probably a good idea to hide the car so we have plenty of room to work in or you can model the tire in a separate Hexagon file and then bring it into the car file. From the Vertex Modeling toolbar select the Grid tool and insert a grid with 18 polygons, as in Figure 11.69a. It is important that you use the same number of polygons and position the edges as in Figure 11.69 so that your results are the same as the tutorial. Next, position the inner edges to form a chevron, as shown in Figure 11.69b.

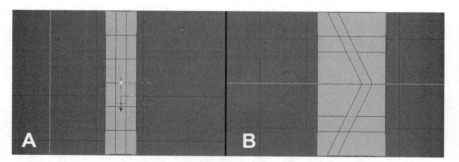

**FIGURE 11.69**   Insert a grid with the Grid tool with 18 polygons. Position the edges to create a chevron.

Select the polygons shown in Figure 11.70a and extrude as in Figure 11.70b. Make sure to extrude at least three times so the added edges will form a more stable shape once the tire is smoothed.

In the next few steps you will shape the once flat grid and extruded chevron into what will become the tire's cross section. Use the Move and Rotate tools to position the polygons and edges, as in Figure 11.71. The polygons that make up the outer parts of the chevrons will need to be rotated about 45 degrees and the inner polygons about 33 degrees as you reposition them.

Once you have the tire cross section modeled, make a copy by either copying and pasting or by selecting the tire and pressing Ctrl/Command-D. Move the copy so that it butts up against the original, as in Figure 11.72a. Try to position the edges of the two objects so that they are very close together or share the same space. With both objects selected, click once on

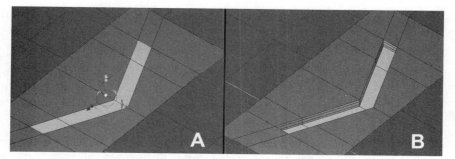

**FIGURE 11.70**    Extrude the chevron shape.

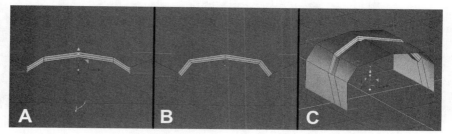

**FIGURE 11.71**    The flat polygons are shaped into an inverted U cross section.

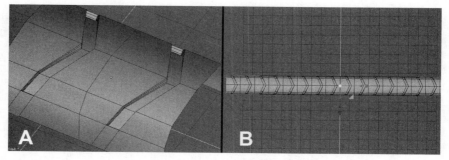

**FIGURE 11.72**    Duplicate or copy and paste the first object and position the copy. The initial tire is modeled flat.

the Average Weld tool, from the Vertex Modeling toolbar, and then click on it once more to bring up the Tolerance value in the Tool Properties. If the Tolerance value is at 0, press the up arrow once or twice to increase it to about 4. Notice that vertices along the seam are welded, forming one object. If you keep increasing the Tolerance value, you will begin deforming the object, so don't increase the tolerance too much. Repeat the copy and weld process until the object looks like Figure 11.72b. This should proceed quickly, as each time you copy and weld you are copying and welding several instances of the original cross section at once.

You have probably figured out by now that what you have modeled is the tire, but flattened or unraveled. The flattened tire is reminiscent of tank tracks, but in the next few steps we will take the flat tire and turn it into a round tire. From the Line toolbar select the Circle from Center tool and insert a circle with about 40 points (see Figure 11.73a). Now, deselect the circle and select the flat tire. In the Utilities toolbar locate the Bend tool and click once on the circle. Viola! The once flat tire is instantly turned into a round tire, as in Figure 11.73b.

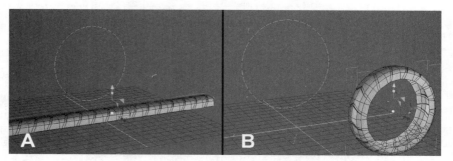

**FIGURE 11.73**    Insert a circle with about 40 points. Use the Bend tool to bend the flat tire into a circle.

If you inspect the tire closely, you will find that the ends of the once flat tire are very close together but not welded. With the Weld Points tool weld the ends of the tire to form a continuous tire. With the last weld done, the tire is done. Next we will model the wheel (see Figure 11.74).

Wheels come in all shapes, sizes, and designs, and with Hexagon you model all of them. For our concept tire we want a slick wheel design. The general wheel shape will be modeled by creating a cross section and profile with the Line tools. Then we will use the Surfacing tools to create the geometry of wheel. First, insert a new circle into the scene. This will be the cross section of the wheel. To create the profile, select the Curve tool and create a short curved line and position it as in Figure 11.75a. Select the short curve and from the Surface Modeling toolbar choose the Sweep Line tool and click once on the circle. The result should look like Figure 11.75b. Add thickness to the wheel thickness by selecting the outermost edge and extruding as in Figure 11.75c.

The wheel pattern in the tutorial was created by inserting a sphere and scaling, duplicating, and positioning the spheres as in Figure 11.76a and then using a boolean subtraction function to carve the pattern into the wheel mesh. The wheel hub is a simple cylinder that has been extruded inward. When finished, the wheel and tire should look like Figure 11.76c.

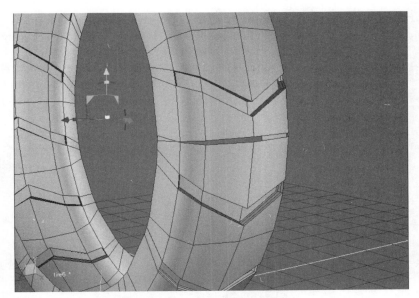

**FIGURE 11.74**    Weld the ends of the tire together to create a continuous object.

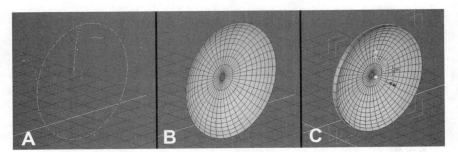

**FIGURE 11.75**    Insert a circle for the cross section and curve for the profile. Use the Sweep Line tool to create the surface of the wheel. Select the outermost edges and move them back to create thickness.

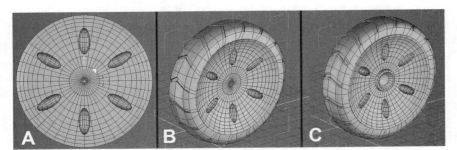

**FIGURE 11.76**    (a and b) The wheel pattern is created by subtracting five modified spheres from the wheel mesh. (c) The completed tire and wheel.

Duplicate the tire and wheel to create four wheels and position them in the wheel wells as in Figure 11.77. With the tire and wheel complete, we are finished with this tutorial. This tutorial was designed to be challenging and to help you practice what you learned in the first tutorial in this chapter, add new modeling skills and, of course, increase your experience with Hexagon.

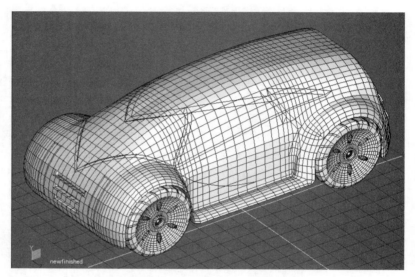

**FIGURE 11.77**   The completed concept car model.

## SUMMARY

You may be asking why there are two Hexagon modeling tutorials in a Carrara book. First, Hexagon features modeling tools that Carrara does not yet have, so modeling with Hexagon can sometimes be more efficient. Second, since Hexagon was developed by Eovia, it is designed to work closely with Carrara—so much so, that Hexagon can output models in Carrara's native file format. You could think of Hexagon as just one more of Carrara's modeling tools. Third, we know that many Carrara users are already using Hexagon for modeling, and these tutorials will not only help you become proficient with Hexagon but will help you learn modeling techniques not found in Carrara. When you are finished modeling Raul and the cool concept car in Hexagon, simply go to the File menu, select Save As, and choose the Carrara file format for import into Carrara.

# PART
# IV

# TEXTURING
# WITH CARRARA

# 12

# TEXTURING WITH CARRARA

## In This Chapter

- Projection Mapping, Bump Maps, Color, and Layers
- Texturing with Shading Domains
- Texturing with the UV Editor

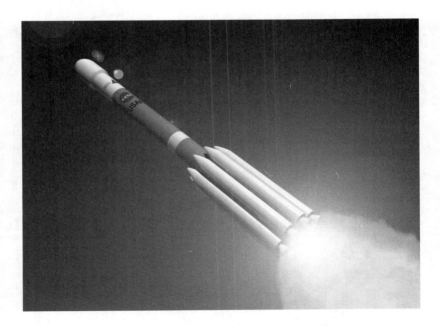

I n this chapter we will work with the model of the Delta rocket from Chapter 9 and the model of Raul from Chapter 11 to learn how to texture different models using the various texturing methods available in Carrara. In the first tutorial we will texture the Delta rocket with projected color maps, bump maps, layers, and color shaders. In the second tutorial we will introduce shading domains and use flat colors to give Raul's face color (Figure 12.1). In the last tutorial we will use UV mapping to apply more detailed textures to Raul's face.

**FIGURE 12.1**   Raul textured with textures applied with UV mapping.

ON THE CD

All of the textures used in these tutorials are provided for you in the Chapter 12 folder on the accompanying CD-ROM. Also provided are untextured models ready to be finished and the fully textured models ready for your inspection. If you get stuck or don't understand how something works, take a moment to study the finished models provided on the CD-ROM.

**TUTORIAL 12.1**   **PROJECTION MAPPING, BUMP MAPS, COLOR, AND LAYERS**

ON THE CD

In this tutorial we are going to texture the Delta rocket modeled in Chapter 9. If you haven't worked through Chapter 9 yet but want to complete this tutorial, you may use the untextured model of the rocket found in the Chapter 12 folder of the accompanying CD-ROM. All textures that will be applied to the model are also provided for you in the same folder (see Figure 12.2).

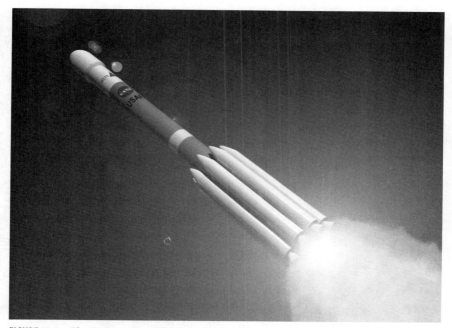

**FIGURE 12.2**    The Delta rocket fully textured.

In this tutorial you will learn to build shaders that use image-based maps, bump maps, color, and layers. Texturing concepts were covered in detail in Chapter 2, so you may want to review that material before beginning this tutorial.

## Building a Shader with Texture Maps

ON THE CD

Open the file rocket-notexture.car found in the Chapter 12 folder in the book's CD-ROM. Surface textures provide valuable information about an object's material makeup and properties. Since the rocket in the file you just opened has an unremarkable gray finish, it is difficult to discern anything about it other than its basic shape (see Figure 12.3). We will correct this by applying textures to all of the surfaces.

To begin texturing the main rocket, select it in the scene or from the Instances list in the Properties tray and then click on the Texture room button in the upper-right corner of the Carrara interface. Carrara will ask if you want to Edit the Master shader or Create a New Master shader. Select Create a New Master shader and click OK, as shown in Figure 12.4. This will create a new shader, leaving the original gray shader unchanged.

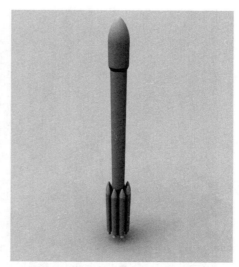

**FIGURE 12.3**   Without any textures it is hard to tell much about the rocket.

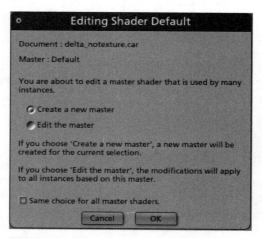

**FIGURE 12.4**   Select Create a New Master shader when creating a new shader.

The Texture room has very specific tools for building simple or complex shaders. The main component in the Texture room is the Shader tree. The left side of the Shader tree displays all of the channels and layers available. The right side of the Shader tree displays detailed information about a selected channel or layer. Another important component of the Texture room is the Preview window. The Preview window displays a real-time preview of the texture applied to the object being textured. The Preview window can also display the standard materials sphere instead of the object being textured. In the Texture room the Properties tray often displays information on the shading domains of an object (see Figure 12.5).

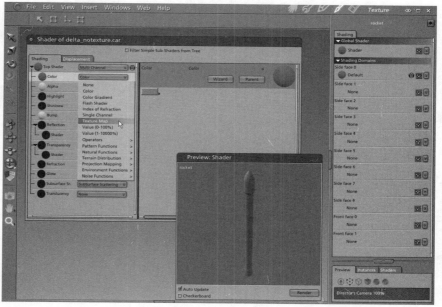

**FIGURE 12.5**   The Texture room has all of the tools needed to texture an object.

### Defining the Projection Mapping Type

The rocket will be textured using an image-based texture map, a grayscale bump map, and layers. The texture map will provide the surface colors, the bump map will simulate 3D surface details that were not modeled, and the layers will allow us to place markings on the rocket's surface. However, the first thing we will do is set the type of projection mapping that will be used to apply the textures. Defining the type of projection mapping helps eliminate distortions and problems when projecting textures on to the surface of a model. Since the rocket is cylindrical, we will use Cylindrical projection mapping. Select the Top Shader by clicking on it once, open the menu labeled Multi-Channel, select Projection Mapping, and from the submenu select Cylindrical Mapping, as in Figure 12.6. Next, in the Cylindrical Mapping details set the Direction to Y.

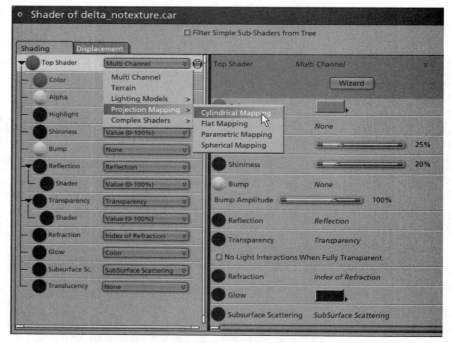

**FIGURE 12.6**   Setting the projection mapping type to cylindrical.

### Applying the Color Texture

Now we are ready to apply the textures. The Delta rocket has a white and green painted finish, so we will use an image-based texture to create the paint job. Select the Color channel, open the menu labeled Color, and select Texture map. When prompted, browse to the file rocket-color.jpg on the CD-ROM and click OK. When Carrara asks if you want to load the tif, click OK again. Notice that the Preview window displays the rocket with the texture applied. However, when a texture is initially applied, it may not be oriented correctly. In the case of the rocket it is flipped upside down. The Texture Map details, on the right side of the Shader tree, provide three buttons to orient a texture. The buttons are Flip Vertical, Flip Horizontal, and Rotate 90 degrees. To correctly orient the texture on the rocket click once on the Flip Vertical button (see Figure 12.7).

### Applying a Bump Map

A bump map is an 8-bit grayscale image map that Carrara uses to create the illusion of relief on an object's surface. Black creates a raised area, white creates a depressed area, and shades of gray create intermediate levels of

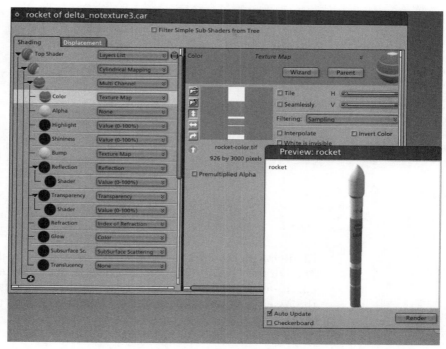

**FIGURE 12.7**    The color texture applied and flipped to orient it correctly.

relief. Bump maps are commonly used to add details to an object's surface that would be time consuming to model. For example, to model a golf ball you would have to a model a sphere with dozens of dimples. Instead, you can apply a bump map to create the illusion of dimples. The drawback to using a bump map is that the relief created by the bump is only an illusion. In other words, the surface, or topology, of the object is not altered. For example, a golf ball that has been modeled with actual dimples would have a silhouette that shows the dips of the dimples. However, a golf ball that has a bump map looks perfectly smooth when viewed in silhouette.

We will use a bump map to apply minor surface details to the rocket. For example, the payload (the tip of the rocket) has shallow, vertical ridges all the way around. We could have modeled the ridges, but it is more efficient and less time consuming to use a bump map in this case. The bump map also creates details along the rest of the rocket, as shown in Figure 12.8.

The bump map is applied to the rocket exactly the same way as the color texture was applied, except that instead of using the Color channel we will work in the Bump channel. Open the menu in the Bump channel and select Texture Map. Browse to the file rocket-bump.jpg found in the

**ON THE CD**

**FIGURE 12.8** The bump map we will use to create surface details.

CD-ROM. Remember to flip the map as you did with the color texture. Though the Preview window will display the bump map, it may be difficult to see, so to better see the result of the bump map jump back out to the Assemble room and use the Test Render (X) tool to do a quick render of the rocket (see Figure 12.9).

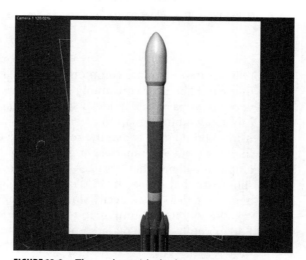

**FIGURE 12.9** The rocket with the bump map applied.

### Applying Details with Layers

Layers allow you to create special effects on the surfaces of objects. We will use layers to apply markings on the rocket's surface. We could have used a color texture that had the markings on it already, but that would require a precisely sized texture to prevent distortion. In addition, layers provide more flexibility, in that layers can be scaled, moved along the surface of the rocket, or overlapped, something you can't readily do with a single texture map.

Working with layers requires using the specialized set of tools found in the upper-right corner of the Texture room (see Figure 12.10). The Select Layer tool allows you to move and scale layers, the Rectangle Layer tool creates rectangular layers, the Polygon Layer tool creates layers with multiple sides, and the Oval Layer tool creates round layers. We will use the Rectangle Layer tool to create three layers and the Select Layer tool to position and scale the layers.

**FIGURE 12.10**    The layer tools.

The layer tools work in conjunction with the Preview window, so use the camera navigation tools to position the rocket in the Preview window as in Figure 12.11a. Select the Rectangle Layer tool and in the Preview window click and drag on the rocket surface to create a rectangle (see Figure 12.11b). Switch to the Select Layer tool if you want to move or scale the rectangle on the rocket's surface.

At the bottom of the Shader tree a new layer has been added, and the Top Shader has changed from Multi Channel to a Layer list. A layer may contain any of the standard shader channels. For our purposes we will load an image into the new layer. Click on the Shader channel of the new layer, open the menu labeled None, and select Complex Shaders. From the submenu select Single Channel. Though the single channel can be different types of channels, it defaults to a Color channel, which is what we need. Click on the menu labeled Color and select Texture Map. When prompted, browse to the NASA.jpg file. Notice in the Preview window that the NASA logo appears in the layer on the rocket's surface, as shown in Figure 12.12. If the image is not oriented correctly, use the Texture Rotate button in the Texture Details part of the Shader tree. Once the image is oriented correctly, you can use the Select Layer tool to position and scale the image.

The rocket has two other markings on its surface, so repeat the steps from above to apply the USAF and Delta II markings. When finished, the layers should look similar to Figure 12.13. The last thing you may want to do is adjust the Highlight and Shininess values to give the rocket a more metal-like finish. Values around 20% for both will create distinct highlights.

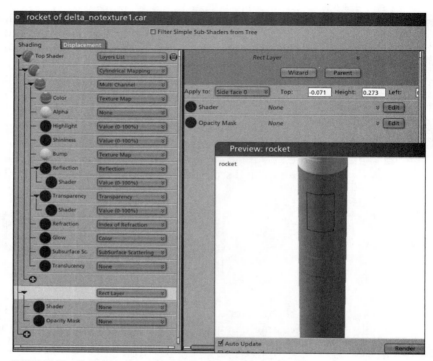

**FIGURE 12.11** Position the rocket in the Preview window so you can see where you will be working. Use the Rectangle Layer tool to create a new layer.

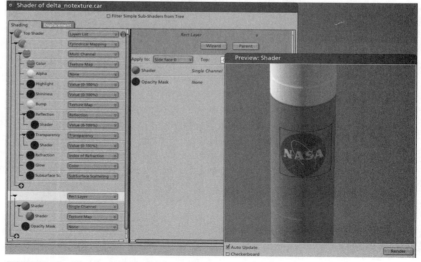

**FIGURE 12.12** The first marking in place.

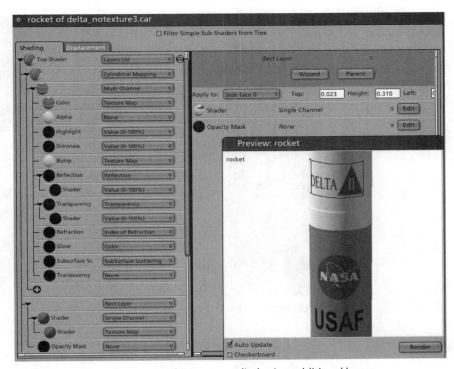

**FIGURE 12.13**    The other two markings are applied using additional layers.

## Custom and Stock Color Shaders

Now that the main rocket has been textured, we will move on to texturing the booster rockets. The booster rockets are made of metal painted white, so they have a somewhat metallic finish. To get started, go to the Edit menu and choose New Master Shader. Notice that in the Shader tab of the Properties tray there is a new shader. Rename it "white metal" and double-click on it to jump into the Texture room. In this shader we will work with four channels: Color, Shininess, Highlight, and Reflection. Click on the Color channel and in the Color section (right side) of the Shader tree click once on the color chip to bring up the Color Picker. The Color Picker is set to the HLS color wheel by default. To select white, move the small black circle over to the white area of the triangle. The Shininess, Highlight, and Reflection channels will simulate the specular properties of metal. Click on the Shininess channel and set its value to about 15%. Set the Highlight value to about 58% and the Reflection shader value to around 10%. Notice that these changes make the materials sphere appear metallic (see Figure 12.14).With the white metal shader done, jump back into the Assemble room so that the shader can be applied to the booster rockets.

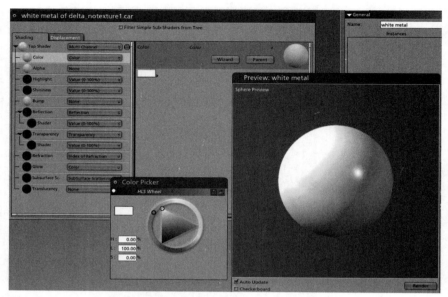

**FIGURE 12.14**  The white metal shader.

### Applying the White Metal Shader

Applying the new shader to the booster rockets is very easy to do. However, Carrara's drag-and-drop feature to apply shaders has a new twist. In previous versions of Carrara when a shader was dropped onto an object in the scene, the entire object took on the properties of the shader. In Carrara 5 when you drag a shader over an object, you can select which shading domains to drop the shader on. Each shading domain will be highlighted in red to indicate that it will accept the shader. If you want to apply the shader to all shading domains at once, all you have to is hold the Shift key as you drag and drop.

To apply the white metal shader you just created, click on the Shader tab in the Properties tray to display all available shaders. Hold the Shift key down and drag the white metal shader onto each booster rocket in the scene. The nozzle of each booster is also white, so apply the white metal shader there too, as in Figure 12.15.

### Using a Stock Shader

The main engine nozzle has an unpainted metal finish, so you can use one of the stock metal shaders that come with Carrara instead of having

**FIGURE 12.15**    The booster with the white metal shader applied.

to make one from scratch. At the very least, you can use the stock metal shader as a starting point for your own shader. To apply the metal shader, open the Sequencer tray, click on the Browser tab, and open the Basic Metal Shaders section. Drag the Anodized Aluminum shader onto the nozzle—that's all there is to it (see Figure 12.16).

At this point the texturing is just about complete. All that is left to do is to apply color shaders to the base of the nozzle, which is white, and to the direction vectors, which are green. The green shader is basically the same as the white metal shader, except that it is green, of course. When you are done the rocket should be similar to Figure 12.17.

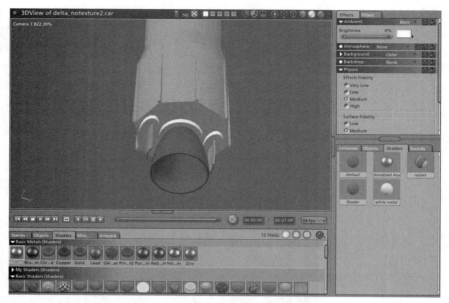

**FIGURE 12.16** Using a stock metal shader to texture the nozzle.

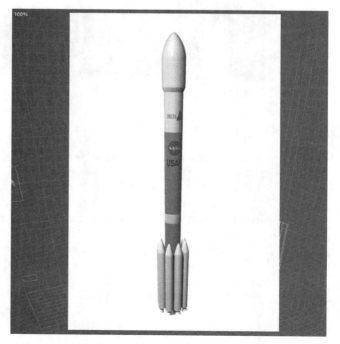

**FIGURE 12.17** The finished rocket.

**TUTORIAL 12.2**    **TEXTURING WITH SHADING DOMAINS**

In this tutorial we will use shading domains to add color or texture to specific areas of the Raul's face. For instance, the lips, skin, hair, and eyes are distinct areas that have different colors. Trying to color or texture Raul's facial features in the same manner we textured the rocket in the previous tutorial would be very difficult because unlike the rocket, which has separate parts, Raul's facial features are all part of one object. Shading domains allow us to group and name sets of polygons on an object and then apply different texturing methods to just those areas. In this tutorial we will create the shading domains and then add color only. Often all you need to texture a character in a convincing manner is flat colors, especially cartoon or caricatured characters like Raul.

### Creating Shading Domains

ON THE CD

Launch Carrara and open ShadingDomainStart.car. You should see Raul's untextured head in the scene as in Figure 12.18. Take a look a the Instances tab in the Properties Tray and note that Raul is made up of several parts, such as the eyes, teeth, and tongue.

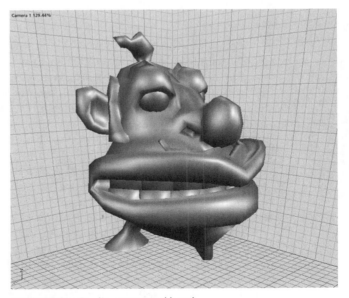

**FIGURE 12.18**    Raul's untextured head.

All of the tools to create shading domains are located inside the Vertex Modeler, so double-click on the head object to jump into the Vertex Modeler. We will start by creating a shading domain for the lips and inside of the mouth. Choose the Move tool from the toolbar and select all of the polygons that make up the lips and inside the mouth as in Figure 12.19.

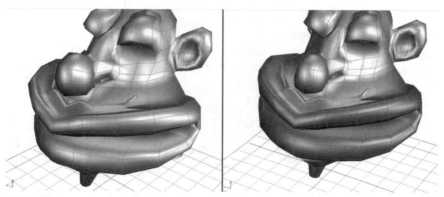

**FIGURE 12.19**   In the Vertex Modeler select all of the polygons that make up the lips and inside of the mouth.

Once all of the polygons for the lips and mouth are selected, click on the Global tab found in the Properties Tray and scroll down to the Shading Domain Management section. With the polygons still selected, click on the Add button and when prompted by Carrara with "Set the new shading domain on the current selection?" click Yes. Notice that a new shading domain named Texture 1 is created. Rename the new shading domain "Lips" in the Name field. You have just created the first shading domain (see Figure 12.20).

Next select the polygons that make up the mustache, goatee, and hair tuft on top of the head, as in Figure 12.21. As with the lips, click on the Add button in the Shading Domain Management section to create the new shading domain. Don't forget to name the new shading domain.

The last shading domain to create is for the skin. However, the skin has many polygons, which can be a chore to select one by one. There is a quick way to select all of the polygons for the skin. Aside from allowing color and textures to be applied on specific areas of a model, shading domains can also be used as selection tools. In this case we will use the two shading domains for the lips and hair to help us select the skin. We are still working in the Vertex Modeler, so make sure nothing is selected. Go to the Selection menu and choose Select By... and from the submenu

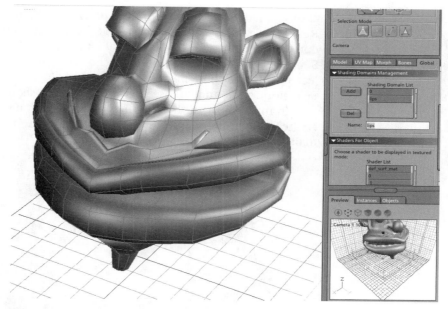

**FIGURE 12.20**    The first shading domain for the lips.

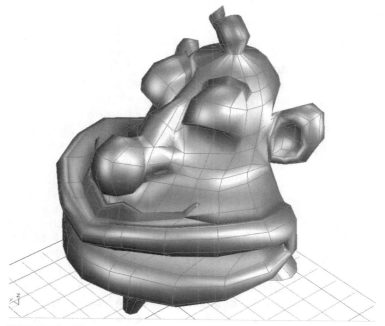

**FIGURE 12.21**    The next shading domain is for the hair.

choose Shading Domain. From the prompt click on lips and click on OK. Repeat the process, but this time hold the Shift key and select the shading domain for the hair. The polygons and the hair and lips will be selected. Some polygons between the mustache and lips may be inadvertently selected. Unselect those polygons for now (see Figure 12.22). Next go to the Selection menu and choose Invert Selection. This will reverse the selection from the lips and hair to the polygons that make up the skin. Now create a shading domain for the skin. Now there are three shading domains: one each for the skin, lips, and hair.

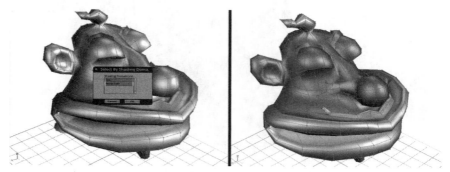

**FIGURE 12.22**   The polygons for the skin selected.

Now that all of the shading domains for the face are created it's time to assign a color to each. Like with the rocket, the color work has to be done in the Texture room, so jump out of the Vertex Modeler and into the Texture room. You can do this simply by clicking on the brush icon in upper-right corner of the Carrara interface. When prompted, if you want to Create a New Master or Edit a Master, choose Create a New Master and click OK. This creates a new shader for the face and allows you to jump into the Texture room (see Figure 12.23).

In the Texture room you will see the shader tree for the new shader. However, at this point the Top Shader is set to Multi Channel so there is no place to assign color to the shading domains we created in the Vertex Modeler. To fix this we have to switch the Top Shader to Layers List in order to see the shading domains. Click on the Top Shader menu and choose Complex Shaders and Layers List from the submenu. Notice that the shader tree changes and now displays a small cross inside a circle as part of the shader tree. This is the Layer icon. The Layer icon also appears on the right side of the Shader interface. Click on either icon and select Basic Layer from the menu, as seen in Figure 12.24.

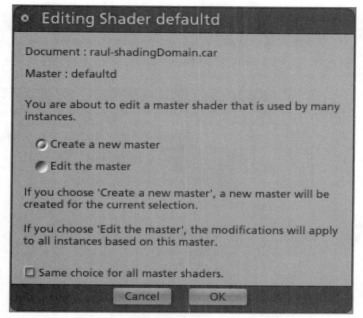

**FIGURE 12.23**    Creating a new shader for the shading domains of the face.

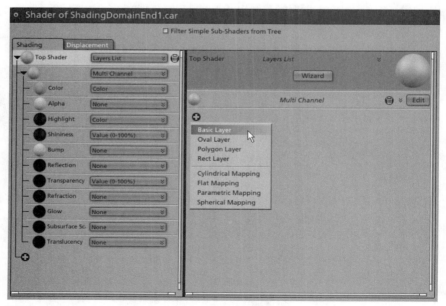

**FIGURE 12.24**    Creating a new Layer for a shading domain.

Once the Basic Layer has been created, click on the menu labeled Whole and select Lips from the menu (see Figure 12.25). This assigns the new layer to the lips shading domain. Click on the Layer icon two more times to create the layers for skin and hair (see Figure 12.26).

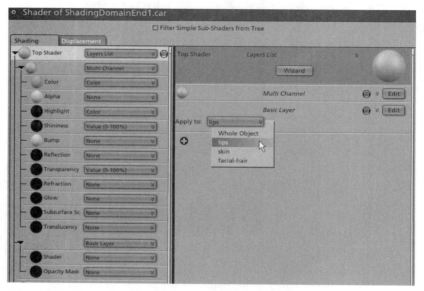

**FIGURE 12.25**  Assigning the new layer to the lips shading domain.

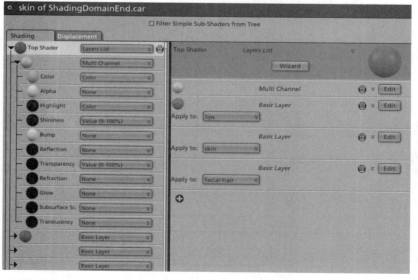

**FIGURE 12.26**  Layers for the lips, skin, and hair.

We are now ready to begin assigning colors to the layers and shading domains. Let's start with the lips. On the left side of the shader interface click on the Shader channel of the first Basic Layer and select Multi Channel (see Figure 12.27). This will assign the standard shader channels such as Color, Alpha, Highlight, Shininess, and so on. Click on the Color channel and choose Color from the menu. Note that the lips become red—the default color for a new shader. On the right side of the shader interface click once on the color chip to bring up the Color Picker, as in Figure 12.28. Choose the lip color you want for Raul's lips. Keep and eye on the Preview window, as it will show the colors as they are applied to Raul's face.

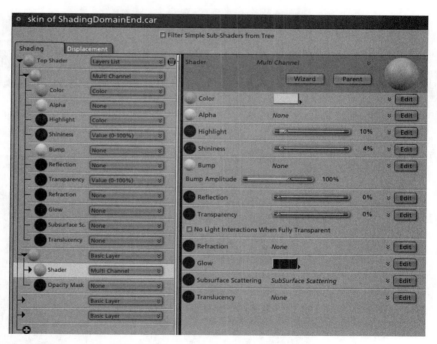

**FIGURE 12.27**    Assign a Multi Channel shader to the Lips Basic Layer.

When you are done with the lips, move on to the next Basic Layer on the shader tree and repeat the previous steps. The hair is black and the skin is a light brown (see Figure 12.29).

Now that the face has color via shading domains it's time to do the same to Raul's eyes. If you jump out into the Assemble room, Raul looks like a zombie because his eyes have no color. Double-click on one eye to jump into the Vertex Modeler. Select polygons for the iris and create a

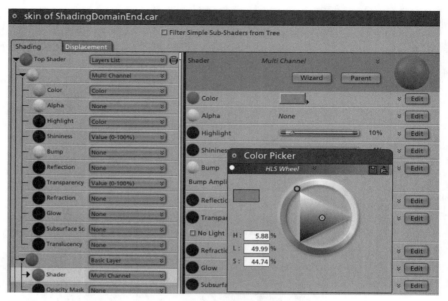

**FIGURE 12.28**    In the Color channel select a color for the lips.

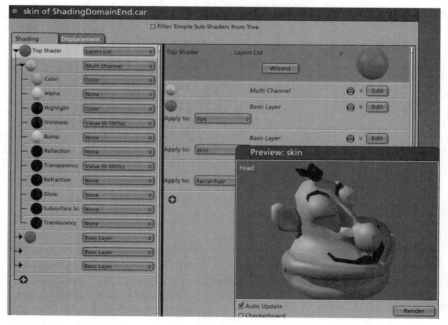

**FIGURE 12.29**    Finish adding color to the shading domains for the skin and hair.

new shading domain, as in Figure 12.30. Don't forget to create a shading domain for the pupil and white of the eye. Once you are done with the shading domains, create a new shader for the eye and assign colors to the iris, pupil, and white of the eye. You don't have to repeat this for the second eye. Simply delete it and copy the eye with color and replace the deleted eye.

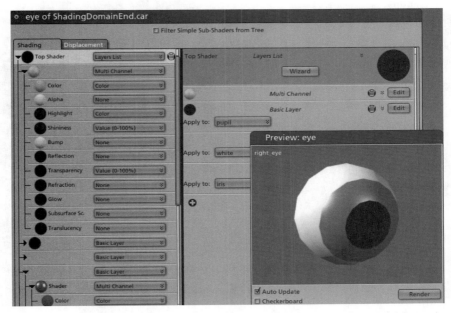

**FIGURE 12.30**    Once shading domains for the eye are finished, create a new shader and apply color to the parts of the eye.

Though we are done with the face and eyes, we still have to texture Raul's teeth and tongue and the patch of hair at the back of his head. Since these separate objects are all one color, there is no need to go through the trouble of creating shading domains. Simply create shaders for each object. For instance, select the hair at the back of the head and jump into the Texture room; choose Create a New Master and click on OK. Once in the Texture room, keep the Top Shader at Multi Channel, assign a color in the Color channel, and set values for the other channels if you so decide. Once you are done, Raul will look something like Figure 12.31.

We have now added shading domains to our texturing toolset. Shading domains make it easy to assign shaders to specific areas of an object and serve as selection tools. In the next tutorial we will take shading domains to the next level and use them to help UV-map Raul.

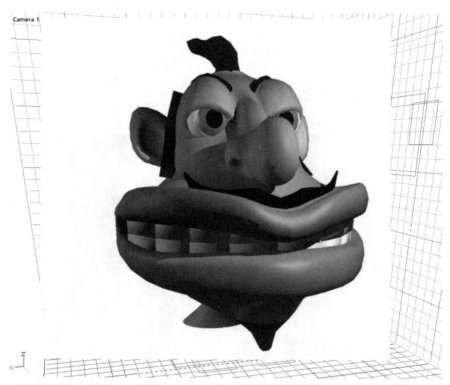

**FIGURE 12.31**   Raul completely shaded with shading domains and color shaders.

| TUTORIAL 12.3 | **TEXTURING WITH THE UV EDITOR** |

UV mapping is a texturing process in which an image-based texture is applied, not projected, onto the surface of a 3D object. The texture is precisely applied onto the surface of an object by using the UV coordinate system. In other words, each pixel of the texture has a corresponding UV coordinate on the surface of the object, which makes the texture "stick" to the object. UV mapping is a popular method for texturing models, so it is important to have a good understanding of how it works. As we will see, UV mapping requires the creation of a UV map and a texture map and application of the texture onto the model, as seen in Figure 12.32.

Carrara's UV Editor is found within the Vertex modeler, so only polygonal models can be UV mapped. If you want to UV-map any other type of model, such as a spline model, you must first convert it to a polygonal model. The ability of UV mapping to precisely position textures on the surface of any model with little or no distortion makes it tempting to

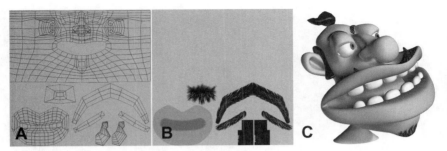

**FIGURE 12.32**    (a) UV map. (b) Texture map. (c) Texture applied to model.

use it on everything you model. However, UV mapping can be a tedious process, requiring much planning, texture creation, and editing and the eventual manipulation of dozens if not hundreds of UVs. For that reason you may want to consider using UV mapping only for models that cannot be textured any other way. For instance, Raul's teeth and some of his hair can be easily textured with separate color shaders, so UV mapping is not necessary. Conversely, Raul's head and face would be next to impossible to texture with basic shaders, so UV mapping is required. In this tutorial we will be only UV mapping Raul's head and face.

### UV-Mapping the Face and Head

ON THE CD

Open the file UVstart.car found in the Chapter 12 folder of the companion CD-ROM. This file contains a model of Raul that is completely untextured but that has shading domains already created. We are not going to repeat the creation of shading domains in this tutorial because you just completed that exercise in the previous tutorial. However, we will use shading domains to facilitate the UV mapping process. All of the textures used in this tutorial have been provided for you and can be found in the Chapter 12 folder on the accompanying CD-ROM.

To get started, double-click on Raul's head in the scene or in the Instances tab of the Properties tray to jump into the Vertex Modeler. Once in the Vertex Modeler, click on Global in the Properties tray and scroll to the Shading Domain Management section. There should be three shading domains listed: skin, hair, and lips, as seen in Figure 12.33. These are the areas that we will UV-map so that we can apply image-based textures.

Press Ctrl/Command-A to select all of the mesh in the Vertex Modeler, click on the UV Map tab in the Properties tray, and then press the UV Editor button. To make sure we start at the same place, go to the Edit tab, uncheck the Show All option in the Shading Domain List, and click once on the "skin" shading domain. The UV map should like Figure

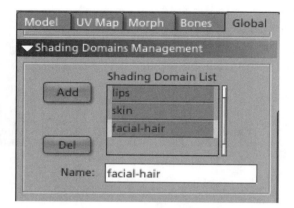

**FIGURE 12.33** The shading domains that we will use to facilitate UV mapping.

12.34. The jumble of lines and points (the points are the UVs) in the UV map is a projection of the mesh in the Vertex Modeler. However, the projection is not the mesh itself, so any changes made to the projection in the UV map will not affect the mesh in the Vertex Modeler.

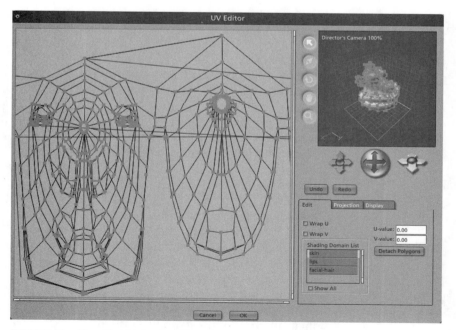

**FIGURE 12.34** The skin UVs in the UV map.

To begin unwrapping the skin UVs we will assign an appropriate UV projection. First, check the Wrap U and Wrap V options in the Edit tab. Next, click on the Projection tab, and from the small menu on the left select Cylindrical. Set the direction of the projection by clicking once on the Z arrow and press Apply. The result should look like Figure 12.35.

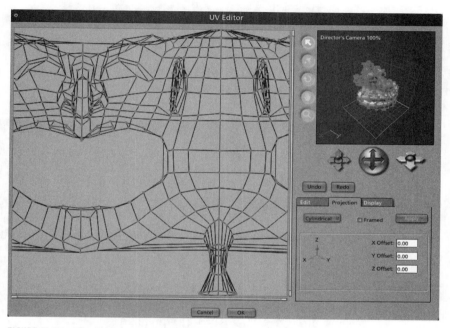

**FIGURE 12.35**    The initial attempt at unwrapping the mesh with a cylindrical projection.

Though the initial UV mapping is pretty good, it needs to be refined. First, let's spread out the UVs a bit more by using the Offset options. In the Y Offset field type "-1.6" and then press Apply. Notice that the UVs do not overlap as much and that there is more space between most UVs, as seen in Figure 12.36a. We want the UVs to overlap as little as possible and be spread out as uniformly as possible to help with the texture painting and application process. Next, click on the UV Editor's Move tool and drag the UVs to the right so that the seam created by the edges of the UV map is at the back of the head (see Figure 12.36b).

At this point the UVs are sufficiently unwrapped that you can apply a simple skin texture without any problems, as seen in Figure 12.37. However, if you were to planning on creating a complex texture for Raul's face, for instance a texture with scars or other markings, you would have to take the time to continue to move the UVs so that there are absolutely no overlapping UVs.

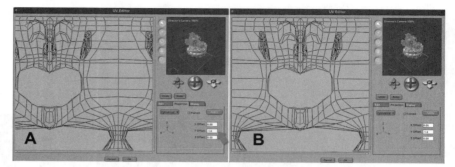

**FIGURE 12.36**    (a) Use the Y Offset to spread out the UVs. (b) Drag the UVs so that the seam is at the back of the head.

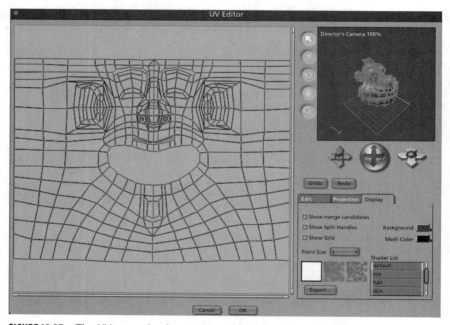

**FIGURE 12.37**    The UVs completely unwrapped by moving each UV.

Next, we will UV map Raul's lips. In the Edit tab select the lips shading domain. Once the lips are displayed in the UV map, click on the Projection tab and select Planar from the Projection menu, click on the y axis arrow,  select No Split, and click on Apply. The result should look like Figure 12.38a. The lips are on their left side, so click on the UV Editor's Rotate tool, hold the Shift key, and rotate 90 degrees to the left. Select the UV Editor's Scale tool and scale the lips down (see Figure 12.38b).

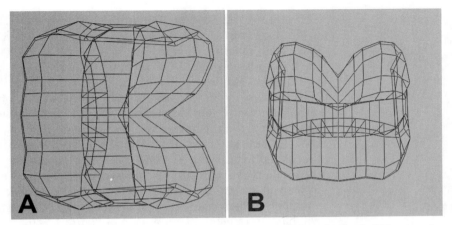

**FIGURE 12.38**    (a) The initial UV mapping projection for the lips. (b) The lip UVs rotated.

The automatic UV mapping tools in Carrara have done all they can to unwrap the lips, and because we are using simple colors to texture the UV-mapped areas, you can leave the lips as they are. However, this is a good opportunity to practice moving the UVs to get a better result. Use the UV Editor's Move tool to further unwrap the lip's UVs as seen in Figure 12.39. Unwrapping the UVs simply means that you will unravel the UVs so that they don't overlap and are as flat as possible.

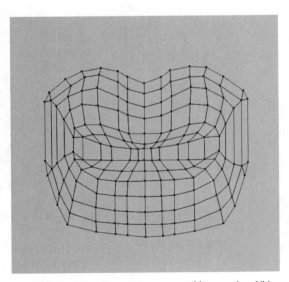

**FIGURE 12.39**    The lip UVs unwrapped by moving UVs with the Move tool.

Next we will UV map Raul's mustache, eyebrows, and goatee and the tuft of hair on top of his head. In the Edit tab of the UV Editor select the facial-hair shading domain. In this case we cannot simply select all of the UVs and apply one UV projection, because mustache, eyebrows, goatee, and hair have different shapes and positions. Instead, we will select each object and apply the UV projection that best fits that object. Select the tuft of hair on top of Raul's head and apply a Planar projection along the *y*-axis. Scale down the hair so you can continue working with the rest of the UVs. Carrara automatically UV-maps objects when they are loaded into the UV Editor. Usually Carrara's attempts need some refining. However, the initial UV mapping by Carrara works for the goatee and the eyebrows, so we will leave those as they are for now. Next, select the mustache UVs and apply a Planar projection along the *z*-axis. To finish the mustache you will have to move the UVs as seen in Figure 12.40.

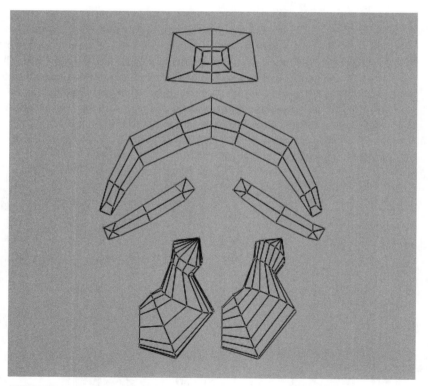

**FIGURE 12.40**    UV-mapping the facial hair and the hair on top of the head.

### Packing the UVs

The next step in UV-mapping Raul's face and head is a process called *packing* the UVs. When you pack the UVs in the UV map, you arrange all of the UVs so that they don't overlap and take up as much of the UV map area as possible. To pack the UVs use the UV Editor's Move and Scale and Rotate tools to fit the all of the UVs, as in Figure 12.41.

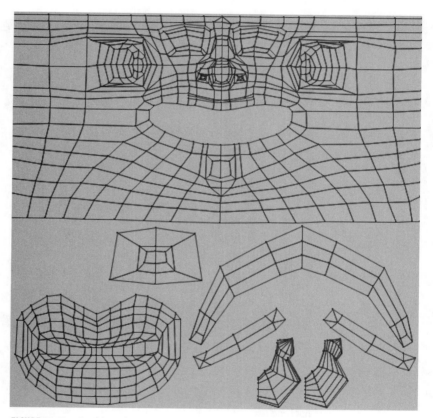

**FIGURE 12.41** Packing the UVs.

### Exporting the UV Map

Once all of the UVs are packed, it's time to export the UV map as an image so that it can be used as a template to paint the texture. To export the UV map click on the Display tab and press the Export button. In Carrara UV maps are exported at 72 dpi, but you can choose from six sizes starting at

128 pixels and ending at 4096 pixels (128 stands for 128 × 128 pixels and so on). Unless you are trying to keep memory use low, as in real-time 3D applications, you typically want to export a map that is at least 1024 × 1024 pixels. If your work will be printed, you may consider using a higher resolution. From the Map Size dialog box choose 1024 and then save the file (see Figure 12.42). Open the map in your favorite graphics program and paint the textures, as seen in Figure 12.43.

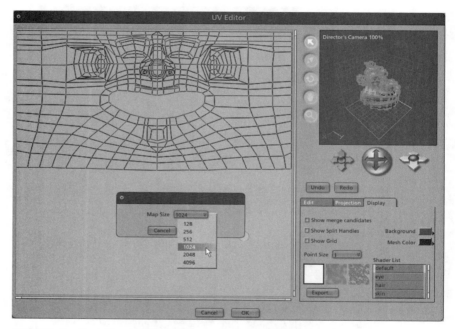

**FIGURE 12.42**    Exporting the UV map as an image to be used as a template in painting the textures.

### Applying Textures to UV-Mapped Objects

Once the textures are painted, it's time to apply them to Raul's head and face. In the Assemble room select Raul's head and jump into the Texture room. When prompted, choose to create a new shader. Select the Color channel, open the menu labeled Color, and choose Texture Map. In the Texture Map details browse to the file UVtexture.tif. Jump back into the Assemble room and do a quick test render to see your work. It should look similar to Figure 12.44.

ON THE CD

**FIGURE 12.43**    The texture map painted using the UV map template.

**FIGURE 12.44**    Raul's face textured using UV mapping.

**ON THE CD**

Open the file UVend.car to see the completely textured model. Double-click on one of Raul's eyes to examine how they have been UV-mapped. The eye texture is provided for you, so all you have to do is UV-map the eyes and apply the texture.

## SUMMARY

Carrara provides you with just about all of the tools you will need to texture any model you create. The tutorials in this chapter are designed to introduce you to the most common methods used for texturing models. However, by no means are these methods the only way to texture models in Carrara. For instance, the flexibility of shading domains and UV mapping can be combined to selectively apply textures to certain areas of the model and use procedurals or color shaders on other parts of the model. In the next chapter we will cover two new tools in Carrara 5: subsurface scattering and displacement mapping.

# ADVANCED SHADERS: SUBSURFACE SCATTERING AND DISPLACEMENT MAPPING

## In This Chapter

- Subsurface Scattering
- Displacement Mapping

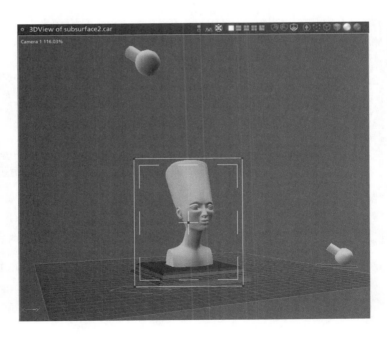

In the previous chapter we covered standard texturing methods such as UV mapping, bump mapping, image-based textures, and shading domains. While the standard texturing methods can take care of most texturing tasks, in some cases you will need Carrara's more advanced materials features. The two tutorials in this chapter will cover subsurface scattering and displacement mapping. Subsurface scattering is a special effect that simulates more realistic interaction between light and certain materials. Displacement mapping is, believe it or not, a modeling process that quickly creates detailed models.

| | |
|---|---|
| **TUTORIAL 13.1**  | **SUBSURFACE SCATTERING** |

All nonmetal materials have some level of *translucency*. When light strikes the surface of a translucent material, some of the light is reflected but some of the light is transported into the material, is scattered, and then exits at a different point from where it entered. The result is that translucent materials such as skin, wax, marble, plastic, and wood appear emit a subtle glow in certain lighting conditions. In computer graphics this process is known as *subsurface scattering*. Sometimes when computers render translucent materials without taking subsurface scattering into account, the results may appear dull or in the case of organic materials lifeless (see Figure 13.1). Until recently subsurface scattering was something that only proprietary software and hardware were capable of simulating because of the computer power required, but as personal computers have evolved, programs like Carrara can also offer subsurface scattering effects. However, as with all high-end effects, subsurface scattering will add considerably to the amount of rendering time required. For the most part, subsurface scattering is a very subtle effect, so you have to weigh any benefits of using it against the additional time required for rendering.

*Subsurface scattering is subtle effect. To best see the effects of subsurface scattering in the following figures, view the figure files in the Chapter 13 folder in the companion CD-ROM.*

ON THE CD

To become familiar with subsurface scattering we will work with a model of a sculpture of Queen Nefertiti. As you can see in Figure 13.1, when the sculpture is textured with a marble procedural shader it looks pretty good, but the problem is that marble is translucent, as are many types of polished stones.

**FIGURE 13.1**    Traditional render of the sculpture using a marble shader but no subsurface scattering.

**ON THE CD**

To get started, open the file subsurface.car found in the Chapter 13 folder of the companion CD-ROM. Do not change the position of the sculpture, cameras, lights, or the scene properties. They are set up so that the effects of subsurface scattering can be easily seen. That is, the sculpture is positioned between the light and the camera. At this point there is no subsurface scattering in the scene, so before moving on let's do a quick test render so we have a control image to compare with the subsurface scattering image we will render. Press Ctrl/Command-R to render the scene. Notice that because the scene is back lighted, the sculpture is barely visible and the scene is very dark. Now let's add subsurface scattering to the sculpture and see what happens. Select the sculpture in the scene and click on the Texture room button to jump into the Texture room.

In Carrara subsurface scattering is implemented as a channel in the shader tree. To display the subsurface scattering controls click on the Subsurface Scattering channel at the bottom of the shader tree and from the menu labeled None select SubSurface Scattering (see Figure 13.2). Remarkably, for such a complex effect Carrara's subsurface scattering controls are simple and straightforward to use.

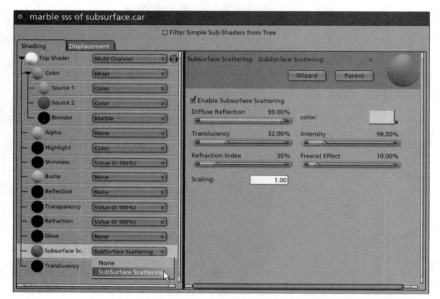

**FIGURE 13.2**    The subsurface scattering controls are a channel in the shader tree.

Before enabling subsurface scattering let's adjust some of the controls. Click on the color chip and in the HLS color wheel select a light beige color (e.g., H8, L80, S33). Choosing the right color in the subsurface scattering settings is important, as this is the color that the translucency will take and often the color in the subsurface scattering settings will override the color in the Color channel. Next, set the Translucency value to about 25%, check the Enable Subsurface Scattering option, and then press Ctrl/Command-R to render. Notice that in the new render the sculpture is translucent; the light behind the sculpture is actually coming through the sculpture making it glow subtly. The translucency is most apparent in areas that are not thick, like the nose (see Figure 13.3).

**FIGURE 13.3**    With subsurface scattering enabled, the sculpture is clearly visible and appears translucent.

Subsurface scattering is a subtle effect that is affected by the lighting in the scene and by the point of view of the camera in respect to the surface being lit. For instance, if the scene has bright lighting, any subsurface scattering effects may be washed out. If a camera is looking directly at a lit surface, markings, color, or specular properties may also diminish subsurface scattering effects. In this tutorial we are working with standard lights, but in Carrara subsurface scattering also works well with advanced lighting such as global illumination. Also, subsurface scattering will drastically alter the surface characteristics of an object. Particularly, the intensity and definition of shadows cast on objects with subsurface scattering will tend to diminish, thus reducing detail and possibly making objects appear flat. To see how lighting affects subsurface scattering, in the Top camera view move the light so that the sculpture is no longer back lighted but lighted from the front and move the camera so you can see the sculpture from the front as in Figure 13.4. Render again to see how just changing the light position changes the subsurface scattering effects.

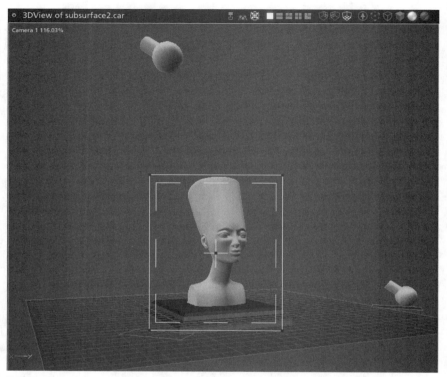

**FIGURE 13.4** Many variables, including lighting and camera position, affect subsurface scattering.

ON THE CD

Now that you have some experience with subsurface scattering, let's set up a scene in which subsurface scattering is obvious but the sculpture of Nefertiti is at a more normal point of view. For this part of the tutorial open the file subsurface2.car. As before, first create a control render without subsurface scattering. Press Ctrl/Command-R to render. The image looks dark and hard, as in Figure 13.5a. Now select the sculpture and jump into the Texture room and select subsurface scattering from the SubSurface Scattering menu. Adjust the subsurface scattering properties as follows: Diffuse Reflection: 99%, Translucency: 32%, Intensity: 98%, Refraction Index: 30%, and Fresnel Effect: 10%. Set the subsurface scattering color to H8, L80, S30 and render (see Figure 13.5b).

Here are some quick tips on using subsurface scattering: leave Diffuse Reflection between 90% and 100%; lower values will reduce the subsurface scattering effect substantially. Translucency is the degree to which light will penetrate and should be between 25% and 50%; lower values will increase brightness, and of course higher values will diminish brightness.

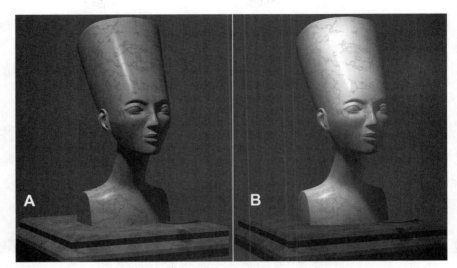

**FIGURE 13.5**    With subsurface scattering, the sculpture has a soft glow and is lit by the translucency of the material.

Keep Intensity around 100%. Keep Refraction Index around 30%. When the camera is looking directly at the object and there is direct lighting, increase the Fresnel Effect between 10% and 20% to maintain translucency. When using subsurface scattering, decrease the specular properties, Highlight and Shininess. High specular values interfere with the subsurface scattering effect. Finally, pay close attention to scene lighting conditions. Subsurface scattering is more evident in indirect lighting, which is balanced with the subsurface scattering settings. Subsurface scattering works very well with Carrara's advanced lighting such as Global Illumination. Working with subsurface scattering takes considerable preparation and experimentation to get it just right. Nonetheless, the effort is well worth it to attain the unique effects achieved with subsurface scattering.

Click on the Shaders tab in the Properties tray. There you will find wax, plastic, and alabaster subsurface scattering shaders that you can experiment with. Each shader is a great starting point to create your own subsurface scattering shaders. To apply the shaders simply drag and drop the shader onto the sculpture and render. 🪃

**TUTORIAL 13.2**    **DISPLACEMENT MAPPING**

The term *displacement mapping* can be misleading. Displacement mapping is a form of modeling using a grayscale image instead of traditional modeling tools. Simply put, in displacement mapping a 256-level grayscale image is used to *displace* the polygons of a mesh. Figure 13.6a shows a smooth sphere. When the displacement map seen in Figure 13.6b is applied, the result is a sphere that has had its surface remodeled with dimples, as seen in Figure 13.6c. With displacement mapping, complex and intricate modeling can be accomplished with relatively little effort.

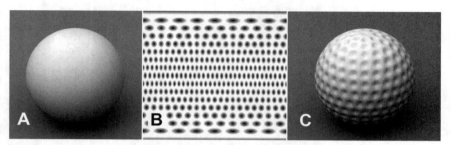

**FIGURE 13.6** The grayscale displacement map in panel b is applied to the smooth sphere to model the dimpled ball.

Much of the work and time involved in modeling with displacement mapping goes into creating a good displacement map. For best results with Carrara, the base color of the displacement map should be gray (R128, G128, B128). This level of gray causes no displacement; white causes raised areas and black, lowered areas. To achieve subtle effects when painting the displacement map in your favorite graphics program, use a low opacity, soft-edge brush, and to get stark differences in displacement use an opaque, hard-edge brush. A high-resolution displacement map of at least 1024 × 1024 pixels gets better results than lower resolution maps.

In this brief tutorial we will revisit the model of Queen Nefertiti, except that instead of rendering a translucent marble sculpture, this time we will make her into an ancient mummy. When you think of mummies, you probably imagine a human face disfigured by decaying or desiccated flesh and sunken skull-like features. It would take hours if not days of detailed modeling to convert the smooth face in the model from the previous tutorial to the face of a mummy ravaged by time. Fortunately, we don't have to wait days to model the mummy. Instead, we will use a carefully painted grayscale map to instantly disfigure the smooth face (see Figure 13.7).

ON THE CD

Open the file displacement.car found in the Chapter 13 folder in the companion CD-ROM. This version of Nefertiti is a bit different than the model in the previous tutorial. For instance, the head dress and the face are two separate objects and the shoulders have been omitted for simplic-

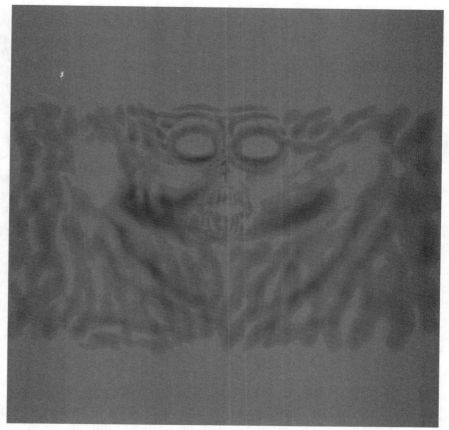

**FIGURE 13.7**    The displacement map we will use to instantly model a mummy.

ON THE CD

ity. Click on the face and jump into the Texture room. Click on the Displacement tab. In the shader tree select Displacement and from the menu labeled None choose Texture Map. Load the displacementmap.tif file, also found in the Chapter 13 folder. Next, click on the Top Shader to display the Displacement Mapping settings. Make sure the Preview window is displaying the face. Check Enable Displacement to apply the displacement map to the face. In a few moments you should see that results of the displacement mapping in the preview window (see Figure 13.8).

Just as important as a good displacement map is a good model that has enough polygons for you to be able to use the grayscale information in the displacement map. In other words, to get good results from

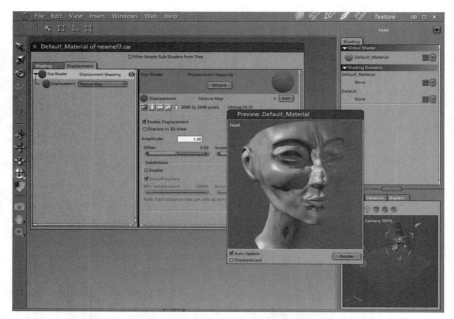

**FIGURE 13.8**   With the displacement map applied, the smooth face becomes disfigured.

displacement mapping, the model should be a high polygon count. However, in Carrara the displacement mapping function has a property that can automatically subdivide the model to get the best results, so you can use a low-poly model and increase its polygon count within the Displacement Mapping controls. In the Subdivision section check the Enable checkbox to smooth the model. This should improve the displacement. To get even better results bump up the Min. sample count from 10,000 to 20,000, as in Figure 13.9.

## Considerations When Using Displacement Mapping

Displacement mapping can be combined with any of the shader channels. To achieve the final results seen in Figure 13.10 a Turbulence component was dropped into the Bump channel to get the leathery skin. To attain just the right color for the skin a separate color map was loaded into the Color channel. The Highlight and Shininess channels were adjusted to create a sheen on the skin. The Displacement channel has all of the shading components available to all the other shader channels, so you are not

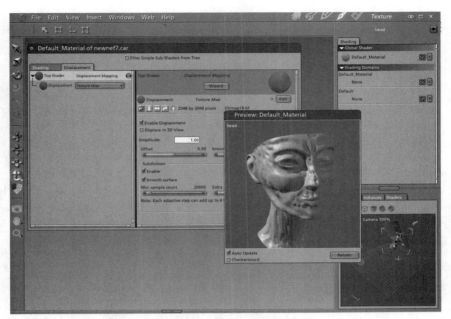

**FIGURE 13.9**    Carrara's displacement mapping can subdivide the model to get better results.

limited to a painted displacement map like we used in this tutorial. You could also use any procedural such as Cellular, Checker, Tiles, and so on to achieve the results you want. Lighting is also an important consideration when using displacement mapping. You will want to turn off ambient lighting in the Scene properties, as it reduces the effect of shadows, and position lights in the scene to create the most contrast between light and dark areas to bring out the displacement details.

The displacement mapping function has a Displace in 3D View option that will displace the surface of model in the Assemble Room. Unless you are exporting the model out of Carrara, you do not need to enable this option because Carrara will render the displacement mapping results regardless of the setting of the Displace in 3D View option. In addition, enabling the Displace in 3D View option will greatly slow down changes you make as you refine the model, so if you are going to enable Displace in 3D view do it last. The model of Nefertiti is UV-mapped to help accurately paint the displacement map. Not all displacement mapping requires a UV-mapped model, but it helps with detailed models (see Figure 13.10).

**FIGURE 13.10**    The final results of using a displacement map to model the mummy.

## SUMMARY

Not only does Carrara feature powerful shaders to simulate just about any real texture and lighting interaction, but as you have seen, Carrara's shader and materials tools are easy and fun to use and experiment with. In this chapter we covered subsurface scattering, which effectively creates ultra-realistic images that are almost indistinguishable from photographs. In the second tutorial we learned that in Carrara modeling is not limited to the modelers, but that very intricate models can be created by using displacement mapping.

# V

# ANIMATION
# WITH CARRARA

# ANIMATING WITH MORPH TARGETS

## In This Chapter

- Creating Morph Targets
- Lip Synching with Morph Targets

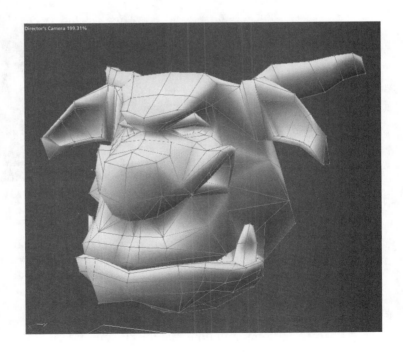

Have you ever watched a TV show with the volume turned down but you could still make out what the person on screen was saying? Or maybe your significant other mouthed "I love you" across a room and you understood without hearing a sound? From a very early age we learn to pick up the subtle nuances in body language and facial expressions, which includes the shape of the mouth, to understand what a person is saying. Because of our natural skill at understanding the unspoken word, successful character animation must take into account our shared and individual mannerisms and gestures. However, animating facial expressions or speech by repeatedly moving dozens of vertices manually each time you needed a blink, frown, or smile would be next to impossible. With morph targets the modeling needed to create a smile has to be done only once. The smile morph target stores the vertex positions for the smile, which can then be effortlessly recalled during animation as often as needed with only a mouse click and drag (see Figure 14.1).

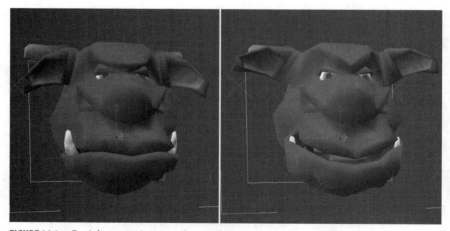

**FIGURE 14.1**   Facial expressions can be easily recreated with morph targets.

In facial animation morph targets can also be used to create the distinctive positions of the mouth, lips, teeth, and tongue during speech. In computer graphics these distinctive mouth positions are called *phonemes*. In English, and other languages of course, most sounds made during speech have a unique phoneme. For instance, say the word "fall." When the "f" sound is made your lower lip is tucked under you upper teeth. Now say "long" and note that the "l" sound is made only when your lips are parted, and your tongue moves up, making contact with your upper teeth, and then down. Some phonemes are similar, for example "f" and "v" have similar lip positions. Vowels also have unique phonemes. Try reciting the vowel alphabet, "a, e, i, o, u" paying attention to the position of your tongue and lips as you say each letter. Now that you are aware at a conscious level of the complexity and variety of facial expressions caused by emotion and speech, you can begin to appreciate the amount of work that morph targets save (see Figure 14.2).

**FIGURE 14.2**    Morph targets can also be used to create phonemes. The troll is saying "fall."

ON THE CD

Carrara has had some form of morph targeting since its early versions. However, older versions of Carrara used a cumbersome method of morph targeting in which facial expressions and phonemes required a unique mesh. That could mean having to model and keep track of dozens of different meshes. Carrara 5 uses a very efficient method of morph targeting that requires only one mesh. Instead of storing expression and phonemes in separate meshes, only the vertex positions for the different shapes are stored as morph targets. If this doesn't make sense yet, it will by the time you are done with these tutorials. For now open the file troll-morphed.car in the Chapter 14 folder of the book's CD-ROM. Click once on the head and notice that in the Properties tray there is a list of morph areas and morph targets. A morph area is a section of the troll that has morph targets applied to it. For instance, the troll has morph areas for the mouth, blink, and ears, among others. A morph target, on the other hand, is the actual change in position. A morph area can have one or many morph targets. Click on Mouth Morph Area from the Area List and notice that several morph targets appear in the Current Area. Move the oo slider all the way to the right to purse the troll's lips, as shown in Figure 14.3. In Carrara all

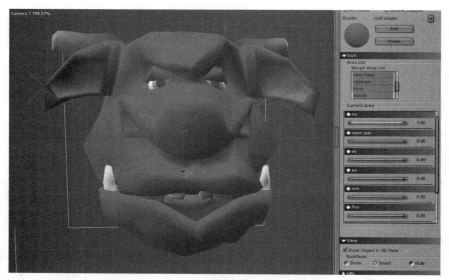

**FIGURE 14.3**   Carrara allows morph targets to be mixed in any combination to create variation.

morph targets can be mixed. For example, you can mix the open jaw and smile morph targets to create variations of the specific morph targets. Experiment with the different morph targets available to see how many different expressions you can create.

The excellent model of the troll we will use in the following tutorials was designed by Dough Dworkin and modeled by Dr. Michael Reiser. Morph targeting, like any other type of animation, requires planning. First, a well-built model designed with morph targeting in mind is a must. The troll is a low-poly model that has enough polygons to allow good morphing but not so many that it is difficult to work with (see Figure 14.4). Second, you should know your model very well before you begin morph targeting so you can decide how the model can be morphed best. Third, you should know in advance what morph targets you will need to create to accomplish your animation. Creating morph targets for every possible phoneme and expression would be a daunting task and is usually not necessary. The file troll-morph.car has 16 morph targets—enough to create many different expressions and phonemes. It is important to note that the eyes are separate objects from the head and are animated with a target object instead of morph targets.

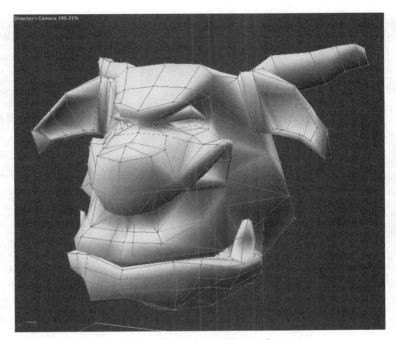

**FIGURE 14.4**    The model we will animate with morph targets.

| TUTORIAL 14.1 | **CREATING MORPH TARGETS** |

ON THE CD

Open the file troll-start.car in the Chapter 14 folder of the book's CD-ROM. This file is similar to troll-morph.car, except that there are a couple of morph targets missing. In the next few steps you will recreate the morph targets. Select the troll and double-click on his head to jump into the Vertex Modeler. Since the model already has morph targets, the Vertex Modeler will be in Animation mode. The initial selection for morph targets has to be done in the Modeling mode, so at the top of the Properties tray find the Edit Mode section and click on the first button to switch to Modeling mode. Next, open the Selection menu and choose Select By and from the submenu select Name. In the Select By Name dialog box click on Right Ear and press OK. The troll's right ear should become selected (see Figure 14.5).

Now, click on the Morph tab in the Properties tray. As in the Assemble room, the Morphs tab has two sections: Area List and Current Area. The Area List displays the areas of the model that can be morph targeted,

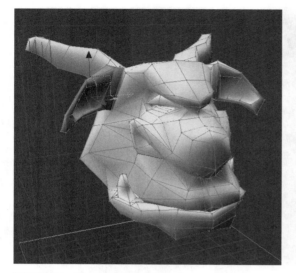

**FIGURE 14.5**   The right ear selected.

**FIGURE 14.6**   Naming the new morph area.

and the Current Area displays the actual morph targets. With the ear selected, click on the Create button in the Area List. Carrara will immediately create a new item in the Area List. Rename the item "right ear" in the Current Area name field, as in Figure 14.6. The initial position of the ear will be the starting point of the morph target, so the end-position morph target has to be created. Click on the small menu to the right of the name field in the Current Area and choose Create Target (see Figure 14.7). In the New Target Name dialog box give the new morph target a descriptive name like "right ear wiggle." Click on the Edit button next to the slider to create the ear morph target, as in Figure 14.8.

Zoom in on the ear and switch to the Left camera view. With the Move and Rotate tool (or the Universal Manipulator) position the ear as shown in Figure 14.9 and click on the Valid button back in the Current Area. The morph target is now complete. Switch to the Animation mode and move the slider back and forth to test the morph target.

Jump back out to the Assemble room and select the troll; in the Properties tray the new morph area "right ear" should be listed. When the right ear area is clicked, the Current Area will display the "right ear wiggle" morph target (see Figure 14.10). Move the slider to see the troll wiggle his right ear in the Assemble room.

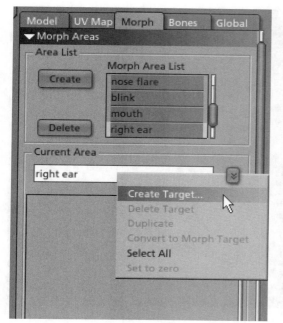

**FIGURE 14.7**　Creating the ear morph target.

**FIGURE 14.8**　The new ear morph target.

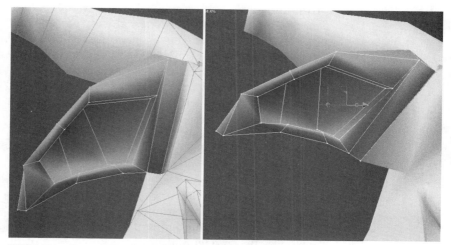

**FIGURE 14.9**　Repositioning the ear to create the morph target.

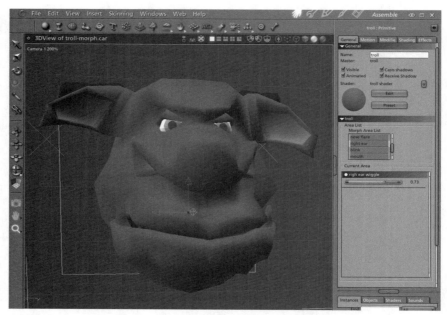

**FIGURE 14.10**    The ear morph target control in the Assemble room.

Let's create one more morph target to make the troll smile. Select the troll and jump back into the Vertex Modeler and switch to Modeling mode. The area to be morphed already exists because the troll's mouth has several morph targets assigned to it. Click on the Morph tab in the Properties tray and in the Area List click on the mouth item. Notice that there are many morph targets in the Current Area list, as shown in Figure 14.11. To add a new morph target for the mouth click on the small menu next to the name field in the Current Area, select Create Target, and name the new target (see Figure 14.12).

As in the previous exercise, name the new morph target when the New Target Name dialog box comes up. "Smile" would be a good name for the smile morph targets. Click on the Edit menu next to the smile morph target. This will allow you to shape the mouth's polygons into a smile. With the Move or Universal Manipulator tool shape the corners of the mouth and lips as shown in Figure 14.13. Modeling the morph targets is the most time-consuming part of creating morph targets. This is where a well-designed model and intimate knowledge of the model helps create good morph targets. When you are done modeling the smile, click on the Valid button next to the new morph target in the Properties tray. Jump back out to the Assemble room, click on the mouth area in the Area List,

**FIGURE 14.11**    The existing morph targets for the mouth.

**FIGURE 14.12**    Select Create Target to start creating the new morph target for the mouth.

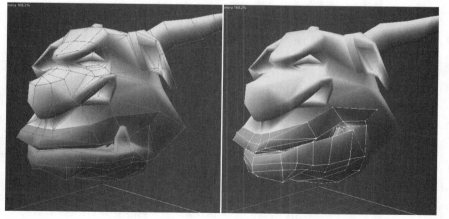

**FIGURE 14.13**    Use the move or Universal Manipulator tool to shape the mouth and lips.

scroll down to the smile morph target in the Current Area list and move the slider to make the troll smile (see Figure 14.14).

As you can see, creating morph targets is not difficult at all and can be a lot of fun, provided that your model is carefully designed so it can be easily morphed. In the next section we will make the troll talk by synching the phrase "Hello, love" with the mouth and facial morphs.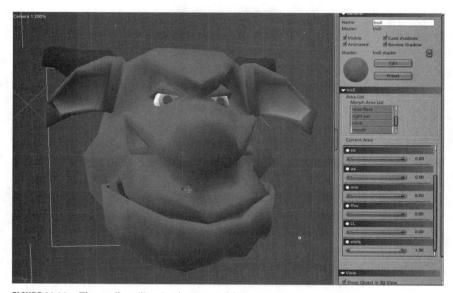

**FIGURE 14.14**   The troll smiling in the Assemble room.

---

**TUTORIAL 14.2**   **LIP SYNCHING WITH MORPH TARGETS**

By far the most common use for morph targets is facial animation, which includes speech. As you have seen from the previous exercises, creating morph targets for facial expression and mouth position or phonemes is a straightforward but time-consuming process. Once all of the morph targets have been created, you are ready to begin animating. The file troll-morph.car, in the Chapter 14 folder in the book's CD-ROM, has all of the morph targets we are going to use to make the troll speak.

ON THE CD

The first thing you need to know is that Carrara is not a lip-synching program, which probably sounds a bit odd in a tutorial about lip-synching with Carrara. With Carrara you can create the phonemes for speech and you can even load a sound file, but lip-synching has to be accomplished with some creative methods. It helps to have a program such as Adobe Audition® or Sony® Sound Forge® (you may download trial versions of either program at its respective Web site) to edit the sound file and to become familiar with the sound waveform. For this tutorial the sound file hello3.aif has been provided in the Chapter 14 folder of the CD-ROM.

ON THE CD

When you listen to a sound file and see the waveform, it is not difficult to discern where the phonemes start and end (see Figure 14.15).

**FIGURE 14.15**    The "Hello, love" sound waveform in Sony Sound Forge.

In this tutorial we will create a 1-second animation in which the troll will say "Hello, love" with a British accent. The phrase "Hello, love" has three syllables, he-llo-love, so to make the troll say "Hello, love" with a British accent we have to use the phonemes for *e, l, oo, l, a,* and *f,* among others. In addition we also have morph targets for facial expressions such as blinking, brow movements, smile, and ear movements.

Animating the with morph targets involves adjusting the morph targets in the Properties tray, previewing in the camera views, and setting key frames in the timeline. However, key frames for the morph targets are set at the master object level, so in the Sequencer tray scroll down until you see the troll master object and click on the white arrow pointing to the right. Keep clicking on the white arrows until you see all of the morph target areas. To see the individual morph targets click once more, as in Figure 14.16. Set the animation length to 1 second by either moving the yellow time marker to 1 second, or by inputting 00:01:00 in the timeline's clock. Check the Snap option at the top of the Sequencer to facilitate setting key frames.

**ON THE CD**

One last thing before animating. Click on the Sound tab in the Properties tray, press the Add button, and browse to the file hello3.aif in the Chapter 14 folder in the book's CD-ROM. Once the file is in the Sound tab, drag it to Channel 1 of the Soundtrack as seen in Figure 14.17.

With all the preparation done, we are ready to animate. The first syllable in the phrase "Hello, love" is *he,* which can be created by mixing the

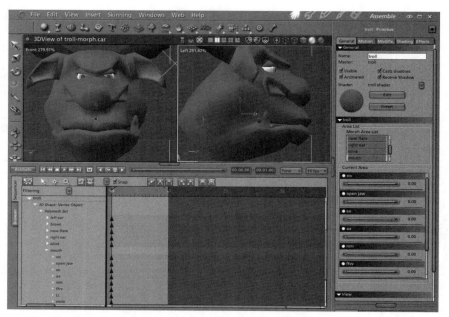

**FIGURE 14.16**    Morph targets are seen at the master object level. Set the animation time to 1 second and check the Snap option.

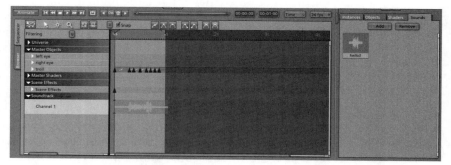

**FIGURE 14.17**    Importing a sound file into the Sound tab and placing it in the Channel 1 of the Soundtrack.

morph targets oo, ee, and open jaw. Move the time marker to 00:00:07 so that it lines up with the beginning of the waveform in the soundtrack. In the Properties tray click on the mouth item in the Area List and in the Current Area set the following morph target values: oo: 0.70, open jaw: 0.31, and ee: 0.38. Notice that there are now key frames in the timeline and that the troll's mouth parted and the lip shape changed (see Figure 14.18).

**FIGURE 14.18**    The first phoneme, *he*, is set at time 00:00:07 to match up with the waveform.

Next, move the time marker to about 00:00:09 and set the following morph target values: oo: 1, open jaw: 0, ee: 0.70, and LL: 0.4. Notice that the troll's mouth is now pursed and the tongue has moved. To complete "hello" move the time marker to 00:00:12 and zero out all of the morph targets so that the troll's mouth is closed (see Figure 14.19). Notice again that each syllable, or phoneme, is matched with the waveform in the soundtrack. To see the animation thus far, move the scrubber back to frame 1 and scrub forward or use the play controls.

The morph targets we will use to form the word *love* are the open jaw, smile, ll, aa, and ffvv. Move the time marker to 00:00:15 and set the following morph targets to LL: 1 and smile: 0.30. At 00:00:17 set the morph target aa to 1, open jaw to 0, and smile to 0.30, as in Figure 14.20. Move the time tracker to 00:00:19, zero out all other morph targets, and set ffvv to 1 and smile to 0.30 to finish the *v* sound. Finally, move the time marker to about 00:00:21 and zero out all of the morph targets except the smile, which you can increase to 1 to finish with a smile. If you are having trouble with the exercise, there are incremental files for this exercise that you can explore in the Chapter 14 folder of the CD-ROM.

ON THE CD

Now that the morph targets have been synched with the waveform in the soundtrack, it's time to see what the result looks like. Press Ctrl/Command-R to render. The render settings are adjusted to output a

**FIGURE 14.19**    The end of "hello" is set at time 00:00:12 to match up with the waveform.

**FIGURE 14.20**    The *aa* sound in "love" is set at time 00:00:17.

**ON THE CD**

QuickTime movie at 24 frames per second. QuickTime is the only format that supports sound. Compare your results with the movie test-talk.mov in the CD-ROM (see Figure 14.21).

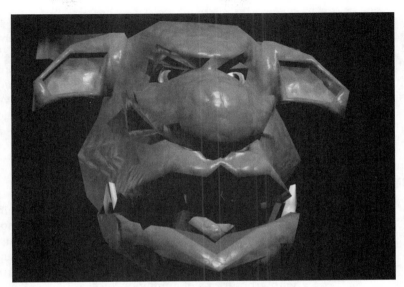

**FIGURE 14.21**    The troll in the process of speaking, but somewhat stoic.

Because no one speaks with their heads perfectly still or without blinking, the only thing left to do is to add a little personality to the speech, so go back and add gestures to the troll's speech by moving his brows, ears, and eyelids and by nodding his head, as in Figure 14.22. The brows, eyelids, ears, and nose are controlled by morph targets, but the head is animated by moving it with the Rotate tool and the eyes are controlled with Target Helper Objects. To animate the head and eyes you have to work in the group named troll in the Universe section of the Sequencer.

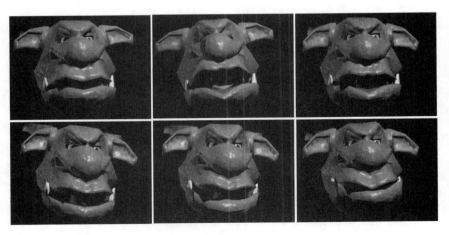

**FIGURE 14.22**    The troll speaking, but with gestures.

Animating the gestures works exactly the same as animating the phonemes we just completed. Move the time tracker to a point in the timeline, adjust the morph target, and repeat. Take a look at the file troll-finished.car, and movie of the same name, to see an example of added gestures. Included in the CD-ROM is a 3-second sound file named hello2.aif that says, "Hello, love, my name is Nigel, it is." When you are up to the challenge, try lip-synching to the longer sound file. The file troll-long.car has the completed 3-second speech by the troll.

ON THE CD

## SUMMARY

Facial expression is where most of the life in an animated character resides, so animating facial expressions and speech with morph targets is one of the most rewarding things you can do. In Carrara animation with morph targets is very easy to do. However, like any animation it takes planning and patience, but the results are truly incredible. Morph targets can be mixed with other forms of animation such as bones. For instance, you can create an entire character with his body controlled by bones and his face with morph targets. In the next chapter you will be introduced to animating with bones.

# ANIMATING A WALK CYCLE WITH BONES

*by Peter MacDougall*

## In This Chapter

- Rigging a Character with Bones and IK
- Animating a Basic Walk Cycle with Bones and Kinematics
- Refining the Walk Cycle
- Happy and Sad Walks

C arrara has all the tools necessary for character animation built right in, and these tools will be the focus of this chapter. In this chapter you will learn how to rig a character with bones, use forward kinematics and inverse kinematics (IK), use the IK Chain tool, apply constraints, work with IK and Target modifiers, and learn how to create a basic walk cycle.

To work through these tutorials you will need a single-mesh two-legged or biped character. You can model your own character or work with the one provided for you. For the model to work with bones in Carrara it has to be a native Vertex Modeler object. Ideally the model should have enough polygon density around joints where the mesh will be distorted the most during movement, yet not so much density that the model takes up too much computer memory and slows down.

When modeling the character, it is important to keep in mind how it will be animated. Since our character will be walking, he is modeled in an upright position with arms extended out, palms down, and slight bends at the elbows, hips, knees, and ankles in what is called the neutral pose. If the character is only going to be sitting, then it would be reasonable to model it sitting rather than modeling it in a standing position.

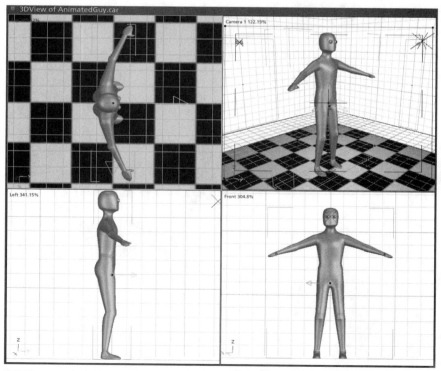

**FIGURE 15.1** The Animated Guy model in Carrara ready for rigging and animating.

A low-poly character is provided for you in the book's CD-ROM in the Chapter 15 folder (see the file AnimatedGuy.car). The character is modeled with just enough polygons so that it will deform well. He also has simple eyes made from grouped vertex spheres and half-spheres that are controlled with a Target Helper object. Eyes are included in this tutorial to show how they can become part of the underlying bone skeleton, and there is a plane primitive to serve as the floor (see Figure 15.1). Incremental files are also provided for each major step in the tutorials and can be found in the same folder with descriptive file names. It may be a good idea to study the incremental files before getting started with the tutorials to help you get oriented. There are also finished movies showing the different parts of the walk cycle.

---

**TUTORIAL 15.1**    **RIGGING A CHARACTER WITH BONES AND IK**

---

### Basic Principles

The process of adding controls to a model to allow it to be animated easily is called *rigging*. Rigging 3D models for animation is an art, as it requires animation controls that are easy to use yet allow you to move the character the way you want. A good rig allows animators to spend their time thinking about the character's movement and not about the tools. A single character may also use multiple rigs. Often an animator will produce variations of the same character with different rigs for specific types of action.

Carrara has two main tools for controlling an animated character: morph targets (covered in the Chapter 14) and bones. Bones are nonrendering helper objects that complement morph targets by allowing you to manipulate the mesh as if it had an internal skeleton. Bones are excellent for animating backbones, limb joints, and other appendages that need to sweep through an arc of movement. Bones can also be used for holding parts of the character in place relative to the other parts, such as holding the eyes in their sockets. Bones are created, assembled, and attached, or *skinned*, to a model in the Assemble room. How much each bone influences the parts of the character, a process known as bone *weighing*, is established and controlled in the Vertex Modeler.

A character rig can be simple, including only the lowest number of bones required to move the character, or very complex, with controls to move the character in a more realistic manner. For this tutorial we will create a basic bone skeleton designed for a walking biped character such as a human.

### Creating Bones

ON THE CD

If you don't have it open already, browse to the file AnimatedGuy.car found in the Chapter 15 folder in the book's CD-ROM and open it in Carrara. This file includes a simple polygonal character with separate eyes made of spheres and half spheres grouped together. The character should be in the middle of the scene in a neutral position: facing front, arms out to his sides but bent slightly in the usual direction of motion, legs shoulder-width apart, and knees slightly bent. This pose was chosen so his joints bend appropriately when they are moved. To properly place the bones you should at least be able to see the Left and Front views in the Document window. To get started, click on the Bone Tool on the right end of the row of object icons at the top of the screen as shown in Figure 15.2.

**FIGURE 15.2** The Bone Tool. Once it is active, you can add bone helper objects to the scene and easily create chains of bones to form a skeleton.

In the Front view click and hold the mouse button down at approximately the middle of the figure, about where the tail bone would be, under the top of the hip. When you click, a bone appears and, with the mouse button held down, you can move the bone into position. If you then hold down the Shift key before you release the mouse button, you can resize the bone. Releasing the mouse button sets the bone position and size.

If you click on the bone again, you can move it. However, if you click anywhere else, you will create another bone linked to the first one. The bone tool will create a new child bone off of any selected bone. This makes it quick and easy to set up branching chains of bones; create a bone, click where the new bone has to go, hold down the mouse button to move the new bone, hold down the Shift key to resize it, and repeat. It is worth experimenting with the bone tool to get the hang of making bone skeletons.

If the first bone is not in the right place, use the Move Tool to move it until it is just inside the back of the figure, roughly where the end of the spinal column would be. The file on the CD-ROM has the first bone at X = 0, Y = −0.85, and Z = 6.75, as shown in Figure 15.3.

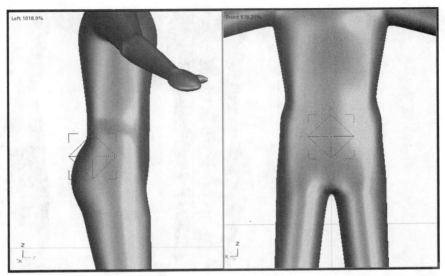

**FIGURE 15.3**    The position of the first bone as seen from the Right and the Front. It will become the parent of all the other bones.

You may need to resize the bone in the Properties tray or with the Scale tool so that it fits comfortably in the figure. Use the Properties tray to set the X coordinate to zero so that it is centered in the figure. Then rename this bone "Hip."

The position of the bone relative to the vertices of the model determines what parts of the model the bone will influence. The bone's size has no effect on bone influence, so it is not necessary that the bone be resized to fit entirely inside the figure. Resizing bones makes it easier to manipulate them. For instance, you may want a big bone in the center of a figure so it is easy to click on, but you may want small bones in the fingers or limbs so that you can keep closely spaced bones from overlapping and being difficult to select.

The Hip bone will be at the top of the bone hierarchy. The Hip will be the parent bone of all the other bones. Moving the Hip bone will move the whole figure. The hip is the typical parent bone, as it represents the center of gravity of the figure. The legs will come off the bottom of the hip, and the spine and arms will come off the top.

With the Hip bone selected, click on the Bone tool again and then click at the top of the left leg about where the hip joint ought to be. Carrara automatically creates a link to the Hip bone and makes this new bone a child of the Hip (see Figure 15.4).

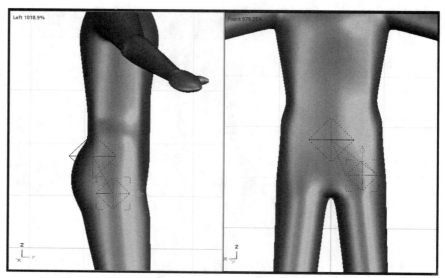

**FIGURE 15.4**    Placement of the second bone at the center of the hip joint.

Move and resize the bone so it fits in the middle of the space of the hip joint. Repeat this process of clicking, moving, and scaling to create joints at the knee, the ankle (where the calf meets the foot), the ball of the foot (just in front of the middle of the foot), and the end of the toes. The knee bone should be slightly forward of the hip and ankle joints to provide a very slight bend that will aid in control of the joint later on. The position of these bones is shown in Figures 15.5 and 15.6. Rename the new bones "HipJoint L," "Knee L," "Ankle L," "Foot," and "Toes L" (the L stands for left). Feel free to use your own nomenclature for the bones.

One of the key points to remember in creating bones is that you should scale and move the bones as you create the hierarchy. If you scale or move a parent, that will also scale and move all of its children. If you decide that the knee is it too big or needs to be moved over, you will have to rescale and move the ankle and foot bones as well.

Once you are satisfied with how the leg is set up, select the Hip bone once more and in the Left view create a bone above the Hip bone around the level of the middle of the abdomen. Click again at the point toward the back of the shoulders. Click once more at the middle of the neck and the base of the head. Finish by selecting the head bone and clicking in the center of the left eye. Using either the Align menu command (Edit > Align) or the Properties tray, change the eye bone's center to be the same as the left eye object. Name this eye bone "Eye L." This bone will be used to hold the eyeball and eyelid objects onto the head. These bones are shown in Figures 15.7 and 15.8.

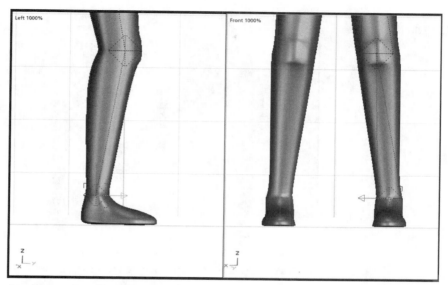

**FIGURE 15.5**    The knee and ankle bones.

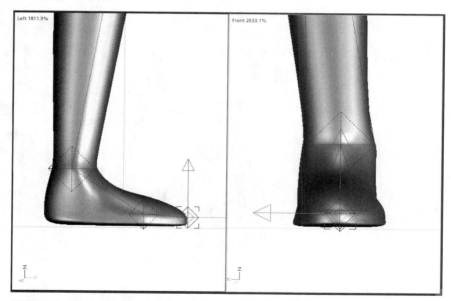

**FIGURE 15.6**    The ankle, foot, and toe bones.

The new back bones should line up along the S-curve of the spine of the character, but inside the character. By using the Left view, these bones should be centered in the *x*-axis, but if they are not, use the Properties tray to set their X coordinates to 0. The new bones are the points

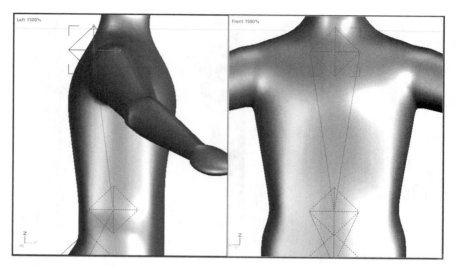

**FIGURE 15.7**    Placement of the abdomen and chest bones.

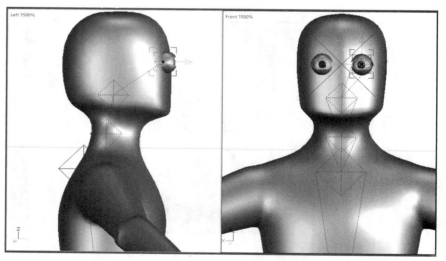

**FIGURE 15.8**    Placement of the neck, head, and eye bones.

that will move the shoulders, abdomen, neck, and head. Name each bone appropriately. Position the bones carefully, following the shape of the back, as this produces a more realistic result than putting the bone straight down the middle of the figure.

In a real human being the spine is made of 24 vertebrae. This character simulates the many vertebrae, using only four bones: the Abdomen, Chest, Neck, and Head bones. When posing the trunk and upper body, it will be necessary to rotate each joint to get a natural pose. For example, when posing the character's head, you will want to rotate both the Neck and Head bones to get the best-looking deformation.

To create the arm bones, select the bone between the shoulders, and use the Bone tool to create the clavicle joint (just to the side and forward of the Chest bone), shoulder joint, and elbow joint, as shown in Figures 15.9 and 15.10.

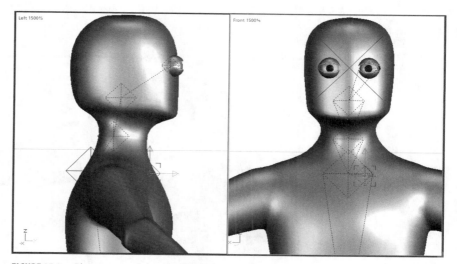

**FIGURE 15.9**    Placement of the clavicle bone.

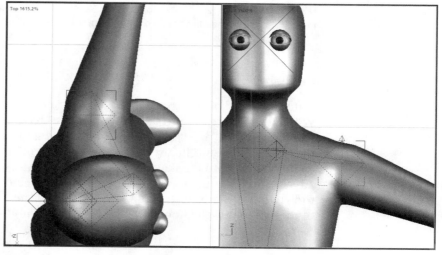

**FIGURE 15.10**    Placement of the shoulder bone.

At this point the elbow bone should be rotated so that its axes of rotation are oriented parallel and perpendicular to the arm as shown in Figure 15.11. The bone for the elbow joint also should be pushed toward the back of the joint, where the bony prominence of the elbow sticks out in a real person. Once the elbow is set, create the wrist, hand, and finger tip bones following down the arm. While creating the arm and hand bones, move and scale them so that they are easy to manage, as in Figure 15.12. Name the bones "Clavicle L," "Shoulder L," "Elbow L," :Wrist L," "Hand L," and "Fingers L" (see the file AnimatedGuy-HalfSkeleton.car).

**ON THE CD**

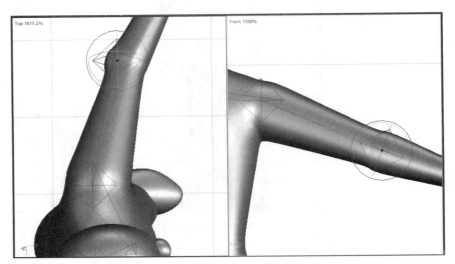

**FIGURE 15.11**   Placement of the elbow bone. Note that the elbow bone is rotated to be in line with the plane of the arm for easy manipulation later.

## Constraints

With half the skeleton created, it is appropriate to set up joint constraints. When Carrara creates the skeleton, the bones have no restriction on their movement. You can stretch them apart or bring them together and rotate them through ±180° in any axis. Although this might be useful for elastic characters, it would make controlling the character with IK difficult. The advantage of setting up the joint constraints when only half of the skeleton is built is that the constraints will be duplicated when we create the other half of the skeleton using the Duplicate with Symmetry command.

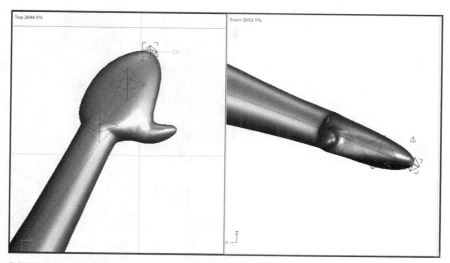

**FIGURE 15.12**    Placement of the wrist, hand, and fingers bones. Note how they inherit the rotation of the elbow.

Aside from adjusting bone influence, creating constraints can be one of the most time-consuming parts of the creating the rig.

Constraints can be used to limit a child object's position and rotation with respect to its parent. For example, an elbow can be made to only bend in one direction and not move side to side or twist unnaturally. Constraint settings are set in the Motion tab of the Properties tray. You can set constraints to None no limits, Lock no movement, 2D Plane movement in only one plane, Slider movement all planes but with limits, Axis movement around one axis, Ball Joint movement around all axes, Shaft rotation around and movement along a single axis, and any custom combination of the above. An example of the Ball Joint Constraint is shown in Figure 15.13.

Because the Ball Joint and Custom constraints allow movement in all three axes, the constraints allow the rotation order to be set. Joint rotation order determines which axis is the main axis of rotation and which axes are for secondary rotation. For example, for a character facing forward (Y direction), the ankle's main rotation is to bring the foot up and down ($x$-axis); the secondary rotation is to bend the foot from side to side pointing the sole toward the other foot or out ($y$-axis); and any twisting motion, making the foot in-toeing or out-toeing, would be along the $z$-axis. Rotation order is important in how the joint moves when using IK and limiting Gimbal lock. Gimbal lock is the undesired situation where rotating a joint along one axis causes its orientation to flip into another

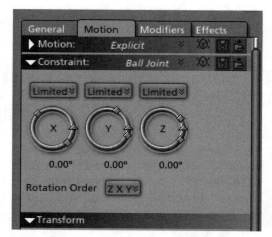

**FIGURE 15.13** The HipJointL bone has a Ball Joint Constraint to allow it to rotate but not to move relative to the Hip bone.

very different orientation. Well-designed constraints and rigs can minimize Gimbal lock.

In this character most of the joints can be properly controlled with the Ball Joint constraint with limited rotation on each axis. If you were animating limbs that can stretch or squash, then the Custom Constraint would allow you to set limits on how the bones can move relative to each other.

A quick way to add the Ball Joint constraint to all the bones in the model is to select the Hip bone and then choose Set IK and Constraints from the Skinning menu as shown in Figure 15.14.

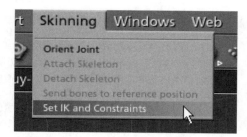

**FIGURE 15.14** You can add a constraint to a bone and all of its child bones quickly using the Set IK and Constraints command.

If you leave the option "Affect children of selected trees" checked, all the bones coming off the Hip (in other words, all the bones), will be changed. Since we want to set up the IK separately, make sure you uncheck the "Change the IK settings" check box. "Set the following constraint on each tree" should be selected by default. From the pull-down menu of constraints choose Ball Joint and set all three axes to Limited and the Joint Rotation order to XZY, as in Figure 15.15.

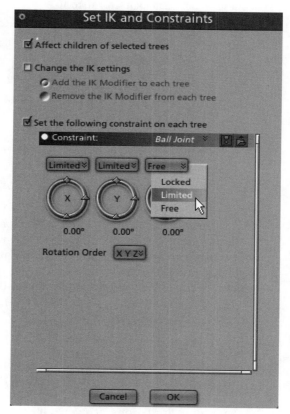

**FIGURE 15.15**    The Set IK and Constraints dialogue box indicating that a Ball Joint constraint with limited rotation on each axis will be added to the Hip and all of its children.

When you click OK for the limited Ball Joint constraint, with the default −90° to +90° rotation, limits for each axis are added to every bone.

These default-limited ball joints are a good start, but each joint needs to be adjusted further for easy realistic motion. It can take some experimenting, but Table 15.1 the values appropriate for this model and skeleton:

**TABLE 15.1    VALUES FOR THE MODEL AND SKELETON**

| BONE | CONSTRAINT TYPE | X ROTATION LIMITS | Y ROTATION LIMITS | Z ROTATION LIMITS | JOINT ROTATION ORDER |
|------|-----------------|-------------------|-------------------|-------------------|----------------------|
| Eye | Lock | | | | |
| Head | Ball Joint | 30 to 30 | 30 to 30 | 45 to 45 | ZYX |
| Neck | Ball Joint | 60 to 45 | 60 to 60 | 60 to 60 | ZYX |
| Chest | Ball Joint | 10 to 10 | 15 to 15 | 15 to 15 | ZYX |
| Clavicle | Ball Joint | Locked | 5 to 30 | 30 to 5 | XZY |
| Shoulder | Ball Joint | 60 to 60 | 100 to 90 | 135 to 60 | XZY |
| Elbow | Ball Joint | 90 to 90 | Locked | 145 to 5 | XZY |
| Wrist | Ball Joint | 90 to 90 | 90 to 90 | 20 to 20 | XZY |
| Hand | Ball Joint | 0 to 30 | 135 to 35 | 30 to 30 | XZY |
| Fingers | Lock | | | | |
| Abdomen | Ball Joint | 90 to 30 | 25 to 25 | 60 to 60 | ZYX |

These values are close to what is typical for a person. Some exaggeration in the joint limits can be helpful in animation, so the limits are somewhat generous.

The clavicle bone could be omitted and the shoulder bone could be allowed limited movement along the *x*-, *y*-, and *z*-axes in addition to rotation using a Custom constraint to simulate the effect of movement at the clavicle and sternum. For this model, at this size, allowing limited movement along the *z*-axis from −1.0 to +1.0, along the *y*-axis from −0.3 to +1.0, and along the *x*-axis from 0 to +1.0 in addition to the previously mentioned rotation limits would allow you to mimic shrugging shoulders. However, this will not provide as good results as having an independent joint for the clavicle.

Once you have set up a series of joints, you can reuse constraints by dragging them to the Constraints tab of the Browser window. This comes in handy if you are building a series of skeletons that need to share the same joint limitations or even for setting up the two halves of a biped model. The Constraints for the Animated Guy skeleton are stored in the Chapter 15 folder in the AG Constraints subfolder on the book's CD-ROM. Copy the AG Constraints folder to the Carrara Presets folder on your hard drive to add that folder to your Browser. This will allow you to drag and drop the Constraints onto the appropriate bones for this part of the tutorial rather than inputting all the limits manually.

**ON THE CD**

However, at the moment you cannot drag and drop a constraint onto an existing constraint and have it be applied. The bone's constraint has to be set to None before you can drag a constraint from the Browser onto the object (see Figure 15.16). If you already set all the joints to a limited

**FIGURE 15.16**    The Animated Guy's joint constraints in the object browser ready to be dragged and dropped onto their respective bones.

ball joint and want to use the prepared constraints in the browser, select the Hip bone, go back to the Skinning menu Set IK and Constraints command, and set all the bones constraints to None. Then drag and drop constraints from the Browser.

If you are having trouble moving any of the joints after applying the constraints, make sure that the constraints are set up as detailed in the table. The wrong rotation order can lock a joint.

### Completing the Skeleton with Duplicate with Symmetry

To get the other leg, arm, and eye bones, we will use the Duplicate with Symmetry command. For the command to work, you have to turn off Use Constraints in the Assemble room either from the View–Use Constraints or from the icon attached to the document window (see Figure 15.17).

Select the Left Hip bone HipJoint L, go to the Edit menu, and select Duplicate with Symmetry. Because the figure is facing Front (+Y), duplicate along the *x*-axis (see Figure 15.18).

When you click OK, the right leg bones should pop into place, with constraints already set. The right side bones will need to be renamed to "HipJoint R," "Knee R," "Ankle R," "Foot R," and "Toes R." Repeat the same process for the arm and the eye by duplicating with symmetry the Shoulder L bone for the arm and duplicating the Eye L bone. Rename these new bones for the right side as well.

Once all of the bones are created, make sure Use Constraints is turned back on. If you ever need to reposition bones, you will need to turn Use Constraints off, move the bones, and turn it back on again. Save your progress so far. Figure 15.19 shows the complete skeleton without the Animated Guy model, and Figure 15.20 shows the bone hierarchy of the complete skeleton.

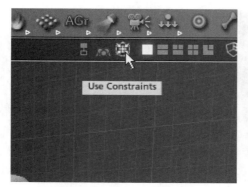

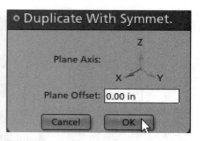

**FIGURE 15.18**    Duplicate with Symmetry dialog box. Select the *x*-axis to mirror the leg, arm, and eye bones from the left side to the right.

**FIGURE 15.17**    The Use Constraints icon is useful for telling Carrara to pay attention to or ignore constraint settings on objects. Use Constraints needs to be turned off for repositioning bones that have had constraints applied.

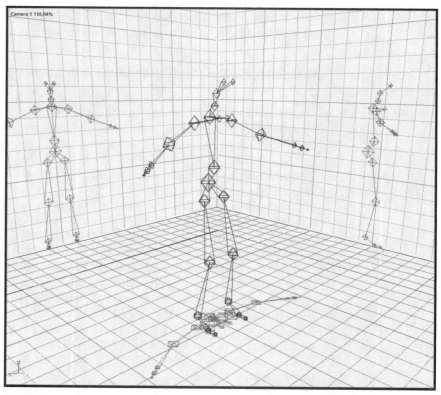

**FIGURE 15.19**    The completed skeleton with the Animated Guy model hidden.

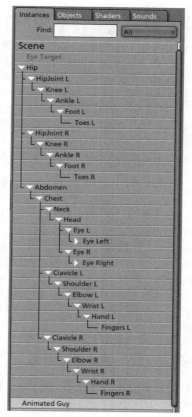

**FIGURE 15.20**   The completed skeleton hierarchy with the Hip bone as the topmost parent and all other bones and bone chains as children.

## Skinning and Attaching Eyes

Once the skeleton is complete, the next step is to attach, or skin, it to the model. Alternatively, you could have finished the skeleton, attached it to the model, and then set up Constraints and IK settings, or even set up IK before skinning. The main point to keep in mind is that once the bones have been skinned by attaching the model to them, the model cannot be edited without first being detached from the skeleton. Another point to note is that if your model is a Spline model or Metaball model, the skinning process will convert it to a vertex model, so make sure you save a copy of your original model before attaching it to its skeleton. Props such as the eyeballs should be kept separate from the skinning process and attached to the bone skeleton afterwards, as we want the bones to hold them in place but not to deform them.

Skinning is a straightforward process. Select the character and then with the Shift key held down, select the Hip bone. This will select all of the skeleton and the model we want to attach it to. Go to the Skinning menu and select the Attach Skeleton item. A dialog box comes up telling you that once you have attached the skeleton, you will permanently lose any animation information for the model. Since this is exactly what we want to do, click OK.

You do not need to check "Only attach selected objects" in this case since we do not have any other objects, such as clothing or jewelry, as children of the character. By default, the skinning process will add any child objects to the bones and those objects would be deformed by the bones just like the parent object would. If we had modeled props and attached them to the model, this check box would allow us to include or exclude them from being skinned.

Now that the model has been attached to the skeleton as a skin, it is time to add the eyeball groups to the eye bones. By excluding the eyeball groups from the skinning process, we ensure that they will keep their shape no matter how the bones deform the model. Select the Eye Left group, which includes the Upper and Lower lids and the eyeball itself, and make it a child of the Eye L bone by dragging and dropping the Eye Left group onto the Eye L bone in the Instances hierarchy. Make the Eye Right group a child of the Eye R bone. After these changes the hierarchy should look like Figure 15.21.

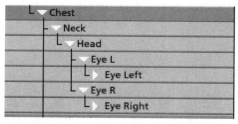

**FIGURE 15.21**   The eyeball props as grouped objects attached to the Eye R and Eye L bones so that they follow the head as it moves.

To test the rig so far select one of the bones in the hierarchy and rotate it. You should test each joint to see how it is deforming (see Figure 15.22).

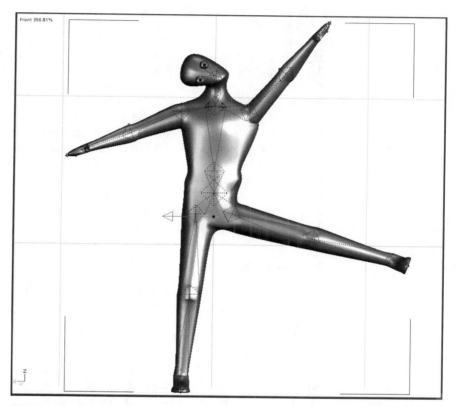

**FIGURE 15.22**   The effect of the initial bone influence settings calculated by Carrara.

The first thing you will notice is that the head, neck, shoulders, and hips are not behaving as you would expect. Carrara does a good job of calculating which bone will affect which vertex and by how much, but in some areas Carrara has trouble coming up with the best solution, especially around limb girdles where a joint bone meets a nonmoving bone (like shoulder to chest, neck to chest, or hip joint to hip) and where several bones are close together but affecting different parts of the figure, such as with fingers or the head.

Once you see how the unrefined skeleton is affecting its attached skin, you can undo all the testing by selecting the character model alone in the hierarchy and then selecting "Return bones to reference position" in the Skinning menu. This will make all the bones jump back to the positions they were in when you skinned the model.

You cannot modify the model while it is skinned to the bones. If you think you need to edit the model so that it deforms better when the bones are moved though their paces, the Skinning menu also allows you to detach the skeleton from the model. Before you detach the skeleton it is important to send all the bones back to their original positions. Select the model and choose "Send bones to reference positions" from the Skinning menu. Once you have detached the model, you can modify it in the Vertex modeler. Once the modifications are done, the skeleton can be reattached to the altered model in the usual way.

For problem areas, where the bone influence is not calculated ideally, it is possible to modify the extent to which individual bones contribute to a vertex's position. Modifications to bone influence are made in the Vertex Modeler. Adjusting bone influence can take some time to get good results, especially if you have a model with a large number of vertices. This is one reason for keeping a model at a relatively low resolution and using Subdivision surfaces for adding smoothing. This model was kept deliberately simple to make the bone weighing manageable (see the file AnimatedGuy-CompleteSkeleton.car).

**ON THE CD**

## Bone Weighing

With the character model selected, jump into the Vertex Modeler. To modify bone influences, select the vertex or vertices you wish to adjust and then click on the Bone tab in the Properties tray as shown in Figure 15.23. The list will display all the bones that Carrara thinks should be influencing the selected vertex's or vertices' position. For all the bones contributing, the total sum of the influences must equal 100%, so increasing the proportionate influence of one bone decreases the influence of others and visa-versa. The Add Bone and Remove Bone menus can add or remove bones from the list of bones influencing a vertex or set of vertices. If you have trouble removing a bone, set its influence to 0%, or if you have only two bones left, set the one you want to keep to 100%.

**ON THE CD**

Note that since bone influence is always based on bone placement, the influences you see calculated for the character and skeleton may differ from this tutorial, as you are likely to have placed your bones in slightly different positions. Some experimentation will be required to find the best set of influences for your character and skeleton. If you need further guidance, the AnimatedGuy-BoneInfluence.car file contains the model and skeleton as set up in the next part of the tutorial.

## Head

The skull makes up most of the head, leaving only the ears, eyelids nose, jowls, and lips as readily deformable skin. It articulates at the top of the

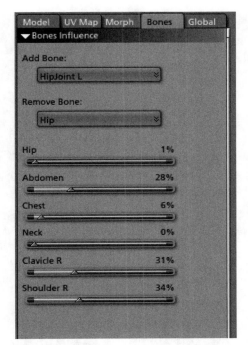

**FIGURE 15.23**    The Bone Influence controls.

spine halfway between the shoulders, roughly just below and behind where the ears ought to be. The Head bone was placed for realistic bending of the head. However, if you rotate the head bone it deforms the head as if it were putty.

In the Vertex Modeler zoom in on the figure so that you can see the character's head in detail. Select all the vertices from the upper ring forming the chin to the top of the skull. Add the three front vertices that make up the lower part of the chin in the lower ring connecting the head and neck. In the Bone tab of the Properties tray, Carrara will show that for these vertices it has calculated that the Chest, Neck, Eye L, and Eye R bones should be influencing their position as shown in Figure 15.24. To get a rigid skull, the other bones need to be removed. Click on the Remove Bone drop down-list and remove all the bones but Head.

If you go back to the Assemble Room and rotate the Head bone, the vertices we selected now follow the bone without deforming. There is still some work to be done on the upper neck, as bending the head forward causes the skin under the chin to fold. In the Vertex Modeler select the row of vertices that make up the lower limit of the skull and jaw but exclude the three vertices making up the bottom of the chin, as shown in Figure 15.25.

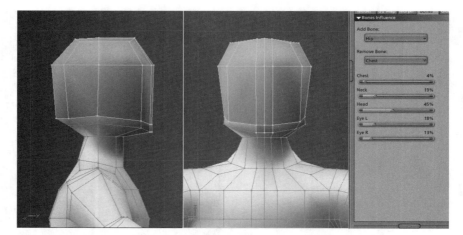

**FIGURE 15.24**   These are the vertices to be assigned exclusively to the Head bone to create a rigid skull (Subdivision Surfaces Smoothing is turned off).

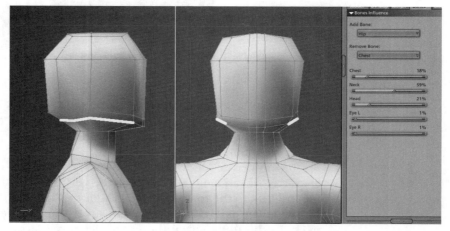

**FIGURE 15.25**   The vertices to select to adjust the influence of the bones at the top of the neck.

Again remove the Chest, Eye L, and Eye R bones, leaving only the Head and Neck bones. Slide the Neck Bone slider to about 20%; the Head Bone slider rises to 80% to compensate. Go back to the Assemble Room to see the result. Now the bottom of the head stretches the neck nicely but does not deform easily.

## Shoulder

Because the chest is a relatively rigid structure, it should not be bent out of shape by the shoulder bones. However, with the default setup, the chest collapses in at the side when the shoulder is rotated down toward the body and puffs out when the shoulder is rotated up. Ideally we would like the vertices in the arm pit to move somewhat with the shoulder but still keep most of the chest stationary. Select the three vertices just under the left armpit, the ones in line with the breast (see Figure 15.26).

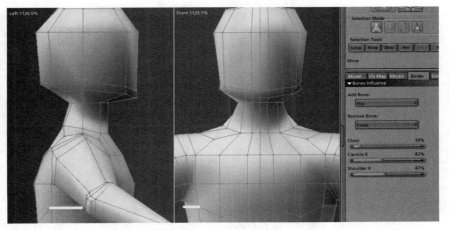

**FIGURE 15.26**    The vertices to select to adjust the influence on the side of the chest.

Add and remove bones until the list includes just the Chest, Clavicle, and Shoulder bones. Increase the influence of the Chest bone and decrease the influence of the Clavicle and Shoulder until the Chest has the majority of the influence (about 70%) and the Shoulder and the Clavicle each have about 15%. Repeat the same steps for the left side.

It is difficult to get a shoulder that moves and deforms exactly like a real shoulder without creating a complicated setup. If your character was going to spend a good deal of time in a pose with an extreme arm position, such as above the head, it would be best to have an alternate character and rig where the figure is modeled with the arms up over the head and the bones are set up to accommodate this position.

## Abdomen

Between the semi-rigid chest and the rigid pelvis is the very flexible abdomen. The default influences that Carrara calculates do a good job but create problems at the hip when the character bends forward. Shifting the influence to favor the Hip bone for the vertices that make up the pelvis will fix this and will help with the legs as well. Select the three vertices on the left side of the hip, as in Figure 15.27.

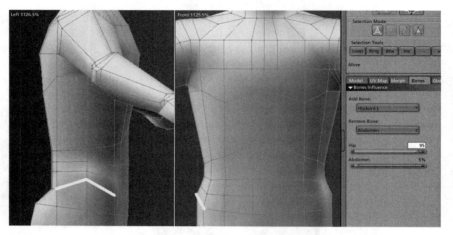

**FIGURE 15.27**   The vertices to select to adjust the influence for the top of the hip.

These vertices correspond to a boney prominence known as the *iliac crest* and are essentially immobile. Remove the HipJoint L and reduce the Abdomen bone influence to only 5%, leaving the Hip with 95%. Repeat these steps for the right side.

From the front view, select the five vertices in the middle, crossing the pelvis, that make up the lowest ring of the three rings of polygons that make up the abdomen. Remove the HipJoint L and R bones and set the Hip bone influence to 70% and the Abdomen to 30%. Select the next five vertices down and set the Hip bone influence to 80% and the Abdomen to 20%. Select the next five vertices down and set the Hip influence to 70% and each HipJoint bone to 15% each. These vertices are shown in Figure 15.28.

Although the abdomen still deforms when the character bends forward, it does not lose all volume and gives the sense of an underlying pelvic bone.

## Hips

With the hip joint coming straight off the Hip bone, raising the leg makes the pelvis and lower abdomen cave in. Select the three vertices on the left side of the hip, in the row below the peaked iliac crest row. Remove the HipJoint L bone, leaving the Hip bone influence at 100%. Repeat for the

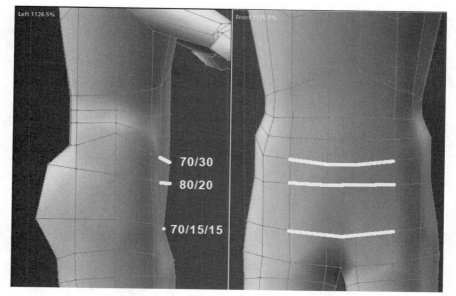

**FIGURE 15.28**　The vertices of the abdomen and pelvis that need adjusting.

right side. Select the next three vertices in a row below that row. Set the Hip influence to 80%, leaving 20% for the HipJoint L bone (see Figure 15.29). Repeat for the right side.

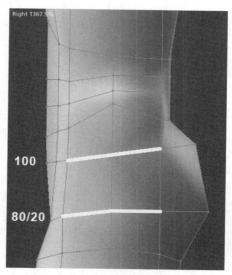

**FIGURE 15.29**　The vertices that need to be adjusted on the side of the hip.

To keep the tutorial simple, the above instructions have included only the most necessary weighing changes to make the figure workable. With some patience and time, setting better bone influences for each vertex can result in a figure that deforms more realistically (see the file AnimatedGuy-BoneInfluenceSet.car).

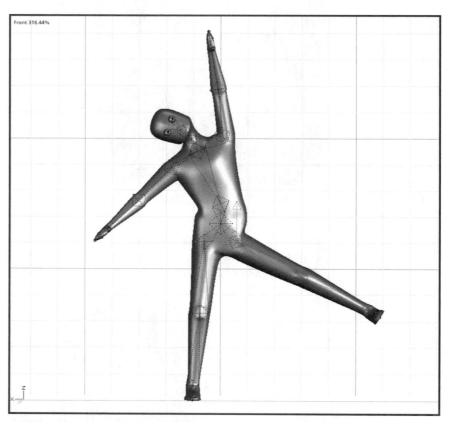

**FIGURE 15.30**   The result of adjusting the bone influence on selected vertices is more natural deformation.

**TUTORIAL 15.2**   **ANIMATING A BASIC WALK CYCLE WITH BONES AND KINEMATICS**

### Forward Kinematics and Inverse Kinematics

Forward kinematics (FK) is the default control method for the skeleton and is in place when the bone skeleton is created. FK means that each child object inherits the movement and rotation of its parent object. For example, if we rotate the shoulder forward, the elbow, wrist, hand, and fingers follow. The movement information is propagated down the hierarchy, in this case the bone skeleton.

Inverse kinematics (IK) is the opposite of FK. In IK the child object determines the position of its parent object. For example, with IK controlling the leg, we can position the foot and have the ankle, knee, and hip bend automatically to compensate. One advantage of IK is that it is possible to fix the position of a child bone, like the foot, and have the rest of the figure move. This makes it much easier to create walk cycles without the foot slipping along the floor. With FK we would have to readjust the hip joint, knee joint, and ankle joint with each frame to get the foot to stay in one place.

IK is added to a skeleton by one of three methods: adding the Inverse Kinematics modifiers to bones individually, adding IK to chains using the Set IK and Constraints item from the Skinning menu, or by using the IK Chain tool.

With Carrara you can mix FK and IK on the same bone chain. You can also toggle tracking an IK target on and off. This allows you to mix tools for posing a limb throughout an animation, using whatever method is easiest for animating the skeleton.

The tracking of the IK modifier can be key framed: you can turn the tracking on and off during an animation. This can be useful for movements like tripping, where an arm might swing freely with a walk but then needs to stay fixed to a support object when the character slips. It can also be handy during the animating process: you can animate part of a body first, without worrying about an attached limb going out of position because of the IK target, then re-enable tracking and animate the limb afterwards.

## IK Chains with Targets

One of the main problems to overcome when animating a walk cycle is preventing the feet from slipping as the body moves forward. To accomplish this task the feet must be pinned with the aid of a target. The best way to accomplish this is with the Create IK Chain tool, as in Figure 15.31.

Select the HipJoint L bone and then click on the IK Chain tool and click on the left Ankle bone. This creates an IK chain from the HipJoint to the Ankle bone, creates a target object—represented as a box with a line extending to the center of the target—at the center of the bone, and adds the IK Terminator modifier to the HipJoint L bone and the IK modifier to the Ankle bone while setting the chain to follow the IK Target box. The IK Target box is too large, so in the Motion tab of the Properties tray, set its overall scale to 20%. The result of these steps is shown in Figure 15.32.

**FIGURE 15.31** The IK Chain tool for creating IK chains with Targets to control them.

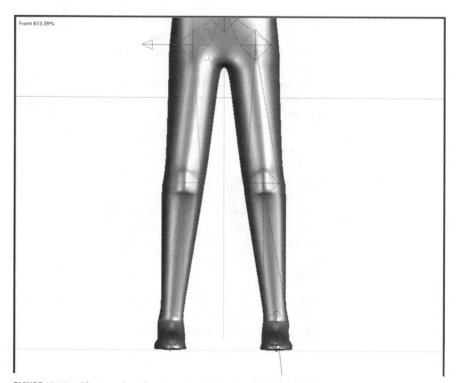

**FIGURE 15.32** The results of using the IK Chain tool after clicking on the left HipJoint and then the left Ankle bone.

Repeat these steps for the right side. Rename the IK Target and IK Target 1 objects something more meaningful such as "IK Target Leg Left" and "IK Target Leg Right." The boxes coming off the IK targets are sometimes off center but the IK targets themselves work just fine.

## IK Chains with No Targets

While the character is walking, the arms and hands will be swinging freely at the character's side. Therefore, it would be easier to animate them without an IK target. The IK Chain tool could be used again on the arms, from the Clavicle bone to the Wrist bone and then the tracking in the IK modifier for the Wrist bone could be turned off. However, it is just as easy to add the IK Terminator modifier to the Clavicle bone as shown in Figure 15.33 and the IK modifier to the wrist as shown in Figure 15.34. This will produce an arm that can be animated by FK from the Clavicle down or by IK from the Wrist up without having the arm locked to a target.

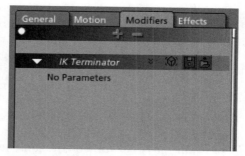

**FIGURE 15.33**   The IK Terminator modifier on the Clavicle bone to stop IK calculations starting at the Wrist from affecting the rest of the body.

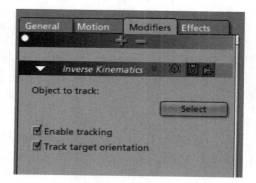

**FIGURE 15.34**   The IK Modifier on the Wrist bone to allow the arm to be positioned by moving the Wrist bone.

An IK chain could also be added to the model, extending from the Hip bone to the Chest or Neck bones. You could then grab the character by the Chest and have the Abdomen contribute to the motion automatically without key framing it as well.

## Testing IK

ON THE CD

With the model's skeleton and controls complete, it should be ready to animate. It is likely, however, that during the process of creating the animation you will find flaws or limitations in the model or the rig that will need to be fixed. It is useful to test the rig, putting it through the rough motions and extremes of motion, before you are several hours into animating a sequence that cannot be completed because of a flaw in the model or the rig (see the file AnimatedGuy-IK.car).

## Character Animation Basics

Animating a character is a challenging task, but starting with a well-designed model and an efficient rig greatly simplifies the process. One of the first tasks a beginning animator must master is the basic walk cycle. Of all possible acts a character can go through, why choose to master walking? Though complex, a basic walk cycle is a manageable animation. It requires and develops an understanding of the basics of motion including weight, timing, force, arcs, readable poses, overlapping motion, and emotion. Walking is a very common action, so an animator will have to make many characters walk. Also, since we are all familiar with how people walk, it is also obvious when the animation is not working. In the end, though, animators must learn to walk before they can run.

The walk cycle will be animated by creating key frames at key positions in the walk cycle. Figure 15.35 shows the character poses through half a walk cycle: contact, weight down, pass position, weight up, contact with the opposite foot. Each position will be created with a series of key frames for each part of the character. Carrara will fill in the in-betweens between key frames.

In a walk cycle most movements trace out arcs. For instance, the body and the limbs will swing, starting and ending at the same spot but following a curved path or arc. This seems obvious for the arms and legs but is also true of the body and head even though they seem to only be moving up and down.

A single walk cycle has a natural beat lasting about a second, so adjust the animation length to 1 second and set the frames per second to 24. You can make these adjustments in the timeline. Also check Snap in the Sequencer so that current time bar jumps to each frame rather than between them. In the preferences (File > Preferences) set the default

**FIGURE 15.35**    Some of the positions in a simple walk cycle.

tweener to Linear. Though the Bezier tweener can be used for the continuous steady motion of a basic walk cycle, the linear tweener works best. Finally, when working on the animation, it is best to have at least two views available—usually front and side views (see Figure 15.36). For reference purposes the completed walk cycles are available as movies and Carrara files in the Chapter 15 folder of the companion CD-ROM.

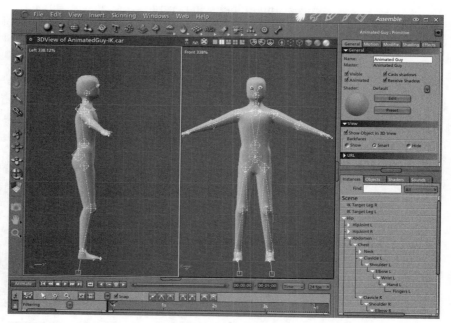

**FIGURE 15.36**    A good animation setup for the Document window, Sequencer, and Properties Tray.

## Walking in Place

### The Hip

The first body part to start animating is the Hip bone. The Hip is the center of gravity and the parent of all the other body parts, so its position affects all the others. Next to be animated will be the legs, as they support the weight. After that the body, the arms, and finally the head, as they compensate for the shifting weight.

Select the Hip bone and then click on the Motion tab of the Properties tray to see its initial values. It is important to follow the values in the Rotation and Move fields, as these will update as the Hip moves. The walk cycle will start and end with the figure in the contact or neutral position, where the hip is neither at its highest or lowest. The neutral pose is a good pose to end with if we want to transition from walking to another activity.

The default pose has the legs nearly straight, so the character is at its tallest. We need to get some more bend in the legs. To do this, move the Hip bone slightly down in the Z direction only. The Hip bone in the default position should be at about 6.75 in the Z direction, so move it down to about 6.5. Since the legs are held in place by the IK target and IK, the hips, knees, and ankles will bend to compensate. Since the cycle will start with the right foot forward, also rotate the hip slightly about 10° on the z-axis so that the right side of the pelvis is ahead of the left side. Moving the Hip bone automatically created a key frame, but since this is a cycle, we need the last key frame to be in the same pose. Set the time to 1 second (frame 24 or the end of the cycle) and set another key frame for the hip position by clicking on the Create Key Frames button. The Create Key Frames button is the small button with a key on it in the Sequencer shown in Figure 15.37.

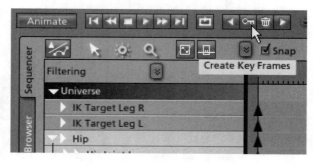

**FIGURE 15.37**   The Create Key Frames button in the Sequencer is useful for creating the same key frame at different parts of the cycle.

Finally, set the current time to halfway through the walk cycle at frame 12 and rotate the hip on the z-axis so that the left side of the hip is now forward the same amount (10°) as the right side was at the first and last key frames.

We also need to get Carrara to set a key frame for the Hip height and only the height at this frame. There are a couple of ways to do this. First, drag the hip up and down, releasing it at the same height as where you started, or set the key frame manually along the z-axis. To set the key frame manually we have to drill down to the z-axis object of the Hip. In the Sequencer there are two white triangular arrowheads beside Hip bone. Click on the rightmost arrow (the one right beside the word *Hip*) to reveal all the attributes that can be key-framed for the Hip. Next, click on the arrow beside Motion Method: Explicit, then the one beside Transform, and finally click on the Position entry to select it. Finally, click on the Create Key Frame button again. This will create a key frame for just the Hip position (see Figure 15.38).

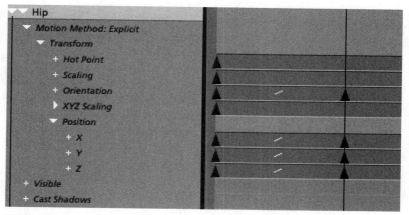

**FIGURE 15.38**    You can set key frames for individual object properties in the Sequencer by opening up the object properties hierarchy.

Next, set the current time to frame 3. Lower the Hip bone slightly more, to a height of about 6.3. Repeat this step at frame 15. These represent the down position, where the leading leg takes the weight of the body before propelling it up and forward.

To set the up position, where the leg is fully extended and the body is at the height of its arc, set the time to frame 9 and move the hip up to 6.75. The feet briefly leave the ground, but we will fix this later by rotating the ankle and foot down to keep contact with the ground. Repeat this step by setting the Hip height to 6.75 at frame 21. These steps have essentially created the contact, down, and up positions for the Hip for the walk cycle. Carrara should automatically create the mid-step Pass position for us from the up and down positions without it having to be created explicitly.

This is a good time to adjust the tweeners between key frames. Although the linear transition from one position to another provides a pretty good result, tweaking the tweeners can refine the walk. The character movement should slow down in and out of the down and up positions, as this is where the character changes direction, and the figure should keep on a steady speed when moving through the contact and pass positions. With this in mind, click on the tweener for the Hip between frames 1 and 3, as shown in Figure 15.39.

**FIGURE 15.39**   The tweener properties are accessed by clicking on the bar between key frames for the object you are working with.

The Properties tray will display the properties of the tweener and show that it is set to Linear with no Ease In-Out. Pull the rightmost marker on the slider, the Ease Out marker, down to 60. This will make a curve that is linear from the start and gradually curves to flat. Change the tweener between frames 12 and 15 the same way.

Select the tweener between frames 9 and 12. Since this transition is from the up position to the contact position, the Linear tweener should be set to gradually accelerate into the new pose. Shift the leftmost marker on the slider, Ease-In, to 40 to produce a gradually rising curve that continues on a straight trajectory at the end. Repeat this change for the tweener between frames 21 and 24.

Finally, the shift from the down to the up position needs to ease in and out, with a linear section in between. Select the tweener between frames 3 and 9 and pull the Ease-In marker up to 30 and the Ease-Out marker to 70 to create a flattened S curve, as in Figure 15.40. Repeat this tweener change for frames 15 to 21.

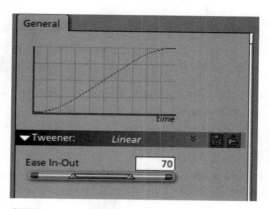

**FIGURE 15.40**    The linear tweener, with Ease-In over the first 30% of the time between key frames and Ease-Out from 70% to 100% of the time, producing a smooth transition between key frames.

This completes the essential movements of the hips. More detail could be added such as rotating the hips around the *y*-axis to make them tip down on the side where the foot lifts or tipping the hip forward for a faster walk or run. This is a good place to save your work (see the file AnimatedGuy-Anim-Hip.car).

ON THE CD

### The Legs

Because the legs are set up with an IK chain and an IK target, it is the IK target movement that will be animated to make the legs move. When positioning the IK targets, we will reference their Hot Points rather than their centers, as the IK calculations use the hot point.

Set the current time to frame 1. Select the IK Target Leg R object. Shift it slightly toward the middle of the body in the −X direction so that it is under the body at about X = 0.45. Then move it forward until the leg is almost straight. The Target hot point (not the center) should be at about Y = 1.50. Finally rotate it around the *x*-axis (to about −135°) so that the foot is at about a right angle to the shin. Set the time to frame 24 and create a key frame for the Target in the same position (see Figure 15.41).

Go back to frame 1 and select the IK Target Leg L object so we can set the left leg positions. Pull the Target back and up slightly so that the left foot is slightly above the floor and the left leg is extended nearly straight. Shift the target slightly toward the body as well so the Target's hot point is approximately at X = −0.45, Y = −3.20, and Z = 0.9. Rotate the target along the *x*-axis so that the foot is touching the ground, with the toes poking through, or about −45°. Go to frame 24 and create a key frame for this target.

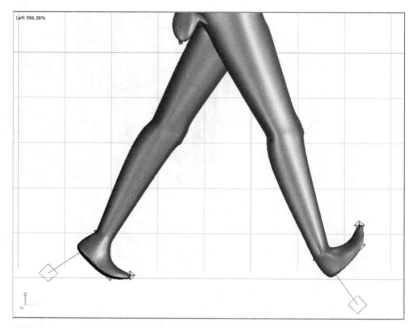

**FIGURE 15.41**   The Leg IK Target positions for frame 1.

Mid-way through the cycle, or at frame 12, the contact positions are mirrored with the left leg forward and the right leg back. There are several ways to do this: you can simply copy the X, Y, and Z position values from one target to the other, you can use the align tool to align one target with the other in the $z$ and $y$ axes and then manually input the other values, or you can just drag the targets to roughly match the right positions. Any way you do it, you want the legs to be roughly mirrored (see Figure 15.41).

Instead of creating the leg positions for the down and up stages of the walk cycle as we did for the hip, we will create the leg positions for when the legs are directly under the body, one bearing all the weight and the other one lifted on its way forward to continue the walk.

Set the time to frame 6. Select the left leg IK Target and move it up so its Z position is about 2. Also move it slightly out from the body so its X position is about −1.00. Finally, rotate the target around the $X$ axis to about −100° so that the foot is dragging behind the leg movement, pointing the foot toward the back.

Next, select the right leg IK Target. Drag it down and back so that the bottom of the foot is against the ground. The X position should be about 0.58, and the ankle should be in line with the buttocks at about −1.00 for the Y position (see Figure 15.42).

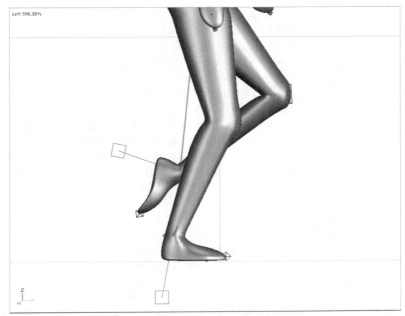

**FIGURE 15.42**    The leg IK Target and leg positions for the Pass position.

Repeat these changes, mirroring the legs, at frame 18. At frame 18, the right leg should be lifted up and moved out, with the right foot bent back, and the left foot should be flat on the ground under the body just in line with the buttocks. The feet still need some work, but if you render the animation so far, the lower half of the body is mostly complete.

Finally, the toes need to be adjusted so that they are not penetrating the floor. Toe position is set by the rotation of the Foot L and Foot R bones. Scrub to frame 1. The toes of the left foot need to be rotated flat with the floor, so select the Foot L bone and rotate it on its x-axis so that the toes are flat on the floor instead of through it (45° in x-axis in the Constraint settings). You can rotate the foot with the Rotate tool or by setting the rotation in the Properties Tray using the Constraint dial for the x-axis in the Motion Tab, Constraint subsection (look back at Figure 15.13; the rings with X, Y, and Z in their centers allow you to set not just the limits of rotation, but the actual rotation at any key frame). Set the time to frame 24 and create a key frame for Foot L. Back up the current time to frame 12 and create another key frame for the foot. Move the time forward to frame 18 and rotate the foot again until the toes are flat to the ground (to 0°). Finally, set the time to frame 6 and rotate the foot so that the toes are pointing backwards, toward where the foot used to be (−30°).

This process needs to be repeated for the right Foot bone. Because the right side is half a cycle out of phase with the left side, start at frame 1 with rotating the foot so the toes point up (about 45°). Move to frame 12 and create a key frame and then create another key frame at frame 24. Frame 6 should have the right foot rotated down (0°) so that the toes are flat, and frame 18 should have the foot rotated even further so that the toes point backwards (−30°).

Although the feet could be slightly improved by adjusting the tweeners, they look good as they are. You could adjust the tweener of the rotation of the foot to make the foot lag even further behind the movements of the leg. This essentially finishes the work on the legs, and you should save your work (see the file AnimatedGuy-Anim-Hip-Legs.car).

**ON THE CD**

### The Body and Head

As the legs move back and forth, the body twists and the arms swing to counterbalance the weight and momentum of the legs. By rotating the abdomen around the z-axis, we can counteract the rotation of the hip and add some momentum to the arms.

Set the time to frame 1 and select the Abdomen bone. Instead of using the rotation tool to rotate the Abdomen, use the Constraint dials in the Properties Tray again. Either click on the small triangle between the two diamonds on the ring with the Z in the middle or click on the number below the ring. This number represents the rotation of the Abdomen with respect to the Hip bone. In contrast, the Rotation numbers in the Transform subsection of the Motion tab represent the rotation with respect to the Universe. Since the Abdomen is a child of the Hip, the animation of the Abdomen is controlled not by the Transform settings but by the Constraint settings. Set the rotation for the abdomen around the z-axis so that the left chest and arm are slightly forward of the middle of the body, to a rotation of about −15.0°. Set the time to frame 12 and set the z-axis rotation to 1° so that the right arm is slightly forward when the left leg is forward. Finally, set the time to frame 24 and again set the relative rotation to −15°.

The rotation of the Abdomen should slow down as it changes direction, so the tweeners need to be adjusted with Ease-In and Ease-Out. Select the Abdomen tweener for frames 1 to 12 and set the Ease-In to 30 and Ease-Out to 70. Repeat this procedure for the tweener between frames 12 and 24.

To keep the Head pointing straight ahead, you can use two techniques: create a Target Helper object for the head to point at like the one used for the eyes or manually set the head and neck rotations. The advantage of using a target is that it automates the process. The disadvantage is that it only controls head rotation, and for some movements you need both head and neck rotation to get a good result, meaning you will still have to manually key-frame the neck movement anyway.

To add a target helper object to the scene go to the Insert menu and choose Target Helper Object from the menu or click on the button shown in Figure 15.43 and rename it "Head Target."

**FIGURE 15.43**    The Target Helper Object button.

Position it in front of the head, at eye level in the middle of the head (about X = 0, Y = 7, and Z = 11). Select the Head bone and Click on the Modifiers tab in the Properties tray. Then add a Point At modifier to the Head bone, type in the Head Target as the object to point toward, and select the $y+$ axis (the Y+ direction is the front of the head and we want the face to point at the object rather than the ear, back of the head, or so on) as the axis to follow (see the file AnimatedGuy-Anim-Hip-Legs-Body.car).

ON THE CD

### The Arms

The arms follow the motion of the chest, which in turn follows the abdomen. The arms swing in arcs back and forth opposite the legs moving back and forth. There is a lot of room for emotion in the arm movement, depending on how the arms are carried. We will animate a basic arm swing that can be modified later for different effects.

Although an IK modifier has been added to the arm from the Clavicle to the Wrist and is handy for certain poses, the swing of the arms are best animated by using FK. With FK, the parent bones, in this case the Clavicle, Shoulder, and Elbow, are animated to position the end of the arm. To do this, it is best to have at least three camera views available: Left, Front, and Top. When you are setting any of the joint rotations, they should all be set in the Constraint Control dials in the Motion tab of the Properties tray and not set in the Rotation fields of the Transform section. All of the rotations will be with respect to the parent bone, as we want the arms to inherit the motion of the Hip and Abdomen.

Set the time to frame 1 and select the Clavicle R bone. The clavicle should be rotated slightly back, approximately −5° around the $z$-axis. Remember to use the Constraint dial. Select the Shoulder R bone and rotate it down on the $y$-axis and back on the $z$-axis so that in the Constraint control, the $x$-axis is −40°, the $y$-axis is −40°, and the $z$-axis is −50°. The Elbow

R bone should already have key frames set with all rotations set to 0°. To maintain a smooth cycle, the bones have to return to their original position at the end of the animation. They each need a key frame at the end of the animation identical to the key frame at frame 1, so set the time to frame 24 and create a key frame for the Clavicle R, Shoulder R, and Elbow R bones.

Next, set the time to frame 12. When a person is walking, the arms move across in front of the body as well as forward. Select the Clavicle R bone again and set the $z$-axis rotation in the Constraint dial to −15°. Select the Shoulder R bone Constraint dial rotations to $x$-axis = −10°, $y$-axis = −60°, and $z$-axis = −5°. Finally, for the Elbow R bone, set the $z$-axis rotation to −30°. Figure 15.44 shows the arm positions for frame 1, where the right arm is in the starting position for the arm swing, fully back, and the left arm is at the end of the swing, fully forward.

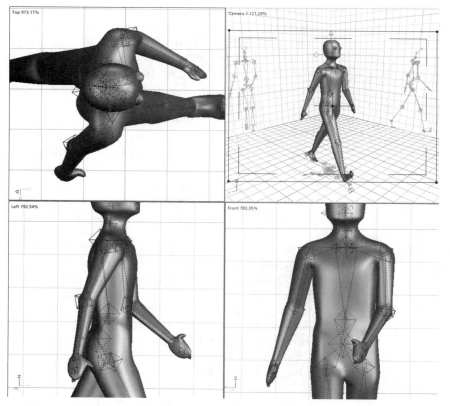

**FIGURE 15.44** The start and end positions for the arm swing as shown by the right arm (start) and left arm (end).

To add some swing to the dangling forearm, set the time to frame 3, select the Shoulder R bone, and set the z-axis rotation to 45°. Select the Elbow R bone and set the z-axis rotation in the Constraint dial to 0°. This will delay the forearm behind the upper arm from moving forward, giving a sense of weight and momentum. Next go to frame 15 and select the Shoulder R bone again. Set the z-axis rotation to 0°. Select the Elbow R bone and set its z-axis rotation to −30°.

The arms change direction and speed around the Hip down positions at frames 3 and 15. Some Ease-In and Ease-Out before and after each of these key frames would add smoothness to the motion. Select the Shoulder R bone tweener for frames 1 to 3. Drag the Ease-Out marker down to 70%. Select the tweeener for frames 3 to 12 and set the Ease-In to 30%. Repeat the process for frames 12 to 15, setting the Ease-Out to 90%, and 15 to 24 where the Ease-In should be about 10%. Then repeat the same tweener changes for the Elbow R bone. The Tweener Iterator plug-in by Michael Gochoco (found at *www.associatedfx.com/plugins.html* or in the Yahoo Groups Carrara mailing list file area) can make this procedure much easier by allowing you to change several tweeners at once. It inserts itself as an option in the Sequencer on the Hides-Displays Tracks drop-down list under the Play button.

Finally, repeat the previous steps for the left arm, keeping in mind that the arm positions are half a cycle out of phase: the left arm starts forward at frame 1, is back at frame 12, and is forward again at frame 24. Frame 3 for the left arm is the same as frame 15 for the right and vice versa. This completes the basic walk and is an excellent time to save your work and do a test render (see the file AnimatedGuy-Anim-Hip-Legs-Body-Arms.car).

**ON THE CD**

## Repeating the Walk Cycle

After all the work we put into the previous exercise, all we have is a 1-second, or 24-frame, animation of a character walking in place. Don't feel too bad, because it is typical to spend days on just a few seconds of animation. However, you can copy the key frames created thus far and repeat the walk cycle to make the character walk in place for as long as you need. For instance, if you want to repeat the walk cycle a couple times, extend the animation time to 3 seconds, or 72 frames. Next, select all the key frames for all of the bones and IK targets, including the key frames at time 0. To select all the key frames you will have to expand the bones groups in the Sequencer so that each bone and its key frames are visible and draw a marquee box around the key frames. When selected, the key frames turn yellow. Then, from the Animation Options drop-down menu in the Sequencer, choose Repeat (see Figure 15.45). In the Repeat dialog box enter 2, leave the Delay before Repeat at 00:00:00, and press OK (see

Figure 15.46). Notice the new key frames in the timeline. Now play the animation to see the character walk through three walk cycles (see the file AnimatedGuy-Anim-RepeatCycle.car).

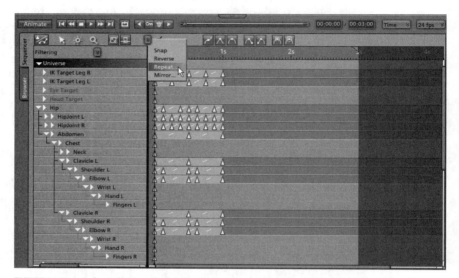

**FIGURE 15.45**   Select the key frames you want to repeat and then choose repeat from the Sequencer menu.

**FIGURE 15.46**   Enter the number of times to repeat the walk cycle.

## Moving while Walking

Walking in place is a good way to learn to create a walk cycle, but the purpose of creating a walk cycle is to move. Next we will explore two methods (but by no means the only methods) to move the character forward, with two variations of the second method. The first method is to manually key-frame each leg and hip cycle as the character moves forward. This method gets good results but can be very time consuming. The second method is to group the bones and IK Targets and move the entire group as the walk cycle repeats. The first variation of the grouped method is to allow the feet to slip during the walk cycle, and the other variation is to pin the feet to the ground using a second IK modifier and Target on that Ankle bone. The feet slip in the first variation of method 2 because there is nothing to pin them down as the character moves forward. However, foot slippage can be minimized by carefully timing the distance the character walks against the walk cycle.

### Method 1

To prevent the feet from slipping during the walk cycle you will have to key-frame each step, moving the hip joint bones and feet IK targets as needed for each cycle. The process is much the same as animating a walk-in-place sequence, except that when setting the first two key frames for the Hip, one for each contact position, the Hip is moved forward one stride length for the next key frame. Then you animate the rest of the hip motion and leg motion. The animation cycle of the Abdomen and its children, including the head and arms, does not have to be key-framed since they are not controlled by separate targets. Instead, the key frames for the Abdomen and its children can be repeated using the Repeat function as described in the repeating the walk cycle section.

### Method 2: Variation 1

If the feet are not going to be seen clearly or are not seen at all in the animation, then some slippage is not a problem, and you can simply group the bones and targets and then move the group forward.

First, select all of the bones and IK targets and group them (see Figure 15.47). Then move back to frame 1 and position the group at the starting point of the walk. Next, move to the last frame and move the group to the end of the walk. Reset to frame 1 and play the animation. You should see the character move forward as he walks, although he may walk a bit funny because the timing is off (see Figure 15.48).

You can time the steps to the distance covered by experimenting with the starting and ending points. However, since the foot positions are controlled to some degree by the Ease-In and Ease-Out of tweeners, the feet will still slip as the group is moved forward at constant velocity. To minimize the slip even more use the Tweener Curve Editor plug-in to provide better control and to create a tweener where the forward movement slows mid-stride to match the leg movements better (see the file Animated-Guy-Anim-MoveGroup.car).

**ON THE CD**

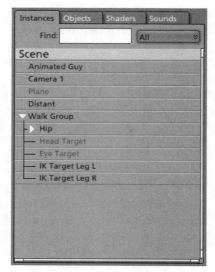

**FIGURE 15.47** Group the bones and targets.

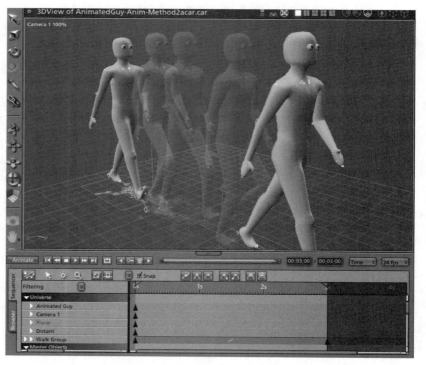

**FIGURE 15.48** Once the grouping is done, reset to frame 1 and position the group at the starting point. Then move to the last frame and position the group at the end of the walk.

**Method 2: Variation 2**

Finally, it is possible to repeat the walk cycle and pin the feet to the ground on each step. To do this, you need to add a second Target Helper Object for the Ankle bones to follow. This second Target is kept separate from the grouped skeleton and Leg IK Targets. A second IK modifier is added to the Ankle bone and is then set to track the new target as shown in Figure 15.49.

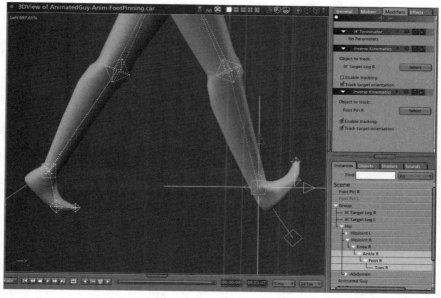

**FIGURE 15.49**   Two stacked IK Modifiers on the Ankle allow you to switch between one target and another for cycling the walk and pinning the feet to the ground.

When the foot contacts the ground, the new Target is aligned with the Ankle and the original IK Target. The Ankle then has the tracking of the original IK Target disabled and tracking for the new Target is enabled. Once the foot leaves the ground again, tracking is re-enabled for the original IK Target and disabled for the new Target. The group is then moved forward one stride length. The new Target is then aligned to the position of the original IK Target for the next time that foot contacts the ground. This process is repeated for each foot and each step. For example, in this walk cycle, at frame 1 when the right foot contacts the ground, the original IK target is disabled in the Ankle Modifier list in the Properties tray and the new Target is enabled. At frame 12 this is reversed. The original target is enabled and the new target is disabled. Frame 24 is then like frame 1. In essence, the IK Target grouped with the skeleton controls the leg position while the leg is lifted in the air, and the Target that is separate from the group controls the leg when it is in contact with the ground. To see this animation method in action take a look at AnimatedGuy-Anim-FootPin.car.

Any way you look at it, it is going to take time and experimenting to get accurate motion over distance. If you have gotten this far in this tutorial, pat yourself on the back. Congratulations on learning fundamental animation techniques for creating a basic walk cycle. The following are some quick tips on refining the walk cycle.

## Refining the Walk Cycle

The previous exercise creates a very neutral walk with little or no personality and emotion. However, it is a good starting point to create a variety of different walks. To make the walk less stiff, some tilt, or rotation around the y-axis, could be added to the hips so that they rotate slightly up on the side of the leg that is supporting the figure's weight. Then the chest could tilt in compensation, tilting down on the same side. The head could then tilt slightly as well. Changing the position of the key frames, either advancing or delaying them by even a frame or two can add some "pop" to the walk. Adjusting the tweeners and using the Bezier tweener for finer control can also smooth or sharpen the movement. Finally, altering the length of the stride, the distance of the arm swing, the posture of the spine, and the duration of the cycle will add feeling and personality to the walk.

## Happy and Sad Walks

From the neutral walk it is easy to edit the body positions at the key frames to change the whole feel of the walk. The following recipes will create a happy walk or a sad walk.

For an energetic or happy walk, try this:

- Make the hip rise higher in the Up position.
- Rotate the hip further forward with each leg swing.
- Lift the legs higher in the Pass position.
- Tilt the abdomen back to thrust the chest forward.
- Bend the neck forward but tilt the head up so that the chin is pointing up and out.
- Rotate the shoulders and clavicle further forward and backward.
- Swing the arms higher and make the arms cross further over the front of the chest.

Take a look at the Carrara file AnimatedGuy-Anim-HappyWalk.car or the Quicktime movie happy-walk.mov in the Chapter 15 folder in the CD-ROM (see Figure 15.50).

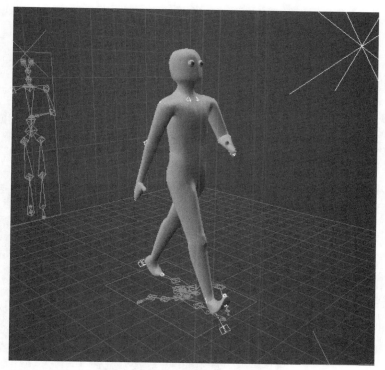

**FIGURE 15.50**    A happy walk has distinct characteristics.

For a lethargic or sad walk try this:

- Drop the hip slightly lower overall and decrease the amount it moves up and down.
- Decrease the hip swing (rotation) as the legs move.
- Make the stride length of each step shorter.
- Barely lift the feet off the ground in the Pass position.
- Tilt the abdomen, chest, neck, and head slightly forward to make the figure hunched and looking at the ground.
- Make the arms swing less, to the point where they are barely drifting back and forth.
- Drag all the key frames out so that a cycle takes two seconds rather than one to slow the pace.

ON THE CD

Open and study the Carrara file AnimatedGuy-Anim-SadWalk.car or take a look at the Quicktime move sad-walk.mov (see Figure 15.51).

If you are interested in learning more about walk cycles, *The Animator's Survival Kit* by Richard Williams covers various techniques to create different types of walk cycles such as female, male, or child walks and

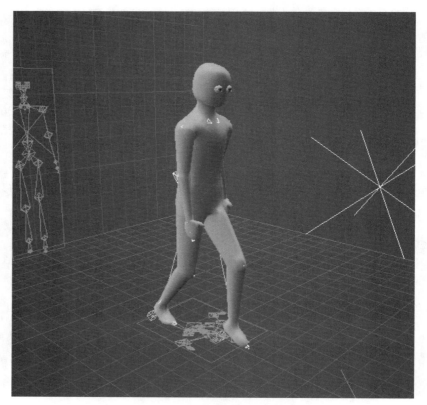

**FIGURE 15.51** A sad walk also has distinct characteristics.

even how to make a figure run. However, no book can replace careful observation of the subtle differences in how people walk, experience, and simply practicing the craft of animation.

## SUMMARY

Animation makes it possible to create a character that appears to feel, think, and move. Though learning to animate takes time, Carrara has all of the tools for creating simple or complex character animation. Remember, the steps are model the character, rig the character with bones, apply constraints to the bones, apply IK controls to bone chains to control their position, and finally animate the character according to the fundamental principles of character animation. Don't forget that animation is also fun, so take some time to enjoy your work and get inspiration from the accomplishments of other animators.

# ADVANCED RENDERING

# ADVANCED RENDERING WITH CARRARA

## In This Chapter

- Global Illumination—Indirect Lighting and Skylight
- High Dynamic Range Image (HDRI)
- Caustics
- Motion Blur
- Non-Photorealistic Render (NPR)

One of Carrara's best features is its state-of-the-art render engine. Coupled with powerful modeling and texturing tools, the render engine allows you to create ultra-realistic images or painterly and abstract images. In Carrara the rendering options are Draft, Photorealistic, and Non-Photorealistic render engines. The Photorealistic render engine provides tools for raytracing, lighting, and rendering scenes with global illumination, caustics, and HDRI files to create ultra-realistic lighting. The Non-Photorealistic render engine creates painterly and abstract renders.

Chapter 8 covered the Render room and basic rendering techniques. This chapter will introduce the advanced rendering features in Carrara. As you will soon discover, using the power of Carrara's render engine is deceptively easy. Eovia has neatly tucked all of the highly technical aspects of global illumination, caustics, and HDRI behind a friendly user interface. As a result, using all of the power behind the render engine is more a matter of imagination and creativity than a technical exercise (see Figure 16.1).

**FIGURE 16.1**   With Carrara's render engines you can easily create exceptionally realistic images (Mike Moir).

## TUTORIAL 16.1    GLOBAL ILLUMINATION—INDIRECT LIGHTING AND SKYLIGHT

Carrara has two global illumination tools: Sky Light and Indirect Lighting. These tools produce the best lighting results when they are used together, but they can also be used separately. The Sky Light feature simulates outdoor indirect sunlight that is scattered in the atmosphere. The scattered sunlight creates a soft glow that appears to come from all directions. This scattered sunlight will fill in shaded areas with a soft light and cast an overall light in the scene, as shown in Figure 16.2.

**FIGURE 16.2**    A scene lit with the Skylight and HDRI (Rich Friedman).

Another method of global illumination available in Carrara is Indirect Lighting, which simulates the diffused lighting effects that we see in the real world. For example, much of the light we see in a room comes from indirect lighting. In other words, when light comes into the room, from a lamp or through a window, the light bounces off walls, the ceiling, and furniture. The result is that the bounced light illuminates the parts of the room that are not in the direct path of the light source, as shown in Figure 16.3.

**FIGURE 16.3**    A scene lit with Indirect Lighting (Andrew Vaudin).

Although the lighting effects created by global illumination are great, they will increase render time—so use global illumination carefully. If using standard lights produces the lighting effects you need, you might consider saving the global illumination tools for another time. Global illumination works with all of the Carrara lights, including the Sun Light of the Sky and Realistic Sky. Global illumination also works with the HDRI lighting system to create ultra-realistic lighting.

## Indirect Lighting

Now that we know what global illumination is, let's work through the steps in lighting and rendering a scene with indirect lighting. We'll use the airplane modeled in Chapter 10 as the focus of this tutorial. To save you the time of having to build a scene, open the file global-light.car found in the Chapter 16 folder on the accompanying CD-ROM.

ON THE CD

Notice that the airplane, the main camera, the light, and the background are already set up for you, as shown in Figure 16.4. Also, the Production Frame is turned on so we can see what part of the scene will be included in the final render. The only thing missing is the lighting effects. In this tutorial, we'll simulate the effects of the midday sun. Being very intense, the midday sun creates areas of bright lighting and areas of strong shadows, but even under these harsh conditions some of the sunlight will bounce and light the shadow areas. This scene uses a photograph of an airport as a background. Because the photograph is in the background, the model of the airplane cannot cast a shadow, which would look very strange when rendered. To simulate a shadow cast by the airplane onto the tarmac, a Shadow Catcher object is being used. In this case it is a plane primitive that has the Shadow Catcher shader applied. As you will see, the plane primitive will also help with our global illumination exercise.

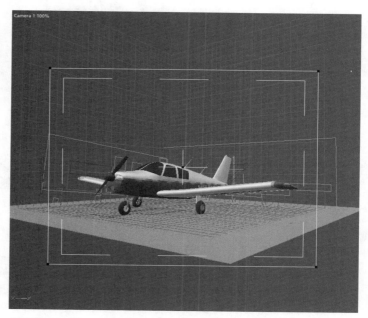

**FIGURE 16.4**    The scene for this tutorial is already set up for you.

The first thing we'll do is create a quick render with normal raytraced lighting. We'll use this image as a control to see the difference between raytracing and raytracing with global illumination. Everything is ready for this first render. Notice that in the Rendering tab of the Properties tray Full Raytracing is checked and that appropriate options for this render are enabled, as shown in Figure 16.5. If you click on the Output tab, the resolution is set at 72 dpi and the render size is modest to keep render times down as we experiment.

**FIGURE 16.5**   The render settings for the first test render.

Click once on the Render button in the Sequencer tray or press Ctrl/Command-R to begin the rendering process. Notice that in the render with no global illumination there are very dark areas around and under the airplane where no light has reached. Without global illumination, fill lights would be used to simulate the effects of indirect lighting. Leave the control render open so we can refer to it later (see Figure 16.6).

**FIGURE 16.6**    With only a single light shining from above, the underside of the aircraft is in complete darkness, which does not occur in real-world lighting.

To simulate more realistic lighting, check the Indirect Lighting option in the Global Illumination section of the Properties tray. Leave the settings at default and render once more. Notice that compared to the first render, in this render the underside of the wings and the underside of the fuselage are lit by reflected light and that overall the lighting is more realistic. This realistic lighting occurs because the light in the scene is bouncing off the surfaces of the airplane and the plane primitive under the airplane (even though we can't see it) (see Figure 16.7).

### Skylight

Next let's try lighting a scene using the global illumination Skylight. Open the file skylight.car found in the Chapter 16 folder in the accompanying CD-ROM. This scene is similar to the indirect lighting scene except that the tarmac is represented by an infinite plane textured to match the background photograph. We are using a textured infinite plane because the skylight cannot cast shadows onto a shadow catcher object. However, Digital Carvers Guild's Shader Plus features the GI Shadow Catcher plug-in that will allow both the Skylight and HDRI lighting to cast shadows on the shadow catcher.

**FIGURE 16.7**  With indirect lighting enabled, light bounces off the surfaces of the airplane and off the plane primitive to light the underside of the airplane more realistically.

As with the indirect lighting tutorial, press Ctrl/Command-R to render the scene and generate a control image. Notice that except for the background everything is dark. At this point there are no lights in the scene (see Figure 16.8a). Now click on the Scene object in the Instances tab of the Properties tray. In the Background section choose Color and leave the default gray. In the Render room check the Skylight option, bump up the Intensity to about 225%, and render. In this new render the scene is completely lit with diffuse lighting and soft shadows, even though there are no lights in the scene (see Figure 16.8b). The Skylight is lighting the scene using the color from the Background.

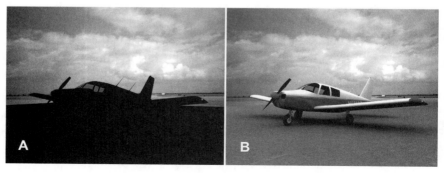

**FIGURE 16.8**  (a) With no lights in the scene, the resulting image is dark. (b) The scene lit only with the Skylight.

If you change the color of the Background, the Skylight will change accordingly. You may also use the Realistic Sky and Sky procedurals to light scenes. The Skylight can also be combined with scene lights and the Sunlight to produce varied results. More important, as we will see in the next tutorial, the Skylight really shines when it is combined with an HDRI file to achieve ultra-realistic lighting.

### Global Illumination Tips

Here are some tips to help you get the results you want with Indirect Lighting:

- To increase the quality of the render, disable Interpolation. Interpolation, enabled by default, speeds the render time at the expense of image quality.
- If you notice any odd artifacts in areas where objects touch or intersect, enable Improved Edges. This will allow Carrara to perform additional calculations to create higher-quality renders. Enabling Improved Edges also increases the render time.
- Change the Lighting Quality from Fast to Good or a higher setting. Usually Fast or Good is all you need to see good results.
- In the Accuracy settings decrease the pixel value to refine the results. The smaller the pixel value, the better the results.
- Increasing the Photon Count will allow Carrara to increase the fidelity of the lighting effects. In other words, a higher Photon Count will allow Carrara to render more precise lighting effects.
- Try using the Show Photon Map feature to gauge where the indirect lighting will fall before creating full Indirect Lighting renders.

To improve performance when using global illumination, optimize the lighting properties by adjusting them to default or lower settings and compensate by increasing the Ambient Light and lowering the shadow intensity. This will produce some of the effects of indirect lighting but renders much faster.

Carrara 5 offers Ambient Occlusion, which is a faster, but not as good, alternative to full indirect lighting. Ambient Occlusion works in conjunction with high Ambient Light settings to approximate indirect lighting. Ambient Occlusion works best for indoor lighting.

**TUTORIAL 16.2**    **HIGH DYNAMIC RANGE IMAGE (HDRI)**

For the novice, HDRI provides a quick and simple way to create realistic illumination in a 3D scene because there is no need to set up 3D lights. For the advanced CG artist, HDRI provides a powerful tool that can be used to create ultra-realistic lighting and facilitate compositing 3D objects into live action film or still images. HDRI is the blend of two separate but complementary concepts. The first is image-based lighting (IBL) and the second is high dynamic range (HDR). Most of the tools and literature about HDR previously available to CG artists are highly technical and intimidating. However, Carrara provides a simple and effective way to apply these complex lighting techniques into your 3D scenes. HDRI will forever change the way you look at illuminating 3D scenes.

Although Carrara does a great job of hiding all of the technical aspects of HDRI behind an easy-to-use interface, it is a good idea to have a basic understanding of what HDRI is and how it works. Therefore, let's review some of the common HDRI terminology and concepts.

**High Dynamic Range (HDR):** The human eye can see many more colors and levels of light than computers, digital cameras, or even the best films can capture. Typically, computers display each color channel (Red, Green, and Blue) as a number from 0 to 255. Levels brighter than 255 are shown as 255, and levels dimmer than zero are shown as zero. HDR is a technique that allows for a larger range of color levels in each channel.

**Image-Based Lighting (IBL):** This is a technique that allows one to illuminate scenes with light captured from a real or previously rendered scene by a light probe. This concept is based on pioneering work done by Paul Debevec and Greg Ward Larson. IBL allows the artist to achieve amazing accuracy in the creation and reproduction of modeled objects. This technique is especially useful in compositing CG objects into real-world scenes. Equally important, it can remove much of the tedious work involved in setting up computer-based lighting systems.

**High Dynamic Range Imaging (HDRI):** This is the technique of expanding the camera's ability to record light by combining a bracketed series of low dynamic range (8-bit) images into one high dynamic range (32-bit) image, as well as the application of these images in IBL.

**Light Probe:** This technique makes use of an omni-directional HDR photograph of a scene, with the important distinction that the pixel values are directly proportional to the scene in the real world. The photo is typically captured with a fisheye lens or a close-up of the reflection from a mirrored ball and assembled in an application such as HDRShop.

**HDR Files:** This is a 32-bit high dynamic range file format designed by Greg Ward for use with the Radiance Lighting Simulation and Rendering System. Carrara uses HDR files in the Latitude Longitude format.

Now that we know a little about the background of HDRI let's light a scene using a light probe provided by Dosch Design (*www.doschdesign.com*). In this tutorial, we'll revisit the airplane scene we illuminated earlier in this chapter, except that this time we'll use an HDRI file to light the scene. The airplane scene is named hdri.car and the light probe is named DH004LL.hdr. Both files are located in the Chapter 16 folder of the accompanying CD-ROM.

With the file hdri.car open, click on the Scene Properties in the Properties tray, open the menu labeled None in the Background settings, and select HDRI from the menu (see Figure 16.9). Next, click the on the button in the File section and browse to the DH004LL.hdr file to load it. Make sure that the Flip Vertical option is checked.

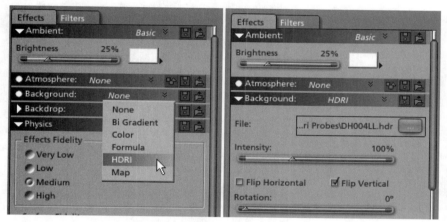

**FIGURE 16.9**    The HDRI settings in the Properties tray.

Now, jump into the Render room and in the Global Illumination section of the Properties tray, check Sky Light. Set the Sky Light Intensity to about 100%. In order for an HDRI light probe to light a scene, the Sky Light must be enabled. Next, click the Render button and watch as the scene is rendered with the HDRI light probe as the light source (see Figure 16.10).

HDRI files may be combined with different backgrounds. Go to the Assemble room and in the Instances tab of the Properties tray select the object tarma1, and in the General section of the Properties tray uncheck Visible to hide it. Select the object tarmac 2 and make it visible. We are switching tarmacs because tarmac 2 works better with the background we are about to load. Next, click on the Scene in the Instances tab and in

**FIGURE 16.10**    The HDRI file lighting the scene and providing a background.

ON THE CD

the Backdrop section load the file airport.jpg. Render that file once more. Notice that while the file is still rendered with the HDRI file, the background is now the airport background, as in Figure 16.11.

**FIGURE 16.11**    HDRI files may be used to light a scene, but not necessarily as backgrounds.

The information used to light the scene is coming directly from the HDRI file loaded in the Background. If you were to change the HDRI file, you would get a different result. Notice that the scene lighting has a volumetric feel to it, as light is coming from all directions. The reflections in the airplane skin and canopy enhance the realism of the entire scene, and the indirect lighting adds the final touch.

### HDRI Tips

- Test the HDRI file by placing a mirrored ball in the center of your scene. Render from several angles. Performing this test will reveal any problems with the HDRI file.
- If you are experiencing problems with the HDRI file, make sure you are using an HDRI file that is oriented in the Latitude Longitude direction. If you are in doubt, use HDR Shop or Photosphere to correct any problems.
- Just a touch of reflection in the objects in the scene, even a small percentage, can boost the interaction of the HDRI with the objects in the scene.
- If you have strange artifacts in the HDRI render and all if else fails, disable Interpolate in the Global Illumination section in the Properties tray.
- If you want to use an HDRI light probe for lighting a scene, but not for a background, load a color or image in Backdrop.

| TUTORIAL 16.3 | CAUSTICS |
|---|---|

*Caustics* is a general term used to describe the patterns of highlights and reflections that are created as light passes through a transparent object or bounces off a surface. Typical examples of caustics can be seen in the patterns of light created on a tabletop as light is reflected off silverware or the light patterns at the bottom of a pool on a sunny day (see Figure 16.12).

Caustics add yet another element of realism, but as with global illumination, caustics lighting effects come at the price of longer render times. In this tutorial we'll create a short animation of a submarine, simulating underwater caustics.

**ON THE CD**

Open the file caustics.car in the Chapter 16 folder on the accompanying CD-ROM. The scene has been set up for you; the only things missing are the caustics effects. The goal of this tutorial is to create an animation of a submarine passing by the camera in an underwater environment. To complete the underwater simulation, we'll add caustics light patterns on the top part of the submarine and on the seafloor. All objects in this scene are kept purposely simple to speed render times.

**FIGURE 16.12**   Caustics are created when light is focused as it passes through a transparent object or is reflected off a shiny object.

First, play the animation in the Assemble room to see the action. Click the Play button in the Sequencer tray and watch as the submarine goes by. Next, jump into the Render room and render the animation; just click the Render button in the Sequencer tray. Because there are no special effects, the animation is rendered quickly. Though a bit dark, the animation looks good (see Figure 16.13). Let's add caustics to make it look even better. Jump back out to the Assemble room, open the Shaders tab in the Properties tray, and double-click on the water shader; this will take you into the Texture room.

Let's take a moment to inspect the shader for the water because it is the object that will create the wave patterns as the light passes through it. A Waves procedural is used in the bump channels to simulate wave crests and troughs on the top Plane primitive. Note that the waves procedural is animated; if you move the scrubber back and forth, you will see the Completion value move back and forth. The Scale value for the waves can be increased or decreased to help define the size of the caustics effect. The

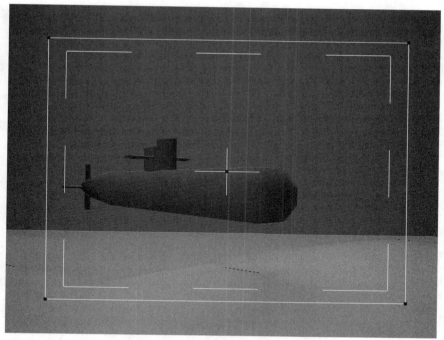

**FIGURE 16.13**   Though the animation looks good, it can look a lot better with caustics enabled.

Transparency channel has a bright blue color to give the water its color, and at the same time the brightness of the color gives the water its transparency level. Finally, in the Refraction channel is an Index of Refraction preset for water that will simulate the way water refracts light. Together, these shader settings will create convincing underwater lighting effects once Caustics has been enabled (see Figure 16.14).

This brings us to the last step in our underwater animation. Jump into the Render room and bring the Rendering tab in the Properties tray forward. Below the Global Illumination settings you will see the Caustics settings. Check the Caustics box to enable it and set the Photon Count to about 180,000. The Output tab should be set to a 12-frames-per-second movie, Cam2 should be selected, and the resolution should be 72 dpi at 320 pixels in width, as in Figure 16.15. These settings will help keep the render time short. All that is left to do is click the Render button in the Sequencer tray and wait a few minutes.

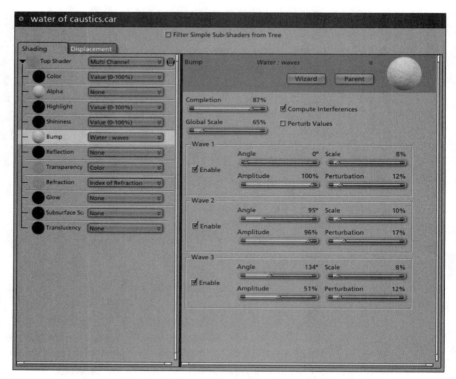

**FIGURE 16.14**    The water shader has been set up to simulate water waves.

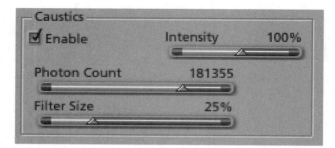

**FIGURE 16.15**    The Caustics render settings.

Once the animation is finished, play it, and you should see the shimmering caustics reflections on the submarine and the seafloor as the light from above is refracted through the water, as in Figure 16.16. If you are not happy with the caustics effects, try increasing the Photon Count and the Filter Size. The Photon Count will increase the number of calcula-

**FIGURE 16.16**   The final animation clearly shows the underwater caustics on the submarine and the seafloor.

tions that are performed to create the caustics effect, thereby refining the final results, and the Filter Size will create more or fewer caustics. Just keep in mind that increasing the Photon Count or the Filter Size will also increase render time.

**TUTORIAL 16.4**   **MOTION BLUR**

If a car speeds past you unexpectedly, all you are likely to see is a fast moving blur. On the other hand, if you see a car speeding toward you and you have time to track the car with your head, you will reduce the motion blur of the car but the background will be blurred. Motion blur is a natural optical phenomenon that we expect to see when an object is in motion. Still cameras and motion cameras also record motion blur. The amount of motion blur recorded is directly related to the shutter speed, with slower shutter speeds producing more motion blur than fast shutter speeds. The movies we watch look natural because cameras record the same motion blur that we perceive in real life. Without taking motion blur into account, computers generate animations where moving objects or camera movements have crisp, clean lines; the result looks unnatural. Luckily Carrara has a rendering filter that simulates motion blur. In the following steps we will experiment with motion blur to achieve that smooth movement of an airplane as it moves across the screen and to prevent strobing of the spinning propeller.

Open the file motionblur.car. In this scene the airplane we have been working with has been animated to move across the camera view. Of course, in order for the plane to move, the propeller has to be spinning, so a Spin modifier of 10 cycles per second has been applied to the propeller and spinner group. Notice that the shadow catcher object moves with the airplane. This is necessary to create the cast shadow on the tarmac as the airplane moves. Press the Play button to see the airplane and the propeller move (see Figure 16.17).

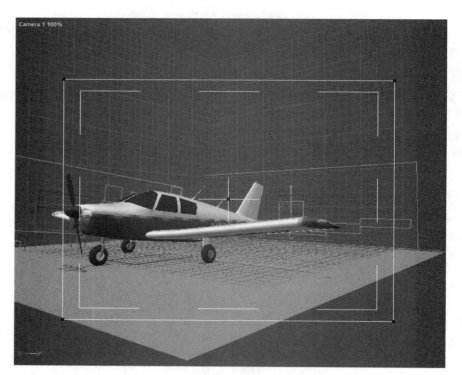

**FIGURE 16.17**    In the motion blur scene the airplane and the propeller are animated.

Jump into the Render room and render the scene. Even though the frames per second are set to 24, the airplane appears to jerk across the screen, especially as it nears the camera and the propeller is strobing. Now let's turn on Motion blur to fix some of the problems with the animation.

In the Motion Blur settings enable Motion Blur, leave the settings at default, and render once more. The results are not much better, but you can see some motion blur in the movement of the airplane and the propeller. Next, increase the Extra Frames from 2 to 6, increase the Blur Intensity to 95%, and render again. Now we are getting somewhere. The propeller is now blurred and the airplane's motion is also blurred, creating more realistic, smoother motion (see Figure 16.18).

**FIGURE 16.18**    Increasing the Extra Frames and the Blur Intensity blurs the motion of propeller and airplane.

In order to get the typical look of the propeller blur, the Extra Frames and/or the frames per second would have to be increased to offset the spin of the propeller. Of course, increasing these variables will also increase render time. To avoid lengthy render times, enable Vector Blur, lower the Extra Frames to 2, and render again. The result of the Vector Blur is a very nice propeller blur (see Figure 16.19). By now you should have some idea of how motion blur works, so you can keep experimenting with the setting to get the effect you want.

**FIGURE 16.19** Vector Blur creates very nice blur effects but does not take as long as regular Motion Blur.

| TUTORIAL 16.5 | **NON-PHOTOREALISTIC RENDER (NPR)** |

So far in this chapter, our goal has been to produce rendered images that are very realistic in appearance and motion. While realism is great, there is also a benefit to being able to create painterly and abstract renders. Painterly renders created with NPR can mimic artistic drawing and painting techniques like chalk, pastels, oils, and pencils. NPR can also create wonderful and whimsical cartoon styles. As with any Carrara render engine, NPR can also be used to create incredible animations.

ON THE CD

For this tutorial, we'll use the model of a girl's face. Open the file npr_girl1.car from the Chapter 16 folder on the accompanying CD-ROM. The scene is set up for you, so all we'll do is create the NPR images (see Figure 16.20). Keep in mind that NPR only recognizes colors, not image-based textures, which is why we're using a model textured with shading domains.

Since NPR is a rendering method, let's jump into the Render room. In the Rendering tab of the Properties tray, select Non-Photorealistic as the render engine. The default render engine is Photorealistic. The first task is

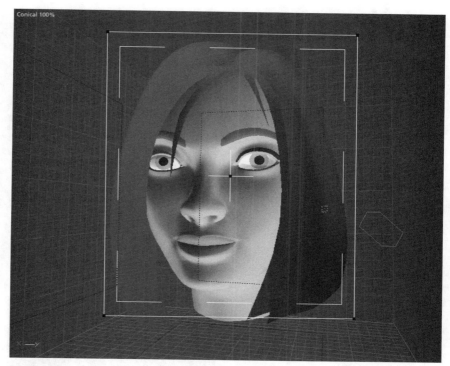

**FIGURE 16.20**    We'll use the model of a girl's head and face to generate the NPR image.

to create a render using just the default settings, so click once on the Render button in the Sequencer tray. The render is set for low resolution, so this should only take a few seconds. Notice that even with just the default settings, the rendered image should look like it was loosely drawn with color pastels (see Figure 16.21).

Now, let's customize the render a bit to add more detail. In the Properties tray enable Highlight, Shadows, and Background and render again. Now the render has more depth to it because we can see light and dark areas. The background also adds a sense of scale and depth. So far, the image looks great, but the brushstrokes are a little too big for this image, so let's edit the brush settings. Change the Max Brush Size to about 2% and rerender the image. The brushstrokes should appear smaller and not as messy as the previous render (see Figure 16.22). If you want to take this a step further, enable Object clipping for each layer and set Antialiasing to Best. These settings will clean up the edges and create a tighter image.

**FIGURE 16.21**    The default NPR settings create a very nice painterly effect.

**FIGURE 16.22**    With a few adjustments, the results can be precisely controlled.

Changing the lighting and colors in the 3D scene can also control the NPR's appearance and quality. For example, if you decrease the Shadow Intensity of the light in the 3D scene, the NPR will render a lighter shadow. If you change the Highlight or Shininess settings of the shaders texturing the object, those changes will be reflected in the NPR image.

Let's try one more experiment with NPR. So far, we have changed the brushstrokes and cleaned up the image a bit. This time, let's create a sepia image that appears to have been hand-drawn with chalk. Because we will not be using the Object Color option in this part of the tutorial, the Shading Domain color information will be lost. Therefore, a new file has been prepared for this section of the NPR tutorial. Locate the npr-girl2.car file on the accompanying CD-ROM. The main difference is that in this file the iris of the eye is a separate object from the rest of the eye so it can be outlined in the render; if we didn't take this measure, the eyes would render blank, and that looks creepy. Additionally, the light source has been changed to help accent the type of render we are about to create.

**ON THE CD**

To keep this brief, we'll run through the NPR settings for this render from the top. Set Antialiasing to Good and leave the Filter Sharpness, the Min and Max Brush Size, and the Paper Color at their default settings. Make sure the Diffuse, Highlights, Outline, Shadows, and Background layers are enabled. Using the Color Picker, set the Outline Color to H10, L18, S85. Set the Thickness to 120% and leave the Length default. Now come the important steps.

In the Diffuse tab select Use Object Color and set the color to H13, L82, S15, which is a warm gray. Click once on the Brush icon and select the Spotted Smudge brush (see Figure 16.23). Set the Intensity to 100% to get a very loose brushstroke. A lower Intensity setting will produce more uniform brushstrokes; conversely, a higher setting will produce more random brushstrokes. Set the Transparency to 30%. The Transparency setting defines how much of the layers underneath you can see through the Diffuse layer. In loose hand drawings, you can always see strokes in the different layers of the drawing, all the way down to the paper. Set the Orientation to Triangle. The different Orientation options will turn the brushstrokes in different directions; there is no right or wrong setting; it's a matter of taste.

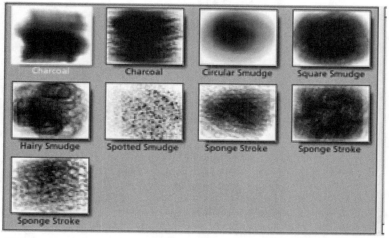

**FIGURE 16.23**  NPR comes with dozens of brushes from which to choose.

The Highlights layer has the same brush as the Diffuse layer, but the color is set to H0, L95, S0, which is almost white. Everything else is default. The Shadow layer uses the Hairy Smudge brush, and the color is set to a warm brown (H10, L23, S75). The Intensity is set to 45%. Finally, the only change in the Background layer is that the Color is set to a dark beige (H12, L51, S17).

For the first render experiments, make sure that the resolution is about 72 dpi and that the image is about 350 pixels in width to keep render times short. All that is left to do is press the Render button. In a few seconds, you should be rewarded with a render that looks just like a sepia charcoal drawing, as shown in Figure 16.24. With NPR renders, experimentation is the norm. Play with the settings until you get the look you want and then set the final render for a high resolution.

**FIGURE 16.24**  By experimenting with the NPR settings you can recreate just about any drawing style.

### NPR Tips

- Work with the 3D scene first to get the correct camera view, lighting effects, and model textures. This will save you a lot of time in creating the NPR render.
- Use the minimum number of lights to light the scene. The more lights you have, the longer it will take to render.
- The underlying mesh of the object will significantly affect how the brushstrokes appear in the render. A dense mesh will be rendered with more strokes.
- When starting out with NPR, work with one layer at a time. The settings and layers tend to affect each other, and it is easy to lose track of which setting is doing what if you move too fast.
- Experiment with the Orientation methods to get the look you want. The different methods affect how the brushstrokes are applied to the model.
- If an object does not render, you might have to switch the Backfaces setting from Smart to Show. The Backfaces option is located in the Properties tray in the Assemble room.
- If an object is only partially rendered in an NPR image, you might have to insert a new camera into the scene and switch to the new camera for rendering. This is a known problem.

## SUMMARY

After hours or even days of working on a 3D scene, there is no greater satisfaction than seeing a wonderfully rendered image or animation. The Carrara render engines make creating incredible animations and images a snap. You don't have to know the technical aspects of HDRI lighting, global illumination, or caustics; just build your scene and let Carrara do the work for you. The lighting techniques and render engines we covered in this chapter can be used together or separately to get the effects you want. Remember to be careful about using these advanced rendering techniques, as they will increase render times. The next chapters will cover how Carrara works with some very popular programs including Poser™ and Adobe After Effects®.

# PART
# VII

# CARRARA AND OTHER PROGRAMS

# CONVERTING CARRARA SCENES TO VECTORS WITH VECTORSTYLE 2

## In This Chapter

- VectorStyle to Flash
- VectorStyle to Illustrator

While VectorStyle™ 1 used licensed Ravix™ technology from Electric Rain™, VectorStyle 2 is developed entirely by Eovia and is much improved. VectorStyle 2 features better shadows, specularity, and reflections and now also supports transparency. Though VectorStyle 2 has many more features than VectorStyle 1, it renders much faster and is better than or at least comparable to Electric Rain's Swift 3D™ (see Figure 17.1).

**FIGURE 17.1**    VectoryStyle produces exceptional vector-based files for use in Flash or Illustrator (image by Jack Whitney).

In a nutshell, VectorStyle exports Carrara scenes to vector-based file formats such as Macromedia Flash, Adobe Illustrator, EPS, and SVG, as seen in Figure 17.2. While 3D animation and illustrations have become very popular, the charming look of outlined, flat colors that VectorStyle produces is also in demand. However, one the most popular uses for VectorStyle is to create Flash content. With VectorStyle you can convert any Carrara scene into an swf file that can be imported into Flash for further development or posted to the Web as is. The *.swf is the native Flash player file format, which will run as a stand-alone file, can be embedded in a Web page, or can be loaded into Flash.

**FIGURE 17.2**    (a) Original Carrara scene. (b) Flat color drawing. (c) Line drawing produced with VectoryStyle.

## TUTORIAL 17.1    VectorStyle to Flash

ON THE CD

Since the focus of this tutorial is VectorStyle we'll begin with a prepared Carrara scene. Locate the vectorstyle.car file (the Carrara file is kindly provided by Jack Whitney) in the Chapter 17 folder on the accompanying CD-ROM. Play the animation to study the action. You should see a PDA-type device swing open as the camera rotates around to the front of the device, as seen in Figure 17.3. The goal is to export this animation for use as a menu in a Flash movie. As we adjust the settings for export from Carrara to Flash, feel free to experiment to get different results.

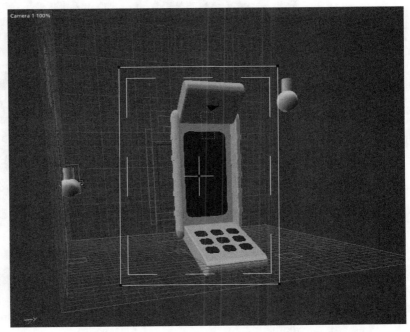

**FIGURE 17.3**    Modeling, texturing, and animation are done in Carrara prior to VectorStyle export.

Since modeling, texturing, and animation are complete, all that is left to do is adjust the settings in the VectorStyle Flash Exporter and export to an swf file. From the File menu, choose Save As, and from the Save As options select Flash (*.swf). Name the file and click Save. Next, you should see the VectorStyle Flash Exporter dialog window. The Flash Exporter dialog window displays all of the possible options for exporting the Carrara scene into an swf file.

Let's take some time to adjust the various Flash export options, as VectorStyle 2 is very different from VectorStyle 1. Before doing anything else, click on the Render button and check Auto Render in the Preview window. This will automatically update the Preview windows as the settings are adjusted. In the Output tab you can adjust the width and height of the exported file. If you change the height and width in the Output tab, it will override the Carrara width and height settings in Render room. For our purposes leave the height and width unchanged. You can also export a single frame or an entire animation by enabling the Export Animation option. Check Export Animation since we are working with an animation. Enabling the Separate Lines/Areas will create separate vectors for strokes and fills. When exporting for Flash leave this option turned off to keep file size down (see Figure 17.4).

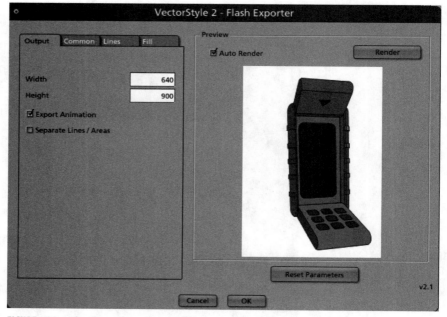

**FIGURE 17.4**   The Output settings adjust general export options such as height and width.

Click on the Common tab to adjust the overall quality and background color of the exported file. Leave the Quality menu at Fast to keep things simple. The different Quality options will produce varying levels of overall vector quality, but for Flash the Fast option works fine. The Curve Fitting option adjusts the smoothness of curves, with higher values producing better curves but also making larger files, so keep the this to about 50%. Include Edge Detail enables VectorStyle to look for edges to outline between polygons. Check the Include Edge Detail option. The Detail Angle setting is similar to the crease angle when modeling. The higher the angle, the smoother the result, so keep this value at about 45 degrees. If the Use Scene Background Color option is checked, then the exported file will have the same background color as the Carrara scene. If you uncheck this option, you can change the background color by clicking on the color chip and choosing a different color. For now leave this option checked, as shown in Figure 17.5.

**FIGURE 17.5**    The options in the Common tab set the overall quality of the exported file.

Next, click on the Lines tab to adjust the stroke properties of the exported file. Though VectorStyle has this section labeled "Lines," in vector-based programs like Flash and Illustrator lines are referred to as strokes. First, enable the Object Outline option to make VectorStyle outline vectors.

If you turn this option off, then all vectors will have color fills only and no strokes. In the Mode menu choose Outline. If you choose the Mesh option, all polygons will be outlined, and that is not what we want for this export, though the Mesh option can produce an interesting wireframe look. Leave the stroke color black and increase the Thickness to at least 0.50. Using values lower than 0.50 for thickness will produce very thin strokes, which can cause problems because they are very difficult to see (see Figure 17.6). The Area Outline option will outline or stroke areas of color, which often produces results similar to the Mesh option in the Object Outline Mode menu. Leave Area Outline off.

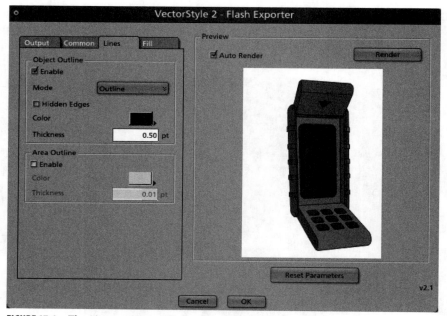

**FIGURE 17.6**   The Lines options adjusts the stroke quality.

Finally, click on the Fill tab to adjust the fill color properties. To create black and white line drawings (see an example of a line drawing in Figure 17.2) you would leave Do Fill unchecked, but since we want color fills, check the Do Fill option. The Mode menu is critical in determining the look and feel of the exported file. Seven levels of color and gradient detail are available, with Average Color being the simplest and Areas Gradient being the most detailed. The only way to know what the different modes will look like on your model is to try them. The Cartoon Average Color option works for most applications, and that is the one we want to select. Check shadows to simulate cast shadows. VectorStyle can now simulate shadows from multiple lights. When enabled, the Specular option will simulate highlights; enable this option. Finally, since the shader on the PDA is reflective, enable the Reflection option and leave Transparency unchecked (see Figure 17.7). The more options you enable, the

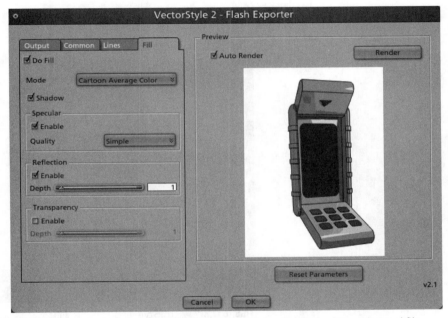

**FIGURE 17.7**    The Fill options are critical in determining the look of the exported file.

larger the file will be and the longer it will take VectorStyle to export the file, so use the Fill options carefully.

When all of the options are set, all that is left to do is click on the OK button. VectorStyle will draw each frame in the animation and export the swf file, as shown in Figure 17.8.

The final step is to import the VectorStyle swf file into Flash. Therefore, open Flash and use the Import command from the File menu to import the VectorStyle swf file. Notice that all of the frames from the swf file appear in the Flash timeline as key frames (see Figure 17.9). Once the frames are imported, you can use the Flash ActionScript language to create interactivity in your Flash export. Play the vectorstyle.swf file provided by Jack Whitney to

VectorStyle 2 Preview

To cancel the export, press the 'esc' key.

**FIGURE 17.8**   VectorStyle exporting to Flash.

see how the Carrara animation was used as a menu for the Flash presentation, as seen in Figure 17.10.

## VectorStyle to Flash Tips

Much of the work in creating a Flash movie is done within Carrara. This means that all modeling, texturing, and animation are done within Carrara, and VectorStyle is only used as a last step to export the Carrara scene into Flash. However, you can do some important things to help the transition from Carrara scene to Flash movie go smoothly.

- Small file-size for fast download is still an important consideration when building a Flash movie. When exporting with VectorStyle,

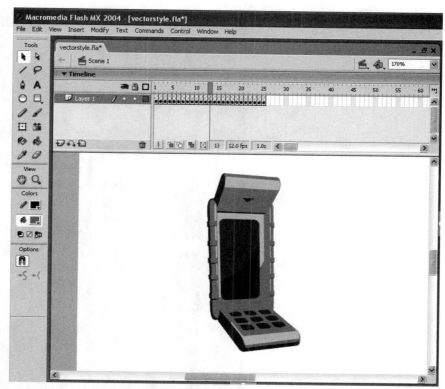

**FIGURE 17.9**   The VectorStyle swf frames in the Flash timeline.

limit the number of fill colors to keep down the number of vector objects that have to be created in the Flash export.

- If you are exporting animation, VectorStyle will use the frames per second set in Carrara. For CD-ROM or Web-based animations, 12 frames per second is sufficient. If you increase the frames per second, you will mostly increase the file size and not the animation quality.

- It is important to be aware of some of the differences between a VectorStyle swf and a native Flash swf file. First, native Flash vector objects are highly optimized for compactness and efficiency. For example, when a square with an outline is created in Flash, only one object is stored in the Flash file. However, a similar square with an outline converted from a Carrara scene with VectorStyle might contain dozens of individual vector objects. Not only does this make the file size larger, but it also makes editing the VectorStyle objects within Flash difficult.

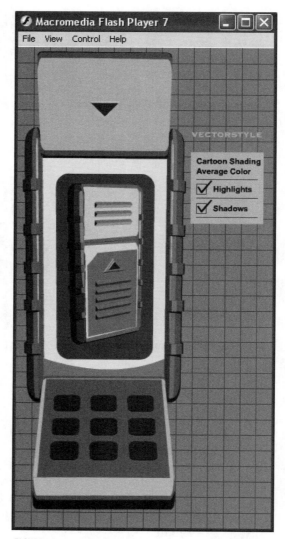

**FIGURE 17.10**   The final Flash movie created with the Carrara animation.

- Flash also has a highly efficient form of path animation called a Motion Tween. This is not too dissimilar in concept from Carrara 's tweeners. However, VectorStyle can only export whole frames of animation, which will correspond to individual frames of animation in Flash. That means that the VectorStyle frames can't be effectively tweened in Flash.

- When importing an swf file created by VectorStyle into the Flash timeline, it is a good idea to create a Movie Clip with the VectorStyle frames and save the Movie Clip to the Flash Library. Use instances of the Movie Clip in the Flash timeline. This will help keep what may be dozens of frames organized and it cuts down on file size if the VectorStyle frames are used more than once.

To avoid problems in Flash with imported VectorStyle swf files, work out all animation within Carrara because it will be very difficult to change it in Flash. Keep the frame count to 12 frames per second and keep export options simple. Most important, be realistic about the limitations of converting a Carrara scene into a Flash movie. Nonetheless, with a little planning you can create dazzling 3D content for Flash with VectorStyle.

**TUTORIAL 17.2    VECTORSTYLE TO ILLUSTRATOR**

Though similar, exporting Carrara scenes for use in Illustrator has different requirements than exporting for Flash. As we have seen with Flash export, the main goal is to produce a manageable file size for download. When you export to Illustrator, there are two typical end uses of the exported file: use of the file as is without editing or more commonly, the exported file being edited in Illustrator. Editing means that you will manipulate the vectors output by VectorStyle with the Illustrator Pen and selection tools, so the aim of exporting for Illustrator is to produce a simplified file that can be edited. There is a trade-off in detail for simplicity. Be warned that VectorStyle will not produce the same type of file you would create if you were drawing from scratch in Illustrator. Editing VectorStyle files in Illustrator or Flash is challenging.

ON THE CD

Open the file vectorstyle2.car. You should see Raul's familiar face. Remember, the goal is to produce a simplified editable file, which means that the VectorStyle file is used more as a template than a finished illustration. First, note that the objects that make up Raul have been subdivided in Carrara. The more polygons there are, the better the results will be for exporting with VectorStyle. Go to File/Save As and choose the AI [VectorStyle].ai option. This will bring up the Illustrator Exporter.

Notice that the Illustrator Exporter Output tab is different than the Flash Exporter Output tab. First, there is no option to create outlined and filled vectors. Only separate objects for strokes and fills can be exported. Though there is an animation export option, it is not very efficient, as it will export separate Illustrator files for each frame. If you want to export an animation, use the Flash Exporter instead (see Figure 17.11).

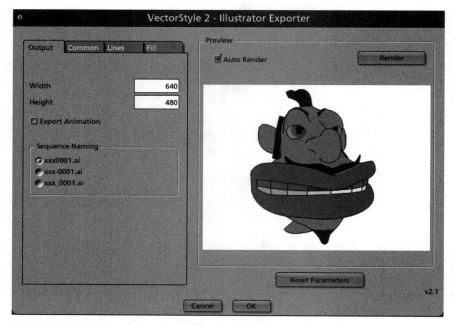

**FIGURE 17.11** The Illustrator Exporter Output options.

The most important option you can enable to get better results for export to Illustrator is to adjust the Quality to Best and increase Curve Fitting to 100 in the Common tab. This will produce smoother curves. This does not mean efficient curves, but smoother at least. Expect to have many control points on the curves. Leave Include Edge Detail off, as having it on will increase the number of vectors exported, and that only makes things more difficult for editing, as shown in Figure 17.12.

In the Fill tab make sure that Object Outline is enabled and that the line thickness is at least 0.5 points. Finally, in the Fill tab choose any of the Fill Mode options except Cartoon Full Color, as this will produce dozens of vectors. Leave all other options turned off. You may also consider turning off the Do Fill option and exporting only a line drawing to be finished in Illustrator. Once all the adjustments are done, press OK and export the Illustrator file (see Figure 17.13). It is important to note that all vectors in the exported file will be grouped; once ungrouped Raul is ready to be edited (see Figure 17.14).

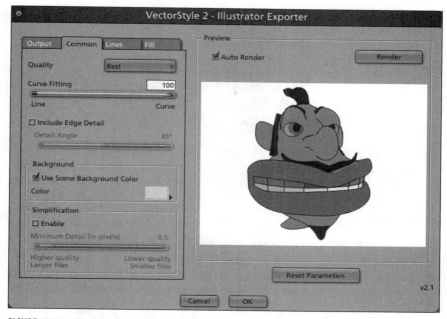

**FIGURE 17.12**    Setting the Quality and Curve Fitting to their highest settings will produce smoother curves.

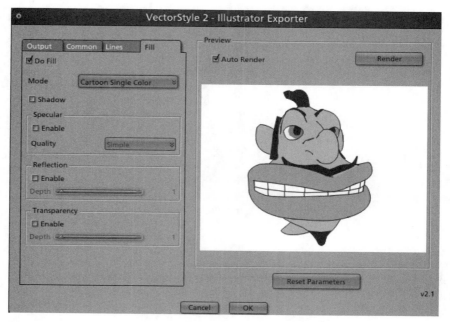

**FIGURE 17.13**    Keep the Fill Mode simple and then press OK to export.

**FIGURE 17.14**    Raul in Illustrator ready to be edited.

## SUMMARY

VectorStyle is definitely a must-have if you will be working with Flash or Illustrator on a regular basis or even you just want a change of pace from the 3D look. VectorStyle 2 is vastly improved from version 1, featuring many advanced options including transparency. Just keep in mind that getting the best results when going from 3D to 2D takes some time and experimentation. Continuing the trend of working with Carrara and other programs in the next chapter, we will learn to work with Carrara and RealViz® MatchMover®.

# 18

# IMPORTING A POSER SCENE WITH THE NATIVE IMPORTER

*by Andrea M. Newton*

## In This Chapter

- Overview of the Poser Workspace
- Creating a Still Image with Poser and Carrara
- Creating an Animation with Poser and Carrara

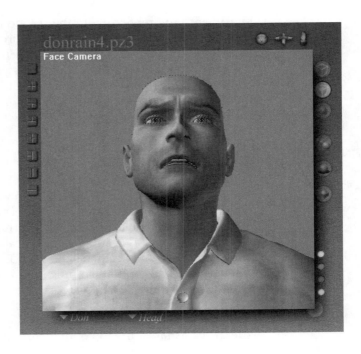

Poser 5 is a 3D graphics program specifically designed for creating images and animations with figures—human, animal, supernatural, or otherwise. Using the standard Poser figures or any of the figures, props, and clothing available through marketplaces like Daz, Renderosity, or PoserPros, you can quickly and easily create scenes without having to model figures from scratch.

Poser is a staple in the workflow of many Carrara users, who use Poser to clothe and pose the figure and then import the scene into Carrara with tools like TransPoser to work on lighting, texturing, rendering, and other more advanced aspects. With Carrara 5, Eovia has added a tool that streamlines the workflow between Poser and Carrara even more: the Native Importer. The Native Importer allows you to import the Poser scene with things such as morph targets, IK chains, and bone setups intact so you can refine your character's pose, expression, and facial and body morphs without having to go back to the scene in Poser. You can also directly import Poser characters, poses, and conforming clothing, and even conform clothing to figures, directly in Carrara 5. Although the Native Importer does not support dynamic cloth or dynamic hair at this time, the advanced capabilities added by the Native Importer, and the time saved by streamlining your workflow, more than make up for that.

In the first tutorial in this chapter, you will create a still image in Poser 5 and then use the Native Importer to open it in Carrara for final adjustments and rendering. In the second tutorial, you'll use the Poser 5 Walk Designer to add a walk to the figure in that same scene and then import the animation into Carrara. By the end of the chapter, you'll know how to use many of the tools in Poser 5 and Carrara 5 and see how together these two programs can help you quickly create images and animations with figures.

## OVERVIEW OF THE POSER WORKSPACE

Before jumping into the tutorial, take a moment to familiarize yourself with the Poser workspace. This will help you work through the tutorials more easily. There are a lot of similarities between Poser and the Carrara interface and a few differences. Like Carrara, Poser uses rooms to separate the different tasks involved in creating a scene. When you start Poser, you're automatically taken to the Pose room, which is where you add and pose figures, add clothing, and add props to scenes (see Figure 18.1). Like Carrara's Assembly room, the Pose room is Poser's base of operations. You do the main work on the scene in the Pose room and only go to the other rooms for specific tasks. To switch to another room in Poser, click its tab at the top of the workspace.

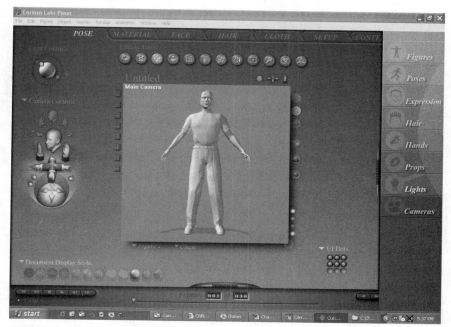

**FIGURE 18.1**    The document window is located in the middle of the workspace in the Pose room, with other tools situated around it. Clicking the tabs at the top of the screen takes you to other Poser rooms.

The document window is located in the middle of the Pose room and is where you construct your scene, positioning and posing figures and props. In other rooms, the document window is a smaller preview in one of the corners. A row of tools located directly above the document window allows you to rotate, twist, or move objects or access advanced tools such as morph putty, magnets, and the group editor. Because the Object Properties palette gives you better control for positioning and posing objects in Poser, and none of the advanced tools are necessary for either of the tutorials in this chapter, you won't use the tools in that toolbar.

Two drop-down list boxes are located directly below the document window. The Current Figure list, on the left, displays the currently selected figure. The Current Element list, on the right, shows the element that is currently selected, which can be a prop, body part of the current figure, or even a scene component such as a light or camera (see Figure 18.2). To select a different figure or element, click the triangle next to that list, referred to as the Browse button, and then select the new figure or element that you want to work with. Poser uses lists and this type of browse button frequently throughout the interface.

**FIGURE 18.2** The Current Figure and Current Element listboxes are located below the document window. To change to a different figure or element, click the Browse triangle next to the list, point to the appropriate subcategory, if necessary, and then click the new object.

Poser also uses palettes to organize tools and content, much as Carrara does. If you click the tab at the bottom of the screen, you can expand the Poser animation palette. The tab on the right-hand side of the workspace allows you to open or close the Library palette, which works much like the Carrara Browser palette. The different figures, props, and poses that you can use in your Poser scenes are accessed using the Library palette; in the Material room the Library palette gives you access to the different textures available. You'll learn how to add items from the Library palette later in this chapter.

The lighting controls are located in the upper-right corner of the workspace. Like the editing toolbar, they won't be used for these tutorials. The Native Importer does not import Poser lights, which allows you to use Carrara lighting instead.

The camera controls are located directly below the lighting controls (see Figure 18.3). The trackball in the center allows you to rotate, or *dolly*, the currently selected camera around the scene. The three small dots around it allow you to change the current camera's focal length, scale, and roll, respectively.

The crossed arm tool directly above the camera trackball allows you to move the current camera along the *x*- and *z*-axes, or in, out, left, and right. The single hand tool above it on the left allows you to move the current camera in the *y*- and *z*-axes, or up, down, in, and out. The single hand tool on the right lets you move the camera in the *x*- and *y*-axes, or up, down, left, and right. Smaller versions of the Camera Dolly, Move X-Z, and Move Y-Z tools can be found above the right-hand corner of the document window.

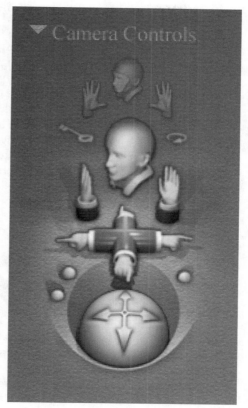

**FIGURE 18.3**   The Poser camera controls, from top to bottom: Select Camera Menu, Right Hand Camera, Face Camera, Left Hand Camera, Animation On/Off, Current Camera, Fly Around, Move Y-Z, Move X-Y, Move X-Z, Focal Length, Scale, Roll, and Camera Trackball.

The icon between the Move X-Y and Move Y-Z camera plane controls represents the camera currently being used. By default, the main camera is used and is represented by a large head. The icon changes as you change to different cameras. You can also click the icon to scroll through the available cameras one by one or click and drag to select a specific camera. It's often easier to select a new camera from the Select Camera list above the camera controls or to click the camera name in the document window and then select the new camera from the list.

Clicking the circular arrow icon on the right-hand side of the Current Camera icon makes the camera fly around the scene. The key icon on the opposite side of the Current Camera icon is used to turn camera animating on and off; when selected, it shows as red and the camera movement can be animated in the scene. Since the Carrara Native Importer doesn't import Poser cameras, you would need to animate camera movement in Carrara after importing the scene instead of doing it in Poser.

The Document Display Style list and buttons at the bottom of the workspace allow you to switch between several display types such as Wireframe, Smooth Shaded, and Texture Shaded. You can either select the display style from the list or click the corresponding button (see Figure 18.4). The textured display style allows you to see how the scene will look with all textures without having to render it, which is helpful when making sure that no body parts poke through clothing; however, it is a much more resource-intensive mode than the other options and can cause your computer and Poser to slow down. Therefore, it's best to do most of your work in one of the other modes and switch to textured mode only for spot checking.

**FIGURE 18.4**   The Document Display Styles, from left to right: Silhouette, Outline, Wireframe, Hidden Line, Lit Wireframe, Flat Shaded, Flat Lined, Cartoon, Cartoon Lined, Smooth Shaded, Smooth Lined, and Texture Shaded. To change to a different style, either click its button or select it from the drop-down listbox.

A series of nine dots, three across and three down, are found in the lower-left corner of the Poser workspace (see Figure 18.5). These dots are called *memory dots*; since Poser can only undo one level of editing, they allow you to memorize up to nine user interface (UI), pose, and camera settings so you can revert back to them if necessary. For example, if you move the figure's head, then move its arm, and then decide that you like the way they were before, you can select Undo from the menu to restore the arm, but you can't select undo a second time to get back to the previous head pose. You have to manually undo that change. However, if you had saved the current pose in a pose dot before moving the head, you could select that pose memory dot to revert back to it. To switch between pose memory dots, camera dots, and UI dots, select the appropriate one from the list. To save a pose, camera setting, or UI setting, click an empty memory dot. To revert to a previous setting, click the memory dot that you saved it to. To erase the settings saved in a memory dot, press the Alt key and then click the dot.

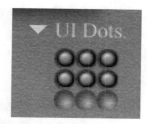

**FIGURE 18.5**    Memory dots allow you to save up to nine settings each for the user interface, figure pose, and camera settings. "Full" dots, like the top six in this screenshot, have settings saved in them. You can also drag the memory dots to a different place on the workspace so you don't have to close the Library palette to get to them.

The buttons along the left-hand side of the document window allow you to switch between full screen and different split screen views. The buttons along the right-hand side control the tracking mode, depth cueing, shadows, collision detection, and the colors for the foreground, background, shadow, and ground in the Poser scene. They are not used in the tutorials in this chapter.

Now that you have a good idea about where things are and how to get around in Poser, it's time to get creative. On to the tutorials!

**TUTORIAL 18.1    CREATING A STILL IMAGE WITH POSER AND CARRARA**

In this tutorial, you'll create a simple scene with one of the standard Poser figures. You'll give him some clothes, pose him, add an expression, and even use the Poser 5 Face Room to change his face so he looks like a whole new person.

When you first start Poser, the default scene opens with the default male figure already loaded. For this tutorial, though, you'll use the Don Nude Hair figure, which not only allows you to add your choice of clothing, but also has a hair skullcap that works well for a short, crew-cut hairstyle. Since you might not want to use the default male figure for all of your other scenes, you can also take this opportunity to change your Poser preferences so your default scene loads without a figure in it. Follow the steps below to delete the default figure from the scene.

### Deleting an Existing Figure from a Poser Scene

1. Click the Current Figure list below the document window and then select the figure that you want to delete, in this case Figure 1 (see Figure 18.6).

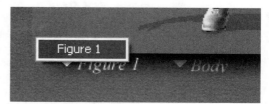

**FIGURE 18.6**   Click the triangle next to the Current Figure list to select a new figure.

2. Click the Current Element list to the right of the Current Figure list, and then select Body.
3. Press the Delete key on your keyboard.

OR

1. Click Figure on the Poser menu, and then select Delete Figure.
2. A message will be displayed asking if you want to delete the current figure. Click OK. The figure is deleted from the scene.

Now that you've deleted the default figure and have a nice, empty scene to start from, you can change your preferences so Poser always starts with an empty scene. Complete the steps below to do that or skip them if you want Poser to continue opening with the default figure in new scenes.

### Setting a New Default Scene in Poser

1. Click Edit on the Poser menu and then click General Preferences. The General Preferences window is displayed (see Figure 18.7).
2. Select Launch to preferred state as the Document Preference option. This tells Poser to open using your preferred document settings instead of the factory default.

*You can revert to the default document settings by changing this option to Launch to factory state.*

3. Click the Set Preferred State button to make the current scene your preferred default scene.
4. Click OK to save the changes.

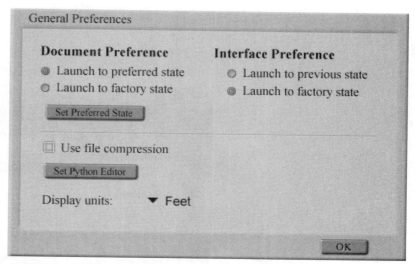

**FIGURE 18.7**    The General Preferences window allows you to set a preferred scene and have Poser use it as the default.

Any new scene you create after changing your preferences will automatically start without any figures in it. You don't even have to restart Poser for the changes to take effect. The next new scene you create will already use the new settings.

Now that you have an empty scene, you need to add Don Nude Hair to it. Like all figures and props that you use in Poser, you add him from the Library palette. The Library palette contains all the categories and subcategories of items you can add to a scene; to add an object or figure, you need to browse to the correct subcategory, select the figure or object that you want, and then add it.

### Adding a New Figure to a Poser Scene

1. Click the tab on the right-hand side of the screen to open the Library palette.
2. Click Figures. The Figures category is displayed.

*If you've been working in Poser already, the library might open to the Figures category or to a different category or subcategory. Continue to step 3 to browse to and select the Don Nude Hair figure if that happens.*

3. Click the Browse button to the right of the current subcategory heading to display a list of all categories. Point to Figures and then click Poser 5 (see Figure 18.8).

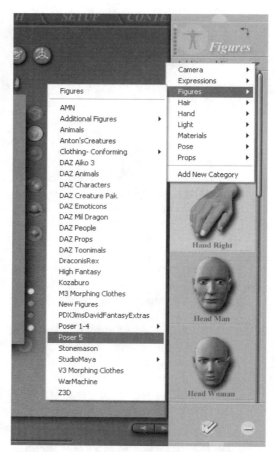

**FIGURE 18.8** Click the triangle next to the current category name in the Library palette to browse to a different category or subcategory.

4. The Poser 5 Figures subcategory is displayed, which shows a thumbnail for each figure it contains. Select Don Nude Hair and then click the Create New Figure button at the bottom of the palette (see Figure 18.9).

**FIGURE 18.9**    After you select the item, click the double checkmark Create New Figure button at the bottom of the Library palette to add it to the scene.

*The Create New Figure button looks like a double checkmark. If you already have a figure in the scene, you'll also see a button that looks like a single checkmark, which is the Change Figure button. Clicking the Change Figure button or double-clicking a figure in the library deletes the currently selected figure from the scene and replaces it with the new one. Get into the habit of clicking the Create New Figure button to add a figure to the scene, even when no other figures exist, to keep from accidentally replacing figures you've already added.*

    5. The Don Nude Hair figure is added to the scene and appears in the middle of the document window.

Don is now part of your scene. If you look below the document window, you'll see that the Current Figure list now reads Figure 1 instead of No Figure. You could complete the scene with Don labeled as just Figure 1, but when you have multiple figures in a scene it can get confusing remembering which figure is which—especially when you're conforming clothing. Before going any further, use the steps below to change Don's name from Figure 1 to something a little more specific.

### Renaming a Figure

1. Click the Current Figure list below the document window and then select the figure that you want to rename, in this case Figure 1.
2. Click the Current Element list to the right of the Current Figure list and then select Body.
3. Click Object on the Poser menu and then click Properties. The Object Properties dialog is displayed (see Figure 18.10).

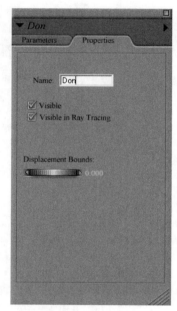

**FIGURE 18.10**    The Object Properties dialog.

4. Click the Properties tab if it is not already selected.
5. Select the text in the Name field and then type a new name for the figure, in this case Don.
6. Press Enter. The figure's name is changed; the heading on the Object Properties dialog and the name in the Current Figure list are automatically updated.
7. Click the Close button in the upper-right-hand corner of the Object Properties dialog to close it.

You now have Don Nude Hair added to the scene and you've given him a name that'll be easier to recognize than just Figure 1 as you continue working. That's a good start to the scene and a very good place to save the file. As with any project, it's a good idea to save often when working on a scene in Poser. Saving scenes in Poser works much like saving them in Carrara or even saving a file in a word processing program. If you're unfamiliar with that, though, use the steps below to save your file.

## Saving a Scene in Poser

1. Click File on the Poser menu and then click Save As.
2. The Save Document As dialog is displayed. Type a name for the Poser scene, such as DonRain.pz3, in the File Name field.
3. Click the Browse button to the right of the Save In field and change to the folder where you want to save the file.
4. Click Save. The file is saved in the directory specified with the name given.

You now have a saved scene with one figure, Don, in it. At this point, you could either start posing Don or you could give him some clothes to wear. If you were using dynamic clothing, then you'd have to pose him first so you could drape the clothing to his pose, but conforming clothing moves with the figure as you pose him, so you get to choose. Since you can add conforming clothes first, and so you can see them move with Don when you pose him later, complete the steps below to add and conform a shirt, pants, and some shoes to Don.

## Adding Conforming Clothing to a Figure

1. Click the Library Palette tab to open the Library palette if it isn't already.
2. To change to the conforming clothing subcategory, click the Browse button. Point to Figures, point to Clothing—Conforming, and then click Clothing–P5 Male. The Clothing–P5 Male subcategory is displayed.
3. Scroll down until you find the P5MaleSlacks. Select them and then click the Create New Figure button (see Figure 18.11). The slacks are added to the scene with the name Figure 1.
4. Make sure that the Current Figure list shows Figure 1 and that the Current Element list shows Body.
5. Click Object on the Poser menu and then click Properties. The Object Properties dialog is displayed.
6. Click the Properties tab if it is not already selected.
7. Select the text in the Name field and then type a new name for the figure, in this case Slacks-Don.

**FIGURE 18.11**   After you select the P5MaleSlacks, click the Create New Figure button to add them to the scene. If you double-click them, they will replace the currently selected figure.

*Although this scene only uses one figure, it's good to get into the habit of including the name of the figure wearing the clothing in the clothing figure's name. When you're working on a scene with two or more figures, this makes it easier to distinguish between each figure's clothing. For example, if you have two figures in a scene who are both wearing slacks, naming the slacks figures "Slacks 1" and "Slacks 2" doesn't make it very easy to know which figure the clothing is for. If you named them "Slacks-Don" and "Slacks-Judy," for example, you could tell at a glance exactly which figure is wearing that pair of slacks.*

8. Press Enter. The figure's name is changed; the heading on the Object Properties dialog and the name in the Current Figure list are automatically updated.

You've added a pair of conforming slacks to Don, but if you click the Texture Shaded button, the scene changes to a textured preview and you can see that part of Don's legs poke through the pants (see Figure 18.12). In addition, if you moved Don's legs, the pants wouldn't move with him. That's because they haven't been conformed to Don yet. Click the Smooth Shaded button to return to the normal scene view, and then complete the steps below to conform the slacks to Don.

## Conforming Clothing to a Figure

1. Select Slacks-Don from the Current Figure list. Select Body from the Current Element list.
2. Click Figure on the Poser menu, and then click Conform To.

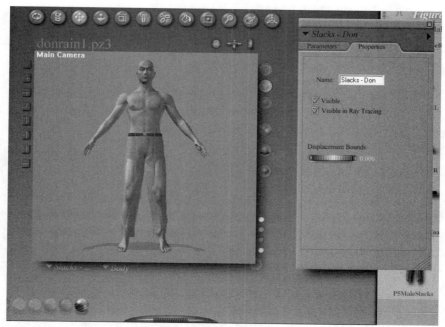

**FIGURE 18.12**   The P5MaleSlacks have been added to the scene but still need to be conformed to Don.

3. The ChooseFigure dialog is displayed (see Figure 18.13). Select Don from the Select Figure to Conform to list and then click OK. The slacks are automatically adjusted to fit the Don figure and are parented to him so they will move how he moves.

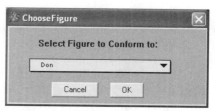

**FIGURE 18.13**   The ChooseFigure dialog allows you to choose the figure in the scene that the clothing should conform to.

4. Click File on the Poser menu and then click Save to save the scene.

Now that you have Don wearing a pair of slacks, use the steps in the "Adding Conforming Clothing to a Figure" and "Conforming Clothing to a Figure" sections to add the P5MaleDressShirt2, P5MaleDressShoe2L, and P5MaleDressShoe2R figures to him. You'll find these figures in the Clothing—Conforming, Clothing—P5 Male library subcategory, the same place from which you added the P5MaleSlacks. Name the P5Male-DressShirt2 figure "Shirt-Don." Name the P5MaleDressShoe2L and P5MaleDressShoe2R figures "Shoe Left-Don" and "Shoe Right-Don," respectively (see Figure 18.14).

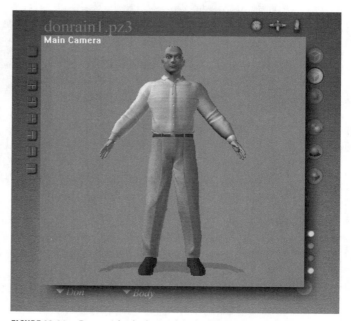

**FIGURE 18.14**    Don with clothes added and conformed to him.

When working with conforming clothing, it's important to remember that each article of conforming clothing is specifically designed to fit a certain Poser figure. You may have wondered why you add conforming clothing as a figure, not a prop. To allow the clothing to fit the character and move when it does, the clothing object is given a bone setup and joint parameters that match that character. Not only does that turn the object into a figure, but it's what defines the clothes as being for that particular character. Since Poser's Don figure has a different bone and joint setup than Michael or Judy, clothes that have a bone and joint setup designed to match Don's won't match Michael's or Judy's. If you try to use conforming clothes that weren't designed for a figure, the clothes won't fit right.

In some cases even conforming clothing designed for the figure you're using might not fit quite right. A little of a shoulder, leg, or other body part might poke through. This happens when the conforming clothing's bone setup or joint parameter isn't created exactly right to fit the figure or if you've rescaled your figure's body parts to be larger. You can see if any body parts are poking through the clothing by switching to texture shaded mode and rotating the camera around the scene. If you see any places that the body pokes through the clothing, select that clothing figure. Select that body part on the clothing and then use the X-scale, Y-scale, and Z-scale parameters to enlarge the clothing to cover the body. If the adjustments are fairly large, you might also need to use the Taper parameter to blend the enlarged clothing section with the sections around it or even adjust the scale and taper on those surrounding clothing parts to blend the changes. This method can also be used, in some cases, to use conforming clothing that isn't designed for your figure. As a general rule, though, if you stick to conforming clothing designed for your figure, you shouldn't have a problem with poke-through.

Even with clothes on Don, the scene would be pretty boring with him just standing there in the default pose, so the next thing you'll do is pose Don in a more interesting manner. For this tutorial, you'll position Don as if he's just felt the first few drops of rain and is holding up his hand and looking at the sky to see if it really was rain that he felt. As mentioned before, you won't use the editing tools above the document window to pose Don. If you use those tools to pose a figure, it's very easy to over-adjust body parts, resulting in arms, legs, necks, or other appendages that are twisted in horribly disfiguring and painful-looking ways. Even undo doesn't always fix the problem.

## Posing Don

1. Select Don from the Current Figure list.
2. Click Figure on the Poser menu. Point to Use Inverse Kinematics; RightLeg and LeftLeg should have checkmarks next to them, indicating that inverse kinematics is active for them. Click RightLeg to deactivate inverse kinematics for it.

 *Inverse kinematics (IK) allows you to position an entire limb by selecting and moving just the last body part on that limb. For example, with IK activated for the right leg, you could click and drag the right foot to a position, and the rest of the right leg would follow. Since you'll be using the parameter fields to position the body parts, though, IK needs to be turned off.*

3. Click Figure on the Poser menu. Point to Use Inverse Kinematics and then click LeftLeg to turn off inverse kinematics for it.

4. If the Object Properties window is not already open, click Object on the Poser menu and then click Properties to display it.

5. Click the Parameters tab.

6. The currently selected element is displayed at the top of the parameters tab. Click the Browse button to the left of it to browse the list of elements. Point to Body Parts and then click Left Shoulder. If necessary, click the triangle at the top of the body parts list to scroll up or the triangle at the bottom of it to scroll down.

7. Left Shoulder should now be listed at the top of the parameters tab, indicating that it is the currently selected body part. If necessary, click the plus sign next to Transform to expand the transformation settings list.

8. Click the Bend dial and then drag it to the left until the value reads −72.

OR

Click the current Bend value, and then type −72 in the field. Press Enter to accept the new value.

 *If you already know the value that you want to change a parameter to, it's easier just to type it in the field. However, using the parameter dials allows you to adjust a body part's position, size, or other setting "by sight," dragging the dial left and right until the object looks how you want it to. You will use both of these methods as you create scenes in Poser.*

9. Click the Browse button, point to Body Parts, and then click Left Collar. The parameters tab should now show Left Collar as the currently selected body part.

10. Select the Up-Down value and then change it to −8.

11. Click the Left Hand Camera icon in the camera controls to change to the left-hand camera. Use the camera trackball to rotate the scene so you can see the back of the hand. Continue posing the left arm and hand, setting the values listed for these body parts:

**Left Forearm:** Side-Side: −7; Bend: −20
**Left Hand:** Bend: −8
**lThumb1:** Bend: 4
**lThumb2:** Bend: 4
**lThumb3:** Bend: 4
**lIndex1:** Side-Side: 16
**lMid1:** Side-Side: 5
**lRing1:** Side-Side: −5
**lPinky1:** Side-Side: −5

*You might have noticed the Spread, Grasp, and Thumb Grasp settings on the Left Hand body part. You also might have wondered why you aren't using those to pose the hand. Although those settings are designed to make it easy to pose the hand, especially when opening and closing it, they don't always position the fingers correctly. If you drag the Spread dial to the left, you'll notice that the middle and ring finger cross each other before the index and pinky fingers are correctly positioned (see Figure 18.15). Because of this, it's easier, in the long run, to manually position the fingers.*

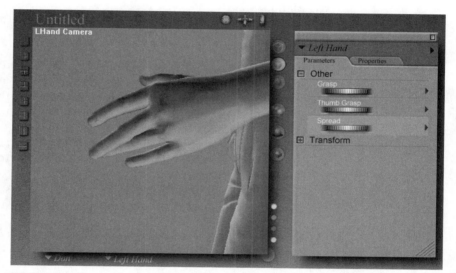

**FIGURE 18.15**   The result of using the Spread setting to pose a hand. The middle and ring fingers are moved more quickly than the index finger and pinky, making them cross through each other before the index finger and pinky are in place.

12. When you've finished posing the left arm and hand parts, select Main Camera from the Select Camera list.
13. Click Figure on the Poser menu. Point to Symmetry and then click Left Arm to Right Arm.

*Poser's symmetry option allows you to copy the pose from one half of the figure to the other. This is useful when both halves will have the same or similar poses. In this case, symmetry allows you to give both arms the same starting pose.*

14. A message is displayed asking if you also want to copy the joint zone setup. Click Yes. The right arm is automatically changed to match the left arm's pose.
15. Click the Browse button on the Object Properties palette Parameter tab, point to Body Parts, and then select Right Forearm. The parameters tab should now show Right Forearm as the currently selected body part.
16. Select the Twist value and change it to −80.
17. Select the Bend value and change it to 91.
18. Click the Browse button, point to Body Parts, and then select Right Hand.
19. Click the Right Hand Camera button to switch to the Right Hand Camera.
20. Select the Twist value and change it to −13.
21. Select the Bend value and change it to −24. Don should now have his right arm raised slightly, with his palm up.
22. Click LHand Camera in the upper-left corner of the document window and then click Main Camera to switch back to the main camera view.
23. To make Don look up at the sky, select Head from the Body Parts list. If necessary, click the plus sign next to Transform to display the transformation settings.
24. Select the Bend value and change it to −25. Don's head tilts back.
25. To move Don to the left side of the scene, click the Browse button and then click Body.
26. Select the xTran value and change it to −1.65.
27. Click File on the Poser menu and then click Save to save the scene.

You have Don's body posed now (see Figure 18.16), but there's more to posing than just the body. A well-done facial expression adds a great deal of depth and emotion to an image; the same scene can convey entirely different meanings just by changing the character's expression from happy to sad. The head morphs built into Poser figures like Don make it easy to add an expression to your character. In the scene that you're creating now, use the steps below to give Don a sad expression to show how distraught he is that it's raining on this of all days.

### Adding an Expression

1. Click the Face Camera button in the Camera Controls section to change to the Face Camera.
2. Select Don from the Current Figure list.
3. Select Head from the Current Element list.
4. If the Object Properties window isn't already open, click Object on the Poser menu and then click Properties to open it.

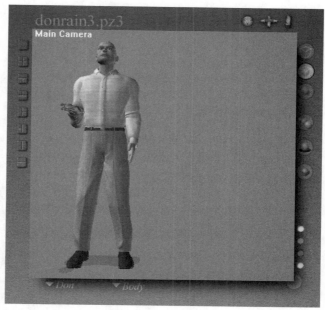

**FIGURE 18.16**   Don with the pose applied.

5. Click the Parameters tab.
6. Click the plus sign next to Full Expression Morphs. Select the Sad value and change it to 0.967.

*The Full Expression Morphs settings are a good place to start when adding an expression. They change multiple facial features to apply the expression. You can then use morphs for individual features, such as Blink and Mouth Worry, to further refine the expression until you have it just the way you want it.*

7. Expand the Eye Morphs list. Select the Blink value and change it to − 0.106. Don's eyes are opened slightly wider.
8. Expand the Mouth Morphs list.
9. Select the Part Lips value and change it to 1.590.
10. Select the Mouth Worry value and change it to 0.383.
11. Expand the Lipsync Morphs list.
12. Select the Mouth O value and change it to 0.268.
13. Select the Open Lips value and change it to 0.186.
14. Click File on the Poser menu and then click Save to save the scene.

As you can see, adding an expression to Don gives the scene an entirely different feel, and with the built-in facial morphs, it wasn't that hard to do (see Figure 18.17). The range of morphs gives you the ability to create any expression that you want, from the most subtle to the absolutely ridiculous.

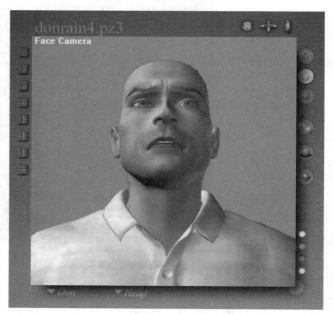

**FIGURE 18.17**   Don's new expression gives the scene a completely different feel.

Even with his expression, Don is still recognizable as Poser Don; to keep him from looking like a clone of a character in hundreds of other images and animations created by Poser users, you can modify his face shape in the Face room. Although many people think of the Face room as just a way to create a character based on a photograph, it's also a handy tool to create a new face using just your imagination.

To change to the Face room, make sure Don is selected as the current figure and then click the Face tab. The first time you go to a room other than the Pose room during a Poser session, a help window for that room is displayed. A shortened version of the information in the Poser user manual, these help windows provide a lot of good information about how to use the different rooms most effectively. The Face room help, for example, provides tips and steps to create a new head shape using reference photos. This information can help you avoid many problems that people encounter in the different Poser rooms. If the Face room help is displayed while you're completing this tutorial, click the red X in the upper right corner to close it.

The Face room displays a sample head shape based on the standard Poser figures; it doesn't include any changes made in the Pose room, so you won't see the expression that you worked so hard to create on Don. However, modifying and applying a head shape from the Face room won't erase the changes that you made in the Pose room, so you don't have to worry about losing your work. As in the Pose room, the Mini Camera Controls are available above the upper-right-hand corner of the document window, so you can move the camera around to better see your changes. You'll be working mostly with the Face Shaping Tool palette, though (see Figure 18.18). Similar to the parameter dials and fields in the Object Properties palette, the Face Shaping Tool morphs allow you to adjust different aspects of the face. You can either drag the dial left and right or click a field and type a new value to change a setting. Most of the face shaping parameters have two possible values; for example, the first morph for the brow ridge is high/low. Dragging the dial to the left or entering a negative value changes the facial shape to have a higher brow ridge. Dragging the dial to the right or entering a positive value results in a lower brow ridge. Complete the steps below to create and apply a new head shape to Don.

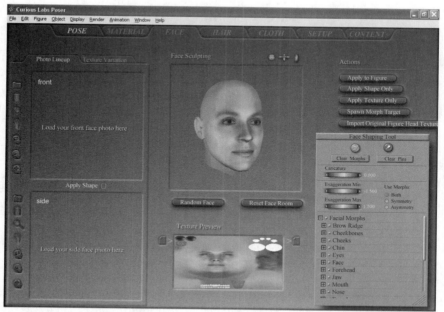

**FIGURE 18.18**   The Poser Face room. The Face Shaping Tool palette in the lower right corner lets you modify a figure's head shape with or without a reference photo. The sample head display shows what your figure will look like with the new shape applied.

### Using the Face Room to Create and Apply a New Head Shape

1. Click the Current Figures list and then select Don.
2. Click the Face tab at the top of the screen. Poser changes to the Face room.
3. Click the plus sign next to Facial Morphs to expand the Facial Morphs list.
4. Click the plus sign next to Brow Ridge to expand the Brow Ridge morphs list.
5. Select the high/low value and change it to 0.390. The sample face in the document window is changed to have a lower brow ridge.
6. Select the inner-up/down value and change it to 0.330. The inner brow ridge on the sample face is moved down.
7. Continue modifying the facial shape, setting the values listed for each of the following morphs:

#### Facial Morphs

**Cheekbones:**   Shallow/pronounced: 0.650
**Chin:**   Pronounced/recessed:  −0.330;  Retracted/jutting:  0.390; Small/large: 0.300
**Eyes:**   Small/large: 1.030; Tilt inward/outward: 0.580
**Face:**   Light/heavy: 0.480; Round/gaunt: 1.050; Thin/wide: 0.320
**Jaw:**   Retracted/jutting: 0.250; Wide/thin: −0.580
**Mouth:**   Drawn/pursed: 0.550; Tilt up/down: 0.350; Underbite/ overbite: −0.500
**Nose:**   Up/down: −0.310; Flat/pointed: 0.460; Short/long: 1.000; Tilt up/down: 0.810
**Bridge:**   Shallow/deep: 0.230; Short/long: 0.150
**Nostrils:**   Small/large: 0.310; Thin/wide: 0.340
**Sellion:**   Shallow/deep: −0.540; Thin/wide: 0.090
**Temples:**   Thin/wide: 0.320

#### Ethnicity/Gender/Age

**Age:**   Younger/older: 1.000

8. Click Apply Shape Only to apply the new shape to the figure in your scene.

*By clicking Apply Shape Only, you apply only the new shape to the figure. The Face room also lets you apply a new texture either from a reference photo or from an imported texture by clicking Apply Texture Only. Clicking Apply to Figure applies both the new shape and the new texture to the figure. If you use the Face room to apply a new texture, bear in mind that it is only applied to the head. You will need to manually adjust the rest of the figure's body texture to match.*

Spawn Morph Target creates a morph target that you can then adjust from the Object Properties palette in the Pose room; however, it adjusts all the settings that you changed at once. You can't change individual ones to tweak them without going back to the Face room.

9. Click the Pose tab at the top of the screen to go back to the Pose room.
10. If it isn't already the current camera, click the Face Camera button to get a better view of the new head shape that has been applied to Don.
11. Because you made the head wider, the skullcap hair doesn't fit correctly now. Click the Current Element list, point to Props, and then click SkullMale4 to select the skullcap hair.
12. Open the Object Properties palette and click the Parameters tab.
13. Select the SkullMale4 xScale value and change it to 113.
14. Select the zScale value and change it to 102. The skullcap hair is resized to fit the new head shape.
15. Click File on the Poser menu, and then click Save to save the scene.

Without having to do any additional modeling or add any morph targets, you have a completely new face for Don, that of an older, more careworn man (see Figure 18.19). You can use morphs in the Object Properties dialog to change other aspects of the face, such as wrinkles, or go back to the Face room to modify and reapply the shape as often as you need until you're happy with the result.

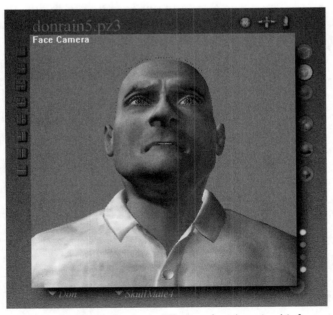

**FIGURE 18.19**    Don looks much different after changing his face in the Face room.

Bear in mind that the Face room is designed to be used with Poser standard male and female figures. While you can try to use it with non-Poser figures like Michael and Vicky, you can get unexpected results, such as a split in the neck. Instead, reserve the Face room for Poser standard figures and use the morphs supplied with non-Poser figures to modify their facial shapes. If you don't see face shaping morphs in the Object Properties dialog for a non-Poser figure, you might need to inject the morphs; if the figure doesn't come with morphs, Poser allows you to create your own.

Now that Don's wearing clothes, is posed to check the sky to see if what he felt really was a raindrop, has an expression to show just how distraught he is that it's raining, and has a unique face all his own, you're ready to import your scene into Carrara. Make sure you've saved the scene after making the last changes and then complete the steps below to bring the scene into Carrara using the Native Importer.

### Importing a Poser Scene Using the Carrara Native Importer

1. Start Carrara 5.
2. Click File on the Carrara menu and then click Open.
3. Click the Browse button to the right of the Look In field and then browse to the folder where you save the Poser file.
4. Select the Poser file and click Open.
5. The Poser scene import dialog is displayed (see Figure 18.20). Select the Native Importer option to import the scene using the Native Importer. This allows you to import morph targets, bone structure, and IK

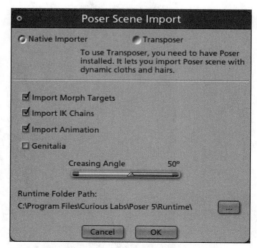

**FIGURE 18.20**   The Poser Scene Import dialog lets you specify how you want to import the Poser scene.

chains for figures so you can modify them in Carrara. The Native Importer does not support dynamic hair or dynamic clothing at this time. The Native Importer dialog has the following fields:

**Import Morph Target:**   Activate this checkbox to import Poser morph targets for figures in the scene. This allows you to adjust morphs in Carrara so you don't have to reopen the scene in Poser to make changes.

**Import IK Chains:**   Activate this checkbox to import the IK chains for figures in the scene.

**Import Animation:**   Activate this checkbox to import animations with your Poser scene.

**Genitalia:**   Activate this checkbox to import genitalia for the figures in the scene.

**Creasing Angle:**   Move the slider to the left to make imported figures less smooth or move it to the right to make them smoother.

**Poser Runtime Folder:**   Click the button to browse to a different Runtime folder location. This allows you to have multiple Runtime folders in different locations and even to use Poser-related content, such as poses, figures, and conforming clothing purchased separately at online marketplaces, without needing to have Poser installed.

6. If necessary, click the Runtime Folder Path button and browse to the location of your Poser Runtime folder.
7. Click OK to import the Poser scene into Carrara (see Figure 18.21).

Now that your scene is in Carrara, you can add textures, backgrounds, terrains—anything that you could do with a scene created entirely within Carrara. For this tutorial, you'll use the default background and the textures imported from Poser, but the Native Importer doesn't import the Poser cameras or lights. The default Carrara light, which points in toward the workspace, will work for this scene, but you need to make some adjustments to the camera. Since lighting and camera placement are easier to do in Carrara, this is actually a good thing.

### Adjusting the Camera in Carrara

1. If necessary, click the tab on the right-hand side of the screen to expand the Properties tray.
2. Select Camera 1 on the Instances tab in the lower half of the Properties tray.
3. Click the Motion tab in the top half of the Properties tray to display the camera properties. If necessary, click the triangle next to Transform to display the camera position and rotation values (see Figure 18.22).

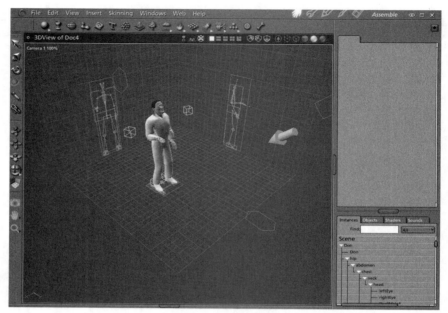

**FIGURE 18.21** The Poser scene after it has been imported into Carrara using the Native Importer. Unlike TransPoser, the individual body parts are retained for the figures and can be selected from the Instances tab so you can change their properties or positions.

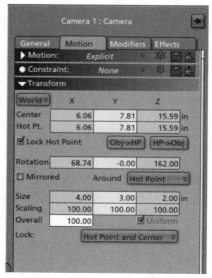

**FIGURE 18.22** Change the position, size, and rotation of the camera or other objects in the scene in the Transform section of the Properties tray Motion tab.

4. Select the value in the X column of the Center field and then change it to 6.06. Change the value in the Y column to 7.81 and the Z column to 15.59.
5. Select the value in the X column of the Rotation field and change it to 68.74. Change the value in the Y column to 0.00 and the Z column to 162.00.

The camera should now be positioned so that Don's upper body, including his upturned hand, are in the middle of the workspace window. This gives a good view of his face so you can show off the work that you did in Poser on his face shape and expression.

Just as when working on a scene in Poser, it's a good idea to save your work frequently in Carrara. Take a minute to do that now. The steps are essentially the same as when you saved the scene in Poser, but you can follow the Carrara-specific steps below to refresh your memory.

### Saving a Scene in Carrara

1. Click File on the Carrara menu and then click Save.
2. The Save Document As dialog is displayed. Type a name for the Carrara scene, such as DonRain.car, in the File Name field.
3. Click the Browse button to the right of the Save In field and change to the folder where you want to save the file.
4. Click Save.
5. The Carrara Export dialog is displayed. Accept the default settings and click OK. The file is saved in the directory specified with the name given.

As mentioned before, one of the best features of the Native Importer is that it allows you to modify Poser figures directly in Carrara. If you look at the Instances tab on the Properties tray, you'll see that not only are the figures listed, but their individual body parts are also. That along with the imported bone setup and IK chains are what enable you to repose the figure in Carrara. This is particularly handy when you need to pose a figure with a prop that you create or add directly in Carrara, or even if you just change your mind about a pose after importing a scene. Complete the following steps to adjust Don's pose in your scene.

### Adjusting the Figure's Pose in Carrara

1. If necessary, click the triangle next to Don on the Instances tab to expand the Don figure group.
2. Select Head.
3. Click the Motion tab in the upper half of the Properties tray and then expand the Transform list.

4. Select the value in the X column of the Rotation field and enter 30. Press Enter to accept the change. Don's head tilts back further.

5. Select rForearm from the Don figure group on the Instances tab.

6. Click the Rotate tool button, which is the third from the top in the toolbar on the left-hand side of the screen. Don's right forearm is surrounded by colored circles.

7. Click the green rotation circle and drag the mouse up. Don's right forearm is moved up. Since his hand is connected to his forearm in the bone setup, it, and all of its child body parts, are moved also.

8. Click File on the Carrara menu and then click Save to save the scene.

As the steps in this section show, you can repose the figure by manually entering a value in a field on the Motion tab or by selecting the body part and rotating it. You can also use the Move tool to manually move the hands or feet, and the rest of the limbs will be repositioned along with them. Although it's not recommended to use the editing tools in Poser to position body parts, Carrara doesn't have the same problems that make it so easy to overpose a part in Poser. In fact, it's easier to use the Rotation and Move tools to pose a figure in Carrara, since that allows you to visually pose the figure, something you need to rely on the parameter dials for in Poser.

Since you selected to import morph targets with your scene, you can also adjust Don's expression, body shape, or anything else controlled by a morph target listed in the Poser Object Properties palette. Unfortunately, that doesn't include the face shaping tools from the Poser Face room, since they aren't part of the figure itself. If you need to adjust the shape of the face directly in Carrara, you can create individual morph targets in Poser or spawn a morph target based on your new head shape in the Face room. Non-Poser-standard figures that can't use the Face room, such as Michael and Vicky, typically have face-shaping morphs available on the Poser Object Properties palette, so those morph targets would automatically be imported into Carrara with the rest of the morph targets.

The biggest difference in using the morphs in Carrara is where you find them. In Poser the morphs for each body part are located in the object properties for that body part. In Carrara all of the morphs are found in the properties for the main figure, with individual groupings there for the ones for each body part. If you select the Don figure within the Don group in your scene, you'll see tabs for General and Morph on the General Properties tab. The Morph tab contains the Areas list and the Current Area list. The Areas lists includes all of the morphable body parts for that figure. If you click a body part in the Areas list, the morph targets available for it are displayed in the Current Area list. To adjust a morph, you just drag its slider left or right. Complete the following steps to add some wrinkles to Don's face using the imported morph targets.

## Adjusting Poser Morphs in Carrara

1. Select Don from the Don group on the Instances tab (see Figure 18.23).

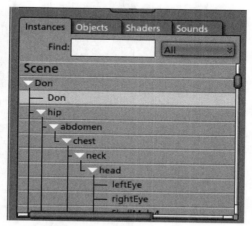

**FIGURE 18.23**   Select the Don figure from the Don group on the Instances tab.

2. Click the General tab on the Properties tray to display the general properties for the Don figure.
3. Click the Morphs tab on the Properties tray General tab to display the morphs available for the Don figure.
4. Select Head from the Areas List. Morphs for the head are displayed in the Current Areas list (see Figure 18.24).
5. Click the triangle to the left of Wrinkle Morphs to expand the wrinkle morphs list.
6. Click and drag the slider for W Forehead until the value reads 0.2.

OR

Click the W Forehead value field and type 0.2. Press Enter to accept the new value.

7. Change the following wrinkle morphs to the values listed:
   **W CrowsFeet R:** 0.3
   **W CrowsFeet L:** 0.3
   **W SidesMouth:** 0.5
   **W SidesChin:** 0.2
   **Wrinkles MouthSide:** 0.5
8. Click File on the Carrara menu and then click Save to save the scene.

**FIGURE 18.24** Poser morph targets are found on the figure's General tab on the Properties tray General tab. You can select a specific body part from the Areas List box and then expand a morph group in the Current Areas list to see the individual morphs in that group.

The wrinkles really add to Don's appearance as a careworn, older man (see Figure 18.25). As you may have noticed, the morph values in Carrara have a maximum setting of 1, but a small change can make a big difference. If you need to use a larger value on a morph to get the look you want, change that setting in Poser before importing the scene into Carrara.

When you have the main figure selected on the Instances tab, you can also import poses and clothing for that figure or conform clothing in the scene to it (see Figure 18.26). With Don still selected on the Instances tab, click the General tab next to the Morph tab on the Properties tray.

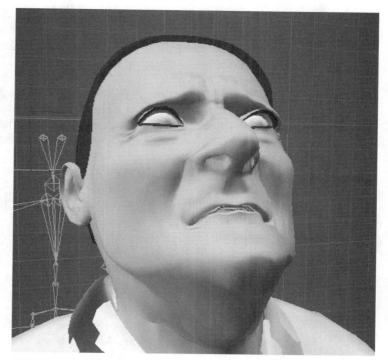

**FIGURE 18.25**    Don with wrinkles added. Using the Native Importer enables you to adjust morphs like this after importing the scene into Carrara without having to go back to Poser.

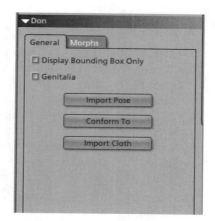

**FIGURE 18.26**    With a figure selected, the General tab allows you to change to bounding box view for that figure, display or hide genitalia, import poses, and conform or unconform clothing already in the scene.

Activating the Display Bounding Box Only checkbox changes the current figure from a smooth shaded display to a polygon box display. That can be useful if you need to limit the system resources used when working on complex scenes. Activating the Genitalia checkbox displays genitalia for the Poser figure, which would be used when creating images with nudes.

Clicking the Import Pose button allows you to browse to a Poser pose file, import it, and have it automatically applied to the current figure. Clicking Import Cloth provides the same functionality for conforming clothing. If the current figure is an article of conforming clothing that hasn't been conformed to a figure yet, the Conform To button enables you to select the figure in the scene to conform the clothing to. It works the same as conforming clothing in Poser, but since the Import Cloth button automatically conforms cloth to the selected figure, you only have to conform clothing if you unconform it from a figure or if you import it from the Carrara menu instead of from the figure properties. If you select an article of clothing that is already conformed to a figure, the Unconform button is displayed instead, which allows you to remove the relationship between that clothing and its current parent figure. You could use these two buttons together, for example, to switch clothing between figures.

At this point your image of Don realizing, to his dismay, that it's starting to rain is complete. All you need to do is render it and save the final image.

### Rendering and Saving a Still Image in Carrara

1. Click the Render button at the top of the screen.

OR

    Click Windows on the Carrara menu and then click Render.
2. Carrara changes to the Render room (see Figure 18.27).
3. If necessary, click the tab on the right-hand side of the screen to display the Render Settings tray.
4. Click the Output tab on the Render Settings tray.
5. Select Camera 1 in the Rendering Camera section.
6. In the File Format section, select the Current Frame option so you only render the current frame.
7. Select JPEG (RD) from the file type list instead of BMP (RD).

*The file type that you select depends on what you'll ultimately use the image for. JPEG files are compressed image files that are commonly used for images that will be viewed on a computer screen.*

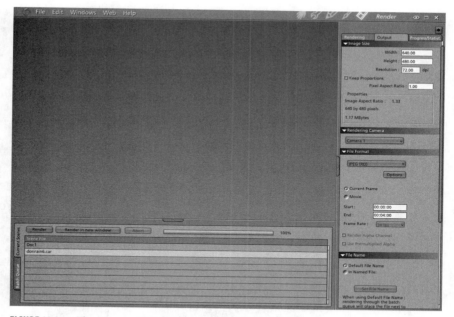

**FIGURE 18.27**    The Carrara Render room. Specify how you want an image or animation rendered on the Render Settings tray on the right-hand side of the screen. The Render tray at the bottom of the screen lets you render to the current window or a new one, abort a render, and view the progress as Carrara renders a scene.

8. Click the tab at the bottom of the screen to display the Render tray.
9. Click the Render button on the Render tray. Carrara will begin to render the image. The status bar on the Render tray shows you Carrara's progress.
10. When Carrara has finished rendering the image, click File on the Carrara menu, and then click Save.
11. The Save Document As dialog is displayed. Type a name for the Carrara scene, such as DonRain.jpg, in the File Name field.
12. Click the Browse button to the right of the Save In field and change to the folder in which you want to save the file.
13. Click Save.
14. The JPEG Options dialog is displayed. Select the image quality that you want and then click OK. The file is saved in the directory specified with the name given.

And there you have it! From the default Poser scene to a fully rendered image with a posed, dressed, and morphed Don (see Figure 18.28). But now that Don realizes it's starting to rain, he'll probably want to get inside—fast! In the next tutorial you'll learn how to take this same Poser scene and turn it into an animation using the Poser Walk Designer.

**FIGURE 18.28**    The final, rendered image.

**TUTORIAL 18.2**    **CREATING AN ANIMATION WITH POSER AND CARRARA**

If you've done any animation work, then you know that one of the more difficult things to animate is a person walking. Fortunately, Poser has the Walk Designer, which makes it very easy—even for novice animators—to create and add a walk, run, or even a strut to a Poser figure.

To start, open the Poser scene from the previous tutorial in Poser. Unless you want your figure to walk in place, the first step to adding a walk in Poser is to create a walk path. This path defines where your figure will walk in the animation. You can make a figure walk from the left side of the screen to the right side, around in a circle, or in any meandering path that you can think of. The only limitation, besides your imagination, is that the path cannot go up or down, so you wouldn't be able to make the figure walk up a hill.

Another important thing to bear in mind is that walk paths and walk designs are intended to be used by bipedal Poser figures. In other words, you can use the Walk Designer to animate Don, Judy, Michael, Vicky, or even the Chimpanzee, but not the Poser Dog or Cat. The Walk Designer expects to find two arms and two legs and expects to apply appropriate motions for them. With a quadruped, though, the Walk Designer finds four legs and no arms. As a result, the leg motions are applied to the back legs and the arm motions are applied to the front legs—not at all what you want. Although there are workarounds for using the Walk Designer with nonbipedal figures, there are no guarantees that they will work correctly, and you will probably have to manually animate parts of the figure.

### Add a Walk Path in Poser

1. Select Don from the Current Figure list.
2. Click Figure on the Poser menu and then click Create Walk Path.
3. The walk path, represented by a line, is created in the scene (see Figure 18.29).

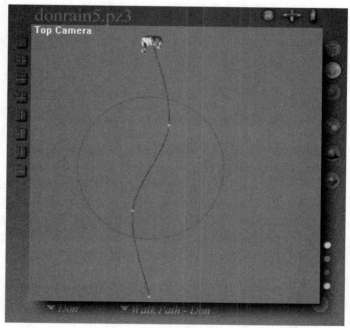

**FIGURE 18.29**    The walk path is represented by a line. Switch to the From Top camera to see and adjust it more easily.

4. If the Object Properties dialog is not open, click Object on the Poser menu and then click Properties to display it.
5. Select Path_1 as the current element on the Object Properties palette. Click the Properties tab and change the Name field to Walk Path— Don.

6. Click Main Camera in the upper-left-hand corner of the document window and then click From Top to switch to an overhead view. This allows you to see and adjust the path more easily.

7. Click the Move X and Y camera control and drag the mouse up until Don is at the top of the document window.

*If you move the camera too far and can't find Don again, you can reset the camera to its original position by resetting its Transform parameter values. Select the From Top camera as the element on the Object Properties palette. Click the triangle to the right of each value in the Transform section and then click Reset Value. Repeat this for any setting in that section that has a value other than zero until you can again see Don.*

You can also use the Camera memory dots to memorize the From Top camera settings before making changes. Then, if you need to revert to the original settings, just click the memory dot in which you saved the original From Top camera settings.

8. Click the Move Y and Z camera control and drag the mouse to the left to pan out until you can see the entire path.

9. Move your mouse over the walk path without clicking. The path will be highlighted, showing white dots at intervals along it.

*If the dots do not appear, make sure the walk path is selected as the current element.*

10. Click the first dot in the middle of the path and drag the mouse to the right. The path is changed so it curves more sharply.

11. To create a new curve in the path, click on the path and drag the mouse. For this scene, click midway between Don and the first dot and then drag the mouse to the left (see Figure 18.30).

12. Click the Parameters tab on the Object Properties palette.

13. Select the YRotate value and then change it to 15 (see Figure 18.31).

*The following limitations apply when editing the walk path properties:*

- *The path can only be rotated in the y-axis. In other words, it can be rotated side to side, but not up or down.*
- *The path can only be scaled in the x- and z-axes. You can change the width and length of the walk path, but not the height.*
- *The path can only be moved in the x- and z-axes. You can move it left, right, forward, or backward, but not up or down.*

14. Click Top Camera in the upper-left-hand corner of the document window and then select Main Camera to switch back to the main camera view.

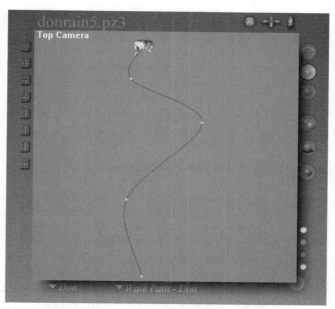

**FIGURE 18.30**    The first curve was added by clicking between Don and the first dot, or *curve anchor*, and then dragging the mouse to the left to add a curve to the walk path. The second curve was made sharper by clicking the existing curve anchor and dragging it to the right.

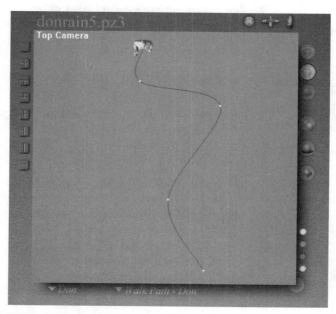

**FIGURE 18.31**    The final walk path.

15. Select Main Camera as the current element on the Object Properties palette.
16. In the Transform section of the Main Camera properties, select the Dolly Z value and change it to 32.
17. Select the Dolly Y value and change it to 5.75.
18. Click File on the Poser menu and then click Save As.
19. Enter a different name for the file, such as DonRainRun.pz3, in the File Name field.
20. Click Save to save the file.

You now have a walk path to guide Don as he walks—or runs—from the rain in your scene. That puts you halfway to animating Don. The next step is to create the walk in the Walk Designer.

Different people walk different ways. Some shuffle their feet; others always have a bounce in their step. The same person will even walk differently depending on his mood. If he's feeling proud, he might strut a little, but if he's trying to slip back inside unnoticed, he'll be very sneaky as he moves. The Poser Walk Designer enables you to create a variety of walks for different people in different situations. The default walk design is just an average walk. You can stick with that or you can adjust the walk settings to customize it. Since Don needs to move pretty quickly to get out of the rain in your scene, some modification to the default walk will be necessary.

### Adding a Walk with the Poser Walk Designer

1. Select Don from the Current Figure list.
2. Click Window on the Poser menu and then click Walk Designer. The Walk Designer window is displayed (see Figure 18.32).
3. Click Walk to see the default walk style.
4. Click ¾, Side, Front, and Top to view the walk from different perspectives, which can help you spot problems with a walk design.
5. Click Stop to end the walk preview.
6. In the Blend Styles section, scroll down until you find the Run setting. Drag the slider or click the buttons to the left and right of it to change the Run value to 50%.

 *You cannot select the value in the Walk Designer fields and manually type the new value, unlike other parameter settings in Poser.*

7. Click the Walk button to preview the modified walk design. Click ¾, Side, Front, and Top to view the walk from different perspectives.
8. In the Tweaks section, change Arm Swing to −30 and Stride to −30.

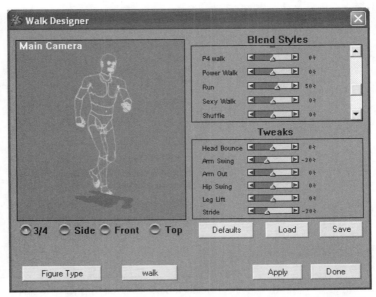

**FIGURE 18.32**    You can preview, modify, and apply a walk to a figure with the Walk Designer.

 *By leaving the walk preview on while changing the Blend and Tweak settings, you can see, in real time, the effect the changes will have on the walk.*

9. Click Stop.
10. Click Apply. The WalkApplyDialog screen is displayed (see Figure 18.33).
11. Verify that Don is selected in the Figure list.
12. Select Walk Path - Don from the Path list. This defines that Don should move along the path defined by the Walk Path - Don walk path as he completes the walk cycle.
13. Activate the Transition from pose at path start checkbox.
14. Click OK to apply the path and return to the Walk Designer window.
15. Click Done to accept the changes and return to the Pose room.
16. Click File on the Poser menu and then click Save to save the scene.

The settings in the Blend section of the Walk Designer window adjust the overall walk design; all elements, including pace, stride, arm swing, and head motion, are affected. Use the Blend settings to create a starting point for your new walk design. Increasing the Run value in this walk design changes the walk to a run. The higher the value, the faster and more pronounced the run.

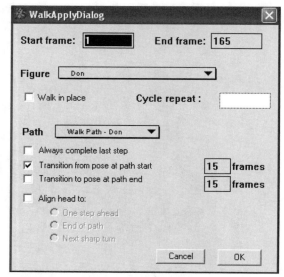

**FIGURE 18.33** The WalkApplyDialog screen defines how you want the walk applied to the selected figure.

The Tweak settings let you further refine specific elements of the walk. Since Don in this scene is older, at least middle aged, he isn't as spry as he used to be, and his run should demonstrate that. Reducing the Arm Swing and Leg Lift values give a sense of heaviness and stiffness when Don runs.

The WalkApply dialog contains a number of settings that control how the walk animation is incorporated into your scene. The Start Frame and End Frame fields are automatically calculated by Poser based on the length of the walk path, the length of the figure's stride, and the speed of the walk design. Essentially, they're determined by how long it takes the figure to get from the beginning of the walk path to the end using the walk that you've designed. By default, the start frame is 1 and the end frame is the last frame necessary to complete the path. However, you can change the start or end frame setting to splice the walk into an existing animation in the scene. For example, you could manually pose the figure to pick up a box, use the Walk Designer to make the figure walk across the screen, and then manually pose the figure to set the box down. The Start Frame would be the first frame after the figure picks up the box, the first frame in which he should start walking. The End Frame would be the last frame in which the figure should be walking, immediately before he starts to set the box down. You can change these fields to incorporate an animation before the walk, after the walk, or both, but make sure that you still include enough frames to complete the walk. For example, if the default starting frame is 1 and the default ending frame is 150, but you want the first 20 frames to be of the figure picking something up, change the starting frame to 20 and the ending frame to 170, so you still have 150 frames to complete the walk path.

If you aren't using a walk path, you can activate the Walk In Place checkbox to make the figure stay in the same place while going through the walk cycle. Enter a value in the Cycle repeat field for the number of times that you want the figure to go through the walk cycle.

The Always Complete Last Step checkbox forces the figure to always finish the last step in a walk cycle, even if he's already at the end of the walk path. That prevents the figure from ending the animation with one foot still in the air. Unless the figure will complete the walk path off screen, it's a good idea to check this box.

Transition from pose at path start and Transition to pose at path end direct Poser to automatically move the figure from the pose he's in when he starts walking or into the pose that he should be in when he finishes walking. This keeps you from having to manually adjust the pose at each frame of the walk. If you change the starting or ending pose after adding the walk, you just need to go back to the Walk Designer and apply the walk again to get Poser to readjust the frames to fit the new starting or ending pose.

Align head to allows you to specify what you want the figure's head to align to as he walks: one step ahead of him, the end of the walk path, or the next sharp curve.

You could import the animation into Carrara right now, but before you do that, take a minute to test the animation in Poser. If there are any problems with the walk, path, or any transition with a starting or ending pose, you can find them and correct them in Poser before going into Carrara. You might have noticed that the changes you made in Carrara to Don's head and arm pose, and even the wrinkle morphs, don't show up when you open this scene in Poser. Carrara doesn't write back to the Poser scene file, so changes made in Carrara won't be seen in Poser. Testing the animation in Poser before importing the scene into Carrara can save you from doing a lot of work in Carrara only to discover that you have to go back to Poser to fix a problem with the walk—losing all the changes that you made in Carrara.

## Testing the Walk Animation in Poser

1. Click the tab at the bottom of the screen to expand the Poser animation palette (see Figure 18.34).

**FIGURE 18.34** The Poser animation palette lets you preview and modify animations. Click the VCR buttons on the left side to return to the first frame, skip to the last frame, stop the animation, play the animation, step back one frame, and go forward one frame. Select the Loop button to play the animation in a continuous loop or clear it to have the animation play once and then stop.

2. Click the Play button to play the animation.
3. Activate the Loop option to make the animation play in a continuous loop or clear it to make the animation play once and then stop.
4. Press the Stop button to stop the animation at any time.

The scene starts with Don standing in the pose that you created in the first tutorial in this chapter; he immediately starts to run, lowering his head and his right arm as he does. Since the animation looks good, you're ready to import it into Poser. You do this the same way that you imported the still image file.

### Importing a Poser Animation Using the Carrara Native Importer

1. Start Carrara 5.
2. Click File on the Carrara menu and then click Open.
3. Click the Browse button to the right of the Look In field and then browse to the folder where you saved the Poser file.
4. Select the Poser file and then click Open.
5. The Poser scene import dialog is displayed. Select Native Importer.
6. If necessary, click the Runtime Folder Path button and browse to the location of your Poser Runtime folder.
7. Click OK to import the Poser scene into Carrara.

Just as with the still image, you'll need to adjust the camera after importing the animated Poser scene. This time, though, you'll set the camera further back, so you can see Don as he runs along the path.

### Adjusting the Camera in Carrara for the Animated Scene

1. If necessary, click the tab on the right-hand side of the screen to expand the Properties tray.
2. Select Camera 1 on the Instances tab in the lower half of the Properties tray.

3. Click the Motion tab in the top half of the Properties tray to display the camera properties. If necessary, click the triangle next to Transform to display the camera position and rotation values.

4. Select the value in the X column of the Center field and change it to −1.42. Change the value in the Y column to 73.89 and the value in the Z column to 11.57.

5. Select the value in the X column of the Rotation field and change it to 89.24. Change the value in the Y column to 0.00 and the value in the Z column to −175.00.

6. Click File on the Carrara menu and then click Save As. Select the folder to save the scene to in the Save In field and then type a name for the file in the File Name field. Click Save.

7. The Carrara Export dialog is displayed. Accept the default settings and click OK. The file is saved in the directory specified with the name given.

Don should now be positioned so he is facing the camera. In a still image, you could reposition the figure to face the camera, but in an animation it's important to adjust the camera. Otherwise, the figure would flip back to the original position in the next frame. You would have to reposition the figure in every frame. Repositioning the camera is a much easier solution; ideally, you should position the figure in Poser so it imports into Carrara facing the way you want it.

All Poser animated scenes import into Carrara with a default length of 4 seconds. Depending on the length of your walk path, the speed of your walk design, and any other animated frames that you have in the scene, 4 seconds might be too short or too long. In this scene, it's about 3 seconds too short. To correct that, click the triangular yellow time marker at 4 seconds on the animation palette timeline and drag it to 7 seconds (see Figure 18.35).

**FIGURE 18.35**    By default, the Poser scene is set to 4 seconds. To change the animation length, click the triangular yellow time marker at 4S on the animation palette timeline and drag it to the correct time. In this screenshot, it has been moved to 7S, or 7 seconds.

Now that the camera is set and you've adjusted the animation length, you're ready to render and save the animation. Again, this is much the same as working with a still image, but a few fields are set differently.

### Rendering and Saving an Animation in Carrara

1. Click the Render button at the top of the screen.

OR

Click Windows on the Carrara menu, and then click Render.
2. Carrara changes to the Render room.
3. If necessary, click the tab on the right-hand side of the screen to display the Render Settings tray.
4. Click the Output tab.
5. Select Camera 1 in the Rendering Camera section.
6. In the File Format section, select the Movie option so you render all frames.
7. Click the tab at the bottom of the screen to display the Render tray.
8. Click the Render button. Carrara will begin to render the image. The status bar on the Render tray shows you Carrara's progress.
9. When Carrara has finished rendering the image, click File on the Carrara menu and then click Save.
10. The Save Document As dialog is displayed. Type a name for the Carrara scene, such as DonRainRun.avi, in the File Name field.
11. Click the Browse button to the right of the Save In field and change to the folder where you want to save the file.
12. Click Save.
13. The VideoCompression dialog is displayed. Select the type of compression you want and then click OK. The file is saved in the directory specified with the name given.

That's it-you've made it! You've created an animation of a man running using both Poser and Carrara. To see your finished animation, click the Play button on the rendered movie (see Figure 18.36).

## SUMMARY

Although the tutorials in the chapter used only one human figure to create a simple still image and animation, you can use multiple figures of many types in your renders, as well as props, backgrounds, terrains, and much, much more to make them even more complex and imaginative.

**FIGURE 18.36**    Click the Play button below the rendered animation to see Don run.

In working through these tutorials, you've used most aspects of the Poser interface. Although not all of the rooms or features of Poser were covered, the tools you used are the fundamental pieces necessary to create any Poser scene—and a few advanced ones, too, like the Walk Designer and the Face room. The latter is perhaps one of the most underutilized tools in Poser; by learning it, you've given yourself a virtually limitless array of figures based solely on the Poser standard figures.

You've also learned to use the Carrara Native Importer to bring Poser scenes into Carrara and the tools it allows you to have in Carrara. You can now adjust the figure's pose in Carrara, modify its morph targets, and even import conforming clothing for it, which requires one less step in Carrara than in Poser. Learning the Native Importer allows you to streamline your workflow so you aren't constantly jumping back and forth between Carrara and Poser to change Poser-related aspects of a figure.

Poser and Carrara are powerful 3D applications. By using them together, you can quickly and easily create great character-based still images and animations—and it all starts with an empty Poser scene.

# POSTPRODUCTION WITH AFTER EFFECTS 6.5

*by David Bell and Lisa Yimm*

## In This Chapter

- Rendering the 3D Helicopter
- Integration with After Effects

C arrara's exceptional modeling, animation, lighting, and rendering capabilities can be combined with Adobe's After Effects to achieve cinema-quality composites. Rendering individual elements in passes allows you to seamlessly integrate Carrara 5 with Adobe After Effects 6.5, giving you maximum flexibility when compositing your files for final render (see Figure 19.1).

**FIGURE 19.1**    In this tutorial we will be compositing animation footage from Carrara with a background scene in After Effects.

As this book is dedicated to showing you how to get the most out of Carrara, in the following tutorial we'll give you an overview of the Carrara side of the equation. You'll be rendering various elements in our scene, which features a CGI helicopter composited into a real scene, with an emphasis on showing how to structure your project for maximum flexibility in your workflow. We have included all of the necessary files in the Chapter 19 folder in the accompanying CD-ROM for you to be able to complete the assembly in After Effects 6.5. If you don't have a copy of After Effects 6.5 installed on your computer, a 30-day demo of the current version can be downloaded from the Adobe Web site: *http://www. adobe.com/products/aftereffects/*.

**ON THE CD**

To begin with, you'll need to copy the project folder CS5_to_AE from the companion CD-ROM onto your desktop. This includes the Carrara working file, cs5_helicopter_proj.car, that will allow you to render out the various passes that we will combine later in After Effects.

As a matter of convenience, we've preloaded all of the textures, backgrounds, lights, geometry, and cameras into the Carrara file, as much of this information is covered elsewhere in this book. Our intention is to make it easy for you to follow the tutorial and illuminate the structure;

feel free to change or alter the settings once you've finished the tutorial. Our goal is to show you just one way that Carrara files can be generated for compositing in After Effects.

## RENDERING THE 3D HELICOPTER

ON THE CD

To get started, double-click on the file cs5_helicopter_proj.car. Figure 19.2 shows the file open in Carrara.

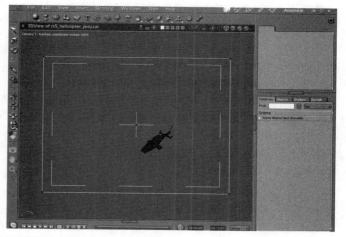

**FIGURE 19.2**    The Assemble room showing our scene in the default work space layout.

The file will open into the Assemble room, showing our scene in the default layout. Our first pass will render the full scene including geometry, textures, lighting, shadows, and background. You'll have a short QuickTime movie of our 3D helicopter composited into a live action scene. We chose this specifically to highlight Carrara's advanced rendering capabilities. However, it's not quite finished. We're going to show you a few tricks that will add details to make our scene so realistic you might be tempted to believe it's real!

### Pass One: The Glory Pass

First, you'll want to double-check to see that the animation timeline at the bottom of your screen is set at the beginning of the sequence: 00:00. This point is crucial to making sure that all of your passes are synced properly and is very easy to overlook. The authors can personally attest to the headaches caused by not checking to see if the timeline is set to zero before getting to work. Then go over to the Properties tray and select Scene Master Null (handle) in the Instances Tab. Click on the triangle to expand the tree; this will expose the various layers used for each pass. Then go up to the General Tab and make sure that Visible and Animated are checked under General. Under View, you'll want to check Show Object in 3D View (see Figure 19.3).

*These three parameters in the General tab, when checked, make the layer visible to the renderer and for our purposes should be considered "on." When unchecked for any layer, these parameters should be considered "off."*

Next, back in the Instances tab, select Support Lighting > Pass 1, 6 and turn it on by making sure that Visible, Animated, and Show Object in 3D View are all checked. Repeat the above actions for Support Geometry > Pass 1.

Now, click the triangle next to Copter Master Null (handle) to expand the tree. Then click on the triangle next to Copter > Animation Null to expand the next set of layers. Select Copter > Textured > Pass 1 and make sure that Visible, Animated, and Show Object in 3D View are checked, and on, for this selection as well.

We're done with our selections in the Assemble room. Now we'll set up to render the first pass. Clicking on the filmstrip icon at the top right of your screen will take you to the Render room.

In the Properties tray, select the Rendering Tab. In the Renderer settings, double-check that the renderer is set to Photorealistic and make sure that Shadows, Reflections, Refraction, Bump, and Transparency are all checked for this pass. We've left Full Raytracing unchecked for the sake of speed in this tutorial. Skylight under Global Illumination and Motion Blur should be checked and preset for this pass (see Figure 19.4).

Next, you'll want to select the Output tab. For this pass we will render without the alpha channel, so you'll need to make sure that Render Alpha Channel is unchecked.

*It's important to remember that in Carrara the Alpha Channel is turned on/off in the Output Tab, not the Rendering Tab.*

Check In Named File in the File Format section of the Output tab and save the file as "01_pass_01_v_001.mov" into the Source folder, which is nested in the Footage folder provided for you in the project folder you copied onto your desktop. This will set up the finished renders for import into After Effects. We like to use leading numbers on our renders, which automatically orders the files and makes it easier to find and locate the files

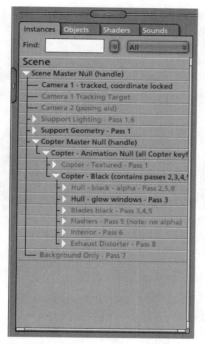

**FIGURE 19.3**   The Instances tab with the Scene tree expanded.

**FIGURE 19.4**   Rendering Tab in the Properties tray showing settings for the first pass.

by pass number. It's also handy to number your versions for easy identification of the latest version. Press on the Render button in the Sequencer tray or press Ctrl/Command-R to render the scene (see Figure 19.5).

**FIGURE 19.5**   Pass one renders the helicopter, complete with textures, shadows, and background.

### Pass Two: Helicopter Hull Alpha Channel

Return to the Assemble room. In the next pass, we will render out the alpha channel for the helicopter's hull. In the Instances tab under Scene Master Null (handle):

- Support Lighting > Pass 1, 6 is off. Visible, Animated, and Show Object in 3D View should all be unchecked.
- Support Geometry > Pass 1 is off. All items above should be unchecked.

Under Copter Master Null (handle):

- Copter > Textured > Pass 1 is off. Items unchecked.
- Copter > Black is on. All items should be checked.

Click the triangle next to Copter > Black to expand the tree. This section contains the elements that will be rendered in upcoming passes. As you'll notice, the layers are labeled not only with the contents of the layer, but also the pass that it applies to. This helps to visually organize the various passes, which in turn makes it easier to diagnose when something doesn't look as it should.

- Under Copter > Black:
- Hull > Black > Alpha: on
- Hull > Glow windows: off
- Blades black: off
- Flashers: off
- Interior: off
- Exhaust Distorter: off

Return to the Render room and in the Renderer section of the Rendering tab.

- Everything under Ray Tracing and Global Illumination should be unchecked: off.
- Under Motion Blur: Enable Motion Blur and Vector Blur should be checked: on
- Under the Output tab, make sure that Render Alpha Channel is checked: on
- Render and save this pass into the Source folder as "02_pass_02_v_001.mov."

Don't be surprised that the result of pass two is all black, as seen in Figure 19.6.

**FIGURE 19.6**    Helicopter Hull alpha channel: like a black cat in a dark room, you can't see it, but you know it's there.

### Pass Three: Helicopter Windows Luminance Mask

In this pass, we render the Helicopter windows as a luminance mask. This will allow the blur of the blades to obscure the windows at the appropriate time in our animation. It also allows you to insert an interior of your choice as well as control the lighting of the interior during final composite in After Effects.

If you expand the layer and really look at it, you'll notice that the number of rotor blades is doubled for a more realistic motion blur and strobe effect.

To set up pass three in the Assemble room:

- Support Lighting: off
- Support geometry: off
- Copter Master Null/Copter > Textured: off
- Copter Master Null/Copter > Black/Hull > Black > Alpha: off
- Copter Master Null/Copter > Black/Hull > Glow windows: on
- Copter Master Null/Copter > Black/Blades black: on
- Copter Master Null/Copter > Black/Flashers: off
- Copter Master Null/Copter > Black/Interior: off
- Copter Master Null/Copter > Black/Exhaust Distorter: off

In the Render room everything is the same: Raytracing and Global Illumination are off, Motion Blur is on, and, as above, the Alpha Channel is on. Render this pass and save it to the Source folder as "03_pass_03_v_001.mov" (see Figure 19.7).

**FIGURE 19.7**    Rendering the cockpit windows luminance alpha mask.

### Pass Four: Helicopter Blades Alpha Channel

Pass four will render an alpha pass for helicopter rotor blades only. By rendering separate alpha channels for the blades and the body, we overcome edge issues generated by Carrara when rendering animation including Motion Blur.

Settings for pass four in the Assemble room:

- Support Lighting: off
- Support Geometry: off

- Copter Master Null/Copter > Textured: off
- Copter Master Null/Copter > Black/Hull > Black > Alpha: off
- Copter Master Null/Copter > Black/Blades Black: on
- Copter Master Null/Copter > Black/Hull > Glow Windows: off
- Copter Master Null/Copter > Black/Flashers: off
- Copter Master Null/Copter > Black/Interior: off
- Copter Master Null/Copter > Black/Exhaust Distorter: off

In the Render Room everything remains the same: Raytracing and Global Illumination are off, Motion Blur is on, and Alpha Channel is on. Render this pass and save it to the Source folder as "04_pass_04_v_001.mov" (see Figure 19.8).

**FIGURE 19.8**    Once again, this alpha pass appears all black.

## Pass Five: The Flashing Beacons Alpha Channel

To add even more reality to our scene, this pass will render out the glare effect for the flashing beacons on the helicopter. The result is pure white. We will add the color and the flashing effect to the lights when doing the final composite in After Effects. This allows us to change the color of the lights quickly and easily without rerendering the entire model.

Settings for pass five in the Assemble room:

- Support Lighting: off
- Support Geometry: off
- Copter Master Null/Copter > Textured: off
- Copter Master Null/Copter > Black/Hull > Black > Alpha: on
- Copter Master Null/Copter > Black/Hull > Glow Windows: off
- Copter Master Null/Copter > Black/Blades > Black: on
- Copter Master Null/Copter > Black/Flashers: on
- Copter Master Null/Copter > Black/Interior: off
- Copter Master Null/Copter > Black/Exhaust Distorter: off

Render settings for pass five in the Render Room:

- Ray Tracing and Global Illumination: off
- Motion Blur: off
- Enable Alpha Channel: off

Render this pass and save it to the Source folder as "05_pass_05_v_001.mov" (see Figure 19.9).

**FIGURE 19.9**    Flashing light beacons in the alpha channel.

## Pass Six: Helicopter Interior

In this pass, you'll render out the interior of the helicopter. It is lit more brightly than the helicopter itself and will be used with pass three in the final composition.

*Instead of removing and reinserting the background for this pass, we simply dropped a large black sphere into the scene that obscures the background, thus saving time and sparing us the work it would take to make sure our background was replaced exactly where it was before removal.*

Settings for pass six in the Assemble room:

- Support Lighting: on
- Support Geometry: off
- Copter Master Null/Copter > Textured: off
- Copter Master Null/Copter > Black/Hull > Black > Alpha: on
- Copter Master Null/Copter > Black/Hull > Glow Windows: off
- Copter Master Null/Copter > Black/Blades > Black: on
- Copter Master Null/Copter > Black/Flashers: off
- Copter Master Null/Copter > Black/Interior: on
- Copter Master Null/Copter > Black/Exhaust Distorter: off

Render settings for pass six in the Render Room:

- Ray Tracing: on
- Shadows: on
- Reflections: on
- Bump: on
- Global Illumination: Skylight: on
- Motion Blur: on
- Enable Alpha Channel: on

Render this pass and save it to the Source folder as "06_pass_06_v_001.mov" (see Figure 19.10).

**FIGURE 19.10**    Interior of the helicopter.

## Pass Seven: Background Only

Now you're probably scratching your head, asking why we should render out a completely separate background-only pass when we already have the background rendered in pass one. The answer is this: a background-only render will be used with the other layers to fake geometry that obscures the helicopter at the beginning and end of the clip. This clever cheat cancels out your need for extra geometry in the scene, thus saving you a great deal of time in modeling, texturing, and rendering.

Settings for pass seven in the Assemble room:

- Support Lighting: off
- Support Geometry: off
- Copter Master Null/Copter > Textured: off
- Copter Master Null/Copter > Black/Hull > Black > Alpha: off
- Copter Master Null/Copter > Black/Hull > Glow Windows: off
- Copter Master Null/Copter > Black/Blades Black: off
- Copter Master Null/Copter > Black/Flashers: off
- Copter Master Null/Copter > Black/Interior: off
- Copter Master Null/Copter > Black/Exhaust Distorter: off
- Background Only > Pass 7: on

Render settings for pass seven in the Render Room:

- Ray Tracing and Global Illumination: off
- Enable Motion Blur: on
- Enable Alpha Channel: off

Render this pass and save it to the Source folder as "07_pass_07_v_001.mov" (see Figure 19.11).

**FIGURE 19.11**  Background footage rendered without helicopter.

### Pass Eight: Exhaust Gas Distortion

This is the last render before we leave Carrara 5 and assemble our final composite in After Effects 6.5. It's an alpha channel render that will be used with the displacement filter in After Effects 6.5 to give our helicopter a realistic exhaust gas heat distortion that will really sell the shot. Although it won't be visible in the render, the Hull Geometry is turned on to obscure the exhaust at the appropriate time and place.

Settings for pass eight in the Assemble room:

- Support Lighting: off
- Support Geometry: off
- Copter Master Null/Copter > Textured: off
- Copter Master Null/Copter > Black/Hull > Black > Alpha: on
- Copter Master Null/Copter > Black/Hull > Glow Windows: off
- Copter Master Null/Copter > Black/Blades Black: off
- Copter Master Null/Copter > Black/Flashers: off
- Copter Master Null/Copter > Black/Interior: off
- Copter Master Null/Copter > Black/Exhaust Distorter: on
- Background Only > Pass 7: off

Render settings for pass eight in the Render Room:

- Ray Tracing and Global Illumination: off
- Enable Motion Blur: on
- Enable Alpha Channel: on

Render this pass and save it to the Source folder as "08_pass_08_v_001.mov" (Figure 19.12).

**FIGURE 19.12**    Exhaust gas distortion alpha channel.

With motion blur enabled, the renderer does five passes for each frame. The particle distortion for our helicopter does not show up until frame 3, so don't panic if you see only black at first.

## INTEGRATION WITH AFTER EFFECTS

You're now done rendering all of the individual passes of the helicopter scene in Carrara. For each of the passes, we've had you save the rendered

QuickTime files into a specific "Source" folder nested within the project folder we've given you. In doing this, we've set our project up so that when you open the After Effects project file the footage will be in the correct place in the folder hierarchy for After Effects to automatically import it into the composition. Paying close attention to how you name and organize your files as you work can shave hours off of your production time.

**ON THE CD**

Double-click the After Effects project file cs5_ae_helicopter_comp. aep. You should see several compositions with all the layers and effects precomposed and ready to render, as in Figure 19.13. This was done so that even if you have no experience with After Effects, you will be able to see the final rendered composite with a few clicks of the mouse.

**FIGURE 19.13**   cs5_ae_helicopter_comp opened in After Effects.

In the After Effects composition window, click on the tab labeled 050 Daylight Final Assembly to make it active. Go up to Composition in the Menu bar on the top of your screen and scroll down to Make Movie. This will bring up a dialog box that says Output Movie To . . . with file already labeled 050 Daylight Final Assembly.mov. After choosing the location in which you would like to save your movie, click Save. This will bring up the Render Queue. We've already preset the render options for a 400 × 300 pixel QuickTime movie. Simply click the button marked Render and you'll have your finished composition (see Figure 19.14).

**FIGURE 19.14**    A still frame from Daylight Final Assembly.

For those with experience compositing in After Effects, please feel free to look at our workflow and experiment with the settings on your own. We've also included a precomposed Day-for-Night version of the movie (Figure 19.15). If you'd like to see it, go back to your composition window and click on the tab labeled 065 Night Final Assembly and repeat the render instructions given above. Once again, all of the pieces are precomposed for final render. Have a look at the individual layers and settings to see what we've done and experiment with the settings yourself.

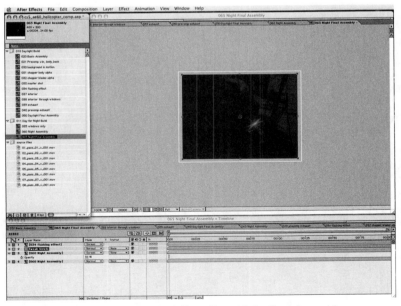

**FIGURE 19.15**    A still frame in After Effects from Night Final Assembly.

## SUMMARY

While many artists will create entirely within Carrara, with this tutorial we hope we've been able to show you that Carrara is also a powerful and easy-to-use postproduction application. Its advanced lighting and rendering abilities integrate seamlessly with After Effects.

 *The authors would like to thank John Hoagland for the great helicopter model. John's work can be found at* www.renderosity.com *under JHoagland.*

# VIII

# CARRARA PLUG-INS

# DIGITAL CARVER GUILD PLUG-INS FOR CARRARA

*by Eric Winemiller*

## In This Chapter

- Making a Fairy Ring with Anything Grows
- Creating Old Chipped Paint with Anything Goos
- Making a Robot Bug Walk with Cognito

O ften, when applications are released they remain static, and no new features are added until the next upgrade is released. For a se-lect few applications, like Carrara, this is not true. Carrara is built so that new tools can be added at any time; these new tools are called plug-ins or extensions. Through the use of a software development kit (SDK), a programmer can build new tools for Carrara, adding new functionality that Carrara's original creators might never have imagined. These tools could be new primitives, shaders, or even a new render engine. The core Carrara program itself is very compact. Most of the features built into Carrara are plug-ins that Eovia has built and provided with Carrara.

This chapter will cover several of the most popular plug-ins for Car-rara, including Anything Grows, Anything Goos, Shader Ops, Shader Plus, and Cognito. All plug-ins covered in this chapter were developed by Eric Winemiller of Digital Carvers Guild. This group is also responsible for several of the tools that are now standard with Carrara such as Toon! and Anything Glows.

You will need a working version of each of the plug-ins covered in this chapter. To purchase Digital Carvers Guild plug-ins, visit *www.digital carversguild.com*. You can find more plug-ins listed on Eovia's plug-ins page at *http://www.eovia.com/products/carrara_addons/carrara_addons.asp*.

---

**TUTORIAL 20.1**      **MAKING A FAIRY RING WITH ANYTHING GROWS**

The first plug-in we will explore is Anything Grows. We'll use it to build a small field of grass and a ring of toadstools, or fairy ring, as seen in Figure 20.1. Anything Grows is a fur, hair, and grass generator for Carrara. How-ever, Anything Grows can be used for much more than that. With its Tip Object functionality, you can use it to randomly distribute objects in a scene.

### Making a Patch of Grass

First, we will start with an easy task and model a field of grass. We could just slap down a plane, apply Anything Grows, shade it green, and call it a day, but for this image we will go a little farther and create a couple of different species of grass.

Create a new Carrara scene. Anything Grows needs something to grow from, so insert a Plane primitive. We are just going to use this plane as a base for Anything Grows; we don't actually want to see it in the ren-der, so disable Visible and Show Object in 3D View for the Plane primitive. Next, Insert an Anything Grows primitive by choosing Anything Grows from the Insert menu. Set the following properties for the new Anything Grows primitive: Base Object = Plane, Width = 0.35 in., Height = 5 in., Strands = 50, Show Base = Unchecked, Segments = 8, Taper = 20%. Click

**FIGURE 20.1**    The goal of this tutorial is to create a fairy ring in a patch of grass using Anything Grows.

on the Anything Grows Wiggle and Stiffness button (the one that looks like three wavy lines) and set the Wiggle = 50% and Stiffness = 40%. This creates a large blade that tapers to nearly a point (see Figure 20.2). You might want to do a quick Area Render to see what the grass looks like.

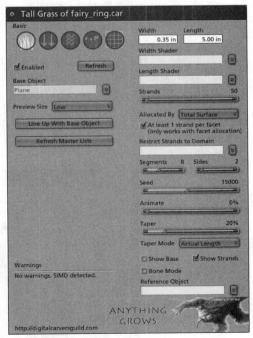

**FIGURE 20.2**    The Anything Grows settings for the first patch of grass.

Jump into the Texture room and create a new shader to texture the grass. A yellowish texture like the one shown in Figure 20.3 would work just fine. It creates variation by mixing a yellow R = 250, G = 224, B = 112 with the dirt256.jpg texture. All textures used in this tutorial are available on the accompanying CD-ROM in the Chapter 20 folder.

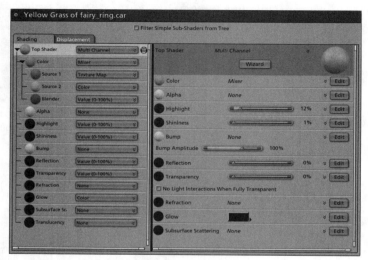

**FIGURE 20.3**    The yellow grass shader.

Now, go back to the Assemble room and center the Anything Grows object in the working box. Rename the new patch of grass "Tall Grass" and rename this Master Object in the Sequencer tray "YellowGrass." Click on the Shaders tab of the Properties tray and rename the new shader "Green Grass." The first type of grass is complete. Do a quick render and you should have something that looks like Figure 20.4.

**FIGURE 20.4**    A test render of the first patch of grass.

For the second species of grass, we'll need a little more variation. Many of the Anything Grows settings can be defined by shaders. For the next species, we are going to use a shader to define the Width and Length. The first thing we'll do is create a new shader by choosing New Master Shader from the Edit menu. Rename the new shader "Noise." Double-click on the new shader and in the Texture room create a noise shader like the one in Figure 20.5.

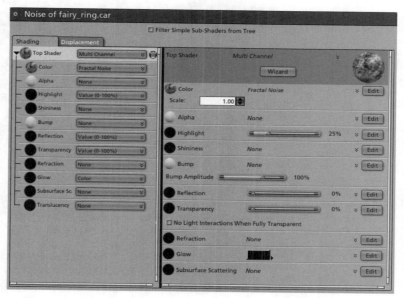

**FIGURE 20.5**   The Noise shader will help define the attributes of the second patch of grass.

With the Noise shader built, we are ready to create the second crop of grass. In the Assemble room insert a new Anything Grows primitive. This new crop of grass will use the same Plane primitive for a base as the first crop of grass did. Set the following properties to create shorter, less tapered grass: Base Object = Plane, Show Base = Unchecked, Strands = 1500, Height Shader = Noise, Width Shader = Noise, Segments = 6, Start Bend Effects at Segment = –1, Seed = 10,000. Stiffness = 30%, Wiggle = 150%. Note that we are using the Noise shader to define the Height Shader and Width Shader properties (see Figure 20.6).

Create a new shader and jump into the Texture room. This new shader, which is different from the Noise shader, will be used to texture the new crop of grass. Mix green R = 124, G = 161, and B = 81 with the dirt256.jpg texture from the accompanying CD-ROM (see Figure 20.7). Rename the new Anything Grows object and Master Object Short Grass and

ON THE CD

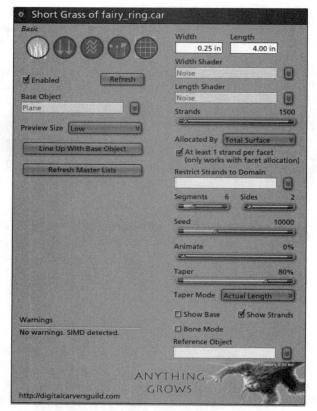

**FIGURE 20.6**   The Anything Grows attributes for the second patch of grass.

the new shader "Green Grass." Also remember to center the new Short Grass object. Do a test render of the scene to see how it is coming along.

### Creating a Grassy Field

Now we have a small patch of grass, but it doesn't exactly fill the screen. The next step is to duplicate the patch so that it appears to be a large field of grass. Select the Tall Grass and Short Grass, group them, and rename the new group "Grass Block." With the Grass Block group selected, select Duplicate from the Edit menu. Click on the Motion tab on the Properties tray and change the Center y to 20 inches. Duplicate the Grass Block three more times. You'll notice that each time the group moves 20 inches, so you don't have to keep editing the Center y value. Select all five Grass Blocks, group them, and rename the new group "Grass Row."

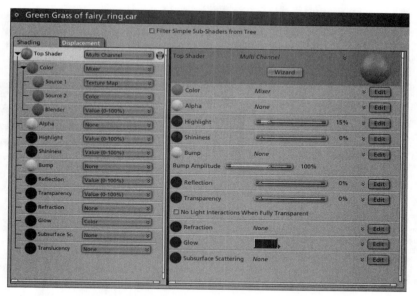

**FIGURE 20.7**    The green grass shader.

Have you figured out what's next? Now, do the same thing we did with the blocks, but in the X direction. Duplicate the Grass Row group and change its Center x to 20 inches. Duplicate three more times. We now have a 100 × 100 inch grassy field—plenty of space for us to build a fairy ring in the center. Group all the Grass Rows, rename the new group "Grassy Field," and make sure the new group is centered in the working box. Do a quick render of your scene; it should look like Figure 20.8.

**FIGURE 20.8**    The Anything Grows grassy field.

In the next section we'll explore Anything Grows a little farther. We'll use the Tip Object to one set of strands to grow some quick and easy mushrooms and use a shader to constrain where the mushrooms grow.

## Creating the Mushrooms

In this section, we'll use the Anything Grows Tip Object feature to create the mushrooms. However, Anything Grows needs the mushroom shape before we can proceed. Therefore, open the mushroom.car file from the accompanying CD-ROM and import the mushroom object into the current file with the grassy field. Like the Plane primitive we used as a base for the grass, we want to hide the mushroom, so make it invisible. Rename the mushroom shape "Mushroom Cap" so we can locate it and assign it as the Tip Object for the mushroom model.

Next, insert a new Anything Grows Primitive and set the following properties: Base Object = Plane, Sides = 7, Width = 3 in., Width Shader = Noise, Show Base = Unchecked, Taper = 50%, Stiffness = 30%, Tip Object = Mushroom Cap, Tip Scale = 35%. To get to the Tip properties, click the Tip button (see Figure 20.9).

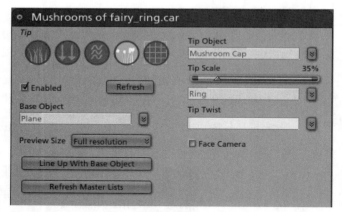

**FIGURE 20.9**   The Anything Grows Tip Object settings for the mushroom model.

Jump into the Texture room to texture the mushrooms. Figure 20.10 shows a mushroom shader you can use. It uses the Spots and Fractal Noise shaders to mix together a few shades of brown. When you are finished shading the mushrooms, jump back into the Assemble room and rename the new Anything Grows object, master object, and new shader Mushrooms. Change the Mushrooms' Z coordinate to 0.

To see how the scene is shaping up, do a quick test render. You should have a field of grass with a big blob of mushrooms right in the middle. Right now, it doesn't look anything like a fairy ring; the mushrooms take up the

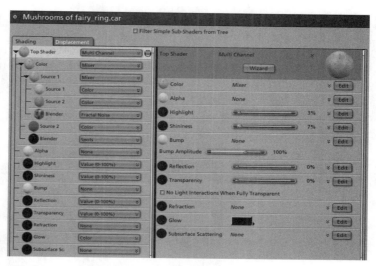

**FIGURE 20.10**    The mushrooms' shader.

whole size of the plane! We'll constrain the area in which the mushrooms grow with a shader. Create a New Master Shader and rename it "Ring." The properties of the Ring shader are shown in Figure 20.11. Once you have completed the new shader, go back to the Assemble room, select the Mushrooms instance, and jump into the Modeling room. Change the following properties in the Anything Grows window: Length Shader = Ring, Tip Scale shader = Ring. All of the black areas in the shader will have no mushrooms, leaving just a ring of mushrooms.

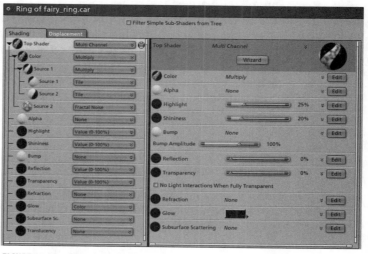

**FIGURE 20.11**    The ring shader.

To finish up, add an Infinite Plane. Create a new shader for the new Infinite Plane and texture it by tiling the dirt256.jpg three times in the Color channel. Drop the same texture into the bump channel. For lighting, leave the default distant light and add a couple more from different directions, each a dark blue. You should end up with something that looks like Figure 20.12.

**FIGURE 20.12**    The finished fairy ring waiting for fairies.

**TUTORIAL 20.2**    **CREATING OLD CHIPPED PAINT AND RUST WITH ANYTHING GOOS**

One of the hardest tasks in 3D is making things look old and worn. It's easy to create a shader for a perfectly painted brand new surface, but when it's time show an object's age, it's nearly impossible to make the aging fit the object without painting custom texture maps. That's where Anything Goos comes in. Anything Goos identifies features of your mesh such as creases, ridges, and perimeters, so that you can shade those features with dirt or wear shaders. This tutorial will take a model of a typical cast iron pipe and shade it to look like it has old chipped paint after years of being neglected.

### Creating the Old Paint Shader

**ON THE CD**

Start by opening the pipe-start.car file located in the Chapter 20 folder in the book's companion CD-ROM. The file has a simple model of a cast iron pipe with a default shader. Select the pipe object and switch to the Texture room. When prompted, choose Create a New Master Shader. Once in the Texture room switch the Top Shader channel to a Terrain shader by selecting Terrain from the channel menu. This will move the current Multi Channel shader down to the Global Shader channel. The pipe surface is painted red but is bumpy from many coats of paint. To simulate the layers of paint select the Color channel and change the default grey color to red: R = 238, G = 25, B = 17. Remember to switch the default HLS color wheel to RGB sliders when entering color values. To give the paint job highlights set the Highlight channel to 30% and the Shininess channel to 5%. The last thing we need to do with the base shader is add the rolling bumps that build up when something is painted over and over again without the old paint being stripped off. Select the Bump channel and choose Natural Functions from the channel menu, then select Cellular from the sub-menu. Check the Fractal option, select the eighth cellular shape option, and turn down the Scale to 24%. The bump is a bit too intense, so select the Global Shader so you can see the Bump Amplitude and turn it down to about 20%. When rendered, the result should like Figure 20.13.

**FIGURE 20.13**   The bumpy, but still freshly painted, pipe.

### Weathering the Paint

In the next few steps we will chip paint off the edges of the nuts and flanges. At the bottom of the Shader tree there is a Plus sign. Click on it and select Terrain Layer (see Figure 20.14). Name this layer "Chipped Paint" in the Name field in the Terrain Layer details. The new Terrain layer will have two subshaders: Distribution and Shader.

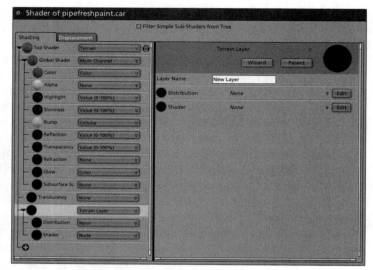

**FIGURE 20.14**    The new Terrain layer.

Click on the Distribution and choose Anything Goos. In the Edges section of the Anything Goos details turn off the Inner and Perimeter options and turn the Edges slider down to about 13. Set the Fall Off to Absolute and the Size to 0.35 (see Figure 20.15). In the Noise channel below the Distribution channel with Anything Goos, open the menu and select Noise Functions and then Noise Factory from the submenu. Leave all options at default for the Noise Factory. If you take a look at the Preview window, you'll see that nothing is happening yet, so let's move on to the next step.

**FIGURE 20.15**    The Anything Goos settings.

Click on Shader below Noise and choose Multi Channel. The following shader recipe will create the bare metal where there is no paint. In the Color channel add a new Noise Factory function and adjust the Noise Type to Perlin, Smoothing to 7%, and check smoothing. In the Highlight channel insert a Fractal Noise function. In the Fractal Noise details select the second fractal pattern. All other values in the shader can be turned off (see Figure 20.16). At this point you should be able to see the chipped paint on the edges of the nuts, bolts, and flanges, as shown in Figure 20.17. You can check your work against the file chippedpaintpipe.car.

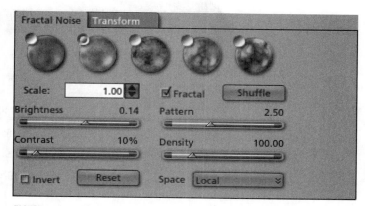

**FIGURE 20.16**    The Fractal Noise component in the Highlight channel.

**FIGURE 20.17**    The pipe with chipped paint around the edges.

## Adding Rust

Next we will add rust to the exposed cast iron. Select the pipe and jump into the Texture room if you are not already there. To begin adding the rust effects click on the plus sign at the bottom of the shader tree to add a new Terrain layer and name it Rust. In the Distribution channel select Anything Goos and set the following settings: Size is 0.30 and Fall Off is Radial. In the Edges section leave Outer checked and move the slider to about 12 (see Figure 20.18). In the Noise channel below Anything Goos add a Noise Factory component and leave all settings at default.

**FIGURE 20.18**    The Anything Goos settings for the rust.

In the Shader channel choose Multi Channel from the channel menu. The following is the shader recipe for the rust. In the Color channel select Operators and then choose Mixer. For Source 1 of the Mixer, select Color and set it to a dark purple: R = 59, G = 25, B = 62; set Source 2 to a grungy orange: R = 161, G = 75, B = 27. In the Blender select Noise Functions and then Noise Factory. Change the Noise Type to Perlin Noise and set the Scale to 10%, The rust has no highlights and isn't shiny, so set Highlight and Shininess to Value 0%. In the Preview window zoom in on the flanges of the pipe. You should see the rust on the bare metal, as shown in Figure 20.19.

**FIGURE 20.19**    The pipe with chipped paint and rust.

Obviously you can do much more with Anything Goos than create chipped paint and rust. With a bit of practice you can create just about any type of weathering. The best part about Anything Goos is that its effects are procedural and not image based, meaning that the effects can be changed at any time—even animated.

| TUTORIAL 20.3 | **MAKING A ROBOT BUG WALK WITH COGNITO** |
|---|---|

Cognito is a mechanical motion choreographer for Carrara. It can be used for simulating synchronized mechanical motions like gears, chains, cross chains, and pistons. Cognito works by setting up relationships between motors and slaves. When you set up a motor, you define which axis it rotates around and how many teeth are on it. The slave specifies what kind of relationship exists between it and the motor through its Linkage setting. Some examples of the Linkages are Chain, Gear, Piston, and Trip Hammer. Using the slave's Teeth and Pitch/Arc settings, you control how motion is transferred from the motor to the slave. Most simple motions can easily be set up using Linkages, and complex motions can be simulated by building up layers of Cognito motion.

### Creating a Walking Robot

In this tutorial we are going to use Cognito to animate an insect-like, robot's walk cycle. The stepping motion will be complex, but we will break it down into two kinds of motion: an up-and-down motion and a side-to-side motion. You'll learn how to combine these two motions to create the complex walking motion. The robot will be an eight-legged robot and it will walk by keeping four legs on the ground while it steps with the other four.

This tutorial should be a lot of fun, but it is also complex, so follow all of the instructions exactly. Pay attention to the numerical values. Be especially careful to distinguish negative numbers from positive numbers and pay attention to the order in which the motions are created—don't skip any steps or improvise until you are done. Once you have completed the tutorial and have a good idea how Cognito works, you can experiment. To help you along, four incremental files have been provided on the accompanying CD-ROM that show important milestones in the building of the walk cycle for the robot. cognito_walker1.car has one leg with the basic walking motion completed, cognito_walker2.car has two legs, cognito_walker3.car has four legs completed, and cognito_walker4. car is the finished robot.

**ON THE CD**

Open the cognito_walker.car file and locate the single robot leg that is prebuilt (see Figure 20.20). Since the first leg is preassembled, let's add Cognito to it right away. There are two things happening in the type of motion we are going to create. First, there is the up-and-down motion of the leg, and second there is the swinging back and forth. For each type of motion, we will need a separate Cognito motor. Let's take a moment to set up the animation; open the Sequencer tray, check the Snap property, and make sure that the frames per second are set to 12 fps. Set the Render Range at the top of the timeline to 10 seconds. This tells Carrara that the animation is 10 seconds long.

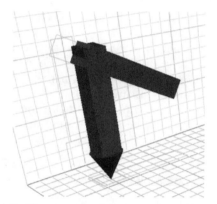

**FIGURE 20.20** The first leg is preassembled, but we still have to add the Cognito effects.

Make sure you are at the beginning of the timeline and insert a Sphere primitive. In the General tab of the Properties tray, rename the sphere "Stepper." Since this primitive will only be used as a Cognito motor, we don't need to see it in the final render, so uncheck its Visible property. Click on the Modifiers tab in the Properties tray and use the plus (+) button to add Cognito from the menu. Now, switch to the Effects tab and check the Motor property in the Cognito Data. We have our first motor.

With the Stepper motor still selected, move the scrubber to the 10-second mark and in the Cognito Data set the Rotation property to 1.0. This will create a key frame at the 10-second mark, which is the end of the animation. Next, move the scrubber to the 00:01-second mark (the second tick mark on the timeline) and set the value to 0.0. This will create a key frame at 00:01. We are creating a key frame at 00:01 because with some types of linkages, Cognito needs a baseline to know its starting point. That baseline is the object's position at 00:00 in the timeline. Not all linkages used in this animation need to have a baseline, but it's a good habit to get into when using Cognito. You should end up with a timeline that looks like Figure 20.21.

**FIGURE 20.21**   The keyframes for the Stepper motor. All motors will have key frames at 00.01 seconds and 10 seconds.

Now, select the Upper Leg and in the Modifiers tab use the plus (+) button to add Cognito. Switch to the Effects tab and set the following properties: Slave is checked, Driver is set to Stepper, Linkage is set to Rocker, and the Pitch/Arc is –0.05. The Driver property defines which motor will control the Upper Leg, and in this case it is Stepper. The Linkage property defines how motion is translated, and Pitch/Arc sets the range of motion. Not all linkages require the Pitch/Arc property; some will use the Teeth property.

If you press Play in the Sequencer tray, you should see the leg move up and down. A couple of problems still need to be worked out. The first problem is that the range of motion for the leg is too long and slow. Second, since the walk cycle we are building will alternate a set of feet in the air and a set of feet on the ground at each step, the leg needs to stay on the ground 50% of the time.

To make this happen, we're going to use a formula. Click on the area between the Stepper motor's two key frames in the timeline. You should see the Tweener appear in the Properties tray. The Tweener is set to Bézier by default. By changing this Tweener, the spin of the Stepper changes, which in turn drives the rocking of the Upper Leg. Select Formula from the Tweener menu, delete the existing formula, and type this exactly as it is shown here:

```
u=(t-tmin)/(tmax-tmin) * p2 * 10 + p1;
u=u - floor(u);
value=((u > 0.5)?u :0.5);
```

ON THE CD

Alternatively, you could load the stepper tweener.cbr using the Load Component button next to the Tweener label. The cbr file is located on the accompanying CD-ROM. Then, set the values p1 .25 and p2 0.40. For this custom tweener, p1 controls how far along in the cycle it is, and p2 controls how many cycles there are (see Figure 20.22).

If you play the animation, the leg will move up and down with pauses between each step. Now it's time to add the second motor to control the back-and-forth swinging motion. Rewind to get back to the beginning of the animation. Insert a new Sphere, change its name to "Swinger," and make it invisible. With the Swinger object selected, add Cognito from the

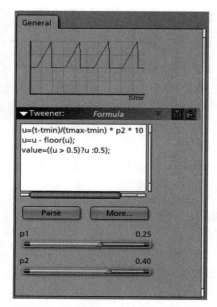

**FIGURE 20.22**    The Tweener formula for
the Stepper motor.

Modifiers tab in the Properties tray and check the Motor property on the
Cognito Data Effect. Move the scrubber to the 10-second mark and set the
Cognito Data Rotation to 1.00. Move the scrubber back to the 00:01-second
mark and set the Rotation to 0.0, just like you did with the Stepper motor.

By grouping objects, you can apply additional levels of Cognito motion. The swinging motion supplied by the Swinger motor will be applied
at the new group level. Therefore, select the Upper Leg group and group
it again by choosing Group from the Edit menu. Rename the new group
"Even Leg." Make sure that the Hot Point of the new group is located at
the base of the Upper Leg object so that it rotates and moves correctly. In
the Modifiers tab, add Cognito once again, click the Around option button next to the z field, click on the Effects tab, and then set the following
values for the Cognito Data: Slave is checked, Driver is Swinger, Linkage
is Rocker, Pitch/Arc is 0.05.

If you play the animation again, you'll notice that the swinging motion doesn't synch with the stepping motion. To fix this, we will use another tweener, but this time, we can use one of Carrara standard
tweeners. Click on the space between the Swinger object's key frames.
Change the Tweener to Oscillate and set the following properties: Saw-
tooth is selected and Up Phase is 100%, as in Figure 20.23. Rewind and
then play again to see the leg step and swing. This completes the motion
for one leg. If you are having trouble getting the leg to move correctly,
check your work against the cognito_walker1.car file.

ON THE CD

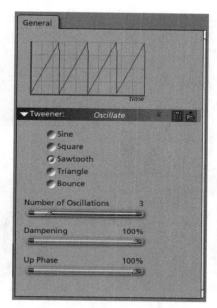

**FIGURE 20.23**    The Tweener for the Swinger motor.

Now we need to set up the new motor for the leg that will step opposite to the first leg. Select the Stepper motor in the Properties tray and duplicate it. Click on the General tab in the upper half of the Properties tray and rename the new copy "Odd Stepper." Click on the Tweener between Odd Stepper's key frames and change the p1 value to 0.75 (remember, this Tweener is defined by a formula).

Select the Even Leg group, duplicate it, and move the new leg group next to the original leg so that it looks like Figure 20.24. The new leg should be behind (farther away from the camera) than the original leg; rename the new copy "Odd Leg." Now we have two legs on the same side. Select the new leg, and in the Effects tab, change the Phase Offset in the Cognito Data settings to 0.50. This will change the Odd Leg so that it is halfway farther along the Rocker cycle than the Even Leg. Select the Upper Leg object in the Odd Leg group. Switch to the Effects tab and change Cognito's Driver to Odd Stepper. Press Rewind and then press Play again; you should see the two legs stepping alternately. If you are having trouble getting this to work properly, take a look at the cognito_walker2.car file on the accompanying CD-ROM and compare it to your file.

Now we are going to create the legs on the opposite side so that there will be four legs. Select the Even Leg and the Odd Leg groups and group them. Rename the new group "Left Side." Move the Hot Point of the new group so that if viewed from above it is centered between the two legs, and if viewed from the front it is about 3 inches outside the group.

Duplicate the new Left Side group, and rotate it 180 degrees around the Z. Rename the new group "Right." Always make sure that the timeline is at 00:00 when you make your changes unless you are setting a key frame. When you are finished, you should have a scene that looks like Figure 20.25.

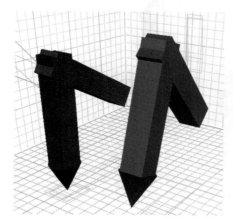

**FIGURE 20.24** The two new legs take alternating steps.

**FIGURE 20.25** The Left Side and Right Side legs.

Now there are two legs on each side, but if you play the animation, you'll notice that it's still not quite right. Because we duplicated and rotated the new set of legs, one pair of legs is walking forward and the other is walking backward. Fixing this problem is easy; open the Right Side group and open the Even Leg and Odd Leg groups. Select the Upper Leg in the Even Leg group and switch the Driver from Stepper to Odd Stepper. Next, select Upper Leg in the Odd Leg group and switch the Driver from Odd Stepper to Stepper. When you play the animation now, you should have four legs that walk forward and are in synch. You can check your work against the cognito_walker3.car file.

**ON THE CD**

To make an eight-legged robot, select the Left Side group and duplicate it and move the new group forward. Do the same for the Right Side group, so that it looks like Figure 20.26. Now there are eight legs floating in air walking nowhere. It's time to add a body and animate the movement.

Insert a cube and scale it along the *y*-axis so that it spans the length of the legs and fits in between the legs and looks like Figure 20.27. Name the new cube "Body." To attach the legs to the body, do the following: in the Instance tab of the Properties tray, select and drag the two Right Side groups and the two Left Side groups on top of the Body object. You should end up with a hierarchy that looks like Figure 20.27 when you are finished.

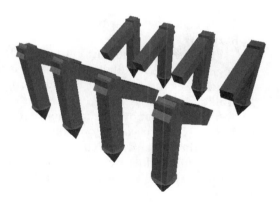

**FIGURE 20.26**    The eight legs in position.

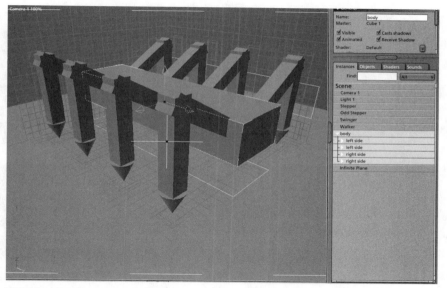

**FIGURE 20.27**    The legs and body in position. The Body group and the Leg group hierarchy.

The body could be animated by creating key frames in the timeline, but since this is a Cognito tutorial, we are going to use Cognito's Rack linkage to create the movements of the body. Insert a new sphere, make it invisible, and rename it "Walker." In the Modifiers tab of the Properties tray, use the plus (+) button to add the Cognito modifier. Switch to the Effects tab and check Cognito's Motor option. This will be the motor that drives the body's movement. Move the scrubber to 10:00 and set Cognito's Rotation to 1.0. Move it back to 00:01 and set the Rotation to 0.0 so that the new motor has key frames that match the other motors. Click on the tweener between the two keyframes and set it to Linear instead of Bézier.

Press the Rewind button to get back to 00:00. Select the Body and add Cognito in the Modifiers tab of the Properties tray. Switch to the Effects tab and set the following Cognito properties: Slave is checked, Driver is Walker, Linkage is Rack, Pitch/Arc is –10. The Pitch/Arc setting tells Cognito how far to move the rack for each tooth of the motor. If the –10 value doesn't work for you, try making it a little higher or lower. This will coordinate the forward movement of the body with how far the legs step. Finally, add the floor by inserting an Infinite Plane. Now for the moment of truth; rewind to the beginning and play the animation. Your robot should now appear to walk forward as the legs step in synch. Use the Production Frame to frame the robot within the camera view and jump to the Render room to create the final animation (see Figure 20.28).

**FIGURE 20.28**    A frame from the Cognito Walker animation.

## SUMMARY

Using just a few of the Carrara plug-ins, we were able to grow a grassy field with mushrooms, weather a pipe, and make a robot walk. Luckily, Carrara is one of the few applications that has its core set of tools and features extended by powerful plug-ins. Beyond providing extra tools, plug-ins are a way to work efficiently and save time. Many tasks that would take days to model in Carrara, such as a grassy field, take just minutes with Anything Grows. Learning to work with Carrara's diverse set of plug-ins is definitely worth the financial and time investment.

# CONTRIBUTING AUTHOR BIOGRAPHIES

This book would not have been possible without the expertise, talent, and generosity of the following artists.

## David E. Bell

David E. Bell is a digital artist and electronic storyteller who takes great pride in unraveling complex problems into workable solutions—be they pixels, electrons, or endless lines of code. He currently lives in the Hudson River valley where he is working on his illustrated novel *Icarus:2300*. David is also one of the founding partners of the post-production house, InDVFX. He can be reached by email at *dbell@indvfx.com*.

## Peter MacDougall

Peter MacDougall is an illustrator, author and instructor. He has held a life-long interest in animation. He works in pen, watercolors, and digital paint, and has been working with 3D since 1994. He is a contributor to 3Dxtract and the previous edition of the Carrara 3D handbook. He lives with his wife and three children on the West Coast of Canada. He has several short film ideas and would love to collaborate on an animated film project. Rumours that he has been cloned not once but several times are completely based on misinterpreted fact.

## Andrea M. Newton

Andrea earned a bachelor's degree in creative writing from the University of Evansville, where she also served on the editorial staff of two of the university's literary magazines. Since then, she has worked as an editor for two non-profit publications. Over the years, Andrea has published writing and artwork in several magazines, and was the editor, illustrator, and co-author of a Call of Cthulhu sourcebook, *Cthulhu Invictus*, in 2004. It was while working on that project that she became interested in 3D graphics. Andrea also worked for several years as an e-commerce technical specialist and EDI mapping developer; that experience, together with her writing and editing background, earned her a position as a technical writer for an international software company. In keeping with her belief that technical documentation should help users learn to use software effectively, Andrea also developed and taught EDI courses while in that position. She now works as a freelance writer in Greensboro, NC. You can find more tutorials by Andrea, along with some of her artwork and other writing, on her Web site, *www.rejectedreality.com.*

### Patrick Tuten

Patrick Tuten is a self employed artist, graphic designer, and sign maker in the Orlando, Florida area where he has operated the "Patrick Tuten Graphics Studio" since 1989. With the help of his wife Jenifer and step-son Justin he designs and produces everything from logos and magazine ads to paintings and 3D artwork for local businesses, individuals, and theme parks. He also does large format printing, vinyl cutting, and outdoor electric sign design.

After working with computer vector files for many years he came across a copy of Bryce 3 and got hooked on 3D, later moving on to Ray Dream, then Carrara, Amapi, and Hexagon. He uses 3D to create images which are used in logos, backdrops, sign previsualizations and fine artworks. Please visit *www.tutengraphics.com* to view samples of his projects.

### Jack Whitney

Jack Whitney was trained as an airbrush illustrator with a passion for sculpting when there was time. 3D programs like Carrara and Hexagon have allowed him to not only illustrate his sculptures, but to animate them as well. He currently runs a solo studio producing illustration, animation, and design for print and the Web. He also teaches traditional and digital mediums and concepts at the college level. He lives with his wife, Lisa, and their four children in St. Louis, Missouri.

### Eric Winemiller

Eric Winemiller is currently almost everything for Digital Carvers Guild; Chief Programmer, CEO and janitor. During the day he dons the roll of his secret identity as a computer programmer for Siemens Medical Solutions Health Services, occasional author, and amateur 3D artist. At night he builds plug-ins for Carrara, makes custom furniture, continues to pretend to be a 3D artist, and spends time with his wife, Judy, two children, Ethan and Anya, and five cats.

Digital Carvers Guild is the largest creator of plug-ins for Carrara, born out of the shareware/freeware community and still devoted to that spirit. If you are interested in building plug-ins for Carrara, we can help; contact us at *http://www.digitalcarversguild.com.*

### Lisa E. Yimm

Lisa E. Yimm, is a San Francisco-based photographer, writer, and visual effects artist who spends her days working in broadcasting and media studies as the Program Director of KUSF 90.3FM at the University of San Francisco. An old school B&W photographer at heart, she is also one of the founding partners of the post-production house, InDVFX. She can be reached via email at *yimm@indvfx.com.*

# B

# ABOUT THE CD-ROM

The companion CD-ROM is full of files that will help you work through the tutorials in the book.

## DEMONSTRATION SOFTWARE

The CD-ROM contains demonstration versions of Carrara 5 Pro for Windows® and Macintosh® OS X and demonstration versions of Hexagon 1.2 for Windows and for Macintosh OS X. The Hexagon tutorials in Chapter 11 use Hexagon 1.01, which is a slightly older version than the demonstration version which is Hexagon 1.2. The minor differences between the two versions should not interfere with the steps in the tutorials.

## CARRARA MINIMUM SYSTEM REQUIREMENTS

### WINDOWS

- Pentium II 300 MHz or better
- Windows 2000/XP/ME (with SP3 or later)
- 128 MB of RAM (256 MB recommended)
- 16-bit color display (24-bit recommended)
- CD-ROM drive
- 300 MB free hard drive space
- 3D graphics accelerator card recommended

### MAC® OS X

- Power Macintosh G3 266 MHz or better
- Mac OS X 10.1 or later
- 128 MB of RAM (256 MB recommended)
- 16-bit color display (24-bit recommended)
- CD-ROM drive
- 300 MB free hard drive space
- 3D graphics accelerator card recommended

## HEXAGON SYSTEM REQUIREMENTS

### WINDOWS

- Pentium or compatible (800 MHz or better)
- Windows 2000/XP
- 256 MB of physical RAM
- 24-bit Color Display
- 3D graphics accelerator card—OpenGL
- 300 MB free hard drive space

### MAC OS X

- Power Macintosh G4/G5 (800 MHz or better)
- Mac OS X 10.2 or later
- 256 MB of physical RAM
- 24-bit Color Display
- 3D graphics accelerator card—OpenGL
- 300 MB free hard drive space

## CHAPTER FILES

The Chapter Files folder on the CD-ROM contains folders for each chapter of the book. Included in each chapter folder are all of the figures in the book in color. If it is difficult to make out subtle details in the printed figures in the book open the corresponding chapter folder and you can view a full color, large version of the figure.

In addition to color figures many chapters include incremental files, support files and start and finish files. For instance, the modeling tutorials in Chapter 10 are very detailed, so to facilitate your progress each tutorial has dozens of incremental files in the chapter folder showing how the model was built. Support files such as reference images, textures, and sound and movie files are also provided to help you complete each tutorial successfully. Also several tutorials have specially prepared start files to provide you with a starting point for completing the lesson, and a finished file which shows you what the final result should look like.

## CARRARA GALLERY

The CD-ROM also has an inspirational gallery of artwork and animations created with Carrara by users just like you. The vast range of work will give you a solid idea of what is possible with Carrara.

All of the files on the CD-ROM are copyrighted and are provided for use in conjunction with this book. None of the files in the CD-ROM may be printed, posted, distributed or reproduced in any form without written consent from the owner of the file.

# INDEX